ARCHITECTURE
IN THE AGE OF DIVIDED REPRESENTATION

THE MIT PRESS ❀ CAMBRIDGE, MASSACHUSETTS ❀ LONDON, ENGLAND

ARCHITECTURE
IN THE AGE OF DIVIDED REPRESENTATION

THE QUESTION OF CREATIVITY
IN THE SHADOW OF PRODUCTION

DALIBOR VESELY

This book was set in Clarendon by Graphic Composition, Inc. and was printed and bound in the United States of America.

Library of Congress Cataloging-in-Publication Data

Vesely, Dalibor.
    Architecture in the age of divided representation : the question of creativity in the shadow of production / Dalibor Vesely.
        p. cm.
    Includes bibliographical references and index.
    ISBN 0-262-22067-9 (alk. paper)
    1. Architecture, Modern—Philosophy. 2. Architecture—Aesthetics.   I. Title.
NA500.V47 2004
720'.1—dc22

                                                                          2003061453

TO MY MOTHER FOR HER GENEROSITY, LOVE, AND SACRIFICE

◂ CONTENTS ◂

LIST OF ILLUSTRATIONS   viii

ACKNOWLEDGMENTS   xvi

INTRODUCTION   2

CHAPTER   1   **MODERNITY, FREEDOM, AND DESTINY**   11

2   **THE NATURE OF COMMUNICATIVE SPACE**   43

3   **THE PERSPECTIVAL TRANSFORMATION OF THE MEDIEVAL WORLD**   109

4   **THE AGE OF DIVIDED REPRESENTATION**   175

5   **THE FOUNDATIONS OF MODERN ARCHITECTURE**   229

6   **CREATIVITY IN THE SHADOW OF MODERN TECHNOLOGY**   281

7   **THE REHABILITATION OF FRAGMENT**   317

8   **TOWARD A POETICS OF ARCHITECTURE**   355

NOTES   390

WORKS CITED   464

ILLUSTRATION CREDITS   492

INDEX   496

‐ ILLUSTRATIONS ‐

1.1   Renzo Piano, Kansai International Airport, passenger terminal 15

1.2   Ludwig Mies van der Rohe, National Gallery, Berlin 17

1.3   Theo van Doesburg, Aubette, cinema and dance hall, Strasbourg (destroyed) 21

1.4   Daniel Libeskind, *The Architect and His Shadow* (1981) 22

1.5   Ivan Leonidov, headquarters of heavy industry, Moscow (1934) 25

1.6   Melanie Young, metaphorical study of the design studio 27

1.7   Ivan Leonidov, United Nations Headquarters (1957–1958) 28

1.8   Hans Scharoun, Berlin Philharmonie, plan 31

1.9   Hans Scharoun, Berlin Philharmonie, interior 31

1.10   Hans Scharoun, *Ich Du, Volkshausgedanke* (1920) 32

1.11   Ludwig Mies van der Rohe, National Gallery, Berlin 33

1.12   Berlin Kulturforum, aerial view 35

1.13   Coop Himmelblau, preliminary sketch (1982) 38

1.14   Coop Himmelblau, conversion of the attic space, Flakestrasse, Vienna (1989) 39

2.1   Louvain (Belgium), street in the center of town 45

2.2   Inverted view of the fountain, Cambridge Botanical Gardens 47

2.3   NASA space laboratory (1973), dining area and docking adaptor 53

2.4   Melanie Young, metaphorical study of the design studio, interior 59

2.5   Bolles + Wilson, Münster library 61

2.6   Bolles + Wilson, Münster library, drawing and model 62

2.7   Chartres cathedral, west front 65

2.8   Chartres cathedral, west rose window 66

2.9   Chartres cathedral, interior 67

2.10   Wells cathedral, tracing floor 72

2.11   Café de Flore, Boulevard Saint-Germain, Paris 78

2.12   Soccer game in progress 81

2.13   *Hortus Palatinus,* view of the castle and city of Heidelberg (ca. 1620) 83

2.14   Würzburg Residence, main staircase 87

2.15   Würzburg Residence, ceiling fresco above the main staircase 89

2.16   Würzburg Residence, caryatids in the vestibule 90

2.17 Johann David Steingruber, *Architectonisches Alphabeth* (1773), plan of a project dedicated to Chr. Friedrich Carl Alexander 93

2.18 Zwiefalten church, detail of the nave fresco and rocaille decoration 95

2.19 Chartres cathedral, west portal 97

2.20 Chartres cathedral, detail of the west portal 98

2.21 Johann Lukas von Hildebrandt, Piaristenkirche Maria Treu, Vienna (1702–1723), south chapel 102

2.22 Christoph Dientzenhofer, St. Nicholas Church, Prague, south side of the nave 105

2.23 Gian Lorenzo Bernini, Fontana dei Fiumi, Piazza Navona, Rome; the allegory of the Danube 107

3.1 Saint-Denis cathedral, choir 111

3.2 Capella Arena, Padua, interior 112

3.3 Cesare Cesariano, edition of Vitruvius, *De architectura* (1521), the multiplication of celestial light 115

3.4 Roger Bacon, *De multiplicatione specierum,* fol. 376, refraction of light 117

3.5 Villard de Honnecourt, sketchbook, pl. 36, diagrammatic figures 119

3.6 Chartres cathedral, Charlemagne window, detail 125

3.7 Roger Bacon, *De multiplicatione specierum,* fol. 270, pyramidal propagation of light 129

3.8 Roger Bacon, *De multiplicatione specierum,* fol. 367, diagram of light mixing 131

3.9 Cesare Cesariano, edition of Vitruvius, *De architectura* (1521), the relation between the celestial light and perspectival vision 133

3.10 Ulm cathedral, tabernacle, plan of the groined vaulting at the base 135

3.11 Francesco di Giorgio Martini, *Trattati,* fol. 33, tav. 61, diagram of perspectival vision 137

3.12 Taddeo Gaddi, *The Presentation of the Virgin* (1328–1334), Santa Croce, Florence 141

3.13 Altichiero, *The Crucifixion* (1373–1379), Chapel of Bonifacio Lupi, Basilica del Santo, Padua 142

3.14 Altichiero, *The Baptism of the King of Cyrene by Saint George* (1384), Oratory of San Giorgio, Padua 143

3.15 Filippo Brunelleschi, diagram of the experiment in front of the Florence baptistery 145

3.16 Leonardo da Vinci, manuscript A 37r (1492), pyramids of vision and perspectival representation 146

3.17 Leon Battista Alberti, *De pictura* (Lucca manuscript), fol. 27r, perspective diagram 147

3.18 Piero della Francesca, polyptych of St. Anthony, detail of Annunciation (1465–1470) 150

3.19 Jean Cousin, *Livre de perspective* (1560), frontispiece 152

3.20 Jacopo de' Barbari, *Portrait of Fra Luca Pacioli with a Young Man* (1495) 154

3.21 Nicholas of Cusa, *De coniecturis,* the pyramids of light and shadow, finitude and infinity, unity and difference 158

3.22 Lorenzo Ghiberti, Florence baptistery, the *Gates of Paradise,* the story of Joseph 164

3.23 Lorenzo Ghiberti, Florence baptistery, the *Gates of Paradise,* the story of Joseph (detail), distribution of grain 165

3.24 Baltimore panel, ideal city with a fountain and statues of the Virtues (late 15th c.), detail 167

3.25 Perin del Vaga, naumachia in the Cortile del Belvedere, Vatican Palace 169

3.26 Donato Bramante, Cortile del Belvedere, Vatican, plan (Codex Coner) 171

3.27 Raphael, Stanza della Segnatura, Vatican Palace, *Parnassus* and *The School of Athens* 171

4.1 Sebastien Le Clerc, *The Academy of Sciences and Fine Arts,* Paris (1666) 177

4.2 Hildegard von Bingen, *Liber divinorum operum simplicis hominis,* fol. 6r, microcosmos 179

4.3 ·Macrocosm, from Aristotle's *De caelo,* ed. Johann Eck (Augsburg, 1519) 181

4.4 Johannes Kepler, *Tabulae Rudolphinae* (1627), frontispiece, the temple of astronomy 182

4.5 *Romani Collegii Societatis Jesu Musaeum Celeberrimum* (Museo Kircheriano, 1678), frontispiece 183

4.6 Donato Bramante, S. Maria presso S. Satiro, Milan, view of the shallow "false choir" 185

4.7 Donato Bramante, S. Maria presso S. Satiro, Milan, plan 186

4.8 Andrea Palladio, Villa Barbaro, Maser, Veneto 187

4.9 Paolo Veronese, Villa Barbaro, Maser, Veneto, Sala dell'Olimpo, ceiling frescoes 189

4.10 Jean-François Nicéron, *La perspective curieuse, ou, Magie artificielle des effets merveilleux* (1638), pls. 66, 67 191

4.11 Johannes Kepler, *Mysterium cosmographicum* (1596), regular solids of planetary model 193

4.12 Guarino Guarini, SS. Sindone, Turin, exterior of the upper dome 197

4.13 Camillo Balliani, the image of the shroud, *Regionamenti di Santa Sindone* (1616) 199

4.14 Guarino Guarini, SS. Sindone, section 201

4.15 Guarino Guarini, SS. Sindone, interior of the upper dome 205

4.16 Guarino Guarini, original drawing for the structure of the upper dome 209

4.17 Guarino Guarini, SS. Sindone, plan 209

4.18 Gregory of St. Vincent, *Opus geometricum quadraturae circuli et sectionum coni* (1647), hexagonal diagram 210

4.19 Gregory of St. Vincent, *Opus geometricum quadraturae circuli et sectionum coni* (1647), frontispiece 211

4.20 Giovanni Battista Pittoni, *An Allegorical Monument to Sir Isaac Newton* (1729) 213

4.21 Zwiefalten, main nave 217

4.22 Zwiefalten, main nave, ceiling fresco 219

4.23 Zwiefalten, detail of the fresco and rocaille decoration 224

4.24 Zwiefalten, the transformations of rocaille 225

4.25 Emanuele Tesauro, *Il cannocchiale aristotelico* (1670), frontispiece 226

5.1 Jacques de Lajoue, *Le cabinet physique de M. Bonnier de la Mosson* (1752), detail 233

5.2 Claude Perrault, *Memoires pour servir à l'histoire naturelle des animaux* (1671), frontispiece 234

5.3 Claude Perrault, *Ordonnance des cinq espèces des colonnes selon la méthode des anciens* (1683), new simplified version of orders 237

5.4 Versailles, Chasses du Roi, the geometrization of the landscape 239

5.5 Claude-Nicolas Ledoux, elevation of the cemetery of the town of Chaux (1804) 243

5.6 Jean-Nicolas-Louis Durand, *Recueil et parallèle des édifices en tout genre anciens et modernes* (1801), frontispiece 245

5.7 Jean-Nicolas-Louis Durand, *Précis des leçons d'architecture données à l'École Royale Polytechnique* (1819), pls. 11, 17 246

5.8 Pierre Patel, perspective view of the chateau and the gardens of Versailles (1668) 250

5.9 Johann Bernhard Fischer von Erlach, *Entwurff einer historischen Architectur* (1721), Dinocrates 252

5.10 Johann Bernhard Fischer von Erlach, *Entwurff einer historischen Architectur* (1721), first project for Schloss Schönbrunn 253

5.11 Ferdinando Galli da Bibiena, *L'architettura civile* (1711), pl. 23, *perspectiva per angolo* 255

5.12 Giovanni Battista Piranesi, *Opere varie* (1750), *capriccio* 256

5.13 Étienne-Louis Boullée, project for the Temple of Reason, section 258

5.14 Friedrich Gilly, perspective study with landscape scene (1799) 260

5.15 Karl Friedrich Schinkel, Schloss Charlottenhof, Potsdam 264

5.16 Karl Friedrich Schinkel, project of the mausoleum for Queen Luise, Schloss Charlottenhof park (1810–1812) 265

5.17 Karl Friedrich Schinkel, mausoleum for Queen Luise, Schloss Charlottenhof park 267

5.18 Le Corbusier, *Vers une architecture,* Parthenon and Delage automobile 269

5.19 Paul Ludwig Troost, House of German Art, Munich (1933–1937) 272

5.20 James Stirling, Stuttgart Gallery, entrance to the lower galleries 276

5.21 James Stirling, Stuttgart Gallery, detail of the main facade 277

5.22   Terry Farell, television studios, Camden Town, London, entry courtyard 278

6.1   Sebastien Le Clerc, representation of the machines used to raise the large stones in the construction of the Louvre fronton (1677) 283

6.2   Leonardo da Vinci, a courtyard of a foundry 286

6.3   David Weston-Thomas, political building, preliminary study of the main entry space 289

6.4   William Cuningham, *The Cosmographical Glasse* (1559), Atlas bearing the heavens 291

6.5   Agostino Ramelli, *Le diverse et artificiose machine* (1588), pl. 9, water-raising machine 294

6.6   Hendrik Bleu (Bles), *Landscape with the Ironworks* (1544) 295

6.7   Pieter Bruegel the Elder, *Alchemist* (1558) 299

6.8   Railway viaducts in Southwark, London, aerial view 302

6.9   Railway bridge in Camden Town, London 303

6.10   Eiffel Tower, the first elevator section, detail 304

6.11   Robert Delaunay, *The Eiffel Tower* (1910–1911) 305

6.12   Virtual reality simulation, NASA 309

6.13   Bryan Avery, IMAX cinema, Waterloo, London 314

7.1   Robert Wood, preparatory metaphorical study for the project of an ecological research center 319

7.2   Abraham Bosse, *Manière universelle de Monsieur Desargues* (1648), pl. 2 321

7.3   Houston, commercial center, view from Buffalo Bayou 323

7.4   Louis Carrogis (Carmontelle), Park Monceau, panoramic view 324

7.5   Park Monceau, naumachia, current state 326

7.6   Johann Wolfgang Baumgartner, Earth rocaille 329

7.7   Karl Friedrich Schinkel, *Gothic Cathedral on a River* (1813) (copy by Wilhelm Ahlborn, 1823) 332

7.8   Paul Cézanne, *La route tournante* (ca. 1881) 335

7.9   Georges Braque, *Still Life with Clarinet and Violin* (1912) 337

7.10   Daniel Libeskind, collage (1980) 341

7.11   Le Corbusier, Beistegui apartment, solarium 345

7.12   Spitalfields project (London), model 347

7.13   Spitalfields project, civic area 348

7.14 Adam Robarts, Spitalfields project, shadow theater, composite study 350

7.15 Christian Frost, Spitalfields project, museum of Surrealist art, composite study 351

7.16 Elspeth Latimer, center for experimental music, interior 352

8.1 Coop Himmelblau, Factory Funder 3, St. Veit/Glan, Austria (1988–1989) 357

8.2 Jean Charles Delafosse, *Nouvelle iconologie historique* (1768), *Spring and Summer* 359

8.3 Kurt Schwitters, Merzbau (Hannover), view of the Gold Grotto, Big Group, and movable column (1930) 362

8.4 Aegina, temple of Aphaia (5th c. B.C.E.) 365

8.5 David Weston-Thomas, political building, metaphorical study of the museum and exhibition space 369

8.6 Adela Askandar, Vienna project, media center, composite drawing of a reading space 374

8.7 Ladislav Žák, Villa Frič, Prague (1934–1935) 377

8.8 Jemal Badrashi, Prague project, institute of medical ethics, demonstration theater, composite drawing 379

8.9 Jacob van Ruysdael, *View of Amsterdam and the Harbor* (1665) 381

8.10 Alberto Giacometti, sculptures in the atelier (1945–1947) 383

8.11 Eric Parry Architects (EPA), Stockley Park (Heathrow), office building 385

8.12 EPA, Stockley Park, initial proposal 386

8.13 EPA, Stockley Park, horizontal window of the first floor (winter landscape) 387

8.14 EPA, Stockley Park, view of the atrium and foyer 388

8.15 Adela Askandar, Vienna project, media center, library interior 389

- ACKNOWLEDGMENTS -

I WOULD LIKE TO say thank you to many people and institutions, not as a formal gesture but to express genuine appreciation for their contributions to the genesis of this book. The word "genesis" is probably the best guide through the sequence of names that I would like to mention.

My architectural horizon was shaped by Josef Havliček, Karel Honzik, and Jaroslav Fragner in Prague, and later by James Stirling in London. Jan Patočka, my teacher and mentor, contributed more than anybody else to my overall intellectual orientation and to the articulation of some of the critical topics (communicative movement, among others) discussed in the book. During my time in Munich, Hans Sedlmayr and Hermann Bauer helped me to better understand the nature of European Baroque, and Ernesto Grassi, the foundations and tradition of European humanism. The interpretations of the main topics of the book were strongly influenced by ongoing conversations with Hans-Georg Gadamer in Heidelberg and Paul Ricoeur in Paris.

The conditions under which it was possible for me to explore and test some of the main issues of the book in the framework of the design studio were created by Alvin Boyarsky at the Architectural Association in London, and later by Colin St. John Wilson at Cambridge.

I have discussed the content of the book on many occasions with Dawn Ades, Peter Burke, Günter Bock, Nick Bullock, Alan Colquhoun, Mark Cousins, Kenneth Frampton, John Gage, Sir Ernst Gombrich, Karsten Harries, Werner Hofmann, Mojmir Horyna, John Dixon Hunt, Luise King, Robert Maxwell, Rafael Moneo, Werner Oechslin, Michael Podro, Pavel Preiss, Colin Rowe, Joseph Rykwert, Graham Shane, Robert Slutzky, Anthony Vidler, Tomas Vlček, and Dame Frances Yates.

A number of the issues in this book were not only discussed but also explored in a creative collaboration with my students in the studio and in seminars. For obvious reasons I can name only a few, but I would like to thank them all. Many of them became permanent friends and collaborators. The first to mention are Mohsen Mostafavi and Philip Meadowcroft, who for many years were the most unselfish partners in running a studio. Among the others, a special thanks for their friendship and help should go to David Bass, Peter Beard, Gabriele Bryant, Amy Catania-Kulper, David Dernie, Robin Evans, Homa and Sima Farjadi, Robert Ferguson, Graham Howarth, Mari Hvattum, David Leatherbarrow for his unique role in our ongoing collaboration, Daniel Libeskind for a very special relationship, Lorna McNeur,

James McQuillan, Jose de Paiva, Alberto Pérez-Gómez, Wendy Pullan, Mary Ann Steane, Carolyn Steel, Gabriela Switek, Chris Tine, and Dagmar Weston.

Institutions and libraries vary in their kindness. I would like to thank those that were most helpful: first of all, the library of the Faculty of Architecture and History of Art and the Newton Library, Rare Books Department, both at the University of Cambridge; the Werner Oechslin Stiftung Library; the Conway Library at the Courtauld Institute of University College London; the library of the Warburg Institute, London; the Biblioteca Laurenziana in Florence; and the Bibliothèque Nationale in Paris. I am also grateful to the institutions most generous in supplying of visual material: the Galleria Nazionale in Perugia, Edizioni Messagero in Padua, the Walters Art Museum in Baltimore, and the Cabinet des Estampes of the Bibliothèque Royale de Belgique in Brussels.

Among those who contributed most directly to the existence of this book I would like to thank first Peter Carl, whose moral and intellectual encouragement and unselfish cooperation over many years remain unique and without precedent. For the same reasons I would like to thank Marion Houston, whose generous contribution is not easy to express in words. The possibility of speaking about imagination, poetry, and meaning in current architecture was supported by an ongoing collaboration with Eric Parry and by the qualities of his work, which shows that such a possibility exists even in the so-called real world.

My way of thinking and its not always easy relation to writing was never better understood than by Robin Middleton. His erudition, patience, and generosity made our friendship truly unique. The text, as it stands, would not be as legible as it is without the rigorous and imaginative editing work of Alice Falk, to whom I am most grateful for her commitment and kindness. For similar reasons I would like to extend my thanks to Tímea Adrián, the designer of this book, for her skill and patience, and to Matthew Abbate for the coordination of the whole project.

For generous support and encouragement in the early stages of writing I would like to thank Maria Becket, Roger Conover, and Georg Galberg.

On the most personal level my last thanks go to my father, with gratitude for the wonderful conversations and for his poetic vision of life, and to Drahosh, my brother, and his wife Mary, for their support and for making a home for me in their own world.

ARCHITECTURE
IN THE AGE OF DIVIDED REPRESENTATION

· INTRODUCTION ·

T HE TEXT OF this book emerged rather slowly, in a process hampered to a great extent by an uneasy feeling that too much is written today about architecture, which should after all communicate visually rather than through words. The issues I am addressing were stirred in the creative atmosphere of design in the studio, where visual communication very often generates questions demanding a more reflective answer. The questions raised most often concern the broader context in which architecture is situated and which is potentially present in our experience and memory. It is not necessary to look deep or far into the past to recover such memories. The architecture of the prewar avant-gardes was, as we know, closely linked with painting and other visual arts, such as the theater and the film, as well as with more distant areas of culture. And yet this was already merely a remnant of a long tradition in which architecture played a far more important role in embodying and founding culture.

The rather narrow contemporary vision of architecture as a discipline that can be treated as an instrument, or as a commodity, is the result of the transformation of the broadly oriented art of building into a separate profession, judged mostly by the criteria of technical disciplines. The inevitable outcome, characteristic of the current profession, is a mosaic of expert knowledge brought together either as abstract systems or as the intuitive improvisations of personal vision. In both cases the work produced falls short of the required conditions and true possibilities of the task. Even the most elaborate systems or most successful personal visions cannot replace the unity of the different levels of knowledge required for genuine creativity. In a spontaneous creative process it is difficult, even today, to separate completely the abstract geometrical definition of a building from its realization in a particular material and from the world of experience of the users. And yet there is a tendency to make precisely such a separation and to judge architecture as one might any other technical achievement, founded on an explicit and universal knowledge.

Attempts to come to terms with this approach force architects to sacrifice all aspects of architecture that do not meet the standards of technical knowledge and, where possible, to compensate for that sacrifice by cultivating personal experiences and visions on the periphery, or by accepting silently the instrumental operations of the current official culture. How close the instrumental values are to the acknowledged relevance of a particular work can be seen in the occasional success of personal visions in penetrating the mainstream of culture. Such success is most often directly related to the marketability of the work and thus to its instrumental value. This is a relatively new phenomenon reflected most clearly in the new relation between the instrumental and the communicative role of architecture, as well as between its aesthetic and its poetic nature.

The distance separating the instrumental and the communicative understanding of architecture represents a wide gap in our contemporary culture. Any serious attempt to bridge this gap requires a new kind of knowledge that can indicate how to reconcile genuine creativity and creative spontaneity with the productive power of contemporary science. The tension between the productive and the creative reality of architecture may be better understood if we examine more closely the nature and role of representation. In a conventional understanding, representation appears to be a secondary and derivative issue, associated closely with the role of the representational arts. However, a more careful consideration reveals, very often to our surprise, how critical and universal the problem of representation really is. What we normally refer to as reality, believing that it is something fixed and absolute, is always a result of our ability to experience, visualize, and articulate—in other words, to represent so as to participate in the world. Countering representation's participatory function is its tendency toward emancipation and autonomy. This is particularly evident in areas where representation has acquired a high level of coherence and relative independence. In design, which can serve as a good example, such coherence is achieved through drawings, models, different projective techniques, and more recently through digital simulation, known better as virtual reality.

The current debate about the status of simulated realities prompts some to believe that virtual reality might be more real than reality itself. Such a view illustrates how close we have come to accepting relatively isolated forms of representation as the sole criteria of truth and what is real. We probably do not yet fully appreciate the true power of representation, particularly in its emancipated form, despite its conspicuous role in forming modern utopias and ideologies, or in economic and political systems. The same is true in the modern arts and architecture. Here the possibilities of creating representations that can be freely manipulated are not limited to the formulation of manifestos and publicity, but extend also to the creation of concrete works and large-scale projects.

The limited range of emancipated representations can be challenged only by different attitudes toward culture, sustained by a different kind of knowledge that is based on the principles of dialogue. Among the many attempts to open such a dialogue, the contributions made by phenomenology, and more recently by hermeneutics, appear to be by far the most convincing in their consistency and continuity. Most relevant here was the discovery of the primacy of the natural world as a ground and framework within which the achievements of modern science and technology could be reconciled with the concrete conditions of the natural world and everyday human life. Such reconciliation is a task that in our own field we have barely begun. This tardiness has, I believe, much to do with the fact that critical cultural awareness is cultivated mostly in the social sciences, humanities, and philosophy, which modern architectural thinkers never take very seriously.

Such a situation is curiously paradoxical if we agree that it is the goal and not the means that defines the nature of a discipline, and that the goal of architecture is human life, while its techniques and instrumental thinking are only means. Architecture has probably never abandoned completely its humanistic role, though in modern times this role has mostly been improvised. That approach may no longer suffice in a changing world increasingly dominated by instrumentally oriented expectations. To preserve its primary identity and humanistic role in the future, architecture must establish credentials on the same level of intelligibility as instrumental thinking, while at the same time it must integrate and subordinate the instrumental knowledge and the technical potential of human beings to their praxis. This is, in essence, my aim in broad outline, developed in the following chapters.

The nature of the task has often forced me to move into areas outside architecture where the level of understanding of my questions was more advanced or appropriate. In part for that reason, the structure of the text is based not on a particular method but on the intrinsic nature of the issues discussed and on the coherence of the argument. The work as a whole can be seen as an attempt to understand the ontological and cultural foundations of modern architecture, and thus the nature and cultural role of architecture more generally. The argument is structured as a dialogue in which the foundations are revealed behind the veil of conventional and very often frozen interpretations. The process of uncovering those foundations leads inevitably into the depth of time, back to the generation of Leon Battista Alberti and Nicholas of Cusa and the formation of Renaissance perspective, the first plausible anticipation of modernity. By examining Renaissance perspective against the background of the medieval philosophy of light, we can come to understand the ontology of architectural space, which is formed by light before it is structured geometrically. The topic of light provides the link with the following chapters; its analysis illustrates the gradual transformation of space, connected originally with the luminosity of the visible world, into space as a pure conceptual construct.

The central part of the text addresses the question of divided representation in the period of the Baroque, when architectural thinking was seriously challenged by the newly emerging modern science and when light still played a very important role, though in a radically modified form. The geometrical interpretation of light known as *perspectiva naturalis*, or more simply as optics, was until the end of the seventeenth century seen as a key to cosmology and as a propaedeutics to the mathematical and philosophical studies. But its original meaning was more or less lost when optics became a foundation of modern mechanics. In the stage that follows, light itself is divided. In the Enlightenment, it is associated both with the intelligibility of reason and with a subjective aesthetic experience, manifested most clearly in the phenomenon of the sublime.

In the final two chapters, I attempt to draw some positive conclusions and to suggest a new interpretation of fragment, leading to the articulation of architectural poetics. To interpret fragment as a vehicle of a potentially positive meaning is only one of many possible ways to move from the level of knowledge to the level of making (poetics). In my approach there is a point where the interpretation (hermeneutics) and the way of making (poetics) come so close to each other that they become fully reciprocal: what we know contributes to what we make, and what is already made contributes substantially to what it is possible to know. Such reciprocity supports my earlier comment about the relevance of any new approach to architecture and its relation to prevailing cultural tendencies. Tendencies do not emerge as a result of individual efforts. They are more complex and anonymous, representing the historical experience of a particular epoch and common expectations. In architecture, expectations largely shape our plans, ideal projects, manifestos, and other statements, while the space of experience consists not only of our own accumulated experience and knowledge but also the experience embodied in previous projects, in treatises and books, in existing buildings and cities, and so on.

As we accept the current dominant tendency toward a technologically advanced design, we should judge the relevance of any attempt to shift and extend the horizon of creativity on two interdependent levels. The first includes knowing and understanding the real possibilities of a particular design task, based on the hermeneutical articulation of the world of contemporary design. The second represents situations that architecture itself creates in a dialogue with the given conditions of everything that already exists, including the natural world. It is mostly at the second level that architecture can make its main contribution by creating conditions that support a different experience, a different way of life, and perhaps even a different way of thinking about the nature of our expectations.

This brings my position close to the current thinking among ecologists, who are pursuing a similar argument. The relation between what is expected of and possible for human endeavors and the conditions under which they can be sensibly completed is subtle and difficult; it is a problem that architecture has addressed since its very beginnings, most recently in the period of the Baroque. In that period, which was already dominated by a highly abstract representation of the cosmic order, it was nonetheless still possible to reconcile such a representation with the reality of the corporeal world—as we can see, for instance, in the works of Guarino Guarini and his contemporaries. Our situation is different, but the problem remains.

The task and dilemma we are facing is how to reconcile the inventions and achievements of modern technology, which have already established their autonomy, with the conditions of human life, our inherited culture, and the natural world. We will find no answer in a naive belief that the difficulty can be resolved by subordinating all knowledge and different ways of making to instrumental rationality and technology. Whole areas of reality are not amenable to such treatment, and perpetuating the belief that they are merely deepens the dilemma.

It is with such ideas in mind that we may turn to architecture and its latent capacity to harmonize different levels of reality, a phenomenon so clearly demonstrated in architectural history. The unifying power that architecture retains even today can be discovered again in the design process, where we find it possible to relate abstract ideas and conceptual structures to the concrete situations of everyday life. It is a part of our task to extend personal experience into the more public domain of shared reality, where it is possible to communicate not only between different levels of reality but also between different areas of culture. The aim is to create a continuum of relations, reciprocities, and comprehensible communication that can be succinctly described as a "communicative space." One of my intentions is to understand the capacity of architecture to create, or at least initiate, the formation of a communicative space—structured not mechanically, to fulfill predictable functions, but more in the fashion of a musical instrument, which can send reverberations through other levels of culture and help to embody them. Restoring the communicative role of architecture is a necessary step toward restoring its role as the topological and corporeal foundation of culture. This role can be best expressed in an analogy discussed later in some detail: what the book is to literacy, architecture is to culture as a whole.

The framework in which the communicative role of architecture can be restored must make it possible to reconcile the abstract language of conceptual constructions with the metaphorical language of the visible world. This was a typical task of poetics, replaced in modern times by the science of poetics (known better as aesthetics), which left the creative principles of making unaddressed. In the concluding chapter I argue why it is important to return to poetics and why a new poetics of architecture, together with contemporary hermeneutics, can provide the most appropriate framework for restoring the humanistic nature of architecture. It is to this goal that my book is primarily devoted, though it can offer only a foundation and outline for achieving it.

· CHAPTER 1 ·

MODERNITY, FREEDOM, AND DESTINY

T HE STATE OF contemporary architecture is to a large extent defined by the general fragmentation of our culture. Any serious attempt to address the key issues must therefore deal first with the nature of the relative and often derivative positions of various architects. This is not an easy task. As Max Stackhouse observes,

> when individuals and groups develop a link between their own imagination and their own reason that serves their own ends, and are not fundamentally concerned with the overall shape of the society, fragmentation inevitably ensues. . . . Everyone emotionally or intellectually, politically or economically grabs his fragment, which is partially real and creates a total reality with it. The splintered identities, the competing ideologies, the fractured parties and the glaring, cluttered advertising of competing businesses assault the person and the society from a thousand sides.[1]

Typically architects are more aware of the differences that separate them, giving their work an aura of novelty and originality. This leaves behind the common references and goals that contribute to the long-term cultural relevance of their work. The emphasis on difference and originality leads not only to results of questionable merit but also to isolation from the world that we all, in one way or another, share. There is an understandable temptation to describe that shared realm as the "given" or "real world." However, using the term "real" becomes problematic when ideologies and opinions are fiercely competing, when even "virtual reality is just another reality" and the "fact that it is computer generated with no physical existence makes it no less real."[2]

We commonly tend to save the meaning of the real by associating it with the practice of the office or with the building process. Such activities are considered radically different from the unreality or lesser reality of a project, from the deep understanding that grounds design problems, or from clearly defined visions. Though there clearly is some truth behind this impulse to differentiate, in most cases it is misleading. Architectural practice is not always practical; in fact, it is more often theoretical. We need only look at the nature of a typical brief or program, the criteria of design, and the conditions of its execution to grasp this elementary truth.

If we take as a basic criterion of reality the horizon of our everyday, commonsense world, a book might usefully be written to explain how the process of design and building relates to this horizon. That book would be devoted almost entirely to the different aspects of representation and to its history. We may already apprehend that representation is not limited to the physiognomy of buildings and spaces but relates more closely to the situational structure and meaning of architecture. Indeed, it is in this relation that the nature and degree of architectural reality can be established. However, before we can investigate the nature, reality, and meaning of modern architecture, as well as what it represents in our contemporary life, we have to understand the role of representation in creating and experiencing architecture in a broader historical context.

THE CHANGING NATURE OF REPRESENTATION

The problem of representation is closely linked with the process of making (*poiēsis*) and with creative imitation (*mimēsis*). Each project, however small or unimportant, begins with a program—or at least with a vision of the anticipated result. Such a program or a vision is formed in the space of experience and knowledge available to each of us. The result can be seen as the single actualization of an infinite number of possibilities. The formation of the program can be modified or improved through words or drawings because they make the potential field of possibilities present and available. Under such conditions, the actual result becomes a representation of the latent possibilities, bringing into focus their typical characteristics and enhancing their presence. Such focus takes place each time we succeed in grasping what is essential to a performance space, a concert hall, a particular urban space, and so on in a project. Thus, as Hans-Georg Gadamer points out, in contrast to the conventional understanding, "representation does not imply that something merely stands in for something else as if it were a replacement or substitute that enjoys a less authentic, more indirect kind of existence. On the contrary what is represented is itself present in the only way available to it."[3]

On this account, representation more or less coincides with the essential nature of making, and in particular with the making of our world. In the original Greek sense, making as *poiēsis* is the bringing into being of

The elevation of technology as a universal metaphysical foundation for a new era of culture was the final step in a process that reduced all that is worth knowing about the making of architecture to transparent productive knowledge. It did not seem to occur to those who believed in such a possibility that technology itself has no particular content: it is only a method of inventive production, and it therefore cannot be a source of order of any kind. Order is always constituted in the communicative space of a particular culture as a whole. When the culture itself is reduced to its most elementary characteristics and is represented in a manner compatible with technical thinking, then and only then it is possible to believe that "technology is far more than a method," that "it is a world in itself."[8]

Under such conditions "architecture should only stand," Mies van der Rohe as well as some members of the avant-garde believed, "in contact with the most significant elements of civilization. Only a relationship that touches on the innermost nature of the epoch is authentic."[9] Mies, whose late work offers the most interesting interpretation of a relationship between architecture and technology, was convinced that technology reveals its nature most explicitly in construction, in large-scale structures in particular; but he also believed that technology might reveal something else (figure 1.2). He describes this enigmatic something "else" as "something, that has a meaning and a powerful form, so powerful in fact that it is not easy to name it."[10]

To explain the enigma, Mies asks what happens to technology when it is applied. "Some people are convinced," he writes, "that architecture will be outmoded and replaced by technology. Such a conviction is not based on clear thinking. The opposite happens. Wherever technology reaches its real fulfillment it transcends into architecture."[11] This conclusion becomes more overt when we realize that the idea of "technological fulfillment" goes back via Gottfried Semper to Goethe and Karl Friedrich Schinkel, where it is known as the idea of material transformation, which reveals the poetic function of architecture.[12] In the process of material transformation, the inner logic of a building and its material realization manifest themselves as an ideal "material form." Such a manifestation corresponds with Mies's own conclusion: "Architecture depends on its time. It is the crystallization of its inner structure, the slow unfolding of its form. That is the reason why technology and architecture are so closely related."[13]

1.2. Ludwig Mies van der Rohe, National Gallery, Berlin.

The primary conditions for a new relationship between architecture and technology were first established in the seventeenth century when a gap opened up between the traditional symbolic and the new instrumental representation. In this period, in the late seventeenth and the early eighteenth century, architectural thinking, which had always been closely associated through its long history with the mathematical representation of its principles, was overtaken by new developments in the natural sciences. Relatively soon, the older approach and the new instrumentism were merged. The eighteenth century saw the foundation of engineering schools, which began to compete with the traditional architectural education; the emergence of modern aesthetics, providing a new formal appreciation of art; and the general formalization of culture, which were the main symptoms of the new situation. Other symptoms, less obvious, were the diminished relevance of tradition, most clearly visible in the ambiguous nature of late classicism, the growing arbitrariness of architectural decision making; and the discontinuity between the means and the content of representation.

The dual nature of symbolic and instrumental representation was long preserved in the cultural memory. It is apparent in all the main architectural movements of the twentieth century—from Constructivism, the Bauhaus, and De Stijl to French Purism—which no longer distinguished the formal representation of reality from the mathematical representation of technical knowledge. Mies van der Rohe himself declared: "our real hope is that technology and architecture grow together, that some day the one be the expression of the other. Only then will we have an architecture worthy of its name. Architecture as a true symbol of our time."[14] This hope did not last long. It was soon evident that not architecture but technology had become the symbol of our time.

That architecture was particularly open to technical interpretation has much to do with the general technization of everyday reality and its new levels of organization and formalization, particularly as related to work, bureaucracy, and domestic life. The level of formalization achieved is reflected in the history of architectural typologies; more broadly, it is seen in the reduction of the purpose of activities originally based on religious, cultural, or other meaning to technically and economically useful standards. These standards govern a period in which technical perfection and economic efficiency are considered to be "the most significant elements of civilization and the innermost nature of the epoch."[15] The technization of everyday life was in turn strongly influenced by the possibilities of representation developed in great diversity and on a large scale in the domains of architecture, urbanism, and landscape design. I am primarily thinking here not of the representational power of perspective, descriptive geometry, topology, and surveying, but of their power to transcend the unity of representation and to establish a new horizon of autonomy.

This development brings us to the very essence of a change that is manifested as a difference between the participatory and emancipatory nature of representation. It is well known that we largely experience the surrounding world, in its plenitude and in its given state, as otherness. I have already remarked that our experience of the given reality is never direct but only mediated, and that the most important role in that mediation is played by representation and its unity. Only the unity of representation can bring us closer to the depth and the plenitude of phenomenal reality, which would otherwise remain inaccessible. A line of poetry or a single painting very often can tell us much of the hidden meaning and beauty of a landscape, just as a light in a sacred space tells us of the intelligibility of the sky and the divine.

The primary purpose of representation, we may conclude, is its mediating role, which can also be described as participatory because it enhances our ability to participate in phenomenal reality. But the process of representation can also move in the opposite direction toward the emancipation of the results and, as a consequence, toward their separation from the original communicative context. This is a tendency that we know well from the attempts of avant-garde movements to create a new language of expression and representation, a language fully emancipated from history and tradition that might support the autonomy of the particular avant-garde position. The most radical manifestation of this type of emancipatory representation can be seen in recent movements that, so many years later, still share the intentions of earlier avant-gardes.[16]

The technical homogenization of whole areas of modern life makes it much easier to share the illusion that even the most abstract architectural solutions, based on narrow technical criteria, may be adequate and appropriate. Human adaptability is an important factor in the cultivation of this illusion. Even more important, however, is the overwhelming and persuasive power of emancipated representation itself, which addresses only the level of reality expressed in technical language. It is extraordinary how many different forms and facades this language can adopt. And yet, behind all the facades we find a common set of characteristics—not only in the areas normally associated with production and technology but also in other fields of creative activity.

CREATIVITY IN THE AGE OF PRODUCTION

The difference between creativity and production largely coincides with the distinction drawn above between participatory and emancipatory representation. Creativity is always situated within a particular communicative context from which it grows and in which the creative results participate. This circular process is not only the essence of creativity but also the essential moment in the disclosure and in the constitution of the human world. Production, in contrast, though it may grow from the same context, separates itself and establishes its own operation in an autonomous domain of reality.

What makes that separation possible is the know-how supplied by technical knowledge and the autonomy of the formal structures embodied in emancipated representation. In real life, the distinction between creativity and production is never absolute: each creative act always contains initial element of inventiveness, and any production—at least in its initial stage—displays a certain level of creativity. However, their goals remain strongly and clearly differentiated. What is produced, unlike what is created, has no communicative relation with its cultural setting: its purpose and meaning are established entirely in accordance with the task's internal logic. Not just many structures and buildings—industrial plants, supermarkets, schools, hospitals, and the like—but also many artworks are produced in the same way as any other industrial product.

Such a product is typically designed for a precise purpose, and at the same time for any place, people, or culture. In describing his vision of the new art, which was to be universal, Theo van Doesburg already in the 1930s used purely productive terms: "The work of art must be entirely conceived and formed by the mind before its execution. It must receive nothing from nature's given forms or from sensuality or from sentimentality. We wish to exclude lyricism, dramaticism, symbolism, etc. In painting a pictorial element has no other element than itself. The construction of the picture, as well as its elements, must be simple and visually controllable. Technique must be mechanical, that is exact, anti-impressionistic"[17] (figure 1.3).

The productive attitude to art and architecture, which profoundly influenced the nature of creativity in the twentieth century, has become particularly dominant in recent decades. One of its main characteristics is a tendency to accelerate the development of "productive" possibilities. This characteristic is directly linked to the nature of emancipated representation, which translates and reduces reality into an image structured more by our inventiveness and visions than by the given conditions of reality itself. To invent or produce under such conditions is like moving at a high speed through thin air. It is perhaps not surprising that in the fragmented culture of the twentieth century it proved to be easier to produce than to create.

Much evidence is available that helps us to see more deeply into the intricate relation between creativity and production. Perhaps most imme-

1.3. Theo van Doesburg, Aubette, cinema and dance hall, Strasbourg (destroyed).

diately enlightening are Daniel Libeskind's drawings, which he himself describes as "deconstructive constructions" (figure 1.4). They consciously explore "the relation between the intuition of geometric structure as it manifests itself in a pre-objective sphere of experience and the possibility of formalization which tries to overtake it in the objective realm."[18] The drawings offer a unique insight into the constructive possibilities on the boundary of actual and imaginary space—in other words, an insight into the representative power of our imagination, challenged by the conceptual power of invention. The transition from actual to imaginary space, from the geometrical representation of actual spatial relationships to their formal equivalents, is in essence a transition from the space of real possibilities to the space of possible realities. In this process, which illustrates the emergence

1.4. Daniel Libeskind, *The Architect and His Shadow* (1981).

of the autonomy of geometrical representation, the original continuity of meaning is replaced by the transformational meaning of the process itself. The open-ended and enigmatic nature of the results is the price paid for the new productive freedom. Such freedom seems to be the demand of the current situation, but why? Libeskind again:

> Contemporary formal systems present themselves as riddles—unknown instruments for which usage is yet to be found. Today we seldom start with particular conditions which we raise to a general view; rather we descend from a general system to a particular problem. However, what is significant in this tendency, where the relation between the abstract and the concrete is reversed, is the claim which disengages the nature of drawing as though the "reduction" of drawing were an amplification of the mechanisms of knowledge.[19]

The tendency to extend and, where possible, to surpass the limits of visual representation is one of the main characteristics of the contemporary avant-garde as it attempts to transcend the confines of traditional culture and the existing human condition. It is perhaps not surprising that geometry and mathematical thinking in general play a key role in such an effort. Mathematics has always been the major instrument of transcendence, because it generates its own development, regardless of whether its results can be directly reconciled with the world of phenomena. The extension of mathematical thinking into a broader sphere of culture brings architecture itself close to mathematics, and thus into the stream of productive thinking. Because architects are not usually much concerned with the sources and the nature of the knowledge received from other fields, tending to view it either uncritically or as a pragmatic tool, they are very often victims of deep confusion.

In the case of mathematics, much effort was invested already in the nineteenth century to better understand its logical foundations and applicability and to gain a more comprehensive vision of the relationship between mathematical representation and reality. In all these studies and investigations, the recurring issues are the ontological nature of the conditions and possibilities of formalization, the nature of formal systems, and the continuity of meaning in mathematical operations (figure 1.5). It is surprising that architects, who encounter practically the same problems in their own work, pay little attention to their nature and their implications—this leads inevitably to confusion. The words of Jean Ladrière, a leading mathematician who is clearly speaking only about his own field, nonetheless apply also to architecture:

> The abstract is not the first. It is by a perpetual return to its intuitive origins and to the reality of its problems, by a close fidelity to the imperatives of this hidden life which traverses theories like fertilizing sap, that mathematical thought reconquers, through the inevitable snares of a necessary abstraction. This original concrete [reality], which is always present, at the core of its movement, and which manifests in most characteristic fashion its permanent activity in the highest moments of creation. . . . To detach itself from these roots, would in reality be to condemn itself to asphyxia, to enclose itself in a kind of mortal solitude which would result in the emptiness of a system void of all content.[20]

The danger of emptiness has haunted modern architecture from its very beginning. However, it is important to realize that emptiness sprang not only from the buildings but also from the absence of an articulated public culture. Once the continuity of shared meaning has been broken into fragments of understanding, it is unrealistic to expect ambitious abstract structures and their implied meaning to be understood as their authors intended. When Mies van der Rohe speaks about the spiritual meaning of construction, or Michel Seuphor praises an "architecture which by the technical and physical methods peculiar to the age, reflects in its particular organization the magnificent order of the universe,"[21] they are no longer convincing.

We may feel, quite rightly, that there is a deep gap in communication, not only between people or between people and buildings, but between different areas of culture itself. The presence of this divide, it seems to me, is illustrated by the sheer amount of verbal explanation and commentary that accompanies the visual arts. Its purpose, no doubt, is to convey the personal meaning of the work to the public. The need for such explication illustrates a much larger problem—the gap between the achievements of modern science and technology, including their deep influence on contemporary so-

1.5. Ivan Leonidov, headquarters of heavy industry, Moscow (1934).

ciety, and the communicative nature of the phenomenal world. This is, reflected most clearly in the difficulty of reconciling the abstract, conceptual
representations of our world and the particular conditions and aspirations
of our lives.

There is a tendency to believe that the emancipation of technological
possibilities and powers affects reality as a whole and uniformly, and therefore leads to human emancipation. That would be true only if life and nature
could be reduced to transparent knowledge; but as we know, such reduction

is impossible. Whole areas of nature and life are beyond our capacity to comprehend—and yet those very areas exert the greatest influence on the nature of our world. Their importance is increasingly underscored by the growing knowledge now being accumulated by anthropology, human ecology, environmental medicine, and so on, as the following statement by the microbiologist René Dubos illustrates very well:

> The evolutionary development of all living organisms, including man, took place under the influence of cosmic forces that have not changed appreciably for very long periods of time. As a result, most physiological processes are still geared to these forces; they exhibit cycles that have daily, seasonal and other periodicities clearly linked to the periodicities of cosmos. As far as can be judged at the present time, the major biological periodicities derive from the daily rotation of the earth, its annual rotation around the sun and the monthly rotation of the moon around the earth.[22]

Dubos briefly describes the conditions under which the regularity of certain vital processes of our lives were constituted and under which they eventually became the source of other regularities and movements that structured the higher, more articulated layers of our life and culture. That the articulation of cultural life is directly linked with conditions that remain relatively unchanged, while at the same time the path of culture that is open to technological transformation has changed radically, creates a tension and eventually a deep void in the very heart of the culture itself.

The vision of modern society undergoing a steady technological transformation en bloc is misleading. There is a great difference between those levels of reality that can be directly manipulated and those that resist such manipulation. In the case of dwelling, for instance, new constructions, materials, and services, are being developed on a different level and at a different rate than the nature and purpose of the dwelling, which are rooted in tradition, customs, habits, and in the relative stability of primary human situations (figure 1.6).

How to reconcile the differences in the nature and rate of development is a question often addressed. The typical answer refers to technology and to the need to adapt to its imperatives. How one-sided and problematic

1.6. Melanie Young, metaphorical study of the design studio.

such an answer is can be demonstrated by the complex history of adaptation going back at least to the end of the eighteenth century, when the total dominance of disengaged emancipated rationality was first seriously challenged by Romanticism and by its influence on later generations.[23] We have to remember and acknowledge that Romanticism was not just a reaction to the Enlightenment, an artistic movement, or an impossible dream but also a science, philosophy, and general attitude toward culture as a whole.[24] In the dialectical development of modern culture during the past two centuries,

1.7. Ivan Leonidov, United Nations Headquarters (1957–1958).

Romanticism—in different forms and under different names—has been the main source of the continuity of humanistic culture, creativity, and the sense of wholeness. It is mostly through its more recent manifestations in Expressionism and Surrealism, but also (though less explicitly) in certain aspects of Constructivism and even in High Tech, that the Romantic tradition has exerted its influence on modern architecture (figure 1.7). It is difficult to find a better example than the work of Hans Scharoun. His whole life was devoted to a thoughtful and highly personal interpretation of culture that, under the relatively narrow label "Expressionism," manifested a rich, long-term contribution from philosophy, literature, theater, and visual arts. In the Expressionist epoch, most German culture was dominated by a desire to transcend fragmentary experience and to attain a vision of the whole, to achieve a union with the inward reality of the world.

Inwardness is the main feature not only of Expressionism but of the twentieth century as a whole. It has resulted from a long-term transformation of European culture, tied to a belief that our life can be entirely represented in terms of scientific, technical rationality, leaving behind all that cannot be subordinated to this vision—mainly the domain of personal experience, praxis, and the natural world. The emancipation of scientific rationality led to a culture with its own criteria of intelligibility and to a new sense of wholeness based on the continuity of the humanistic tradition accessible through personal, introverted experience. In the field of architecture, this mode of culture is typically embodied in the Romantic notion of genius, which reduces the traditional complexity of culture to a single, creative gesture and to direct communication with the assumed creative powers of nature. In his 1925 lecture at the Breslau Academy, Scharoun declared: "The creator creates intuitively in accordance with an impulse that corresponds not only to his temperament but also to the time to which he belongs and with which he is, to a great extent, one. And if we want to explain this impulse, then we must understand the real tasks of our time. The law that drives and leads an architect can perhaps be grasped only metaphysically."[25]

The law that drives and leads an architect is very closely linked with the mystery of architectural form (*Gestalt*) to which Scharoun explicitly refers: "The great mystery in the creative work is undoubtedly *Gestalt*, *Gestalt* in the sense of organic and multiple form."[26] The mystery of form has much to do with the question of authenticity, which for Scharoun was synonymous with the organicity of design, as measured by the correspondence between *Leistungsform* (functional form) and *Wesenhafte Gestalt* (essential form). The functional form is a result of a *Gestaltfindung* (investigation), in which the appropriate solution is determined by the given purpose, material, and construction. Together with Hugo Häring, with whom he shared many ideas, Scharoun believed that the functional or organic form, as he sometimes calls it, is a result of an anonymous process in which the intrinsic laws of nature or human life determine the design. Despite the importance of functional investigation, the goal of each project was the essential form that was supposed to reconcile the formal solution with the spiritual principles of the epoch. However, the presumed anonymity and objectivity of the process were illusory. The determination of design by the laws of nature or human life is conceivable only as an interpretation in which the role of the architect and his or her experience, imagination, and intentions are decisive. Their importance is even more obvious in the search for the essential form, which in the absence or even negation of all precedents requires a great deal of experience and knowledge as well as a high level of inventiveness.

Under such conditions, the task is not only to invent a particular building from one's own cultural reserves but also to invent a culture that would make the building meaningful. The result is a cycle that seals the introverted nature of the creative process and potentially opens the way to arbitrariness and relativism. It is very difficult to imagine how a culture articulated in an inner dialogue can replace the richness and wisdom of a culture that was publicly cultivated and shared for many centuries. This problem is clearly apparent in the discrepancy between Scharoun's buildings and his stated intentions. In the Berlin Philharmonie, for instance, the main hall was no doubt deeply influenced by the history of music auditoria; and yet Scharoun describes the process of its making as a direct dialogue between the nature of music and the nature of space, seen as a landscape (figures 1.8 and 1.9). "The construction," he writes, "follows the pattern of a landscape with the auditorium seen as a valley and there at its bottom is the orchestra surrounded by a sprawling vineyard climbing the sides of its neighboring hills. The ceiling, resembling a tent, encounters the landscape like a skyscape."[27]

The indeterminate, changing perceptual structure of the whole is held together by the constructive imagination of the architect and the musical experience of the audience. It is interesting to see how early Scharoun anticipated the close link between his own imagination and public experience. In one of his drawings for the Glass Chain, he illustrates the place and the role of the artist among the people—the artist's ability to embody and represent their will and elevate it to the higher level of "spiritual" existence[28] (figure 1.10).

It is a sign of the avant-garde mentality that the architect sees him- or herself as a sole agent, fully responsible for everything related to creativity. This illusion culminates in the belief that world is essentially each architect's own world. Everything created under such conditions is bound

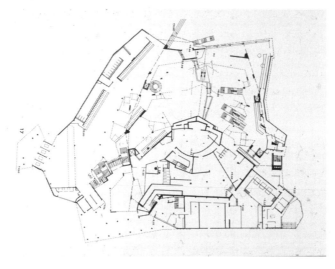

1.8. Hans Scharoun, Berlin Philharmonie, plan.

1.9. Hans Scharoun, Berlin Philharmonie, interior.

1.10. Hans Scharoun, *Ich Du, Volkshausgedanke* (1920).

to be unique, and yet claims are often made for a universal validity. This paradox can be sustained only by a self-centered culture, prepared to share the paradox as a norm. However, this does not resolve the real problem of the relation between the universality and the particularity of design. We can see that problem not only in the architecture of Scharoun but also in the work of his opposite, Mies van der Rohe. The universality of Mies's structure, it is conventionally believed, represents both the universal and the specific aspects of the program and of the broader context of culture (figure 1.11). In fact, the deeper content is present only enigmatically and is accessible only through very cryptic personal interpretations. No amount of wishful interpretation, however, can bridge the gap between the promise of meaning and its fulfillment. In the end, Mies's buildings remain what they are—cultivated material structures, which can at best be appreciated aesthetically. The talk about Mies's classicism and his own arguments about the expression of the essence of the modern epoch through technology are no more than empty intellectual constructions. On the basis of these constructions, the emanci-

1.11. Ludwig Mies van der Rohe, National Gallery, Berlin.

pated and isolated reality of Miesian structures is sometimes situated in a broader sphere of meaning. Such meaning may be available to the architect himself and to those who are persuaded by the thrust of his argument; but to those who are not initiated or have their own critical understanding, the argument must appear hermetic and illusory. It is quite astonishing to see the extent to which the twentieth-century avant-gardes succeeded in fabricating their position—their promises of new meaning, coherence, and wholeness—through publicity, exhibitions, manifestos, and utopian projects rather than through the convincing quality of buildings, to say nothing of cities.[29] In a sense, the career of Mies shows similar characteristics.[30]

The critical role played by the media, the secondary and derivative mode of representation, in the making of modern architecture illustrates how tenuous the link between architecture and its cultural context has become. In Miesian terms, the universality of the solutions is, contrary to the intentions of their author, only a form of universality. In the work of Scharoun, as we have seen, most important is the process of creation starting from and cultivating the particular. "We know," he wrote in the last years of his life, "that all our attempts are only a modest beginning in detail."[31] In the development from the particular and from the detail, there is always a certain anticipation of the result in the form of an idea or conceptual image. However, the aversion toward the a priori presence of all universality leaves Scharoun's work isolated from the broader meaning of the common culture. In that sense, it is complementary to the work of Mies.

THE GRAY ZONE OF CONTEMPORARY CULTURE

By curious historical coincidence, Scharoun's Philharmonie and Mies's National Gallery, the two most typical representations of the polarity in modern architectural thinking, share the same space on the Kulturforum in Berlin (figure 1.12). The gray zone that separates them can be understood both literally and metaphorically.

The space of the forum in its contemporary state is a sad memento of twentieth-century inability to create a genuine public space. That failure is reflected in the broader and deeper metaphorical meaning of the gray zone, which shows the true scale of the gap between the universality of modern culture, represented by modern science and technology, and the domain of introverted culture, represented mostly by the arts, the humanities, and personal experience. Its width was already apparent in the contrast between Mies's conviction that "the individual is losing significance" and "his destiny is no longer what interests us" and Scharoun's doubts about the role of rational knowledge and structured creative process. "Do we reach pure creativity through reflection, through knowledge?" Scharoun writes; "—No—man is the center."[32]

In one sense the gray zone is a metaphor for a deep discontinuity in modern culture; in another sense it is a metaphor for the problematic attempts to resolve the discontinuity from a single, relatively narrow position. The typical example is a loose and arbitrary connection established between a highly personal experience and ideas of universal validity. In the history of modern architecture, the attempts to resolve the problem of cultural discontinuity have resulted in the formation and consolidation of several distinct positions. The most obvious, already discussed, took shape around the belief in the universal role of technology and around personal

1.12. Berlin Kulturforum, aerial view.

expressive epiphanies. Among other formative beliefs might be cited a faith in the restorative power of the vernacular tradition, in classicism, and more recently in the historicizing improvizations of postmodernism and in conceptual deconstructions.

The arbitrary nature of the relation between the sphere of experience and the sphere of concepts or ideas is the main characteristic of the gray zone. It is a source of an unprecedented freedom to produce new works but also of an overwhelming relativism, loss of meaning, and narrowing range of common references—and, as a result, of a general cultural malaise.[33] The nature of this malaise can be easily illustrated by the dilemma facing most contemporary architects. On the one hand, it is assumed that true creative architecture should be free of historical and other unnecessary cultural references in order to be as original and unique as possible. And yet, on the other hand, it is expected that the result should be universally understood, appreciated, and accepted.

In an atmosphere of arbitrariness and relativity, originality of design is manifest primarily in the visibility of the result. Visibility always presumes, even in its most abstract form, some form of continuity with the natural world. That is its main virtue. On the same grounds, visibility can be pushed to its limits and serve as a transition to the derivative quasi-visibility in the conceptual domain. Such a transition is particularly relevant for understanding the fragile nature of visibility in works structured under the strong influence of technical thinking—considered today to be the main source of originality. In many of these works, matters of visibility usually do not precede but instead follow the diagrammatic stage of the project, very often remaining residual.

The residual nature of the primary visibility in modern buildings was anticipated by Mies when he wrote: "The visible is only the final step of a historical form, its fulfillment. Its true fulfillment. Then it breaks off and a new world arises. . . . Not everything that happens takes place in full view. The decisive battles of the spirit are waged on invisible battlefields."[34] These invisible battlefields are the domains of conceptual thinking, calculations, and diagrammatic imagination. The extent to which contemporary architectural projects are conceived on that level can be illustrated by many examples, some of them involving an architecture inspired by no more than structural possibilities.

The fragility of the visible can be extended to other areas of our experience. What we experience in front of an incomprehensible building or structure escapes explicit understanding but is reflected in our tacit response. This dynamic was recognized years ago by apologists of Constructivism, particularly in reference to beauty. "The beauty of the machine," writes the Czech art critic Karel Teige, "is the rational value of an irrational product. . . . Irrationality is the essence of the inexplicable beauty of the machine. It is for that reason that machines can be an example not only of a modern, logically functioning mind, but also of a nervous modern sensibility. There is nothing more nervous than a vibrating dynamo."[35] This understanding of the nature of beauty exemplifies the transformation of modern sensibility in which the richness of a fully articulated world revealed in works of art and buildings has been reduced to a personal aesthetic experience, based on elementary sensations. In the closed world of aesthetic experience, it is virtually impossible to differentiate between the nature of reception and the nature of production or creation.

The concentration on private experience, imagination, and fantasy appears to contradict the very nature of architecture, which is always open to a shared public culture. And yet some architects recently have tended to create architecture in a way similar to the automatism of Surrealism or of action painting. The architects of the Coop partnership are very much aware of this affinity, as they declare: "We conceive of architecture which would engage complicated human procedures and psyches and which would represent a personal statement, with all the attendant strengths and weaknesses implied—not unlike the way art is made" (figure 1.13). The main precondition for taking such an approach is a full emancipation from historical precedents and the continuity of tradition. In their own words, "it is a kind of release from fixed ideas . . . and for that reason we never talk about architecture for fear that inhibitions about what is possible functionally or what others have done before us in similar circumstances will creep in. . . . We have to be self-monitoring, or else we could get side-tracked. We avoid analysis, but remain aware of our bodies and our hearts."[36]

In the spontaneity of the automatic process of design, the content of the project depends, almost entirely, on an internal dialogue with oneself—on the personal and not on the inherited culture (figure 1.14). Is it possible to envisage the genuine content of a work outside inherited culture? This is a question that had already been raised in the early days of Surrealism. Louis Aragon observed, "If you write deplorable twaddle using Surrealist techniques, it will still be deplorable twaddle. No excuses. If you belong to the species of individuals who do not know the meaning of words, it is more than probable that the practice of Surrealism will simply serve to highlight this gross ignorance."[37]

And as Jürgen Habermas notes, "The neo-Avant-Garde moves today within a more or less non-binding pluralism of artistic means and stylistic schools while no longer able to enlist the force of an enlightening originality released in the violation of established norms, in the shock of the forbidden and frivolous, in irrepressible subjectivity."[38] The difficulty of enlisting the force of originality pushes the contemporary avant-garde deeper into a more radical form of self-centeredness and self-referentiality. The result is a higher level of autonomy and separation from everyday

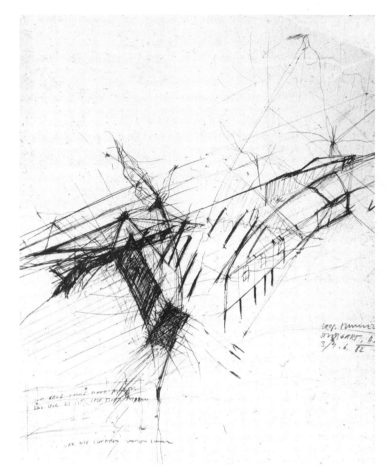

1.13. Coop Himmelblau, preliminary sketch (1982).

reality, accompanied by a desperate search for new sources of originality in current technology and in the domain of private fantasies. Here the difference between the product of imagination and imaginary reality is no longer clear. As artists produce imaginary solutions, they replace the dialogue with phenomenal reality by a monologue of conceptual imagination that relies on the quasi-visibility of geometry as its scaffold. Under such conditions, according to Maurice Merleau-Ponty, "the illusion of seeing is therefore much less the presentation of an illusory object than the spread and so to speak

1.14. Coop Himmelblau, conversion of the attic space, Flakestrasse, Vienna (1989).

running wild of a visual power which has lost any sensory counterpart."
This characteristic loss leads to hallucinations, "because through the phenomenal body we are in constant relationship with an environment into
which that body is projected and because when divorced from its actual environment, the body remains able to summon up, by means of its own settings, the pseudo-presence of that environment."[39]

This sounds like a description of some recent projects oriented toward a creation of virtual reality, which, as is generally acknowledged, is a

consciously structured and controlled hallucinatory world. But hallucinations occur only in certain spaces and media, and cannot be identified with the reality of the whole. Indeed, there are structures in our culture that resist hallucinations. More specifically, Merleau-Ponty writes, "what protects us against delirium or hallucinations are not our critical powers but the structure of our space."[40] The structure of space has its source in the depth of culture and coincides with the overall coherence of our cultural world. Because our existence is always spatial, the nature of lived phenomenal space determines the topography, orientation, meaning, and the sanity of our existence. However, when we speak about the coherence of the cultural world we refer not only to its latent background but also to its visible manifestations, which exhibit a high degree of fragmentation and discontinuity—revealed most dramatically in the gray zone of modern culture.

The distance that separates us from the deeper levels of reality marks the success of the development of the new means of representation. The problematic consequences of this development are the emancipation of representation and the tendency toward self-reference. The emancipated, relatively closed world of representation puts at issue, more radically than ever before, the relevance of communication. How are we to grasp the relation of abstract or simulated space to the space of the everyday life? In the past, such a question would be answered by pointing to a sequence of levels of reality that constitutes a link between universal concepts and the particularity of individual phenomena, thereby creating a continuum of the articulated, communicative space of culture.[41] That this space is accessible to us nowadays only with intense effort remains a challenge for the future.

· CHAPTER 2 ·

THE NATURE OF COMMUNICATIVE SPACE

T HE AMBIGUOUS role of representation in the life of contemporary culture, which is dominated to a great extent by scientific knowledge, is closely linked with the problem of communication, not only between but within different areas of culture. However, the difficulties faced today by the sciences in communicating their results, mutually or to the public, do not seem to disturb us anymore. What do disturb us are issues pertaining to the truth of communication. The possibility that a communication based on emancipated representation can deceive raises a question about how representation may convey or rather obscure reality. The attempt to understand the conditions under which representation contributes to the enhancement of our experience is motivated not so much by intellectual curiosity as by an inherited sense of reality asserting itself, very often against our will. We do not have to look far for examples, which are easily found in our own discipline. From everyday experience we know how wide the gap is between the best possible delineation of a project and the built result. The real intention is most often present in the margin between the design and what is explicitly specified. Each project rests on a network of communication that involves the silent language of craftsmanship and skills, drawings, sketches, and other visual representations as well as verbal descriptions and instructions.[1]

The best possible documentation of a project is only a part of the communication needed for its realization. Attempts to eliminate secondary communication and reduce the process of design and building to that which can be specified a priori are altogether problematic. Attesting to their limits is the fact that most projects do not speak for themselves but require additional explanation. The discrepancy between the a priori representation and the result—the inhabited space—is even more apparent in the concrete experience of a particular space. We do not need specialized knowledge to see how markedly the experience of a space transcends what has been established beforehand. The scale of the space, the texture of materials, the presence and movement of light, the plenitude and simultaneous presence of everything that is visible in the space—these are some of the elements (phenomena) that cannot be directly represented and yet constitute the very essence of any particular space. It would be more appropriate to know more about the situational conditions of our everyday life, about the spatial characteristics of the natural world in which we live and how they are communicated through representation. But in order to obtain such knowledge

2.1. Louvain (Belgium), street in the center of town.

we must first understand how the structure and the experiential content of representation are anticipated in the conditions of the natural world.

To see the problem more clearly, consider the experience of reading the plan or map of a particular place (figure 2.1). To understand the spatial configuration of a town we have not seen before requires a particular effort. Without outside help, only our imagination can guide us through the unknown toward a clearer understanding of the town. It is not easy to explain how such an understanding grows. We certainly do not draw diagrams in our imagination. Instead, the prominence of certain buildings or spaces helps us to move from a random sequence of experiences to a more structured vision of a situational pattern. It is natural but at the same time rather misleading to believe that the simultaneity of vision is a product of our imagination. The sequential nature of the process indicates that the reciprocity between a particular physiognomy of the scene and our imagination is what produces our more coherent vision and understanding. The role of reciprocity becomes even clearer if we make the same effort with the help of the map. The map gives us direct access to a diagrammatic representation of the town, but only on the condition that we can find the correspondences between the conceptual, diagrammatic representation and what we directly see and experience around us.

The task we face in such a situation is not to compare the perceptual and conceptual image but rather to focus our experience and translate it into a conceptual construct, similar to the map. Our experience—which in this case occurs on different levels of corporeal involvement, perceptual experience, conceptual images, and thoughts—is united in one continuous structure of space in which the relationship between the given reality and its representation is mediated and communicated. The nature of the mediation is obscure and not directly accessible to us except in its results. However, when the continuity of mediation is disrupted, insight into its otherwise unavailable workings becomes possible.

THE HIDDEN CONDITIONS OF HUMAN SITUATION AND EXPERIENCE

One of the more revealing illustrations of the working of mediation is an experiment in which the subject wears special spectacles that invert vision while leaving the rest of experience unchanged[2] (figure 2.2). On the first day of the experiment everything in the visual field appears upside down, but the original orientation, manifested most clearly through the sense of touch, remains intact. The arms and legs are localized in two different ways. The body is generally perceived as upright, the space around as upside down. Everything that is touched provokes the old visual image, while the scene, seen directly, is inverted. The whole experience is accompanied by a feeling of dizziness and nausea. Over time, the conflict between the old and the new localizations becomes less explicit and unpleasant. But even on the sixth day a great discrepancy still remains between the original and the new situations. A pendulum, for instance, which appears at first to be upside down, appears upright if suspended from one hand. When the index fingers are brought into the visual field, the right being where the left had been before the glasses were put on, a touch can be felt in either of them, sometimes

2.2. Inverted view of the fountain, Cambridge Botanical Gardens.

in both. It is usually around the eighth day that the visual and tactile fields of experience are more or less reconciled, though even then they never completely agree. The parts of the body that are not directly visible to the subject remain permanently in the old orientation. After the spectacles are removed at the end of the experiment, the visual world becomes straight again almost immediately, but it takes one or two more days before perception returns entirely to normal.

This sequence of rather unusual experiences throws a new light on many important issues, most of all on the intrinsic structure and nature of space. In a conventional understanding of space, its topography and orientation are usually related to a clearly defined set of primary coordinates (absolute space) or to the primary orientation of our body (absolute body).

However, as we have seen, neither is available during the experiment.[3] The question of where up or down is becomes relative; the only absolute is the situated human body and its capacity to constitute a coherent space. That the subject can restore spatial coherence under conditions of spatial ambiguity points toward a more primordial, hidden structure situated in the depths of the human condition. This structure—available to us a priori, as we shall see later—is the result of our earlier involvement with the surrounding world.

The critical phenomena in the formation of space are temporal and spatial continuities of experience. The importance of continuity for the integrity and coherence of space can be illustrated as follows. If we look into a room, accessible visually only through a mirror that is not vertical, everything in the room appears to be leaning to one side. People who walk around the room, as well as all the objects in it, appear to be falling toward the ground. It usually takes several minutes before the room begins to appear as vertical, or at least not in conflict with our own verticality. However, if we physically enter the same room it appears to us as properly oriented regardless of our angle of vision. Seen from a reclining chair or even from a horizontal position the room remains straight. What makes the first experience difficult and problematic is a discontinuity of experience in our effort to inhabit the room. We have to find how to enter and inhabit the distorted space in a way similar to that necessary to reconcile vision with the rest of our experience in the "inverted vision" experiment.

Orientation is not something that can be determined by one of our senses. Merleau-Ponty declares, "What counts for the orientation of the spectacle is not my body as it in fact is, as a thing in objective space, but as a system of possible actions, a virtual body with its phenomenal 'place' defined by its task and situation."[4] The concept of "virtual body," defined by its task and situation, refers to the creative formation of space in terms not only of its topography (as a situated place), or its orientation, but also of its physiognomy. Only with all these aspects of architectural space in mind can we understand the deepest levels of space as it is constituted in the domain of the given natural conditions and human spontaneity. On this level, spatiality is primarily dependent not on the position or direction of the human body, but on the continuity between the actual and possible structures of the surrounding world to which the human body belongs.

The primordial form of spatiality is a "horizon of all our experiences, but it is a horizon which cannot be in principle ever reached and thematized in our express perception."[5] The horizon of all our experiences that cannot be fully thematized in fact defines a world in which space is only a dimension. In this context it would be more appropriate to speak about the spatiality of the world so that the structure, topography, and orientation of space could receive their proper ontological meaning. There is no ultimate origin or ground of space, for the same reason that there is no ultimate ground of the world. Instead there is a continuum of references mediating between the more articulated and explicit form of space and its implicit deep structure. This is well illustrated by a discovery made by the subject in the course of the inverted vision experiment:

> When I stretched out my right hand to pick up a book which was lying to my left on the floor, by chance I discovered a simple method by which I could select the correct hand when picking up objects from the floor, which method I used afterwards with invariable success. If I tapped with my foot once or twice near the object before I bent to pick it up, the appropriate hand came into play. Curiously enough it was still easier to start with the appropriate foot than with the hand.[6]

The tapping on the floor is not just an exercise of tactile experience. It is an articulated mediation between the new, inverted world and its predecessor, which are eventually related through reference to the earth. In this case, the earth functions not as an object or as a center of gravity but as the primary reference of our spatial existence and of our world.

The nature of the world, which I shall discuss in greater detail later, is revealed most explicitly whenever the world itself is disrupted or radically transformed. Such certainly occurs to those, for instance, who are born blind but regain their sight after a successful operation. Today it is widely acknowledged that the world of the blind is structured not only in time series but also spatially; it has therefore its own specific topography, orientation, and physiognomy.[7] In the world of the blind, objects are not only identified and located but also situated in relation to the total world of experience, even though they are recognized mostly through their tactile configuration.[8] The radical difference that exists between the world before and after an operation becomes comprehensible, argues Merleau-Ponty, only through the continuity between them:

> The very fact that the way is paved to true vision through a phase of transition and through a sort of touch effected by the eyes would be incomprehensible unless there were a quasi-spatial tactile field into which the first visual perceptions may be inserted. Sight would never communicate directly with touch, as it in fact does in the normal adult, if the sense of touch even when artificially isolated were not so organized as to make co-existence possible.[9]

We are little aware of the unique contributions that the individual senses make to our normal experience. The encounter with the world of the blind person who has undertaken an operation that restores vision is an opportunity to better comprehend such a contribution. What we discover in the world of the blind is not the loss of a particular ability to experience but rather the consequences of such a loss—confusion, the lack of orientation to and physiognomy of the active space. In the period of recovery after the operation, the formerly blind person lives in a disturbed world, in which sight is possible physiologically but not in reality, because his or her visual field has no physiognomy as yet. At first the discontinuity between things known mostly by touch and those known by visual appearance seems to be total. It is only after a long process of learning, somewhat similar to the process of reconciliation in the inverted vision experiment, that the patient's new visual experience is reintegrated into a unified world.[10]

The world of the blind is not easy for us to understand. However, the enigma of the difference that separates us from the blind can also tell us a great deal about our own world that we would not otherwise know. As one blind person clearly expressed it:

> I admitted to myself that there was in fact a highly important difference of organization between myself and other people. Whereas I can make contact with them by touch and hearing, they were bound to me through an unknown sense which entirely surrounded me even from a distance, followed me about, penetrated through me and somehow held me in its power from morning to night. What a strange power this was to which

I was subjected against my will, without, for my part, being able to exercise it over any one at all. It made me shy and uneasy to begin with. I felt envious about it. It seemed to raise an impenetrable screen between society and myself. I felt unwillingly compelled to regard myself as an exceptional being, that had, as it were, to hide itself in order to live.[11]

After a successful operation, the process of learning begins with confusion. Initially "the newly-operated patients do not localize their visual impressions, they do not relate them to any point, either to the eye or to any surface even a spherical one; they see colors much as we smell an odor of peat or varnish, which enfolds and intrudes upon us, but without occupying any specific form of extension in a more exactly definable way."[12] In the later stages, the identification of objects by color, shape, and spatial position is accomplished first through the help of other senses but eventually becomes almost direct, owing to already acquired experience. One patient, four months after an operation, displays typical progress:

> On subsequent occasions he is able, when helped out by touch, to recognize the objects customarily presented to him, and these latter become points of comparison, standard objects, to which he relates his later acquisitions. And now it becomes possible for him to form associations among images, constituted out of the imagery first acquired and the intuitive images newly presented to him. Instead of hunting over objects by eye, as he did earlier, he now names them approximately and then proceeds to improve upon his first mistaken description, as soon as the objects are placed conveniently for him at a sufficiently short distance.[13]

The most striking characteristic of such transformation and learning displayed in these examples is their systematic nature. It appears quite clearly that the correspondences, reconciliations, and unities of experience are formed according to a preexisting pattern that we have not yet fully identified. So far we have only discovered and established that the nature of space depends on the continuity of reference to deeper structures of the human world, that these structures are in a certain sense related to the earth as a primary reference (*archē*), and that the integrity of space is reflected in the coherence of human experience.

These discoveries are all relevant but are still only general. It would be more useful to find a language that could describe the different modalities of space more specifically. This specificity is possible if we speak about the deep spatial structures in terms of topology (closely linked with the topology of being), about the continuity of references in terms of orientation, and about the explicit manifestation of spatiality in terms of physiognomy. The topology, orientation, and physiognomy of space constitute a unity: the visible aspects of space, its physiognomy, depend on orientation; and orientation in turn depends on the topological character of the surrounding world. This sequence of relationships and dependencies brings us closer to understanding the phenomenon of continuity in its identifiable manifestations.

Such manifestations can be made especially obvious in a space of zero gravity[14] (figure 2.3). For example, one member of the team at the space station recalled an attempt to respond to the sound of the telephone at night: "I had no way of determining up from down, I had no visual reference in the dark. I had to turn on the light, but I just did not know what direction to put my hand in. So I had to feel things to orient myself. I had to use touch instead of sight, but everything felt different because I didn't know my relationship to them." The astronauts used similar language in stressing the importance of natural primary orientation: "You tend to orient yourself when you are in a room even though you are in zero gravity, and when you orient yourself you should find everything is the same. You don't like something up and something under. You like things to be orderly like they always are on Earth."[15] Most of the members of the team turned out to be so reluctant to give up the idea of a single vertical, such as they had enjoyed on earth, that the designers despaired of their more ambitious plans.[16]

The visibility to which this statement refers is not just the visible appearance or surface of things but the visible manifestation of the whole topography of the actual space in which it is possible to recognize the physiognomy of things as well as their place and purpose. The complexity of the problem is revealed in the unfamiliarity that the astronauts felt so deeply, as the lack of overall orientation made any relationship to the things around them ambiguous. It is only through a sequence of approximations that

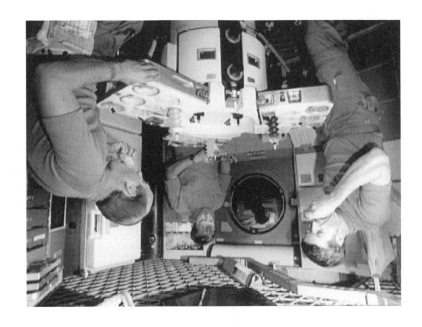

2.3. NASA space laboratory (1973), dining area and docking adaptor.

orientation can be eventually regained. One of those who had lived on the station explained, "It is as though your mind won't recognize the situation you are in until it sees it pretty close to the right orientation and then all of a sudden you get these transformations made in your mind that tell you exactly where you are."[17]

Earlier examples have made clear what these "transformations" are. In this case, they can tell us where we are not absolutely but relatively, in reference to a specific situation. The visible orientation gained by layering the meaning of the remembered space and its coherence is a fragile but plausible substitute for the natural structure of space developed in reference to the earth. In this context it is interesting to learn that the occupation found most satisfying by all members of the team was to observe the earth from the sole window in the living quarters.

It is quite clear that the artificial situation in zero gravity has important links with the natural situation on earth. Take the relation between the physiognomy and the deep structure of space; such links depend not only on continuity of reference to some ground but also on the possibility of simulating natural conditions in space, based on embodied memory. The continuity of reference, as discussed so far, should be seen as a critical link between the natural and artificial structure of space, and more broadly as a link between natural and simulated reality. This brings us close to the essence of representation and also to the nature of architectural space— which is always to some extent artificially created and dependent on the possibilities of representation.

The problem can perhaps be better formulated as a manifestation of the reciprocity of the actual and possible reality of space, where the possible stands for everything that can be achieved creatively in the sphere of human freedom. It is in the tension between the actual and possible reality of space that very urgent questions are currently being raised. For instance, can the possible space be substituted for the actual space, or can it itself become actual? Is there a level of artificiality that can make a living situation uninhabitable? How is it possible to judge when such a limit has been reached?

Under normal circumstances, the relationship between the actual and the possible is a dialogue of reciprocities that are hidden in the depths of our everyday life. It is only under abnormal conditions, when the reciprocity is disturbed, that we become aware of the limits of the possible and its dependence on the actual. The environment in which most of us live is still relatively traditional, despite the enthusiasm of some for creating simulated and virtual realities. So far, the excesses of artificiality evident in such phenomena as alienation, disorientation, and cultural deprivation are largely absorbed in our ability to adapt, and in our disagreements about their possible source and effect. However, there are areas of our life where symptoms similar in their nature, but more radical in their manifestation, seem to point to the same limits in how the possible relates to and depends on the actual. These symptoms arguably include autism, certain types of psychosis, schizophrenia, and a large sphere of disturbances referred to as mental blindness.[18] The cases of mental blindness, particularly as displayed in apraxia and aphasia, are most illuminating for any attempt to better understand the problem of representation and space, and the limits of their artificiality.

In apraxia, the most obvious symptom is the inability to perform purposive acts—dancing, for instance—though the sensory and motor abilities are intact. Those affected can form an idea of action correctly, but they cannot translate it into performance. They cannot situate themselves in an imaginary space and act on what they imagine. For the same reasons they are unable to approach objects that are out of their physical reach. They are fully aware of the aim of a given task, which they can describe verbally; they can sometimes also accomplish it successfully, even using tools as long as the situation is familiar and the tools at hand.

Such disturbances of movement are usually closely linked with disturbances of perception, language, and thought. The inability to grasp an object that is out of reach does not have its source in the movement itself, but results from a more general inability to experience the unity of a situation to which a particular object belongs. The apraxic person is paralyzed because movement is no longer grounded in the unity of situation, and as a consequence it has also lost its physiognomy and meaning. The loss of physiognomy, which is the main characteristic of apraxia, perhaps most clearly manifests the gap between the actual and the possible level of reality in the life of those experiencing it. We can see here a close analogy with the problems suffered in zero gravity, where the lack of orientation was directly linked with the loss of physiognomy of all objects in the surrounding space. As we saw, the residents of the space station learned to reorient themselves and could do so because of the residuum of movement preserved in the memory of space established and cultivated on earth. The residuum of movement in the life of those with apraxia positively affects the whole domain of their possible life. However, the character of their language and thought is changed much as is the nature of their movement. It becomes "akin to the highly technical univocal language of science which having been disengaged from its original hold on life-world structures, can now be employed only mechanically according to the rules of the game like cards or chess."[19]

The ideas of the apraxics are linked together, like their words, only by actual and explicit meanings. In a way, their world as a whole is paralyzed by the unbridgeable gap between the actual and possible levels of their life. The actual takes on an unnatural and strange concreteness, without clear physiognomy and plasticity of experience; the possible becomes a quasi-cybernetic manipulation and decoding of ideas and concepts. The main source of the discontinuity in apraxia is, it appears, the loss of existential (situational) orientation that normally is rooted in the unity of the lived human context. That necessary orientation was described by Merleau-Ponty as an "intelligent arc" that "projects round about us our past and future, our human setting, our physical and moral situation which results in our being situated in all these respects."[20]

THE PRINCIPLE OF CONTINUITY AND THE STRUCTURE OF SPACE

Insight into the discontinuity between the actual and possible levels of reality in the lives of those who are so explicitly disoriented is an invaluable foundation for better understanding certain disturbing tendencies in modern culture, such as ethical disorientation, alienation, loss of meaning, and nihilism. There may be a close analogy between these tendencies and mental blindness, and they may have a common ground in the discontinuity of situational orientation; but such hypotheses are only preliminary and need further elaboration.

What is most interesting in the cases of mental blindness is the similarity of the symptoms, which points to the same source of discontinuity in human existence, differentiated as a result into rather predictable domains of actual and possible behavior. The terminology employed is not yet sufficiently precise, because the phenomena are not themselves sufficiently understood, but some authors—Kurt Goldstein and Merleau-Ponty, for instance—speak of "concrete" and "abstract" or categorial attitudes.[21]

The symptoms of mental blindness cannot be altogether explained physiologically as phenomena immanent to the human body. Too many of them display characteristics beyond the corporeal or physiological. Mental blindness can be partly cured, and the cure has much to do with a change in environment. In his last reflections on the problem of mental blindness, Goldstein, who contributed more to its understanding than has anyone else, observes:

> The mentioned behavior forms have usually been considered as the effect of the use of the mental capacity of a subject. I came to the conclusion that I am not determined by consciousness and that it would be meaningless to call them memories. They represent living events and are not the result of intellectual activity. I could no longer accept the assumption that experience is a product of mind or brain functions alone, especially after it became my conviction that the external world is always connected with it. Pathology has shown how important the world is for understanding at all. Man cannot live without the world and the world does not exist without man. The study of the world of the brain-injured proves to be no less important to our knowledge than the study of the disturbance of the performance. Indeed, though the patient's behavior is certainly determined by the brain defect, it can only be understood as a phenomenon going on in the totality of his modified personality in relation to the world.[22]

The situational character of the symptoms can be illustrated by a well-known case of temporary apraxia. The neurologist Oliver Sacks was recovering from a serious inability to coordinate the movement of his leg with the rest of his body, and therapy was progressing slowly; but he was eventually exposed to the sound of music, which enabled him to regain the ability to walk normally in a very short time.[23] What is surprising is not that music, generated itself by movement, could contribute to the coordination of movement but that the source of movement and change was in the situation and not in the brain or in the body of the patient. The connections of mental blindness to the external environment appear even stronger in cases of aphasia, in which language and thought are more directly involved.[24]

There are a number of things that we can learn from the examples discussed. First, the world as it is given to us in our experience is structured as an articulated series of mediations between the given conditions of our existence and the possibilities of freely developing these conditions through our imagination, language, and thought (figure 2.4). Second, the mediated unity of the result—a coherent world—is rather fragile and more vulnerable than we are usually prepared to accept. And finally, the unity and coherence of our world are neither given, as ready, nor constituted in our experience only. The discovery of the situational structure of the world may help us to distance ourselves from the fictitious, artificially constructed representations of the world as external and only loosely related to the interiority of our existence.

The duality of "man and the world," most often discussed as the duality of "man and the environment," is an old trope. It is cultivated still, even though it obscures rather than clarifies the true nature of environmental conditions. Its origins coincide with the foundation of modern science and with the Cartesian representation of reality as *res cogitans* opposed to the *res extensa.* It is only in this idealized and mathematically constructed model of reality that duality of the internal and external world (environment) makes any sense (as is discussed in more detail in chapter 6).

We have seen that the environment has the character of a world in which the given conditions and our experience belong together in a relation of reciprocity, understood as the reciprocity of the actual and the possible. In a broader sense, the environment can be taken as manifesting the reciprocity of necessity and freedom, where "necessity" represents a given reality—the inevitable, necessary condition of our freedom and creativity. This may suffice as a point of departure, but we may go further and express more precisely the intricate nature of the environment and particularly the depths of our involvement in the surrounding world viewed as apparently neutral and objective—a belief characteristic of most contemporary environmental studies, which rely almost without exception on the methods of natural science.

Most environmental research is focused on biological problems; even human ecology is studied as an extension of biologically oriented disci-

2.4. Melanie Young, metaphorical study of the design studio, interior.

plines.[25] In a situational understanding the environment appears as the embodiment of our life, very much like a body, which sustains our common existence. Given such an understanding—once we have left behind the distinction between external and internal reality—it becomes very difficult to decide what is and what is not "environment." Are we, as corporeal beings, in the environment, or are we an indivisible part of it? Is it not true that our own bodies are in fact the environment of our feelings, imaginations, and thoughts? These critical but important questions can be partly answered by a careful reading of a simple scenario.

When we are involved in the process of drawing, the table in front of us is no doubt part of our environment. The drawing, not as a sign on a piece of paper but as an event leaving traces behind, is also an environment. It would be too simplistic to describe the act of drawing, which is an extension of our intentions and of our visual thinking, as an interaction with the environment. Is it possible to tell what is interacting with what? The act of drawing is anticipated by the informed gesture of our hand, and the visible results in turn inform the hand's movement. The intentional experience and the environmental side of the situation belong together in a unity that cannot be understood by an analysis of the individual components. To be sure, a distinction between the inside and the outside of this scenario can of course be made, but it remains a secondary, derivative representation based on the primary given reality, which can be best described as an articulated continuum, or simply as the natural world.[26]

At this stage it is sufficient to emphasize that the structure of the world is never homogenous. In the continuum of the world there is always a tension between the actual and the possible, the sensible and the intelligible, the known and the unknown, and the private and public levels of reality. It is interesting to note that most of the tensions that develop into real discontinuities seem to coincide with the discontinuities described above in the cases of mental blindness.

This brings us to the first important conclusion. The problem of environment, seen most often as the relationship between human and external reality, is primarily an outgrowth of the structure of our world, which may best be described as a continuity of articulation and embodiment.

A comparison of different experiences of the same building can serve as a preliminary illustration (figure 2.5). The memory of a building that we know from a previous encounter can be convincing and vivid, not only overall but also in its detail. And yet we cannot observe it with any precision; many of its aspects remain obscure and inaccessible, and a general sense of distance separates us from the image. It is difficult for instance to recall exactly the number of individual elements, such as windows, columns, and the like.[27] The situation is fundamentally different when we are looking at a photograph, a drawing, or a model of the same building; but even here we are to some extent prisoners of an abstracted and mediated view (figure 2.6). True, we can focus differently and see things precisely, but only with the help of our imagination as the main source of concreteness and embodiment. It is only in perceptual experience that we can freely and fully observe, explore, and move around the building; interrupt the exploration by closing and opening our eyes; or continue the exploration some other time,

2.5. Bolles + Wilson, Münster library.

without any serious doubt that we are experiencing the same building. These are all possibilities that imagination does not offer. Imagination has a different depth of duration (temporality). It is not stable enough to be explored. Indeed, most of our energy and attention is spent merely sustaining its presence.

That imagination is transitory and vulnerable and perception is more deeply rooted and stable can be taken as a key for understanding the rest of our experience. On the level of representation, the tension between imaginative articulation and perceptual embodiment becomes the main structuring

2.6. Bolles + Wilson, Münster library, drawing and model.

principle of culture as a whole. This principle is very close to what modern anthropology has described as a law of relief (*Entlastung*).[28] Relief is a deep-seated tendency in human life to move beyond the immediacy of the given situation, to concentrate on the typical and the essential. In everyday experience we do not perceive things in their entirety; instead, in the course of our development the perceptual field becomes largely symbolic.[29] In this shift, we concentrate increasingly on the more conscious, intellectual functions that represent the primary experience only suggestively. According to the philosopher and sociologist Arnold Gehlen,

> In order for the lower functions to be directed and utilized, the higher ones must take over certain tasks which were previously the province of the lower ones. Above all these are the variations and combinations of movements. The higher functions however do this in a suggestive predominantly symbolic form. They are therefore conscious. This mechanism is in fact the basis for categorizing the functions as lower or higher.[30]

The relationship between the higher functions, which contribute fundamentally to the articulation of our world, and the lower ones, which contribute to its embodiment, is initially symbolic. Only in symbolic articulation are we informed about the richness of events that take place in the depths of our human situation and experience. As Gehlen points out, "We have no knowledge of the irresistible complexity and perfection of the vegetative and motor processes; consciousness is apparently not able to inform us about these."[31] A typical example of relief is our ability to draw a plan of a building that does not exist yet. This is quite clearly a symbolic operation in which every move is suggestive of a content that only a complex background can provide. The availability of the content depends on the conditions of translation—in other words, on how far we succeed in seeing the diagrammatic drawing (a plan for instance) as the concrete building itself. However, it also depends on the cultivation of the background, which decides how rich and concrete the content is and how it is structured by its possible translation into more articulated levels of experience and meaning. Only under these conditions can the background serve as a basis for the free play of our imagination and thought, for experimentation, invention, and creativity, as well as for evaluation and critical judgment. The higher levels of experience are more autonomous and free; they contain new structures that cannot be derived from the lower strata and in that sense they are richer. Yet the cost of that richness is weakness, a dependence on the existence and structure of the lower strata of experiential reality. To better understand how the relationship between articulation and embodiment is manifested in architecture, consider the following example.

The west facade of Chartres cathedral is dominated by the rose window summarizing the iconographic program and the overall meaning of the facade (figure 2.7). Its primary theme is the Last Judgment, centered on the figure of Christ in his second coming (Parousia).[32] The Parousia of Christ is the final stage of his coming, which began with the incarnation of the word, continued with his descent into death, and will end in the resurrection and the outpouring of the light that completes the transformation of the world. The return of Christ marks the arrival of all things at their final destination. It is interesting to note that at Chartres the Last Judgment was elevated to the upper part of the facade and thereby incorporated into the solar symbolism of the cathedral.[33] This was an innovation that reflected the newly emerging tendency in scholasticism to make visible the mystery of light and treat it as a mediating corporeal form. In the Chartres rose window, the story of the gospel is interpreted as an image embodied in the colored glass, which is in turn embodied in the shape of the window, in the composition of the wall, and finally in the structure of the church as a whole. These embodiments also represent a corresponding sequence of articulations.

The body of the church articulates the global meaning of the facade through its topographical arrangement and the character of its space. The facade itself is defined only in general terms, referring in one sense to the domain of sunset and death, to an entry into the celestial city in another. The topography and orientation of the cathedral represent only the preliminary meaning of the whole. What is more important is that the body of the cathedral provides a background for the articulation of the more explicit meanings visible in the physiognomy and iconography of the sculpture and colored windows.

The light that penetrates the colored glass reveals the different levels of the articulation most clearly (figure 2.8). On the highest level, light is the visible manifestation of its invisible source (*lux*), which is closely linked

2.7. Chartres cathedral, west front.

2.8. Chartres cathedral, west rose window.

with the intelligible meaning of Scripture. In a less elevated sense, light shows itself in the luminosity of the terrestrial elements and as a mystery of incarnation. Finally, on the lowest level, light demonstrates the ambiguity of shadows and the disappearance of light in the impenetrability of matter. The relationships between these levels of articulation and their equivalent modes of embodiment are brought together in the east to west movement of the sun, the visible source of light, which culminates in the sunset. The correspondence between the Last Judgment in the rose window and the sunset

2.9. Chartres cathedral, interior.

illustrates very beautifully the link between the invisible phenomena of death and resurrection, their visible representation in the window, and their embodiment in the hierarchical structure of the cathedral, animated by the movement and light of the sun. The crucial observation at Chartres is how the body of the cathedral, itself abstract and silent, is capable of revealing and supporting a very subtle and highly articulated meaning of salvation—a meaning that can be brought down to earth tangibly and concretely (figure 2.9).

The example of the highly developed space of a medieval cathedral brings to the fore a number of important but difficult questions. What is the nature of the relationship between the verbal articulation of the program, painting, sculpture, and the body of architecture? Are the more articulated possibilities of expression anticipated or prefigured in architecture, or is architecture only a passive receptacle for the more expressive possibilities of sculpture, painting, and the spoken or written word? Is there anything in architecture that can be seen as its communicative power; if so, can it be treated, literally or metaphorically, as a form of language or text? The distance that separates the domains of the spoken or written language and of architecture represents a continuity of meaning that is largely hidden from view. Even today, we can understand a very complicated theological, philosophical, and political program and penetrate the intentions behind a complex iconography of sculpture or painting; but when we come to architecture, the task is usually reduced to structural or formal interpretations that in most cases do not go beyond a tectonic or morphological understanding.

The nature of this anomaly is reflected in the well-established distinction between architecture and the fine arts, and even more explicitly in the current division of art historical writing into separate fields: painting, sculpture, applied arts, and architecture.[34] Modern iconographical and iconological studies are focused on figurative arts, mainly on sculpture and painting; architecture is addressed in the new concerns only sporadically.[35] The key to addressing the problem is clarifying how the established discipline of iconology sees the nature of art and its relation to the more explicit workings of language.

THE SITUATIONAL NATURE OF COMMUNICATIVE SPACE

Our understanding of the continuity of meaning between architecture and the more articulated levels of culture is greatly hampered by a lack of evidence for the communication we know to have existed between clients, clerics, humanists, intellectuals, artists, and architects in the past.[36] The space of communication—where the program, the purpose, and the overall meaning of a building or architectural complex were established and where the translation of a particular content from one medium into another was made possible—can be reconstructed only indirectly, by relying on contextual evidence and by understanding the meaning mediated and shared by the different disciplines and different strata of culture. The key to the phenomena of mediation is language, not in its ordinary sense but as a medium in which culture on all its different levels is articulated.

In order to grasp this dimension of language we have to move beyond viewing it as an explicit and self-sufficient mode of verbal communication. The deep background of language and the conditions that give it life and meaning must be rediscovered. We have seen how in amnesic aphasia, the discontinuity between the possible and actual reality of words, between their concrete and abstract meanings, destroys the physiognomic qualities of experience, perception, and language. The loss of physiognomic qualities is directly related to the loss of categorial background,[37] affecting language and perception. Both linguistic and perceptual experience change similarly, suggesting to Kurt Goldstein "that they express one and the same basic form of behavior, which has been disrupted, a general attitude toward the external world which has been severely altered."[38] This shows just how critical is the communication between articulated, conceptual experience and its background; even more important, it shows that the background is common to our experience as a whole, including our language.

The nature and the role of the background can be gleaned from many contexts, but they probably are revealed most clearly in the acquisition of language. In the early stage of life, before the first words can be articulated, a child is able to produce a considerable number of sounds when pointing or grasping; expressions of mood and of relations to other people and things are as yet undifferentiated. At this same stage, however, the infant displays a remarkable ability to experience similarities and differences between phenomena and to recognize certain critical identities. In the absence of a clear concept that would be at once sufficiently universal and sufficiently concrete, modern phenomenology speaks here of a categorial intuition, which plays a decisive role in our global preunderstanding of the world.[39] Categorial intuition is not based on intellectual ability. It belongs to the spontaneity of our lives; it retains and remembers experience, using this "partial detachment" to recognize similarities, differences, and identities in the continuum of our surrounding world. In this preverbal world, reality is already structured as a communicative space in which we are totally involved; here, all the richness and subtlety of the sensory-motor equivalents of the senses and spheres of our experience are played out until they can be expressed through significant movements and gestures, and eventually through words.[40]

The preliminary articulation of the world that precedes the acquisition of verbal language provides vital background to the life and meaning of language. Verbal language represents another order but only in that it offers a higher level of clarity, greater transparency of meaning, and a more explicit mode of articulation. As we have already seen, the life and meaning of verbal language depend on the presence of a "total language." The relationship between a verbal and a total language can be discussed in terms of communicative movement—as a gestural communication or, more precisely, as a reciprocity of articulation and embodiment.[41] We already know what happens to language when this reciprocity is disturbed, as in cases of aphasia. Its crucial role may be illustrated by the response of Albert Einstein to an inquiry about the nature of creativity:

> The words or the language, as they are written or spoken, do not seem to play any role in my mechanism of thought. The psychical entities which seem to serve as elements in thought are certain signs and more or less clear images which can be "voluntarily" reproduced an combined. . . . The above mentioned elements are, in my case, of visual and some of muscular type. Conventional words or other signs have to be sought for laboriously only in a secondary stage, when the mentioned associative play is sufficiently established and can be reproduced at will.[42]

The laborious search for words and the associative play of visual and muscular activity give evidence of the intimate link between nonverbal experience and verbal language.

We can focus more narrowly on the problem of language by asking a more direct question. How does the presence of language and the possibility of naming the features of architectural space—for instance, its primary materiality, texture, light or purpose—change the reality of the space? Words have the power to reveal the essential characteristics of nonverbal experience—its situational structure; they thus become a vehicle of idealization and stabilization of meaning. Yet the revealed structures of space originate not in language but in the dialectics of language and the experience of the natural world. The higher concepts made available to us by words transform the meaning of the lower ones. However, as Lev Vygotsky observes, a child or a deaf person who acquires higher concepts or their equivalents "does not have to restructure separately all of his earlier concepts. . . . Once a new structure has been incorporated in his thinking[,] . . . it gradually spreads to the older concepts as they are drawn into the intellectual operations of the higher type."[43] The move to the higher concepts does not eliminate the lower ones; in fact, it is the concreteness and the richness of the lower order that give power and meaning to the higher. The process can be seen as a dialogue in which there is tension between the lower and the higher, the concrete and abstract mode of articulation, but there is also room for their positive reconciliation. Such an outcome is particularly apparent in the sign language of the deaf, which relies on movements of hands that inseparably unite experience, intentions, and thought. It is impressive to see abstract concepts and even propositions expressed through no more than mimetic and iconic gestures.[44]

The iconicity of sign language reveals a great deal about design, about the role of sketches and drawings, and eventually about the nature of geometry. In each instance the ideal meaning is defined by the conditions and limits of the iconic representation. The figuration of meaning is directly related to the movement of our body and hands, which may be seen as a work (*ergon*) leading to a more precise definition of gestures and signs. There is a close affinity between the figures of sign language, sign writing, and geometrical operations.[45]

It is possible, I believe, to say that what logic and grammar are to verbal language, geometry is to the visible world. The ontological nature and universal meaning of geometry have been lost in post-Enlightenment culture, and they can be partially recovered only through a historically informed understanding and through hermeneutically consistent inquiry. Geometry is subtly linked to language by movement and gesture. Gestures outline and to some extent define our experience in a way that eludes direct description but can be compared to the process by which movement and sound articulate the meaning of a piece of music. It is through such articulation that the explicit contents of words or geometrical constructs receive their deepest meaning. It is perhaps not unreasonable to claim for geometry

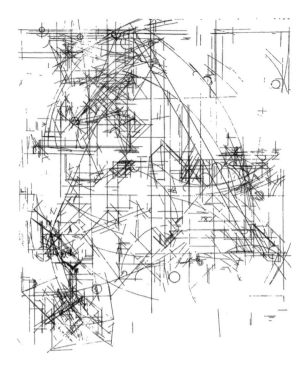

2.10. Wells cathedral, tracing floor.

what Merleau-Ponty has claimed for verbal language—that "the spoken word is a genuine gesture and that it contains its meaning in the same way as the gesture contains its own."[46]

In everyday life, gestures represent an important step in the mimetic formation of typical human situations and in the formation of space. In structured events such as ritual, dance, and drama, the meaning of gesture is largely stabilized by the content of the words, songs, or music. Similarly, the content of geometrical constructs can be stabilized by verbal or visual representations. One example is provided by the rhymes memorized by medieval stonemasons to help them in executing fundamental geometrical operations.[47] Even at its most abstract level, geometry depends on certain basic movements and gestures, such as measuring and drawing, visual analysis, and making models. However, geometry could never have become an ideal discipline without the decisive contribution of conceptual thinking that relies on a highly differentiated language and on idealizing reflections[48] (figure 2.10).

The role of gesture and language in the operations of geometry is hidden behind the apparently neutral and silent results. Yet in design and in the process of building, we do not find it difficult to use geometry analytically or as a visual representation, to discuss it in ordinary language, or to employ it as a practical tool in construction. Today we are largely unaware that each of these possibilities represents a different aspect of geometry, related to a different mode of its articulation and embodiment. That geometry can represent the essential structure of so broad a spectrum of reality, together with its position on the boundary between visible and invisible realities, made it in the past a decisive paradigm of symbolic representation; until the eighteenth century, it was a dominant manifestation of order. Rather than discuss the history or the paradigmatic nature of geometry, I shall here simply refer to a text that may serve as the introduction to such a discussion.

In his commentary on the first book of Euclid's *Elements,* Proclus expounds on the meaning of geometry:

> Let us now turn back for another look at the science of geometry as a whole, to see what its starting-point is and how far it ranges from it, so as to get a view of the ordered cosmos of its ideas. Let us note that it is co-extensive with all existing things, applies its reasonings to them all, and includes all their kinds in itself. At the upper and most intellectual height it looks around upon the region of genuine being, teaching us through images the special properties of the divine orders and the powers of the intellectual forms, for it contains even the ideas of these beings within its range of vision. Here it shows us what figures are appropriate to the gods, which ones belong to primary beings and which ones to the substance of souls. In the middle regions of knowledge it unfolds and develops the ideas that are in the understanding; it investigates their variety, exhibiting their modes of existence and their properties, their similarities and differences; and the forms of figures shaped from them in imagination it comprehends within fixed boundaries and refers back to the essential being of the ideas. At the

third level of mental exploration it examines nature, that is, the species of elementary perceptible bodies and the powers associated with them, and explains how their causes are contained in advance in its own ideas. It contains likenesses of all intelligible kinds and paradigms of sensible ones; but the forms of the understanding constitute its essence, and through this middle region it ranges upwards and downwards to everything that is or comes to be. Always philosophizing about being in the manner of geometry, it has not only ideas but pictures of all the virtues—intellectual, moral, and physical.[49]

Geometry is the paradigm of symbolic representation but does not exhaustively describe it. As we have seen, representation takes place in language, understood in the broadest sense as a linguistic structuring of culture.[50]

So far we have been trying to understand the conditions under which representation takes place. Among our main discoveries are the complex nature of human space, the importance of the continuity between the possible and the actual level of reality, the reciprocity between articulation and embodiment, and the situational character of representation. Perhaps most crucial is the recognition of the universal role of language in the articulation of culture, which includes architecture. What we have accomplished is a kind of outline of the problem of representation. We have thought little as yet about representation as a process and how the different levels of reality involved in representation are actually related and how they communicate. Traditionally, the question of representation is described as "symbolization." I have no difficulty with the term, but feel that because primary representation is already symbolic by definition, the description adds nothing.

THE ROLE OF COMMUNICATIVE MOVEMENT

What makes primary representation and symbolization interchangeable is a communicative movement common to both. Communicative movement is neither physical, physiological, nor subjective; it is ontological and situational because it animates and transforms human circumstances as a whole. For example, it enabled Helen Keller, though early in her life deaf and blind, to acquire verbal language. We may recall the critical moment when the movement of writing on her hand, together with the movement of the water in the garden fountain, produced a miraculous understanding of the meaning of a word.[51] We may also recall that the understanding of a number of other words quickly followed, all in the same setting. However, learning in a different setting was not immediately successful.

Does this suggest the possibility that a situation and its spatial setting are as important a background for learning as it is for memory, imagination, and thought? Such a conclusion would not be surprising. To the extent that all these processes depend on some form of communicative movement, they also depend on the ground that serves as a reference for such movement. Their reliance on background is closely analogous to that observed in examining the transformation of space in inverted vision and the problem of orientation in zero gravity.

Studies of sensory deprivation seem to throw some light on this little-understood phenomenon.[52] Participants in these experiments expect that they will find the state of almost complete isolation from the outside world conducive to concentration and clear thinking. However, such expectations are fulfilled only at first and briefly; there soon follows an inability to keep one's thought focused on a particular subject and finally a gradual disintegration of thinking into fragments—similar to daydreams or hallucinations.

Why does our thinking disintegrate under these conditions? What is the power of the situational background that gives our articulated life its integrity, vitality, and meaning? A case of profound amnesia well documented by A. R. Luria may help us to an answer. The conscious life of a university student who lost his memory after being wounded during the Second World War disintegrated to a state of fragmentation that "affected all aspects of his life. He suffered intolerable, constantly shifting visual confusion. Objects in his visual field were unstable and got displaced so that everything appeared in a state of flux." His sense of space and of his own body was severely impaired: "Sometimes he thought his leg is above his shoulder, possibly above his head." But even more serious was the fragmentation of his memory, language, and thought. He could neither read properly nor remember what he had written; he could only—with great difficulty and very slowly—write down fragments of memories and thoughts as they occurred to him at random. However, through perseverance he managed to write several thousand pages over a period of twenty years and then "to arrange them and order them and thus recover and reconstruct his lost life, making a meaningful whole from the fragments."[53]

By painfully interpreting the discontinuous fragments of experience, the patient succeeded in reappropriating the continuity and sense of the natural world needed to restore the sense of his own life. The slow construction of the narrative proved to be a decisive step, bringing together elements that in isolation were almost meaningless. The text itself was not the missing ground, but it was a mode of embodiment in which the temporality and spatiality of the natural world were directly related. In the life of the patient, the text played the role of a bridge between the communicative power of language and the communicative nature of everyday circumstances, which were thus reintegrated into the continuity of the real world. As a result, the restored memory was not just a memory of the text but a memory of life in its setting—the natural world.

I have from the outset used the term "natural world," but it is only now that I can more explicitly outline its characteristics and meaning. The term itself overlaps with "lived world" (*Lebenswelt*), a concept developed in the phenomenological tradition.[54] To speak about a lived world became necessary in a world increasingly dominated by a scientistic vision of reality, as awareness of the limits of such a vision grew. There is no need to describe here the history of this development, which has already received considerable attention.[55] It is more important instead to comprehend the depth of the problem of the natural world and how architecture may not only benefit from but also contribute to an understanding of it.

Making any discussion of the lived or natural world exceptionally difficult is the fact that we are always situated within it. The world is not a thing or plurality of things that can be explicitly seen or studied. It is more like an articulated continuum to which we all belong. The main characteristic of the natural world is its continuity in time and space and its permanent presence, as can be seen most clearly in language. In language we can move into the past or future, survey different regions of reality, refer to almost anything in our experience, and translate the experience into specific languages. Broadly speaking, these include the languages of painting, music, dance, and architecture and ultimately that of the visible reality itself.[56]

What is revealed in language points to a deeper level of articulated background, the result of our involvement in the structuring of the natural world. I am using the term "natural" here to emphasize the importance of the domain where language meets the natural conditions, the given reality of embodiment in its most elementary form.[57] The structure of the natural world is very often described as a totality of references.[58] I am trying to go a step further by emphasizing how the continuity of references and their communicative nature relate directly to our involvement as corporeal beings. In this view, the natural world appears less as a revelation through language and more as an embodiment of the reciprocity of language and the otherness of the given natural conditions. These background references which enable continuity and communication are potentially present even in situations in which we may not expect them.

Consider a staircase and its space, designed for efficient movement between two levels of a building. What is in one sense a pure object, intended to serve a clearly defined purpose, is at the same time a field of relationships—not always visible and obvious, but permanently available. These relationships are available in all our preliminary design decisions, including those about the staircase's general character and overall spatial arrangement. When we speak about the character of the staircase as being domestic or public, simple or monumental, we have in mind a quite precise relationship between the space, the light, the size and material of the staircase, and the movement that occurs on it. There is a striking contrast between the inexhaustible richness of possible interpretations and the limited number of plausible or optimal solutions. This limitation is even more puzzling in more complex designs such as those of residences, libraries, theaters, and concert halls. Most spatial situations show a remarkable level of identity that cannot be derived from simple characteristics alone; it is something more complex and enigmatic.

If we look closely at a concrete example—a French café, for instance—it is obvious that its essential nature is only partly revealed in its visible appearance; for the most part that essence is hidden in the field of references to the social and cultural life related to the place (figure 2.11). Any attempt to understand its character, identity, or meaning and its spatial setting that uses conventional typologies, relying solely on appearance, is futile. Its representational, ontological structure can be grasped through a preunderstanding that is based on our familiarity with what is being studied and with the segment of world to which it belongs. Preunderstanding in

2.11. Café de Flore, Boulevard Saint-Germain, Paris.

this case is a layered experience of the world, acquired through our in-volvement in the events of everyday life.[59] The identity of the French café is to a great extent defined by the café's institutional nature, rooted in the habits, customs, and rituals of French life.[60] Its identity is formed in a long process during which the invisible aspects of culture and the way of life are embodied in the café's visible fabric, as if they were a language conveyed in written text. The visible "text" of the café reveals certain common, deep characteristics, such as its location, its relation to the life of the street, its transparency of enclosure, a certain degree of theatricality (the need both to see the life of the outside world and to be seen in it, as if the café-goer were an actor), an ambiguity of inside and outside expressed not only in the transparency of enclosure but also in the café's typical furniture, and so on. These are only some of the characteristics that contribute to the identity and meaning of the French café as a culturally distinct typical situation.

How is it possible to explain the relationship between cultural conditions, memories, expectations, the visible physiognomy of the space in question, and the spatial structure of a typical situation? Some understanding can certainly be gained through recourse to metaphors, analogical reasoning, continuity of references, or more explicit correspondences, but only because all these avenues depend on the communicative movement that is the source of their structuring power and meaning. Communicative movement is the source not only of mediation but also of identity and constancy (the latter is discussed in more detail below). This may seem a paradox, if we do not realize that identity and constancy are aspects of a sameness that depends on temporal sequence. Identity is not a property of things or structures; it is constituted in the continuity of references to the ultimate sameness of the most regular movement in reality as a whole—that is, to the celestial movement, measured by the stability of the earth.

However, the nature of communicative movement needs to be understood better and more thoroughly.

For some time already, many authors have been claiming that the "objectivity of the world of things becomes a reality only in relation to the structure of reflected movement."[61] Recent studies have shown that experience and movement belong so closely together that one can stand in for the other. This may explain why our neglect of movement has been largely overlooked. Arnold Gehlen writes, "much too little attention has been given to the ability of human beings to enjoy a wide range of possibilities for movement, unknown among animal species. The combinations of voluntary possible movements available to man are literally inexhaustible, the delicate co-ordinations of movements unlimited."[62] Movement coordinates not only all that accompanies it but also further imagined movement and its articulation in language and thought. The mediating and creative role of movement is apparent in how we acquire skills and learn to perform more generally.

One way to see the mediating role of movement and its power to co-ordinate the richness of events and the identity of space is to observe games, especially ball games (figure 2.12). Here the topography of the ground, the rules, and previous experience constitute a preunderstanding of the game. Against this background the actual game, initiated by explicit movement, takes place. The role of each player underscores the problem of coordina-tion, which depends on the global background, the position and movement of other players, and the movement of the game itself. In contributing to the game, each individual relies on an understanding of a complex relationship between visual, tactile, and kinesthetic experiences in a constantly chang-ing situation, while anticipating the next moment of action. Astonishingly, each is able to translate the kinesthetic reality into its visual equivalents and, conversely, respond kinesthetically to a situation that can be assessed only visually. Even more surprising is the contrast between the constant changes in the game and the stability of the field to which each player refers at all times. This contrast reveals the role of our corporeal scheme, some-times less appropriately referred to as a "body image."[63]

The corporeal scheme—to offer a precise but still broadly applicable definition—is a spatial and temporal unity of sensory-motor experiences that is anterior to any new synthesis and coordination of movement and ex-perience. It can be appreciated each time we move through a small door or drive a car through a narrow gate. In such circumstances, the corporeal scheme shows itself as an ability to come to terms with the spatial condi-tions of the situation as a whole; we possess it because we are corporeal be-ings and because "the body is our general medium for having a world."[64] The corporeal scheme is flexible because it is not an image of a particular pattern or a physical configuration but a "scheme of possible action."[65]

The different manifestations of the corporeal scheme can teach us much that is relevant for a better understanding not only of our actions, ori-entation, and movement through space but also of the rather mysterious phenomenon of the unity of our senses and our experience. In other words, we can learn why our visual, tactile, and kinesthetic experiences do not show any contradictions, why the marble that we see as cold on the wall re-ally is cold when we touch it, and why we anticipate the slippery surface that we see in front of us by changing our body's movement.

2.12. Soccer game in progress.

The unity of senses is usually discussed as a matter of synesthesis. I would like to emphasize the spatial character of this unity and the role of communicative movement, which makes the unity possible. A key question is: What makes movement such a universal phenomenon? To answer it, we have to leave behind the usual approach—which knows only the movement of parts, elements, and bodies in anonymous quasi-mathematical space—if we are to discover a more fundamental mode of movement that is directly involved in the qualitative transformation of reality and thus can be seen as creative or, more precisely, as ontological.

In the activity of an artist or craftsman we find a context similar to that of the players in the game examined above, though the role of movement in their work is less explicit and the unity of their experience is more focused on the tactile domain. This brings to light more clearly the elementary forms of creative movement and its power to animate all around it. The psychologist and philosopher Erwin Straus notes, "Sensuality and motility are coordinated in the tactile sphere in an especially striking fashion. We pass our fingers over the table-top and apprehend its smoothness as a quality of the object. The tactile impression results from the completion of the movement. When the tactile movement stops, the tactile impression dies out."[66]

The work of a good craftsman is always shaped by a deep dialogue between the material, which belongs to the otherness of a situation, and the intentions of the hand. In this dialogue the creative movement finds a new imaginative possibilities, and it is in the same dialogue that the elementary structure of space is revealed in the form of a corporeal scheme. According to the philosopher Hans Jonas,

> The motor element [movement] introduces an essentially new quality into the picture: its active employment discloses the spatial character-istics in the tactile object which were no inherent part of the elementary tactile qualities. Through the kinesthetic accompaniment of voluntary motion the whole perception is raised to a higher order: the touch qualities become arranged in a spatial scheme, they fall into the pattern of *surface* and become elements of *form*.[67]

The same animating power of movement that transforms the tactile experience into a proper "sense" also forms, and in a rather special and pre-cise way informs, our vision. A continuation of the same articulated and in-formed movement is what makes us see the hard and rough surface of the stones or walls, the fragility of glass, and the softness of the ground in a garden. This communication between different kinds and modalities of ex-perience does not result from our decision or will; it takes place in the pre-reflective sphere of our life. It is an impersonal, anonymous process, like the beat of our heart. As Gehlen puts it, "The subject of the process is in fact not so much the individual person as the situation itself—the event involving person and things."[68]

That the primary domain of experience, its unity and order, is already established on a prereflective level is a direct challenge to the conventional view, which attributes that unity and order to intellectual synthesis. Pre-reflective experience overlaps considerably with the classical notion of practical life (*praxis*), particularly in its openness to what is given in the

2.13. *Hortus Palatinus,* view of the castle and city of Heidelberg (ca. 1620).

conditions of our existence. In much the same way as the world of praxis, the prereflective world is structured as a qualitative and communicative reality that is only to a limited extent accessible to reflective understanding. The implicit (tacit) level of the prereflective world is highly structured, but not articulated in a way possible to express in language and thought. We may be able to produce a drawing or play a piece of music with great skill, but we are not always able to explain how we do it. The same is true for other skills and indeed for much of our everyday life. We are largely unaware of the richness of articulation and the potential meaning of what is shaped by spontaneous movement, communication with other people, objects and tools, and the given conditions of our existence. Taken together, common situations can best be described as the latent world, to be understood more explicitly only under certain conditions. The process of bringing the latent world to visibility is most clearly demonstrated in the design of gardens, where the given cosmic conditions are revealed in a visible order (figure 2.13). The order is always a result of a dialogue between the representative structure of space and the spontaneity of the natural change, manifested in the changing nature of the seasons, growth and decay of the flora, and changing weather.

Most important in raising implicit, prereflective experience to the level of the better-articulated and more explicit world is language. We have already seen that the mediating power of language depends on movement, which animates our life on all its levels. In addition, a special role is played in the process of mediation, particularly on the boundary of implicit and explicit meaning, by the imagination and vision. Their unique characteristics enable us to understand the structure of space in relation to the flow of spontaneous experience, contributing to the simultaneity of perception and observation and to the greater stability of spatial relationships.

Visual experience represents a decisive step toward emancipation, insofar as what can be seen does not have to be done. We can understand the implications of this statement by returning to the phenomenon of relief, where the powers of imagination become free to move into higher orders of articulation, which reveal—as does a mirror—the hidden content of prereflective reality. It is in the dialectics of imagination and its hidden content that our vision becomes an ongoing and inexhaustible process. The visible world opens around us a visual field that we tend to see as a field of potential action, even in silent observation or contemplation. The nature of vision manifests itself in its most elementary form as a tendency to experience reality in terms of visible patterns and identifiable configurations, a tendency conventionally described as eidetic vision or Gestalt. Unfortunately, many interpret Gestalt principles as if they were a law establishing the formal identity of objects or objectlike structures, forgetting that Gestalt is always situated in the intentionality of our life and therefore closely linked with the meaning of some potential or actual action. We must ask again: What gives our vision its specificity, meaning, and visible stability and constancy? It is obvious that when we walk around a building and see it from different perspectives, it does not change its primary configuration or physiognomy and does not disintegrate into separate experiences. We know that the green leaves of a tree remain green even in a changing light, just as white objects remain white in a deep shadow. But the phenomenon of constancy has yet to be satisfactorily explained.[69]

Rather than attempting to understand the phenomenon of constancy as formal law, we must see it as the result of a dialectics or reciprocity between the articulating movement and its visible manifestation. The unique quality of our sight lies in the combination of the inexhaustible richness of visual exploration and the stability of spatial structure, which itself becomes visible because of the link that exists between physiognomy, orientation, and the structure of space; thus the vividness of what we see depends on the articulating power of ontological movement and on the stability of the visible field. There is no such thing as pure visibility: there is only visible experience, which is always synesthetic. And yet, for reasons that have in part been discussed, the visible is the most conspicuous manifestation of the natural world. It is not an original or primary reference of our experience, as empiricists believe, but a privileged horizon in which our world has its most explicit level of embodiment.[70]

The horizon of visibility displays a synthesis of the prereflective experience and of the achievements of reflection insofar as they preserve ontological continuity with the visible. It is perhaps not an exaggeration to say that our cultural existence and identity depend on the continuity of a dialogue with the conditions of our embodiment, a dialogue whose stability rests on the horizon of visibility. It is for these reasons that visibility can be seen as a criterion of embodiment itself and as a domain that preserves the mediated unity of culture. Its function is clearly apparent in the history of the visual arts and their reception, and it is even more dramatically highlighted in the disputes concerning the visual culture of our own time.[71]

There is no doubt that visible reality is also the most important domain of symbolic representation. The mediating role of imagination and its ability to cross the boundary between visible and invisible reality brings it close to the classical definition of symbolism—the visualization of the invisible (*per visibilia ad invisibilia*).[72] It is only under certain conditions that visible phenomena acquire the status of a symbol, which is a special manifestation of meaning, acting not in isolation but as a nucleus of a broader symbolic field.

Symbols are formed through interpretation, which is largely anonymous and leads to a differentiation both of distinct areas of meaning and of distinct modes of representation. The same body of meaning is clearly interpreted differently in painting, sculpture, and architecture, and the differences are inevitably reflected in the nature of a particular representation and its mode of visibility.[73] In examining the particular modes of representation, we find not only what is specific and unique to them but also what they share in common and what can therefore serve as a ground for communication between them.

THE SILENT LANGUAGE OF ARCHITECTURE

We have seen in the above discussion of Chartres cathedral that the situation defined by liturgy and worship is represented in the topography, in the organization of space by the body of the building, and in a more detailed articulation of iconography in the sculpture and colored windows. Ultimately, the conceptual meaning of the cathedral as a whole is represented by the philosophical and theological text. If we extend the notion of representation beyond the areas of the individual arts to the world itself, we can describe a hierarchy of representation, mediating between the universal and the particular (abstract and concrete) levels of reality of our culture.[74] However, because the problem of representation is a historical one, it is inappropriate to discuss it in general terms. Instead, I have chosen an example from the Baroque period, when the hierarchy of representation reached a peak and was made more explicit than at any other time.

The bishop's residence in Würzburg is one of the last examples of a successful collaboration of a group of artists in the late Baroque. Its success is manifested not so much in the richness as in the unity of its interior spaces, as is particularly apparent in the main staircase hall[75] (figure 2.14). There we are quite clearly aware of the unity of the space, though it is far from obvious what constitutes the unity and what determines the nature of the space. Is it the monumental architecture of Balthasar Neumann or the large fresco by Giovanni Battista Tiepolo on the ceiling? Does the iconography of the four continents and the elaborate program behind it also contribute to the unity of the space? A conventional understanding of the synthesis of arts as *Gesamtkunstwerk* sees the problem of synthesis and unity in terms of immanent experience. Such experience does tell us something about the relationship between the individual arts, but it does not address the most important question: how the arts are related such that one art participates in the reality of the other—which is exactly what is happening in this space. We can speak about the relationship between arts and

2.14. Würzburg Residence, main staircase.

about experience, and we can play with the translation of words into images, but that is not what we see.

What we see is the manifestation of the program and its content in the visual representations. In other words, we see the program situated and embodied in the painting, and we see the painting in the context of the room. We cannot understand what we see by reducing it to an immanent experience, because our experience itself is situated in a way that is never fully transparent to us. What we can understand through our experience is the structure of the articulated world in which we can directly participate. This is precisely what we do when we move through the foyer and enter the ceremonial stair hall. The staircase itself is aligned with the movement of the sun, represented in the fresco by the chariot of Apollo; this gives orientation not only to the staircase but to the room as a whole (figure 2.15). As we ascend to the first landing and turn, the staircase becomes part of the structure of the room; the four walls transform themselves into four continents and eventually disappear in the light of the ceiling.

The sequence can be interpreted as a movement from the domain of architecture to the domain of painting and to the idea of the program, but doing so tells us very little about the nature of the space and even less about its unity. We must be able to see both how the structuring power of architecture determines the nature of the painting and of the program and, at the same time, how the idea of the program determines the meaning of the architecture. The unity of space, as we already know, depends on the continuity of references, which in our case is the continuity of embodiment understood not as the materiality of a particular art but as situatedness and participation in movement—culminating in the constancy of an ultimate reference to the earth. But how is this reference to the terrestrial order mediated through the space? We can see the first indication of such mediation in the figures of Atlantes carved out of the bosses in the vestibule (figure 2.16). They appear as an iconographic theme that is present in the latent meaning of the supporting columns, the piers, and so on. The Atlantes belong not only to the building's body but also to its idea.[76] What brings the scene into visibility is our imagination, which has its source in the materiality of the building. Gaston Bachelard calls this aspect of imagination "material": "Material imagination, this amazing need for participation which, going beyond the attraction of the imagination of forms, thinks matter, dreams in it, lives in

2.15. Würzburg Residence, ceiling fresco above the main staircase.

it or in other words materializes the imaginary. . . . Whenever images appear in series they point to a primal matter, a fundamental element."[77]

The articulation of a theme, potentially present in an element of the building, reveals the tension between the anonymity and silence of the architectural body and the iconicity that can be anticipated. This tension—characteristic throughout architecture's history, particularly in the iconoclastic periods—tells us more about the unity of space than do many detailed studies. The universality of the imagination that plays a dominating role in

2.16. Würzburg Residence, caryatids in the vestibule.

the visual arts is coextensive with the universality of language. Like language, imagination can transform the material into a pictorial image and eventually into the iconicity of abstract concepts. How the imagination can communicate between such different levels of reality and different areas of culture as architecture, sculpture, painting, language, music, and dance is still little understood. The already discovered role of communicative movement and its close links with imagination may help us here.

We can easily imagine a scenario in which one person dictates a text to another, who writes it down and later reads it back to us. In such a situation we don't translate what we hear into the movement of our hands and then into a visual representation that we can read. We recognize the physiognomy of the audible and visual patterns in such a way that the sequence of hearing, writing, and reading becomes a modulation of the audible, motor, and visual space, all of them sharing a common articulated movement and "without there being any need to spell the word or specify the movement in detail in order to translate one into the other."[78] The translation is more like a melody played in different keys. This example suggests how a space articulated in abstract language, visual representation, and tactile experience can represent a unity. The subtlety of that unity becomes clear when we recognize that particular music does or does not belong to a particular space. We can recognize the difference because a reverberation takes place on the boundary of the acoustic and visual space.

The phenomenon of reverberation brings to light the aspect of movement that makes movement truly communicative. It is for this reason that the French psychiatrist Eugène Minkowski chose resonance (*réverbération*) as a paradigm of communication in his own studies of the poetic image:

> If, having the original image in our mind's eye, we ask ourselves how that image comes alive and fills with life, we discover a new dynamic and vital category, a new property of the universe, reverberation. It is as though the sound of a hunting horn reverberating everywhere through its echo made the tiniest leaf, the tiniest wisp of moss shudder in a common movement and transform the whole forest, filling it to its limits, into a vibrating, sonorous world. . . . It is the dynamism of the sonorous life itself which by engulfing and appropriating everything it finds in its path, fills the slice of space, or better the slice of the world that it assigns itself by its movement, making it reverberate, breathing into it its own life.[79]

We have not, as it might first appear, moved far from architecture. The phenomenon of resonance makes clear the communicative nature of movement, imagination, and language. It casts light on the spontaneous formation of identities and differences, similarities and analogies, and more generally on the metaphorical nature of all communication. At the same time, it is closely linked with rhythm, proportion, and harmony. It is well known that the primary meaning of proportion is analogical;[80] and while analogy belongs to the metaphoricity of discourse, proportion more explicitly represents its structure, which can be eventually expressed in numbers. We do not need to be reminded that proportion was, until recently, at the center of thinking about architecture and its order. But it is not always understood or acknowledged that proportional thinking itself was prima-rily a mediation between the idea of the potential unity of the world and the uniqueness of a particular situation or phenomenon. In the history of West-ern culture, this process became a mediation between the celestial and the terrestrial order, between divine and human reality, and finally between the universal and the particular in the understanding of the world.

The process of mediation found its fulfillment in the hierarchy of rep-resentations, which is most explicitly reflected in the hierarchy of the arts. Architecture, sculpture, painting, poetry, and music, and indeed philos-ophy, each have certain possibilities of articulation, determined by the con-ditions of their embodiment. In philosophy or poetry, it is possible to speak about the idea of world unity or move into the domain of metaphysics or the-ology. In painting, this is impossible. Painting always depends for its artic-ulation on the iconicity of verbal language and thought. It has to create its own iconicity, informed by the content that has already been articulated through language. We find a similar pattern in other arts as we move toward architecture. Undoubtedly architecture itself is shaped by abstract con-cepts, geometry, and ideas, but never without mediation. It is difficult and somewhat problematic to realize a conceptual vision, diagram, or abstract thought directly in a building. In design we automatically use a series of mediating steps, such as drawings and models. The mediated nature of ab-stract concepts or ideas in architecture can be seen in the rare examples of buildings with a plan formed as an anagram in the shape of letters (figure 2.17). It is true that both buildings and letters can be constructed accord-ing to the same geometry, but in the former case geometry does not provide a clearly and explicitly articulated meaning. In a typical building, geometry reflects the conditions of the site, the program, and the overall spatial or-ganization. It is absorbed in the material and communicative nature of the space; and though other arts also inform the space, space has the power to situate them. To situate means also to communicate. What communicates and what is communicated in architecture? For the lack of a better term, I shall describe the enigmatic phenomenon of architectural communication as "architectonic" structure.[81]

Architectonics shares all the main characteristics of architectural space, which has an invisible power, communicated through other levels of

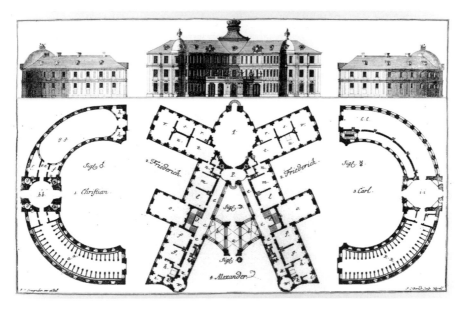

2.17. Johann David Steingruber, *Architectonisches Alphabeth* (1773), plan of a project dedicated to Chr. Friedrich Carl Alexander.

the articulated world. We can identify its structuring power not only in painting or sculpture but also in such areas as poetry, music, and science.[82]

In the Würzburg residence we can recognize the presence of architectonics immediately in the tension between the ascending movement of the steps and the upper part of the hall, but perhaps even more strongly in the hall's situating of the fresco not only optically but also in its physiognomy and content.[83] What has been achieved in the Würzburg stair hall is quite remarkable, though in some ways typical of the period. It is even more remarkable when we realize that the work was collaborative, created by artists who did not even come from the same part of Europe. Such collaboration is obviously possible only in a well-structured communicative space that extends beyond the local situation into the culture as a whole.

On the concrete level of collaboration, one area of creativity seriously misunderstood in the aesthetic interpretation of art is decor. A typical example of decor is stucco, which is supposed to be looked at not as a work of art in its own right but as a mediating link between architecture, sculpture, and painting (figure 2.18). Stucco is a medium that has pictorial character-istics without being a painting, and the same is true of its sculptural and architectural characteristics. As a result, decor oscillates between architec-ture, the visual arts, and rhetoric and thus serves a higher purpose. What is obvious in the example of stucco also holds true, though less visibly, for all the visual arts in their relation to the field of representation as a whole. In that broader context they all play a mediating, decorative role. Gadamer explains,

> The comprehensive situation of architecture in relation to all the arts involves a two-fold mediation. As the art which creates space, it both shapes it and leaves it free. It not only embraces all the decorative aspects of the shaping of space, including ornament, but is itself deco-rative in nature. The nature of decoration consists in performing that two-sided mediation, merely to draw the attention of the viewer to itself, to satisfy his taste and then to redirect it away from itself to the greater whole of the context of life which it accompanies.[84]

The original meaning of "decoration," or decor, adheres closely to that of "ornament," which derives from the Latin translation and equivalent of the Greek *kosmos*—the order of the natural world. In this ontological un-derstanding, order is an implicit and harmonious relationship of parts to the whole, which in our case corresponds to the reciprocity between and re-lationship of individual arts and the unified space. Architecture and the arts take their decorative meaning from their nonaesthetic, mediative role in the process of representation. They are thus closely related to the Greek un-derstanding of representation as *kosmopoiēsis*, the articulation of meaning and order in view of the whole.

Despite the radical shift from the decorative to the aesthetic under-standing of arts in the eighteenth century, the latent decorative nature of the visual arts still asserts itself in many areas: most notably in repeated at-tempts to create a new form of *Gesamtkunstwerk*, and a less obviously in the attempts in modern museums to restore or reinvent a plausible setting for isolated objects. In order to succeed in such a task, Gadamer argues,

2.18. Zwiefalten church, detail of the nave fresco and rocaille decoration.

the concept of decoration must be freed from the antithetical relationship to the concept of the art of experience and be grounded in the
ontological structure of representation, which we have seen as the mode
of being of the work of art. We have only to remember that in their
original meaning, the ornamental and the decorative were the beautiful
as such. It is necessary to recover this ancient insight. Ornament or
decoration is determined by its relation to what it decorates, by what
carries it.[85]

Decor and the decorative meaning of art are thus relational—very
much like the communicative nature of situation. In both cases the individual creative contributions are situated in a sequence of representations in
which the criterion of meaning, relevance, or beauty is not the individual

value but that of the whole. Such an understanding represents a radical departure from the conventional view of architecture and the arts as isolated objects with isolated spheres of meaning and relevance. In a situational approach, individual works of art are mutually interconnected. While preserving their individual identity, they are at the same time linked together through reciprocities much as our sensory experiences are. Under such conditions the problem of representation cannot be reduced to the limited domain of a particular art.

THE PLACE OF ARCHITECTURE IN THE LIFE OF CULTURE

Architecture itself is linked not only to other arts but also to the broader context of life; it is only on that scale that we may understand its specific contribution to the formation of the communicative space of culture. Again, a concrete example will make this clearer.

The sculptures of the biblical patriarchs and prophets on the west portal of Chartres cathedral have taken the place of the columns on the jambs of the portal and become their more articulated equivalent (figure 2.19). Their meaning is derived in the first place from the topography and orientation determined by the overall architectonic structure of the portal, which represents, in this part of the cathedral, the entry into the embodied vision of the heavenly city. The second level of meaning comes from the Bible and its visual interpretation. More important still is the synthesis and reenactment of these meanings in the space of the portal during a simple entry or ceremony (figure 2.20). In such a situation it is not clear where the line between the different modes of representation can be drawn. Architectural embodiment penetrates the whole space. It manifests itself in the vertical organization of the portal, in the spatial arrangement of the iconography, and even in the language that I am using now when I discuss the portal. The same penetration characterizes the sculpture and the meaning of the biblical text. The attempt to identify meaning within a particular mode of representation—architecture, sculpture, or language—and then try to understand how each may be related to the others remains problematic. Such an approach does not give us access to the world where all representations have their origin and find their fulfillment, where there is room for similarity or identity, but not for the autonomy of the individual arts. The meaning

2.19. Chartres cathedral, west portal.

of any work of art that we are trying to understand ontologically and as a part of its setting is always situational. In other words, it is not the representation but what is represented that matters—and what is represented is always a world that the work of art reveals and articulates, at the same time contributing to its embodiment.

We have already seen that architecture is not as crucial in explicitly articulating the world as in embodying and implicitly articulating it. In the past, the role of architectural embodiment was generally recognized, most

2.20. Chartres cathedral, detail of the west portal.

obviously in the long tradition of the art of memory. Though in principle any visual reality might serve as a mnemonic device to stabilize experience, for the most part it is architecture that has been used for this purpose. There are many reasons for choosing architecture, but probably the main one is its comprehensive nature and its proximity to the referential, structuring power of the earth.[86] Thus the historian Frances Yates describes the workings of memory: "Those things are better remembered which have order in themselves. Pure intentions slip out of memory unless they are as it were linked to corporeal similitude. Of those things which we wish to remember, we should place in certain places images and similitudes. The places are like tablets, or paper, and the images like letters, and placing the images is like writing, and speaking is like reading."[87]

Memory brings together most of the points that have been made so far. It is ever present, and it is as central to this argument as is space. It is therefore fair to claim that "what protects us against delirium or hallucination are not our critical powers but the structure of our space,"[88] together with the structure of our memory. Memory has a key role to play, particularly in activities in which we are normally not aware of it, such as recognition, normal perception, imagination, and creativity. By examining these less obvious areas we can gain a better understanding of the structure of memory and see quite clearly that memory is not an isolated ability or power of recollection, and that it cannot be separated from the context of the world and reduced to a physical trace (engram) in the brain.

In the current understanding of memory, dominated mostly by the engram theory, it is taken for granted that a particular impression creates a particular memory image; on this account, the human organism, with its brain, is a passive recipient of stimuli impinging on a sensitive medium or matter. However, as Erwin Straus rightly argues,

> the engram theory proclaims the stimulus the dictator of memory. Impressions, it seems, arrive like the guests in a metropolitan hotel. They come from all directions, lacking any logical connection; rooms are assigned to them just as they happen to be vacant. If this were the way impressions operated, memory would be like a warehouse where the most heterogenous material has been stored in adjacent compartments, but there is no-one keeping a record. Obviously however, the growth of memory in the biographical order of time does not coincide with the temporal sequence of stimuli acting upon sensory organs. Otherwise the first phase of remembering, namely registering, would be completely detached from personal history.[89]

We have already seen the consequences of the separation of memory from personal history in those suffering from mental blindness—particularly aphasia, where memory is split into a concrete memory of simple, everyday tasks and the automatic, mechanical memory of abstract possibilities. This split illustrates the importance of continuity in the normal functioning of memory as it holds together the reciprocity of articulation and embodiment of our experience and of the experienced world. If we acknowledge the impossibility of reducing the sphere of embodiment to the isolated human body or brain, it then becomes clear that memory is—in its very essence—situational. Oral cultures understand this point well: their long narratives are remembered without writing, but always with the help of gestures, rhythm, music, or reference to natural phenomena.[90]

The broader context in which memory is situated is decisive not only for the structure but also for the content of memory. A visit to a familiar building or place, as we often say, "brings back memories." However, it is far from clear what the phrase actually means. What had been forgotten—the building? or the "retained" experience? A similar thing happens when we recognize the face of a friend whom we have not seen for many years. The actual recognition cannot be explained by a correspondence of perception and memory. In this process, what is seen must so organize itself as to present a picture in which we can recognize our former experience. As Merleau-Ponty notes, "the appeal to memory presupposes what it is supposed to explain."[91]

The process of recognition points to a deeper dimension of memory— its ties to the temporal structure of our existence and of our world. This is simply a more explicit formulation of statements made above about the nature of typical situations, the process of symbolization, communicative movement, and communicative space. In this light, it is possible to say that the temporal structure of our existence is the foundation of memory in the same way that spatiality is the foundation of space. However, on a deeper level of understanding, temporality and spatiality belong and appear together as dimensions of a single world articulated by communicative movement. Here memory ceases to be an isolated phenomenon, structured only by time, and becomes itself a dimension of a cultural continuum. To better appreciate this dimension, consider a specific instance of memory at work.

At the beginning of this chapter, I described the problem of the continuity between the experience of a city visited for the first time and its representation on a plan. In such a situation we don't recognize buildings and streets, and yet the place is not entirely unfamiliar. Though it is tempting to believe such familiarity to be directly linked with memory, this is clearly not the case. How can we remember buildings, streets, or anything else in a place that we have never seen before? And yet there is room here for memory, but on a different level. Rather than being associated directly with perceptual experience, what we remember first is linked to the more global and primary aspects of our surroundings. These memories, with the help of imagination, can make the new situation seem similar to others and finally familiar. The question of what it is that we remember and what makes particular buildings or places memorable can be answered only by pointing to the hierarchical sequence of situations in which we are involved and which decide, with only a limited contribution from us, the nature of the result.[92]

That memory is never a memory of an isolated thing—no single phenomenon, shape, color, or sound—is consistent with my earlier argument that physiognomy depends on orientation, and orientation on topology. A leading critic of research into artificial intelligence likewise concludes that human memory "is much more like an implicit and very general sense of appropriateness, and seems to be triggered by global similarities to previously experienced situations rather than by any number of individual facts and features. . . . Lacking access to anything very like the human situation, it is not surprising, that digital computers also lack access to anything very like human understanding."[93]

In other words, no amount of isolated data or "memories" can restore or simulate the concreteness of the human situation.[94] This brings us to the conclusion that memory does not contain "memories"; that its seat is not in the brain, which only contributes to the articulation of remembered experience and to our awareness of the past; that it is mostly latent; and that it is an intrinsic dimension of our world and our ability to understand.

The reason for devoting so much space to this problem is that memory, seen as an embodiment of human experience, probably offers the best approach to the question of the nature of architecture and its role in the making of the world (culture). Given the earlier discussion related to the formation of communicative space, embodiment becomes the problem most central to the very nature of architecture. In terms of articulation, architecture cannot compete with sculpture, painting, or written text, and yet it is present in all of them—not as an explicit articulation but as an articulating embodiment (figure 2.21). It is quite obvious that written text must be situated on a page or screen in order to be legible, and that the page itself must be situated in a setting appropriate for the reading of the text. We already know that the order of the text is determined by a sequence of mediations reaching down to the most elementary situation, which represents the given conditions of the natural world. This is well summarized in Yates's

2.21. Johann Lukas von Hildebrandt, Piaristenkirche Maria Treu, Vienna (1702–1723), south chapel.

statement, quoted above, about the nature of memory: "Those things are better remembered which have order in themselves."

The order of remembered "things" as so mediated is not a formal order. It is closely associated with the content and qualities of the things concerned, and in that sense it is always thematic. Marcel Proust privately confided that his *À la recherche du temps perdu* can be compared to a cathedral.[95] He was referring not to a formal analogy between his text and the structure of a cathedral but to the intimate link between the narrative and memory conveyed in the written text and the deeply embodied writing in stone.[96]

From this rather poetic analogy we can move, again with Proust, to a deeper and more coherent understanding of how memory, personal experience, and identity relate to the structure of a particular place. Proust describes this relation as a reciprocity between memory and "memory-room":

> Even before my brain had collected sufficient impressions to enable it
> to identify the room, it, my body, would recall from each room in succes-
> sion what the bed was like, where the doors were, how daylight came
> in at the windows, whether there was a passage outside, what I had had
> in my mind when I went to sleep, and had found there when I awoke . . .
> the sleep which lay heavy upon the furniture, the room, the whole
> surroundings of which I formed but an insignificant part and whose
> unconsciousness I should very soon return to share.[97]

This few sentences capture the structuring power of space, which asserts itself even in the furthest reaches of our experience. For example, the order of mathematical thinking has its source not in the immanent domain of our mind but in the grammar and syntax of our language. Grammar and syntax, in turn, derive their identity from the constancy and identity of phenomena and things—from the constancy of the primary situations.[98]

What is true for mathematics is also true, less obviously, for other areas of culture, including music, literature, painting, and, in a special sense, architecture. The place of architecture in the continuum of culture is special because its reality coincides with the reality of primary situations and their mode of embodiment. The history of architecture can be seen as a history of attempts to represent the latent order of nature and create a plausible spatial matrix for the rest of culture. The plausibility of the spatial matrix rests on a long process of interpretations and modifications that established an identifiable tradition. In European culture, this tradition was based for more than two millennia on classical cosmology and its Christian interpretation, which preserved its relevance until the period of the late Baroque in the eighteenth century (figure 2.22). We shall have the opportunity to examine more closely the nature of this tradition in the following chapters. For now, the most important aspect of the tradition is the concrete role of architecture in the formation of historical memory and in the spatial structuring of culture as a whole.

We experience the most obvious manifestations of the structuring role of architecture almost constantly in our everyday life. There is hardly a place or circumstance that is not organized by spatial intentions (or, in the case of natural surroundings, experienced as so organized). The encounter with things and their spatial order is an encounter with the otherness of our situation, accessible through the dialectics of revealing and hiding. Straus observes, "In our macroscopic world, things are our partners that respond in their own manner, resisting or supporting our intentions."[99]

It would be interesting to investigate to what extent architecture itself resists or supports typical human situations and how the topography, orientation, and physiognomy of these situations change our life. But while an extensive series of case studies could provide a better understanding of the changes, it would shed little light on the structuring role of architecture. The claim that architecture contributes to the life of our culture as text does to our literacy can be justified only by penetrating more deeply into the mystery of symbolization, mediated by communicative movement.

In a space of a church or a concert hall, where the silence of architecture is complemented by the sound of words carried in music, we can recognize a distinct mode of spatiality in the sphere of words, sung, as it were, from a page. Enhanced by music, the spatiality of language reveals the deep structure of articulation in which words are animated by the hidden communicative movement and meaning of gestures. The gestures themselves belong to a unified corporeal scheme, which not only is a source of order but also provides the structure and content of communication.

As we have already seen in the case of a game, a corporeal scheme has the power to situate and structure the complex, changing world of the game

2.22. Christoph Dientzenhofer, St. Nicholas Church, Prague, south side of the nave.

in the framework of the playing field. If we extend the notion of the playing field to architecture, then it may be possible to say that what the playing field is to the game, architecture is to culture in its broadest sense.[100] This structuring role of architecture is clearly displayed when the same piece of music is performed in different places—leading us to wonder how the architecture of a particular place contributes to the overall musical experience. A similar question can be raised in view of the changing nature of space in film, when the sound turns into silence. Less obviously, we are answering the same question each time we choose the most appropriate place for activities such as work, study, and conversation.

We can speak of "resistance" and "support" when discussing the role of architecture in the communication of order and meaning between the more articulated levels of culture and the more elementary strata of embodiment. However, we need first to see these terms in their dialectical relationship: it is by resistance that architecture supports our intentions and the appropriate meaning of a particular situation. We are aware of this mostly intuitively each time we move up a staircase, travel through uncomfortable corridors, enter rooms with certain expectations, or recognize the purpose of a building from its layout and physiognomy.

There is a close link between resistance and embodiment, and between support and articulation. Resistance, together with materiality and physical presence, is a manifestation of embodiment, while support, together with the actualization of meaning and intelligibility, is a manifestation of articulation. Taking them together, we see that the silence of embodiment is always to a certain extent also a voice of articulation. It is only under these conditions that we can understand the language and the cultural role of architecture (figure 2.23).

This brings the argument very close to Heidegger's effort to grasp the reciprocity between the articulated world and its embodiment, "earth." In his view of the work of art,

the setting up a world, does not cause the material to disappear, but rather causes it to come forth for the very first time and to come to the open of the work's world. The rock comes to bear and rest and so first becomes rock; metals come to glitter and shimmer, colors to glow, tones to sing, the word to speak. All this comes forth as the work sets itself

2.23. Gian Lorenzo Bernini, Fontana dei Fiumi, Piazza Navona, Rome; the allegory of the Danube.

back into the massiveness and heaviness of stone, into the firmness and pliancy of wood, into the hardness and luster of metal, into the lighting and darkening of color, into the clang of tone, and into the naming power of the word.[101]

To appreciate the full meaning of the claim that architecture, as a primary mode of embodiment, is also a voice of articulation, we have to look more closely at the changing role of representation. This is a task addressed in the following chapters.

· CHAPTER 3

THE PERSPECTIVAL TRANSFORMATION
OF THE MEDIEVAL WORLD

EVCLIDES.

T HE MODE OF representation that evolved in the late Middle Ages and
early Renaissance under the name of "perspective" became an influential force in shaping modern European culture. The long and anonymous
process in which the new representation was gradually articulated is often
seen as making possible the breakthrough by a small group of artists and
intellectuals living and working in Florence at the beginning of the fifteenth century. Their contribution—the "invention" of "correct" ("legitimate") perspective construction—is hailed as a unique and unprecedented
event. There is no reason to denigrate the Florentine contribution, but
there is also no need to cultivate the old legend that pictorial perspective
was invented by a few individuals.[1] Scholars and some humanists possessed
enough knowledge of optics to make perspectival representation of reality
a genuine possibility as early as the end of the thirteenth century. However,
much had to change in European culture before such a possibility could become an actuality.

The true nature of pictorial perspective belongs to a world that
emerged in a sequence of important cultural shifts more than hundred
years later. A full discussion of these complex changes is beyond the scope
of this study, but they can, I believe, be collectively characterized as marking the slow perspectivization of the culture as a whole. This process can be
traced back to the new appropriation of nature in the twelfth century, growing individualism in cities, the first signs of a new humanism, and the
change in the nature of knowledge during the thirteenth century—which
includes the return to Aristotelianism and the formation of a new philosophy of light and optics.[2]

The first visible manifestation of a movement toward perspectivity
can be found in the new sense of space in painting, architecture, and the organization of cities[3] (figures 3.1 and 3.2). What is common to all these areas
is a new coordination of space and a representation that takes into account
the position of the spectator and his or her appreciation of the visible unity
and beauty of the setting. The role of the spectator was further cultivated in
the religious plays performed first in churches and then, during the fourteenth century, mostly in the open spaces of the city. The performances in
the open were staged in a setting oriented precisely east to west, in an idealized representation that eventually transformed the whole city temporarily into an ideal city.[4]

3.1. Saint-Denis cathedral, choir.

The religious drama was complemented by processions through the city, very often to its gates, where in some cases the entry into Jerusalem was reenacted.[5] The meaning of urban theater and procession is directly related to the vertical hierarchy of the medieval world, which emphasized the tension between the human and the divine levels of reality. The vivid visualization of the divine order in the theater helped to idealize the everyday life of the city and thus to elevate the city as a whole to the status of a heavenly Jerusalem. The idealized setting became an initial paradigm of

3.2. Capella Arena, Padua, interior.

perspectivity as well as a paradigm of the ideal Renaissance city.[6] However, the most important sources of perspectival thinking were the new developments in the medieval philosophy of light and optics, known then as *perspectiva naturalis.*

Renaissance perspective is conventionally understood as a new representation of space. In this view, perspectival space is assumed to be homogenous, potentially infinite, and in essence Euclidean. Many also believe that perspective reveals the structure of the natural space of the world in which we live,[7] but this belief is somewhat problematic. As perspective was being developed, Euclidean space was available only as an ideal, which could not be realized until the seventeenth century—and then not as an actual space, but only a space accessible to modern philosophy and science.

The notion of a homogenous Euclidean space is a modern invention; it largely coincides with the development of perspective, leading to the formation of the Cartesian space and eventually to the discovery of non-Euclidean geometries. The inadequacy of Euclidean space was acknowledged already at the beginning of the nineteenth century by Karl Friedrich Gauss, who was probably the first to assert the relevance of non-Euclidean geometry.[8] Only much later did Bernhard Riemann convince mathematicians that a non-Euclidean geometry might be the geometry of physical space and that we could no longer be sure which geometry was true.[9]

This development undermined the more than two-thousand-year-old foundations of geometry and the centuries-old faith in the existence of Euclidean space. It is interesting to realize that the original text of Euclid's *Elements* had no room for the modern notion of space. The term that Euclid employed was *to chōrion,* which refers to an area enclosed within the perimeter of a specific figure; it is an abstraction not dependent on the existence of physical space.[10] As a modern invention, cultivated in the development of perspective, Euclidean space was not fully accepted as a structure of the natural world before the seventeenth century, when it became identical with Cartesian space. A more important source for perspective is the tradition, going back to Plato, that space is structured by light; it culminates in the thirteenth century in a synthesis that directly influenced the development of Renaissance perspective.

NATURAL PERSPECTIVE: ITS BACKGROUND AND ORIGINS

The relationship between space and light can be understood only on the level of their common reality. What they share is a continuum of the articulated world in which both space and light appear as dimensions or aspects of the same materiality or corporeality. In a short but precise thirteenth-century formulation, Robert Grosseteste describes the power of light to create and share the continuum of corporeality. "Light," he writes, "which is the first form created in the first matter (*prima forma corporalis*), multiplied itself by its very nature an infinite number of times on all sides and spread itself out uniformly in every direction [figure 3.3]. In this way it proceeded in the beginning of time to extend matter which it could not leave behind by drawing it out along with itself into a mass the size of a material universe."[11]

This understanding of light, which led to the formation of a qualitatively articulated world, coincides with the emergence of a new and more explicit philosophical interpretation of the story of creation.[12] The new philosophical language was based on the older tradition of analogical and dialectical reasoning, but it soon developed into a very sophisticated form of syllogistic reasoning and geometrical speculation that extended into other areas of culture, including architecture.[13]

In the Christian interpretation of Neoplatonic philosophy, light is seen as the paradigm of intelligibility, as divine wisdom, and as a manifestation of the ineffable one—understood as the ultimate good, as a source of creation, or as God. The difficulty of speaking about light has perhaps most to do with the tendency to see light as a separate entity, isolated from the rest of reality that it itself illuminates, as well as with its ambiguity: the invisible source of light (*lux*), which can be named but which cannot be seen, and visible light, which can be seen but which cannot be very easily named. As Plotinus puts it, "Since light, then, belongs to a body you are able to say whence it came because you can say where the body is; but if there is something which is immaterial, and has no need whatever of body because it is naturally prior to body—and does not come from any place or belong to any body?"[14]

Representational symbols have the power to overcome the tension between visible and invisible light, which coincides with the tension between our sensible and our intelligible experience. They also reveal light to be a disclosure of the essential nature of things, the true exemplum of their intelligibility. The link between light and intelligibility is described by Plotinus as follows:

> the depth of each individual thing is matter; so all matter is dark,
> because the light in each thing is the rational forming principle. Now
> intellect too is rational principle. So intellect sees the forming principle
> in each thing and considers that what is under it, is dark because it lies

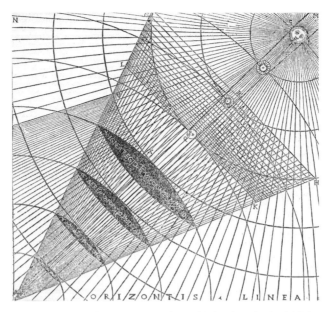

3.3. Cesare Cesariano, edition of Vitruvius, *De architectura* (1521), the multiplication of celestial light.

below the light; just as the eye, which has the form of light, directs its gaze at the light and at colours (which are lights) and reports that what lies below the colours is dark and material.[15]

The close link between light and intelligibility, together with the fact that the main source of intelligibility is language, makes clear the important relationship between light and language. If we move one step further and realize that language, in one form or another, is responsible for the formation of our world, then we can also see how closely linked light is with the structure of our world. This phenomenon can perhaps best be described as the luminosity of the world.

Luminosity is not light; it is the physiognomy of the world structured by the reciprocal relationship between that which is directly visible and that which can be expressed in words and is revealed in light. It is this reciprocity or articulated luminosity that we find behind visual metaphors or behind the iconicity of verbal metaphors, intuitive concepts, and authentic symbols.

That light is manifested as an articulated luminosity can also explain why it is seen as closely related to knowledge and to the formation of the intelligible world.[16]

Similarly, luminosity can be described as a theophany of light (*lux*), which penetrates the world and moves hierarchically through the different levels of reality.[17] The importance given to the phenomenon of light in medieval cosmologies reflects a tendency to grasp the mystery of creation more tangibly, moving beyond poetic and rhetorical language toward a more precise syllogistic reasoning and eventually to a geometrical understanding of light. In this process light ceased to be a mere metaphor for or analogy of intelligibility and became a real natural power—a part of the creative act itself.

The move toward a geometrical representation of light logically followed an attempt to find a more direct form of participation in the essential reality of the divine, closely associated in the twelfth century with mathematics and particularly with geometry.[18] In the treatises of the thirteenth-century perspectivists,[19] the properties of light—not only the physical but also the metaphysical and theological—are discussed almost exclusively in the mathematical language of optics (figure 3.4). This has led modern authors to claim that late medieval optics was an independent discipline, distinct from any broader metaphysical or theological context[20]—a conclusion that is not only wrong but historically impossible. An independent mathematical representation of light is conceivable only in the context of experimental thinking, which was not available before the seventeenth century. Even more important, it defies the representational, symbolic role of geometry in the late medieval and early Renaissance world.

What appears on the surface to be a pure geometrical construction is in reality an intricate and complex mode of representation. We must not forget that in the geometrical representation of light, nothing of its previous, traditional meaning is lost; the task is to see not only what is represented but, more important, how it is represented. For a modern mind, deeply influenced by instrumental, scientific thinking, it is obviously difficult to comprehend how a relatively simple sequence of geometrical lines can represent the content and meaning of a luminous world. The key to such an understanding is the mediating role and the symbolic meaning of geometry in medieval optics.

3.4. Roger Bacon, *De multiplicatione specierum,* fol. 376, refraction of light.

In the earliest commentary on the nature of geometry and optics, Aristotle writes: "the geometer deals with physical lines but not qua physical, whereas optics deals with mathematical lines but qua physical not qua mathematical. Since 'nature' is used ambiguously either for the form or for the matter 'it' can be viewed from two points of view which means that everything in nature can neither be isolated from the material subject in which it exists, nor is it constituted by it." From this, "it seems to follow that physics must take cognisance both of the formal and of the material aspect of nature and further the same enquiry must embrace both the purpose or the end, and the means to that end. And the nature is the goal for the sake of which the rest exists."[21]

Optics, apart from the study of vision, was used to solve astronomical problems; it also provided a model for a more precise understanding of the nature and structure of the universe. Euclid's *Optics,* the first known treatise on the subject, is an extension of his *Elements* and is formulated in the same language of propositions as his geometry.[22] We know that the *Elements* were already taught in the old Platonic academy, where they were supposed to serve as an introduction to the dialectical studies of cosmology through "cosmic figures."[23] The role of cosmic figures is to represent and initiate the mediating movement between sensible and intelligible phenomena in a simulated transition from point to line, to surface, and to solid body. The same process is even more explicit in the structure of the luminous or visual pyramid, where light moves between body and point via surface and lines.

The original meaning of optics is quite clearly cosmological; it is thus not surprising that in the thirteenth century optics becomes the fundamental science of nature, revealing not only the nature of creation but also the mode of all natural actions. It is perhaps not necessary to emphasize to what extent the original meaning of optics depends not just on the presence of the world in which that meaning was originally established, but also on the changing role of geometry (figure 3.5).

In the Platonic tradition, geometry acts as an intermediary that transcends the transitory nature of our visual experience and points toward the clarity of ideas.[24] These are its virtues but also its limitations. Geometry itself cannot grasp the essential nature of things; such understanding is possible only through dialectics, for which geometry is no more than a

3.5. Villard de Honnecourt, sketchbook, pl. 36, diagrammatic figures.

preparation.[25] This conclusion is reinforced by Proclus in his commentary on the first book of Euclid's *Elements:* "Let us then not say that Plato excludes mathematics from the sciences but only that he ranks it second."[26] In the dialectical understanding of geometry and optics we have to take into account the points made in the discussion of geometry in chapter 2, particularly its relation to visual experience and language. The key to this relation is imagination. Imagination gives language iconicity, which can be developed to the level of a full geometrical abstraction; at the same time, it also situates geometrical abstraction in the reality of the visible world.[27] In the dialectical interpretation of optics, geometry preserves its intuitive character and symbolic meaning. It is mainly for this reason that optics can and should be treated not as a separate science but as a discipline linked very closely with physiology and physics, as well as with metaphysics and theology.[28]

The unity of individual disciplines was felt very strongly by the perspectivists of the thirteenth century. In Roger Bacon's view there was only one wisdom, which was unfolded through the different sciences. It is unfolded, as it were, "in the palm with these sciences and yet it gathers within its own grasp all wisdom, since all wisdom has been given by one god to one world for one purpose."[29] The unity of knowledge and wisdom, which was for the thirteenth century the way of salvation, was seen by Bacon and his contemporaries as a goal that could be reached only through a series of steps, beginning with sensible experience and ending with the intelligible understanding of the divine. The typical sequence was a movement, expressed in the progression of knowledge, from physics through mathematics to metaphysics.[30] The central place of mathematics and its mediating role gave it unprecedented prestige.

In reading Bacon's text it takes a strong imaginative effort for us to appreciate how far mathematics was both extended into the physical world and able, at the same time, to sustain communication with the intelligibility of the divine. Its dual nature is, I think, quite apparent in the following two statements. On the one hand,

> mathematical quantity and a physical one are the same as regards being and as regards reality, but they differ only in the point of view, because the geometer considers a physical line, not as it exists in physical matter, and therefore the line is called a mathematical one. And the natural philosopher considers this same line as it exists in physical matter, as in iron, or stone, or other physical object. And because the same thing is, as respects being and reality of existence, physical and mathematical, therefore if there should be here one line or one body mathematically, then in the same way would there be one physically.

And on the other hand,

from the ineffable beauty of the divine wisdom would shine and infinite benefit would overflow if these matters relating to geometry which are contained in Scripture should be placed before our eyes in their physical forms. Therefore I count nothing more fitting for a man diligent in the study of God's wisdom than the exhibition of geometrical forms of this kind before his eyes.[31]

Is it possible to ignore this understanding of geometry when we read the optical texts of this period?

THE OPTICAL SYNTHESIS OF THE THIRTEENTH CENTURY

The names of authors that appear in Lorenzo Ghiberti's third commentary, dealing with the optical sources of pictorial perspective, include Roger Bacon, John Peckham, and Witelo. Their optical interpretations of light have their main source in the work of Robert Grosseteste,[32] whose written work represents the most complete synthesis of the Neoplatonic tradition, the Arabic contribution, and the revived Aristotelian philosophy.

Grosseteste's synthesis is already apparent in his understanding of the nature of light. Starting from the earlier inconclusive debates about whether light is an immaterial entity or a form, a quality or a state of the medium, he came forward with an interpretation that eliminated most of the earlier contradictions. For Grosseteste, light is the first form of corporeality in all material things; it is a source of their activity and the cause of their articulated existence. It is a self-generating corporeal substance, subtle and almost immaterial.[33] In the luminous structure of the world, light is not only a medium that brings the world to visibility or that illuminates the world, as it were, from outside: it is an active power (*virtus activa*), which structures the world from inside and is seen as a primary source of both the differentiation and unity of the world. For Grosseteste and the thirteenth-century perspectivists,[34] light is corporeal, but this does not mean that it has a body. On the other hand, it is not a form either.

In the Christian tradition, everything outside the domain of the divine is by definition corporeal; for that reason, visible light is always united with matter as a substantial form or as a form of luminous bodies. That we think it possible to isolate light from matter in our thought is the main source of confusion in modern discussions of the nature of light. How closely light was associated with matter in the late Middle Ages can be seen in the references to the presence of light in such elementary bodies or matter as minerals, wood, and coal. The fascination with the luminosity of certain minerals, precious stones, and glass made out of dustlike material illustrates how the sense of light had changed. The tendency to see the presence of light in dark matter was a departure from the traditional analogical or metaphorical thinking about light toward viewing the creative cosmogonic role of light, for the first time, as embedded in physical phenomena.[35] Grosseteste was constantly preoccupied with the cosmogonic nature of light, as is seen most clearly in his commentary on Genesis and in his short treatise on light.[36] The line of his philosophical interpretation of light follows very closely the narrative of Genesis. As Augustine explains, in the self-diffusion of light that "multiplies itself from a single point and forms a finite sphere, firmament (*sphaera lucis*), matter becomes dimensional."[37]

The light of the first sphere (the firmament) diffuses itself in straight lines to the center of the universe and reaches the earth in several stages. Each represents a region rarefied by the action of light; once the limit of possible rarefaction is reached, a new sphere is formed. This process of propagation continues through the perfect, incorruptible celestial spheres and culminates in the imperfect, corruptible domain of the sublunar terrestrial spheres identified with the four elements (see figure 3.3). The result can be seen as a continuous space—not a Euclidean space, but a space structured hierarchically between the center and the circumference of the firmament.[38] In this hierarchically ordered space the lower spheres participate through light in the form of the higher spheres in a gradually diminishing intensity, which corresponds to the level of rarefaction and condensation of each sphere.[39]

Grosseteste was probably the first thinker to establish the continuity between the celestial and terrestrial, divine and human realities, assuming the presence of common matter. The unity of matter and the capacity of the elements to communicate with the light of the supralunar spheres are the primary conditions for such continuity.[40] "In this way," he writes, "all things are linked together in the most orderly way by natural connections."[41] Finding unity of matter in the universe and eliminating the traditional difference between celestial and terrestrial phenomena were critical for there to be a unified vision of reality that could, in the future, be represented perspectively. The most important consequence of the new vision was that it became possible to see the presence of celestial order in terrestrial phenomena more directly.[42] This step created new conditions that enabled philosophers to discuss the metaphysical issues of light in the language of physics and eventually in the language of geometry and optics. In his later works Grosseteste characteristically refers not to the firmament, as he had done earlier, but to the visible sun, which he describes in rather poetic terms as the fountain of all light, as the source of visibility, and as a begetter of all corporeal forms impressed in the sun's annual cycle.[43]

Grosseteste was one of the first to stimulate what may be described as "valuational" heliocentrism.[44] A new value was given to the visible body of the sun and to terrestrial phenomena; as a consequence, a new relationship was established between the sun and the human eye, between light and the human intellect. It was this development that opened the way for a new type of anthropology, an anthropology wherein body is no longer a negative residuum of the intelligible world but instead a positive medium of participation in the world. The participation of body or matter in intelligible reality was traditionally seen as a link between body and soul. In Grosseteste's understanding, this link is performed by light, which affects the soul directly through the perception of the visible world. However, this is possible only because the soul has the inner ability to resist the overwhelming power of light by asserting its own freedom.[45]

Because the human body consists of the four primary elements, which are penetrated, as we have seen, by light in direct proportion to their density, the body together with the soul constitutes a unified luminous structure, a mode of being in the luminous world. The layers of luminosity correspond proportionally to the degree of light in the articulated vision and the degree of shadow in the material world. This is—in anticipation— the foundation of the proportional organization of space in Renaissance artificial perspective.

In Grosseteste's anthropology, visual perception is the prime efficient cause of corporeal motion, which is transmitted from vision to the other senses by the nerves and muscles of the body. This rather crude physiological explanation illustrates how light and vision are related to the other senses through the unifying power of common sense (*sensus communis*).[46]

Common sense coordinates individual senses, constitutes their unity, and relates them through imagination to the higher source of light. The concern of Grosseteste and those who closely followed him was to discover the presence of the divine in the most mundane phenomena accessible to the senses, and at the same time to raise vision, through abstraction, to the level of revealed illumination. We shall find similar interests among the perspectivists of the early Renaissance.

The attempt to discover the divine in the directly perceived world was motivated by the conviction that senses give us real knowledge of reality and that it is light which makes the knowledge real, because it simultaneously affects the visual field and vision itself. This was part of the belief in a continuity between light, vision, and intellect, on the grounds that they all share the same source of light and participate in the same sequence of illuminations.[47] The desire to come to terms with revealed illuminations through one's own effort, mainly through idealization and abstraction, represents a new emphasis on anthropology and on a tangible mode of representation based on logic and mathematics. This change laid bare a series of questions. Perhaps the most important concerned representation itself. Is representation only a human construct and heuristic device, or does it reveal an essential truth of reality? How much truth has its source in the luminous world and how much in human intellect? These questions were much debated in the thirteenth century.[48]

We can appreciate the importance of these questions most clearly in front of a stained-glass cathedral window of the period (figure 3.6). In the famous Charlemagne window at Chartres, the translucent layer of colored glass is structured by leading and armature into a geometrical pattern of squares, circles, semicircles, and lozenges, which carry very specific symbolic meanings.[49] The problem of representation demonstrated in the window shows that it is through human effort and in particular through symbolic representation that the visible order and the truth of reality can be revealed. The close link between representation and revelation is ultimately dominated, certainly in the medieval world, by the articulating power of light that stimulates human memory, intentions, and intellect (*irradiatio intellectualis*) through vision, and thus keeps them subordinated to revealed illumination—which may be described, in more contemporary terms, as the light of Being.

3.6. Chartres cathedral, Charlemagne window, detail.

The example of the stained-glass window is a useful reminder that light and vision cannot be understood as separate from the luminous world. What light brings to visibility is a physiognomy of a particular scene, but this physiognomy was formed by a certain program and content. This qualitative understanding of light and vision is clearly apparent in the text in which Roger Bacon describes the action of light: "when a ray passes through a medium of strongly-coloured glass or crystal or cloth, there appears to us in the dark, in the vicinity of the ray, a colour similar to the colour of that strongly-coloured body; and this colour is an opaque substance (that intercepts it), and is called the 'similitude and species' of the colour in the strongly-coloured (transparent) body through which the ray passes."[50]

Species represent the essential character of phenomena; Bacon explains, "they are called species with respect to sense and intellect, similitude or image with respect to thing generating it and virtue with respect to generation and corruption."[51] Sometimes they are also called "impressions," because they resemble impressions made in wax by a signet ring or seal.[52] The creation of species is the first effect of the light-radiating agent, making the recipient similar to itself "because the recipient is always potentially what the agent is in actuality."[53] There is an uninterrupted continuity between the first agent—the source of light (*lux*)—and the last recipient in the universe, and therefore every diversity can be traced back to an original identity.[54]

In the thirteenth-century synthesis, the philosophy of light (optics) became the key discipline of natural philosophy and science. As the most exemplary form of corporeal movement, light was considered to be a special case of the multiplication found also in other phenomena. "We call every multiplication 'radiant,'" Roger Bacon writes, "and we say that 'rays' are produced whether they are light or colour or something else. There is another reason for these names, namely that the multiplication of light is more apparent to us than the multiplication of other things and therefore we transfer the terminology of the multiplication of light to the others."[55] The universal role of species, their power to differentiate and unite phenomena with greater precision, represents a radically new articulation of the inherited, symbolically structured world.

FROM MEDIEVAL OPTICS TO ARTIFICIAL PERSPECTIVE

The emphasis on the more explicit role of light in understanding and representing reality did not in itself introduce a new content. It only helped to make more explicit the existing knowledge, particularly in the sphere of cosmology. The traditional cosmologies, based primarily on Neoplatonic thinking, were at the end of the twelfth century already highly idealized and spiritualized representations in which even material symbols became transparent and nearly dissolved in the subtleties of a poetic language, dominated by abstract metaphors and allegories.[56] The rehabilitation of the natural world together with the more tangible and precise form of representation restored the most important part of traditional symbolism—the visible body of symbols.[57]

The multiplication of species reveals in the visible world whole chains of similarities and identities that link things together and give them a relatively precise place in the overall order of things. Using different language, we can describe the multiplication as a process of symbolization in which a common communicative space is created.[58] For Grosseteste and his contemporaries the equivalent of communicative space was cosmology, seen not as a system but as a framework that could serve as a paradigm of an incomplete project.[59]

The philosophy of light reached its most complete synthesis in the work of Roger Bacon.[60] His interpretation of light, expressed consistently in the language of geometrical optics, established a tradition that played a decisive role in the formation of Renaissance perspective.[61] How the nature of his influence should be interpreted is a question still debated and not well understood. The main source of misunderstanding is, as we have already seen, the geometrical language of optics, which creates an illusion of autonomy and separation from other disciplines, particularly metaphysics and theology.[62]

However, we already know that the separation of optics from other disciplines is historically impossible, and that optics is not a geometry or "physics of causation" of the visible world but a language of natural relations structured by geometry.[63] The role of geometry in the "language of optics" is clearly illustrated in a passage of Grosseteste that must be quoted in full:

> The usefulness of considering lines, angles and figures is very great, since it is impossible to understand natural philosophy without them. They are useful in relation to the universe as a whole and its individual parts. They are useful also in connection with related properties, such as rectilinear motion. Indeed, they are useful in relation to activity and receptivity, whether of matter or sense; and if the latter, whether of the sense of vision, where activity and receptivity are apparent, or of the other senses, in the operation of which something must be added to those things that produce vision. Since we have spoken elsewhere of those things that pertain to the whole universe and its individual parts and of those things that relate to rectilinear and circular motion we must now consider universal action insofar as it partakes of the nature of sublunary things.[64]

The things that can be brought in as intermediaries are lines, angles, and figures. It is with their help that the earlier philosophy of light can be made more explicit. It is interesting to see how closely the geometry of light imitates the articulations already accomplished by the language of natural philosophy. The meaning of the operations can be followed step by step only through the dialectics of the philosophical language and geometry, and the result can perhaps best be described as a philosophy *more optico* rather than as pure optics.[65]

In the treatises of the perspectivists, the geometrical rays of light are discussed as physical. The ray itself is seen as having a thickness and velocity, and as responding to the resistance of a medium and having a generative power.[66] From the large body of optical knowledge of the perspectivists I shall focus on only a small part, directly relevant to the understanding of Renaissance perspective.[67] The perspectivists interpret the radiation of light as taking place primarily on three kinds of lines: direct, refracted, and reflected. The generation of species proceeds along a straight line, "provided the medium in which it is multiplied is uniform as air and water or some other substance and no obstacle is encountered." However, when a species falls obliquely on a medium or body of different density it changes its angle in proportion to the density of the medium (see figure 3.4). "This is properly speaking the refraction of a species. . . . The refracted ray falls between the direct paths and the perpendicular, drawn from the point of refraction." If the second medium is more dense, the ray falls closer to the perpendicular; if less dense, it turns away from the perpendicular. In cases in which the second medium is impenetrable, a species returns by its own power and "multiplies itself in the original medium, forming an angle; and it is properly called a reflected species."[68] This interpretation of light in terms of lines and angles is a preparation for understanding the propagation of light in terms of figures.

The figure that primarily determines the radiation of species is a sphere, "since an agent produces its species everywhere and in all directions and along all diameters. . . . Thus it is necessary that the agent be a centre from which lines proceed in every direction. But such lines are radii of a sphere, and their terminus must be a spherical surface." However, in terms of power the most important figure is a pyramid—"not any pyramidal figure you please, but that having its base on the face of the luminous

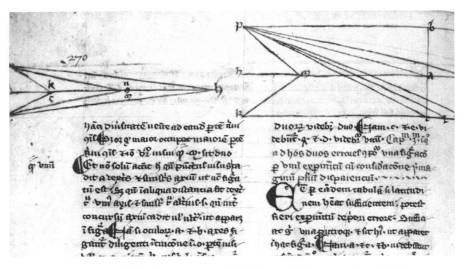

3.7. Roger Bacon, *De multiplicatione specierum,* fol. 270, pyramidal propagation of light.

body and its vertex on the illuminated part of the non-luminous body; for only in this figure are perfect illumination and the action of nature preserved" (figure 3.7). What makes the pyramidal figure unique? Bacon's treatise has a short answer: "if a ray should come from one part of the agent to one part of the recipient, there would be only one ray and that would not be sufficiently active and therefore nature chooses the pyramid."[69] Bacon's definition is taken almost word for word from Grosseteste's longer but much clearer formulation.[70]

The pyramids with their base on the surface of the agent have their apexes projected into individual points of the medium or recipient body. As a result, an infinite number of radiant pyramids is propagated in any one direction. But how can a clearly structured world come into existence from an infinite number of radiations? A deeper understanding of the nature of light and species provides the answer. In such an understanding, which geometry only partly represents, a clear distinction should be established between the essential species represented by perpendicular lines, which are close to the axes of the pyramids, and accidental species represented by oblique lines close to their sides. An even more important distinction should be established between species and genus: species of the same kind in the same genus mix, while species of different kinds remain separate and contingent.

This sequence well illustrates the extent to which the multiplication of species follows the language of natural philosophy and can therefore be seen as a form of a "rhetoric" of light. This relation is clearly demonstrated in Bacon's formulation: "But also the explanation of mixing is entirely true, it contains many apparent contradictions because of the badly understood statements of many authorities. For on the basis of distinct visual perception, those ignorant, judge that all species are distinct in all parts of the medium and that distinct visual perception cannot otherwise be explained."[71] What may be ill-understood and what needs to be explained is the apparent contradiction between the mixing of species and distinct visual perception of distinct entities.[72]

Bacon answers this contradiction with an ingenious explanation; it relies on the human eye's ability to also produce species that mix with the species of luminous objects and, further, on the eye's involvement, because of its unique nature (comparable to the light of the sun), in the principal multiplication that completes the act of vision by concealing, but not destroying, other peripheral, background multiplications (figure 3.8). Nevertheless, the mixed species proceed to the pupil of the observer's eye from the place in the medium where they first mix. One of those species comes directly from the perceived thing itself, falling perpendicularly on the eye and the pupil, while the other comes to the eye along an accidental line. "The latter comes perpendicularly to the eye not from the perceived object but only from the place of mixing. Consequently one of the species arrives with greater strength and conceals the other as greater light conceals lesser light."[73]

The place of mixing, situated in the visual pyramid at a certain distance from the eye, anticipated the pictorial plane in Renaissance perspectival construction. The mixing of species and their transformation into a clear coherent vision was anticipated even more explicitly by the formation of the image in the plane of the mirror, studied in medieval catoptrics.

THE FORMATION OF PICTORIAL PERSPECTIVE

The formation of pictorial perspective, which is sometimes also referred to as *perspectiva artificialis* or *costruzione legittima,* is rightly considered to

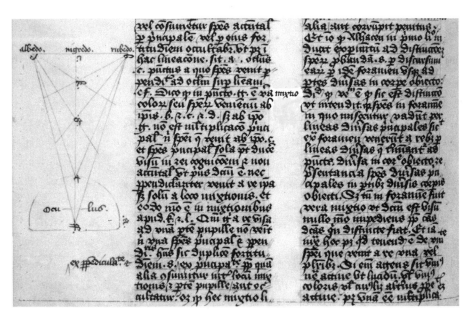

3.8. Roger Bacon, *De multiplicatione specierum,* fol. 367, diagram of light mixing.

be the main characteristic of the new historical era, marking a true revolution in the sphere of visual representation. There is no doubt that artificial perspective represents a radically new way of seeing, with no direct historical precedent. However, the novelty of the new type of representation should not obscure the fact that there is also deep continuity between late medieval and early Renaissance perspective.

The decisive step in the new development—now almost universally accepted as the initiating event—is Brunelleschi's well-known pictorial demonstration of the new perspectival method in front of the Florentine baptistery and in front of the Palazzo della Signoria. There is no need to repeat here the debates about Brunelleschi's contribution or the various conclusions drawn from the numerous reconstructions of his experimental demonstration.[74]

There is a tendency among modern authors to see pictorial perspective as the correct geometrical construction of an autonomous, mathematical representation of vision.[75] But in view of my earlier discussion, and particularly of the conditions under which it is possible to speak about light and vision in terms of geometrical optics (perspective), it is clear that the arguments focused on the pure geometrical nature and autonomy of the new representation are to a great extent misleading. They miss the point, because genuine representation is always situated in an ontological structure of a world: it may not be apparent or explicitly visible, but it is always assumed. Geometrical construction has in itself no empirical content. If the ontological structure of geometrical operations is not taken into account, the representation remains empty and meaningless.[76]

The development of optics (*perspectiva naturalis*), which we have followed thus far, made it possible to determine visual operations by referring not only to intuitive evidence but also to mathematical demonstration. What was to be demonstrated was the "correctness of sight"—but what is the "correctness of sight"? If we take seriously the intentions and contributions of those who took part in forming pictorial perspective during the fifteenth and sixteenth centuries, it is clear that the correctness of sight cannot be reduced to the correctness of optical structures of representation. Correctness, as it was established at the beginning of the fifteenth century, was judged by the degree to which the perfect (divine) order was manifested in representations of the visible world. The efforts that brought pictorial perspective into existence can be seen as the culmination of a trend that began in the generation of Grosseteste, when late medieval culture in general began to turn toward a new appreciation of natural phenomena and the visible world (figure 3.9). We have followed this tendency insofar as it relates to the development of medieval optics. It is only natural to expect that the privileged position given to vision found its fulfillment in the visual arts, most obviously in painting.

The relationship between the nature of perspective in the Renaissance paintings and medieval optics has been discussed many times.[77] But because the arguments that try to clarify and explain this link are none too convincing, the whole issue remains controversial. It is not easy to see how optics, a mathematical discipline cultivated in the domain of theology, cosmology, metaphysics, and physics, could become the foundation of a new, empirically based mode of representation. I believe that the key to a more satisfactory understanding of the continuity between medieval optics and Renaissance perspective lies in the nature of the change in the representa-

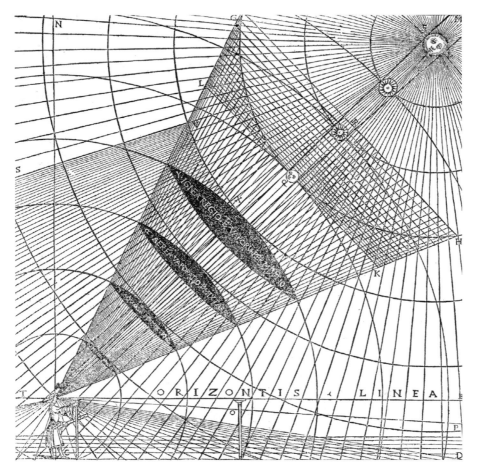

3.9. Cesare Cesariano, edition of Vitruvius, *De architectura* (1521), the relation between the celestial light and perspectival vision.

tion of reality as a whole, including not only architecture and visual arts but also everyday life. It began during the fourteenth century and became fully explicit at the beginning of the fifteenth century.

This change can be characterized as a new tendency to represent the hierarchically structured world as directly accessible and objectlike, a tendency that in the past has been identified with late medieval nominalism or with Renaissance individualism and naturalism.[78] However, I believe that there is a deeper motivation for the change: a strong desire to recognize the presence of light, intelligibility, and order—that is, the divine reality—in the human world and to make it accessible to finite human understanding. This may also explain the apparent contradiction in the character of the visual art of the early Renaissance, which combines illusionistic realism with the abstract mathematical rigor of proportional harmonies and perspectival constructions.

How far this combination was developed is well illustrated in Alberti's discussion of *lineamenti.* "The appropriate place, exact numbers, proper scale and graceful order for whole buildings," Alberti claims, can be determined by lines and angles only. In fact he goes one step further, insisting that "it is quite possible to project whole forms in the mind without any recourse to the material, by designating and determining a fixed orientation and conjunction of the various lines and angles."[79]

The imaginary structure of a possible "form" or building anticipates the Mannerists' notion of *disegno interno,* but remains close to the geometrical principles of medieval optics;[80] it also maintains ties to the use of geometry in medieval architecture[81] (figure 3.10). Much like *lineamenti, disegno interno* belongs to the inventive capacity of the human mind. By means of internal design it is possible to create the image of an ideal world, before such a world is realized. Federigo Zuccaro, the Mannerist painter and writer, left a very vivid description of *disegno:* "Man almost imitating God and emulating nature may produce infinite artificial things similar to the natural, and by means of painting and sculpture make us see new paradises on earth."[82]

The similarity between *lineamenti* and medieval geometry shows very clearly the ambiguity of *lineamenti,* not so much in view of what they represent but in how they represent. Unlike medieval geometry, which determines the nature of a particular configuration, such as a portal, a facade, a window, a wall, or interior space—always in view of a unifying whole and in an open dialectical interpretation—*lineamenti* anticipate the visible unity of the result as a closed system, to which nothing can be added and from which nothing can be taken away.

Seeing buildings as surfaces defined by *lineamenti* was, no doubt, made possible by a long history of geometrical interpretation of primary architectural problems.[83] Such interpretations draw on symbolic meanings associated with geometry and its operations, including the articulation of

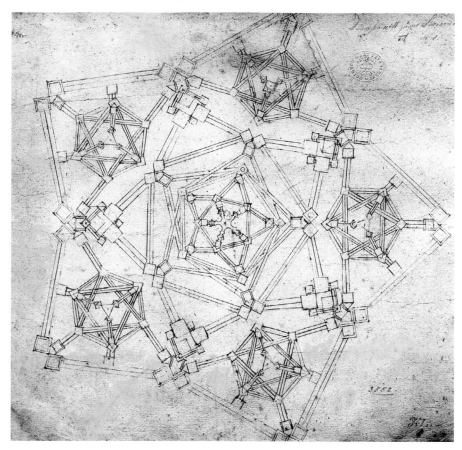

3.10. Ulm cathedral, tabernacle, plan of the groined vaulting at the base.

proportions. It is in the domain of proportions that the difference between *lineamenti* and medieval geometry becomes most visible. In the medieval context, proportions are a direct expression of the hierarchical organization of reality. Thus adapted to the universe of nature, they are the most important means of exploring the secrets of a symbolically structured world. Given all the other options, "the only method which can be at all fruitful in such a case is reasoning by analogy and especially the reasoning of proportion."[84]

The reasoning of proportion follows the articulation of language and, on a more explicit conceptual level, the articulation of light as it is represented in medieval optics. Grosseteste declares, "It is clear that light through the infinite multiplication of itself extends matter into finite dimensions that are smaller and larger according to certain proportions that they have to one another and thus light proceeds according to numerical and non-numerical proportion."[85]

The importance given to proportion may seem misplaced, until we leave behind the conventional understanding of proportion as a visible, quantifiable relation between clearly defined entities and discover that proportion is primarily a qualitative relation and is more universal. In the non-dogmatic tradition of thinking, proportion is—as the original Greek term for the concept, *analogia,* indicates—an analogy. An analogy is a symbolic structure reflecting the resemblances, similarities, and eventually the balanced tension of sameness and difference between individual phenomena. Seen in that light, proportion is a key to the analytical, qualitative articulation of reality and its representation.

The close link between proportion and perspective has been mentioned and emphasized many times. In fact, some authors go so far as to believe that the problem of proportionality is the very foundation of perspective—in other words, that proportion is "a mathematical concept on which Renaissance theory of perspective rests"[86] (figure 3.11). We may agree, but if we do, we have to answer a more fundamental question: How is a world structured by analogical proportions, by medieval optics, and the multiplication of species represented in the geometrical construction of perspective, which does not seem to express any empirical content and is, in accord with conventionally understood intentions, a purely formal and universal mathematical discipline—a "symbolic form"?[87] It is taken for granted that the term "symbolic" refers to a representation of space. However, does not the second term, "form," tell us that the representation refers not to the space of our everyday existence but only to its formal structure? In that case, the question of the world—how it is represented or if it is represented at all—is even more relevant.

In the ongoing discussion about the nature of perspective, it is not clear if perspective is a symbolic form, a scientific mathematical mode of representation, or a rationalization of concrete visual experience. There is a similar ambiguity and disagreement about the origins of pictorial perspective. Almost everyone seems to agree that the workshop tradition of

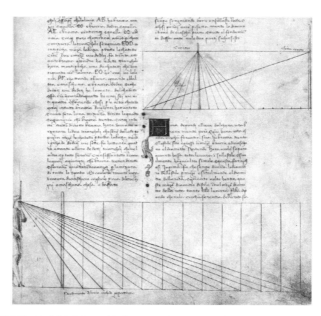

3.11. Francesco di Giorgio Martini, *Trattati,* fol. 33, tav. 61, diagram of perspectival vision.

practical perspective, medieval optics, and the inventiveness of certain artists (including Brunelleschi, Donatello, Masaccio, Uccello, and Alberti) all played an important role; but it is not yet clear what brought the individual contributions together in the decisive period when the *costruzione legittima* was formed. Was it the geometry of the visual pyramid and its projection, the discovery of the vanishing point, or the proportional construction of the foreshortenings? I do not think that the analytical and technical steps themselves can explain the synthetic nature of the new perspective. The discovery of the "legitimate construction" marked a culmination of a long development that was shaped not only by important changes in the nature of visual arts but also by fundamental transformations in European culture as a whole. The terms most often associated with this transformation are *devotio moderna* in religious life, *via moderna* in intellectual life, and *ars nova* in the domain of arts.[88]

For the purpose of my argument I am interested in only one aspect of the change—the tendency to move away from the hierarchically structured world toward a world in which the transcendental, intelligible levels of reality are seen as immanent in what is directly visible in everyday life. The most important role in this change, particularly in the visual arts, was played by the notion of "common sense": the unifying faculty of all senses, the lower unity of meaning, and place of "sensible" judgment. The unity of common sense corresponds to the unity of things sensed in terms of their essential characteristics—common sensibles.[89] Typical common sensibles are movement, rest, shape, unity, number, and magnitude, which includes sizes and distances.[90] The ability to see magnitudes, according to the art historian David Summers, means not that we "can apprehend the exact dimensions or distances of things but that what we apprehend is measurable and corresponds to the measurable." It is for this reason that the history of common sense is closely bound up with optics: "Optics in fact might be described as the science of the common sense par excellence, and provides a clear example of the relation between common sense and reason. We always perceive particular shapes and magnitudes under real circumstances and therefore in a certain sense perceive them 'incorrectly' and optics tells us what we 'really' see."[91]

Because the judgment of sense and the geometry of vision become so closely related, it is possible to discern a new relationship between the principles of medieval optics and the practical achievements of workshop perspective as early as the end of the fourteenth century. A decisive contribution was made by new interpretations of and commentaries on medieval optics. The most interesting, for our purposes, are the commentaries of Biagio da Parma (known also as Pelacani), particularly his unpublished treatise *Quaestiones perspectivae*.[92] In his writings Biagio, who belongs to the late medieval tradition as well as indirectly to the epoch of Brunelleschi, discussed perspective and the questions of vision in a language focused on the tangible visual qualities, on the primary role of common sensibles, and on common sense. In *Quaestiones perspectivae*, Biagio's main concern is correctness of sight (*iudicium sensus*).[93] Such a question can be discussed but cannot be fully answered by verbal argument. For Biagio, the power to decide (*virtus distinctiva*) resided not in the intellect or in words but in sight itself. It is there, in the domain of visual experience, that the question will be addressed by the next generation.

The new relationship between the world articulated by optics and the constructions of linear perspective illustrates the transformation taking place in Florence in the first decade of the fifteenth century. Owing to a unique combination of historical circumstances, it was there that demonstrating the continuity between the optical interpretation of the medieval world (mainly cosmology and the problem of creation) and the perspectival representation of the visible world first became possible. This continuity was largely obscured by the apparent neutrality of the geometrical representation used in linear perspective. The axiomatic nature of geometric operations and their seeming autonomy make it easy, particularly for a modern interpreter, to forget the conditions under which such operations took form or could be taken as truly representing anything. My earlier discussions of geometry and its role in medieval optics have anticipated this problem but more needs to be said, particularly about the assumptions on which the most decisive steps in the development of linear perspective, including the contribution of Brunelleschi and his *costruzione legittima,* were based.

The conventional interpretations, which take for granted that linear perspective is a new representation of space, make sense only in the modern Newtonian world, where space is seen as absolute and as an independent, a priori concept. It is true, of course, that perspective ideally anticipates such space, but in the fifteenth century space is still part of a phenomenal reality in which it cannot be treated in isolation from the conditions of its embodiment. After all, artificial perspective was never supposed to be a purely mathematical or absolute discipline but a pictorial one, representing not a concept of space or abstract structure but a concrete world in its visibility. In such a world, space is both articulated and also embodied and situated, which means that it always has a situational structure as a background to all possible transformations.[94] The development of perspectival representation was closely linked not only with medieval optics, new treatments of proportions, and the imaginary or ideal structure of design (*lineamenti*) but also with surveying, geography, and, most of all, the development of the pictorial space in artists' workshops. The practice of the workshops is particularly important, because it was there that the creative steps of synthesis occurred.[95]

The first signs of the change toward a new type of pictorial space can be seen in the works of Giotto, of his older and younger contemporaries (Cavallini, Cimabue, and Duccio), and of his disciples (Taddeo Gaddi). Changes in the interpretation of space always result from a more fundamental alteration in the intellectual life and sensibility of a particular epoch, and thus these shifts cannot be understood in isolation or as simply formal problems. *The Presentation of the Virgin* by Taddeo Gaddi in Santa Croce in Florence well illustrates such a change in the period of transition from medieval to proper Renaissance representation (figure 3.12). The composition of the painting, dominated by an oblique construction of a temple, is treated in a medieval manner; individual scenes and places are configured in relation to their meaning and not to a unifying space. This approach is underscored by the lack of any clear connections between figures and their surrounding or between themselves, and there is no unity of event, time, and place. Realistic unity or unifying space remains problematic in a world structured in accordance with symbolic topology, where imaginative and not descriptive space is important.

However, the growing emphasis on the concrete representation of directly visible reality, on the realistic interpretation of details and of human figures, contributed decisively to the emergence of a new space. Corporeality became important, with all its typical characteristics—modeling and volume, incidental light and shadow, and so on—simultaneously defining body and space. The new interest in a more precise definition of corporeality led also to a new, almost mathematically clear relation between the body's volume, its surface, and space. This mathematical clarity is most apparent in the geometry of the depicted architectural structures (*casamenti*) and objects. As a paradigm of embodiment and spatiality, architecture became a prime, dominating element in the formation of the new pictorial space and in the process of "perspectivization." What gave architecture such a privileged position was its idealized, quasi-mathematical nature—the main characteristic of perspective itself.

Architecture and perspective share a sense of coherent space, most clearly exemplified in the concept of a "room." The space of a room is obviously not the same as the phenomenal space of the natural world. It is a highly idealized representation that during its long history acquired many of the characteristics of the isotropic space of geometry. The natural per-

3.12. Taddeo Gaddi, *The Presentation of the Virgin* (1328–1334), Santa Croce, Florence.

spectivity of architecture is already anticipated in the prevailing parallelism of columns, pillars, and walls, as well as in the axiality and overall regularity of its spatial arrangement.

It is true that perspectival depth can be represented by other nonlinear means, such as light, shadow, and color, or by perspectival foreshortening of the figures; but in those cases, too, the sense of room seems to play a decisive role. Consider Altichiero da Zevio's *Crucifixion,* which offers an unusual interpretation of space structured mostly by human figures (figure 3.13). Even here, however, the depth of the scene is defined by architectural

3.13. Altichiero, *The Crucifixion* (1373–1379), Chapel of Bonifacio Lupi, Basilica del Santo, Padua.

vistas on the left and right of the picture; it is merely reinforced by figures receding to the horizon.

The level of perfection achieved in the formation of perspectival space without a unifying and precise construction is demonstrated on the walls of the Oratorio di San Giorgio in Padua (figure 3.14). Here, in Altichiero's *Presentation of Jesus in the Temple* and *Baptism of the King of Cyrene by St. George*, we find what may perhaps be described as the limits of the oblique construction of space, where the interiors are still seen from the outside but the figures are already quite convincingly adjusted to the scale and character of architecture.[96]

Surveying the fourteenth-century paintings, we clearly see that the transformation of pictorial space was accomplished mostly through depicted architecture. This points not only to a new, more unified organization of space but also to a new way of representing the traditional medieval order of reality. Medieval structures closely linked the individual elements of architecture with particular themes and their content.[97] Their purpose was to situate important events and their protagonists in the broader context of reality and its meaning. In that sense, the enclosed roomlike space became

3.14. Altichiero, *The Baptism of the King of Cyrene by Saint George* (1384), Oratory of San Giorgio, Padua.

a place where the traditional vertical relations between celestial and terrestrial, divine and human realities could be represented as a horizontal relation between the nearness of the corporeal world and the remoteness of the new, quasi-infinite space.[98] In this light the "discovery" of artificial perspective at the beginning of the fifteenth century is the answer not so much to a mathematical or technical problem as to a deep cultural and ontological question.

One of the main preconditions for the discovery of "legitimate construction" was the radical transformation of late medieval culture, especially the tendency to bring into explicit visibility the highly articulated inherited world, reconciling its reality—very often expressed in the language of mathematics—with the particular, concrete phenomena of finite human lives. Against this background, Brunelleschi's experiments become more comprehensible. The experiments were motivated by the vision of a new coherent space with a structure derived from the geometry of the visual pyramid, correlated with the perspectival organization of the directly visible world. The perspectival organization is not itself directly visible, because it is not an intrinsic characteristic of the visible world, as is very often assumed.

In phenomenal experience, we do not see parallel lines as convergent or as a ready-made geometrical projection on the retina. The distance and apparent size of things are determined not by a perspectival view but by the phenomenal structure of the world to which we belong and through which we move in an essentially nonperspectival manner. As Merleau-Ponty notes, "When we look at a road which sweeps before us toward the horizon, we must not say either that the sides of the road are given to us as convergent or that they are given to us as parallel; they are parallel in depth. The perspective appearance is not posited, but neither is the parallelism."[99] Both are products of a conceptual transformation of the original experience. This is clearly expressed in the notion of the "judgment of sense" (*iudicium sensus*)—a phrase used so often in Renaissance treatises as a reference to judgment and not to the spontaneity of vision. The judgment of sense, I believe, defines the nature of Brunelleschi's experiments. Much has been written already about the technicalities of these experiments, and most of it does not need to be repeated.[100] No one, however, has yet satisfactorily explained their intended purpose. Was it discovery, invention, or demonstration of the vanishing point; legitimate construction of illusionistic space; demonstration of the mathematical nature of vision; or discovery of the truth of vision?

If we take into account all the available evidence, it appears that the main intention behind the experiments was the search for truth, leading not to a discovery or inventions but to an experimental demonstration of its presence in the visible world. What was supposed to be demonstrated was the possibility of a new link between visible reality and its ultimate source in the divine truth. It is not surprising that in the period of a developed *via moderna,* the link was found in the mathematical treatment of light and proportion.[101]

In Brunelleschi's experiment the visible reality of the baptistery and its surroundings, painted on a small panel (*tavoletta*) and reflected in a mirror, is from the beginning seen as a picture; it shows already in its natural configuration certain perspectival characteristics, such as potential lateral points, horizon, symmetry, and the axiality of the line of vision (figure 3.15). Only the anticipation of the results, suggested to some extent by these characteristics and supported by knowledge of the basic principles of optics, could guarantee the relative success of the experiment. In contrast to ear-

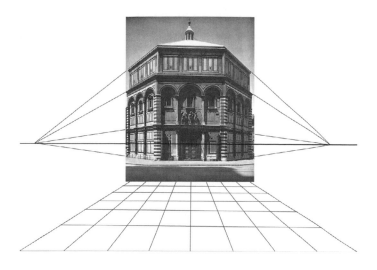

3.15. Filippo Brunelleschi, diagram of the experiment in front of the Florence baptistery.

lier attempts, Brunelleschi's demonstration was systematic and addressed space as a three-dimensional continuum, determined by the geometry of the visual pyramid and its projection first on the surface of the panel and eventually on the mirror. The critical part of the experiment was reconciling the actual setting and its representation, but it rested most of all in the anticipated proportional relation between them. Thus the height of the panel and its distance from the mirror were expected to be in the same proportion as the real height of the baptistery and its distance from the original viewing point.[102]

The mediating role of the mirror is particularly instructive. It illustrates the detached, reflective nature of perspective, manifested most clearly in the ambiguous nature of the plane (intersection) situated halfway between the potential and the actual surface.[103] The intersection of the visual pyramid is the key to all the main issues of perspective. It is where the vanishing point and the horizon are situated and where the pyramid of natural perspective (optics) is reconciled with the visual pyramid in accord with the

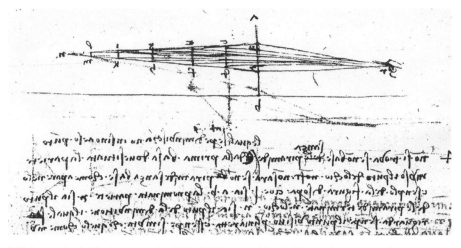

3.16. Leonardo da Vinci, manuscript A 37r (1492), pyramids of vision and perspectival representation.

understanding that, as Leonardo declares, "in the practice of perspective the same rules apply to light and to the eye."[104]

The structural homogeneity of the two pyramids, combined with the empirical identity of the axis of vision, constitutes the essence of pictorial representation (figure 3.16). In his commentary on the conversion of the radiant pyramids emanating from all visible objects into visual pyramids, Leonardo writes that "perspective is a rational demonstration whereby experience confirms that all objects transmit their similitudes (species) to the eye by a pyramid of lines."[105] How the similitudes of objects are transmitted by the pyramids of lines he explains in more detail:

> Perspective in dealing with distances, makes use of two opposite
> pyramids, one of which has its apex in the eye and the base as distant as
> the horizon. The other has the base toward the eye and the apex on
> the horizon. Now the first includes the visible universe, embracing all the
> mass of the objects that lie in front of the eye; as it might be a vast
> landscape seen through a very small opening. . . . The second pyramid is
> extended to a spot which is smaller in proportion as it is further from
> the eye; and this second perspective (pyramid) results from the first.[106]

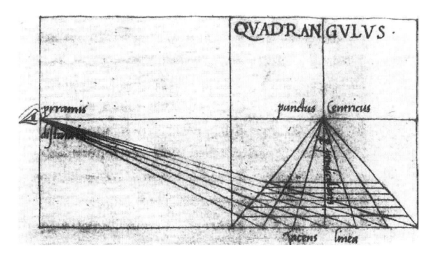

3.17. Leon Battista Alberti, *De pictura* (Lucca manuscript), fol. 27r, perspective diagram.

The experimental demonstration of legitimate construction in which Brunelleschi, to the best of our knowledge, played the most important role was fully articulated by Leon Battista Alberti in his treatise on painting. Alberti completed the process of reducing the paradigm of the perspectival room to its geometrical essence and fully reconciling it with the geometry of the visual pyramid. His contribution can be judged only in the light of the accomplished works of this period of experimentation, which included such impressive achievements as Masaccio's *Trinity* in Santa Maria Novella in Florence, and in the light of the optical knowledge then available in Florence.[107]

In its substance Alberti's contribution offered nothing radically new. However, for its intellectual rigor, conclusiveness, and clarity he deserves much credit. No one before him had had the courage to treat the primary issues of perspective as a purely mathematical problem.[108] Alberti's contribution to perspective was developed entirely around the principles of proportion. The sequence of steps that he followed is based on the understanding that the distance and the size of things, projected on the pictorial plane, represent a definite proportion[109] (figure 3.17). For the same reason, things of the same size appear on the pictorial plane foreshortened in direct proportion to their distance from the viewing point.[110] The proportion

3.18. Piero della Francesca, polyptych of St. Anthony, detail of Annunciation (1465–1470).

the fifteenth century, probably most acutely by Ghiberti, Piero della Francesca, and Leonardo, all of whom also happened to leave behind evidence of their thoughts in writings. Alberti himself, as a humanist, was very much aware of the content implied by his method, which he identified with the concept of *historia*. In fact, he goes so far as to say that "the most important part of a painter's work is the historia."[115] In a broader sense, *historia* is a narrative or program based on the contribution of narrators and poets.

It is typical of Alberti's vision of perspective that he saw the task of representation, including its poetic content, as a quasi-mathematical problem. "Our rudiments," he writes, "from which the complete and perfect art of painting may be drawn, can easily be understood by a geometer, whereas I think that neither the rudiments nor any principles of painting can be understood by those who are ignorant of geometry. Therefore I believe that painters should study the art of geometry."[116] To this end he invented a sequence of steps that made it possible to translate the subtleties of the poetical or rhetorical content into the rigorous language of geometry. The most important role in this translation was played by the human body. The content of *historia* was translated into physiognomic expression, gesture, and movement; the members of the body were then structured in finite proportions of surfaces.[117] The full sequence can be seen as a hermeneutical situation, consisting of a relationship between the parts and the whole. "Part of the historia . . . is the surface, which is defined by lines and angles";[118] in that sense, the surface is a natural element of the geometry of proportion, which means that it can be treated as any other aspect of geometrical perspective. The tendency to translate the content of representation into the language of geometry raises a fundamental question about the status and meaning of geometry and perspective in relation to how they represent phenomenal reality. The discussion of medieval optics above has made clear how a highly articulated content can be symbolically represented in the relatively abstract language of geometry, which can convey most forms of symbolism.

In the perspectival world of Renaissance, new forms of symbolism, based on the achievements of the new way of thinking, began slowly to emerge. It is not surprising that we find their first appearance in the treatises on perspective. One of the striking characteristics of the treatises produced during the fifteenth and sixteenth centuries is the amount of space devoted to representing the five Platonic regular solids. They appear very often as the frontispieces of the treatises, and in many sections of the text they are represented not only in their primary form but also in highly elaborate transformations[119] (figure 3.19). This privileged treatment of the solids, both regular and irregular, cannot be explained as an exercise in the practical use of perspective. There is considerable evidence that the relation between perspective and primary solids is much deeper.

Piero della Francesca, the author of one of the most important treatises on perspective, also wrote separate works on mathematics and on

3.19. Jean Cousin, *Livre de perspective* (1560), frontispiece.

regular solids.[120] That all these treatises were supposed to constitute one body is expressed clearly in Piero's dedication of the *Libellus* of the five regular solids to Guidobaldo, the son of Federigo da Montefeltro, the duke of Urbino. In the dedication Piero asks that the manuscript of his *Libellus* be placed next to his *De prospectiva pingendi,* which was already in the Urbino library.[121] This request was motivated not by a wish to be shown respect but by recognition of the important link between the texts. The content of *De prospectiva pingendi,* which is structured around the relationship between regular and irregular bodies, makes obvious the nature of that link. To reach his primary objective—establishing precise measurements and proportions for all represented elements (*corpi*)—Piero relied on the derivation of all depicted elements, their shape and surface, from the perfect regular bodies.

In the introduction to the second book of the *De prospectiva,* Piero describes the represented elements as objects, bounded by their surfaces. "Objects are of different forms. Some are cubic, tetragonal, and uneven-sided, some round[;] . . . some have many and different sides, such as one finds in natural and accidental things. In this second book, I intend to treat these and their foreshortenings on the determined picture plane as seen by the eye within composite angles, whose bases are formed by some surfaces foreshortened according to the first book."[122]

In the second part of the *Libellus,* written several years later, Piero defines the relationship of one regular body to another; parts 3 and 4 study more complex irregular bodies and their relation to the ideal sphere. The investigation of the progressively more complex solids is a prerequisite for the correct representation of the complex forms of nature. However, Piero does not state his reasons for relying on a geometrical interpretation of natural objects. We must therefore look to others for an explanation—particularly to Leonardo da Vinci and Luca Pacioli (figure 3.20), who are both closely associated with the work of Piero.[123] Leonardo based his interpretation of solids on geometry to allow the transformation of abstract concepts into concrete three-dimensional models. "If by a certain science," Leonardo writes, "one can transform the surface of one body into another and the same science restores such a surface to the original figure, such a science is valid."[124]

Imagining a large variety of solids while preserving their reference to the original figure is an essential aspect of Leonardo's method, which also helped to inspire the content and organization of Pacioli's treatise on perspective, *De divina proportione.* In his treatise, Pacioli is concerned primarily with the perspectival representation of Platonic solids seen as an essential structure in the genesis of the phenomenal world. On one level, the treatise can be read as an exercise in transformational geometry that relates irregular bodies to the regular ones and all of them to a sphere and to the general proportion known as the Divine, or in modern terms as the Golden, Section.[125] However, the same text can also be read as a Christian version of Platonic cosmology in which the transformational geometry represents symbolically the mixing and metamorphosis of the four elements,

3.20. Jacopo de' Barbari, *Portrait of Fra Luca Pacioli with a Young Man* (1495).

thereby leading to the qualitative differentiation of the phenomenal world. There is a certain analogy between the medieval cosmogonic role of light and the geometry of primary solids. Both can be seen as embodying a form (*forma corporalis*), which in the case of the solids is identical with their visible configuration.

What is also common to the light and the solids is the principle of proportionality, which, as we already know, coincides with the very essence of perspective. In the introduction to the third book of the *De prospectiva,* Piero reminds us that "many painters depreciate perspective because they do not understand the significance of the lines and the angles which it produces and by means of which every contour and line can be described in the proper proportion[;] . . . the very nature of perspective shows that it deals with objects seen from a distance and represented within certain given planes proportionately."[126] Here we again have to resist the modern understanding of proportion and remember its original meaning, derived from metaphor and analogy rather than from isolated numbers or geometrical ratios. Analogy opens the horizon of communicative space, which is structured by resemblances, similarities, metaphors, and on a more explicit level by analogies. It is only in such a space that we can understand the thinking of Renaissance authors for whom, as one modern critic explains, "within the realm of the regular bodies perspective and proportion are often but two sides of the same concern."[127]

Pacioli's *De divina proportione,* considered conventionally to be a study of regular and irregular bodies, is in fact a treatise on perspective, as not just its general character but also Pacioli's own words make obvious. In referring to the drawings of the polyhedra, drawn by Leonardo specifically for the treatise, Pacioli specifies that the diagrams are drawn by the hand of a good perspectivist ("per mano de bono prospettivo").[128]

The content of *De divina proportione* is based on the tradition of Platonic cosmology, largely as transmitted through the commentaries of Calcidius and Macrobius, whom Pacioli explicitly mentions in his text.[129] Pacioli was also no doubt familiar, directly or indirectly, with contemporary Platonic thought.[130] In the Platonic tradition, the regular solids (polyhedra) represent symbolically four elements—fire, air, water, and earth—all rooted in the fifth, celestial essence, from which they are generated in proportional relationships. The celestial essence is represented by a dodecahedron inscribed in a sphere; it consists of twelve pentagons, which Pacioli compares with the twelve articles of the creed and the twelve apostles. The pentagons are based on the Golden Section, which, as he says, should be described not as natural but as divine ("non naturali ma divini veramente sonno dappelare").[131]

The divinity of the "divine proportion" is defined by attributes that, in Pacioli's own words, "belong to God." The first is the unity of the divine proportion, "the highest attribute of God himself." The second corresponds to the Holy Trinity because, just as God is one substance that resides in three persons (Father, Son, and Holy Spirit), so the proportion joins three terms.[132] Because God cannot be described directly in clear terms, the divine proportion cannot be expressed by a known number or rational quantity; it is mysterious and inaccessible in the sense that mathematicians describe as "irrational." In Pacioli's view, proportion remains the same and always continues to be invariable because it was created as a celestial virtue, known as the fifth essence (*quinta essentia*), which bestows part of its virtue on the four elements and thus on all things in nature.

Pacioli's interpretation of the five Platonic solids and their privileged status in perspectival representation shows that the goal of perspective is not primarily to create an illusion of visible reality but instead to rigorously portray the generic structure of reality. Perspective made the paradigmatic role of Euclidean geometry in the articulation of Platonic cosmology clearly visible.[133]

The conventional association of perspective and illusion is of a later date. During the fifteenth and sixteenth centuries, perspective shares in the primary ontological task: to reconcile the diversity of the natural phenomena with the universal order, the human with the divine, and terrestrial with celestial reality. At this stage, to see means not to view the surfaces of things but to think the depths of reality—how things are related among themselves and how they are structured by the unifying power of Being. The regular solids play a critical part in this structuring process and constitute, it was believed, a true alphabet of reality. In his treatise on perspective, Wenzel Jamnitzer, a younger contemporary of Dürer, associates the five regular solids with the five vowels.[134] The analogy of geometry and language is also discussed in other treatises, most explicitly in the *Perspectiva literaria* of Hans Lencker, a close friend of Jamnitzer.[135] Lencker argues that letters are true elements of all disciplines.

The tradition in which the regular solids and their transformation were seen as providing the language of reality was an inspiration for Kepler's *Mysterium cosmographicum* and *Harmonices mundi,* and, in its final stage, for the cosmology of Galileo as well.[136] The close association of seeing and thinking was articulated in great depth by Nicholas of Cusa, also known as Nicolaus Cusanus. His philosophy, very often described as perspectival, provides the most valuable insight into the deeper meaning of perspective that was shared not only by the thinkers but also by the artists of the Renaissance.[137] He is known to have been a close friend of Paolo Toscanelli and Alberti, with whom he spent some time in Rome, and with whom he shared his own understanding of perspective.[138]

For Cusanus, seeing and thinking come together in the icon, which as a form of likeness is the only way that we as humans can approach divine things. In the short treatise *De visione Dei,* he structures his argument entirely around the visual experience of a painting by Rogier van der Weyden.[139] Though the painting is only an image, it can serve us in our attempt to grasp the ineffable nature of divine vision. Human vision is limited to the context of a particular place and time, but divine vision transcends such variations and sees all things simultaneously. Cusanus declares:

> Lord, you see and you have eyes. You are an eye, since with you having is being. You thus observe all things in yourself. If in me my seeing were an eye as it is in you, then I should see all things in myself, since the eye is like a mirror. And a mirror, however small it be, beholds in itself the image of a great mountain and of all that exists on the surface of that mountain and so the species of all things are contained in the mirror of the eye.[140]

Cusanus defines the nature of perspective by the tension between the infinity of the divine and the finitude of the human vision. "Lord," he writes, "your essence pervades all things. So also does your sight which is your essence. For even as no created thing can escape from its own proper essence, so neither can it from your essence, which gives essential being to all things. Therefore neither can it from your sight." He beautifully expresses this tension in a single sentence: "If I were to see as I am seen I should not be a creature."[141] To be a creature, according to Cusanus, one has to receive an existence from the seeing God. The importance he gives to sight is characteristic of the new worldview in the fifteenth century, when the creative (cosmogonic) power of light was reinterpreted so that the power of divine and human vision was understood as a more tangible and explicit manifestation of divine light.[142] The closeness of this interpretation of sight to contemporary thinking on perspective can be seen in the diagram that appears near the end of the first part of his treatise *De coniecturis* (figure 3.21), described by Cusanus as paradigmatic. It consists of two intersecting pyramids, one culminating in the light (*lux*) and the unity of being (*unitas*), the other in the shadow (*tenebrae*) and the diversity of the human world

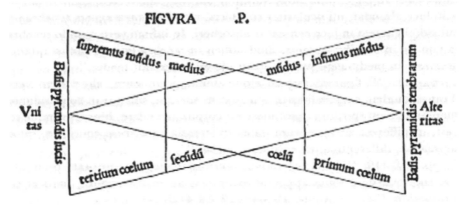

3.21. Nicholas of Cusa, *De coniecturis,* the pyramids of light and shadow, finitude and infinity, unity and difference.

(*alteritas*).[143] The diagram matches Leonardo's description of two pyramids and their role in perspectival vision.[144]

For Cusanus, the intersection of the pyramids represents the dialectics of human and divine vision, described in *De visione Dei* as reciprocity of seeing and being, as being seen by the divine eye.[145] Communication with the divine is possible only through the likeness of human and divine mind. The human mind represents in one sense the unity of vision, in another sense a reference to a measure (*mensura*), which as "the essence of number is the first exemplar of the mind."[146] Because measure is the main characteristic of proportion, the association of human mind and measure also speaks about the proportional structure of mind; and because proportion, as we have seen, is also the essence of perspectivity, the structure of human mind is in Cusanus's understanding perspectival.[147]

Is it possible to assume that this understanding was shared by the artists of his time? To answer this question we have to leave behind some of our modern assumptions, including the belief that modern individualism is in principle the same as Renaissance individualism and that our own sense of authorship and intellectual property existed in the past. It is quite well known that despite a general tendency in the fifteenth century toward individualism and personal fame, the artists still shared the educational advantages of life in guilds and drew on and benefited from collaboration with other artists and intellectuals.

The sharing of knowledge is very clearly demonstrated by the content of Lorenzo Ghiberti's third commentary, which deals with disciplines relevant to understanding vision and perspective. Ghiberti, as far as we know, had only an elementary education from the Scuola del Abaco, whose teaching was intended mostly for merchants and craftsmen. He probably took some lessons in Latin, enabling him to read but not necessarily to understand Latin texts in depth.[148] And yet his third commentary consists of an erudite selection of medieval optical texts, available mostly in Latin. The compilation as a whole, though incomplete and not clearly organized, is a unique perspectival treatise, complementing the tradition established by Brunelleschi and Alberti.[149] Given the complexity of medieval optical thought, it is difficult to imagine how Ghiberti could have accomplished this work on his own. At the time, only a few men in Florence would have been able to understand the task and advise him. One of them was Paolo Toscanelli, who was educated in Padua, the main center of studies in theoretical perspective. Toscanelli brought to Florence several texts on perspective on his arrival in 1424; soon he was collaborating with a number of artists, some of whom were close to Ghiberti. The likelihood that Ghiberti and Toscanelli were friends and collaborators is heightened by their having shared quite a few friends not only among the artists but also among the humanists.[150]

Ghiberti's close ties to contemporary humanism may throw some light not only on the contents of his treatise but also on the proper understanding of its meaning. Ambrogio Traversari, the author of the program for Ghiberti's *Gates of Paradise,* was a follower of Luigi Marsigli, a member of the theologically oriented circle of humanists in Santo Spirito.[151] These links, we may assume, set the terms of the debates in which some of the issues that Ghiberti addresses were discussed. The deeper philosophical and theological meaning of Ghiberti's text may not be immediately apparent, as it is certainly nowhere explicitly stated, but it is preestablished by the context. In a sense, Ghiberti's treatise demonstrates the same approach already encountered in Alberti, who declared that the broader and deeper meaning of his treatise was left to the philosophers to discuss.[152] In delegating that responsibility, he was referring to the collaboration expected in humanistic circles in the fifteenth century.

It is only in the light of such collaboration that we can understand Ghiberti's choice of texts—taken from the writings of Alhazen, Averroës, Avicenna, Bacon, Witelo, Peckham, and Vitruvius—intended to acknowledge and reveal the medieval background of Albertian perspective. This background was, no doubt, known and discussed earlier, but it had never before been incorporated into an artistic treatise.

RETURN TO PHENOMENA AND THE JUDGMENT OF SENSE

The texts in Ghiberti's treatise are almost exclusively concerned with the relating visual experience to the judgment of sense (*virtu distinctiva*).[153] Because any discussion of geometrical optics and linear perspective is conspicuously absent, the work is sometimes dismissed as backward-looking.[154] Yet Ghiberti had very little intention of returning to medieval perspective per se. His interest was in grasping the phenomenal level of perspective prior to its mathematization and in articulating a transcendental nature of vision on the level of directly visible phenomena.[155] Ghiberti's interest is apparent not only in the overall organization and content of the treatise but also in his own comments, which, though meager, show his priorities quite clearly.[156] Most important to him was the proportionality of human body, discussed at the end of the unfinished treatise; Ghiberti links it closely with the discussion of how perspective affects the apparent size and distance of bodies in space, a problem to which he returns several times. The phenomenon of perspectivity, in Ghiberti's understanding, depends largely on the proportional distribution of light and shadows over the surfaces of bodies.

In discussing the role of light in human vision in the opening section of the treatise, Ghiberti makes a distinction among three kinds of bodies according to how they relate to light. The first are bodies that radiate light (*corpi luminosi*), such as the sun, fire, or some precious stones. The second are bodies that are opaque (*corpi umbrosi*), do not accept light, and come mostly from the earth as solid and dark matter. The third, situated as it were in between, are diaphanous bodies (*corpi diafani*), such as air, water, glass, crystal, chalcedon, and beryl, through which light can penetrate.[157]

It is quite obvious that the diaphanous bodies played a key role in Ghiberti's visual thinking. Their ability to receive and mediate light resembled the movement of light on the surface and in the hollows of sculpted volumes. The texts selected by Ghiberti, particularly the long quotations from Alhazen, say much on this subject, and yet it is not clear what light really meant in Ghiberti's understanding of vision. We can certainly exclude the possibility of a purely aesthetic or instrumental view of light, which would break with the tradition to which Ghiberti belonged and which he brought to a new level of interpretation. Ghiberti treats the medieval tradition of the divine origin and meaning of light as a problem of human knowledge and wisdom, as a new relationship between thinking and seeing, giving the visible phenomena a new importance. It is revealing that in the discussion of his favorite subject, the refraction of light in semiprecious stones, Ghiberti uses the term "beryl," which does not appear in the literature to which he directly refers—but does figure prominently, as it happens, in the work of Nicholas of Cusa, who dedicated an entire treatise to the subject.[158]

For Cusanus, "beryl is a clear, bright, and transparent stone to which is given a concave as well as a convex form, and by looking through it one can see what was previously invisible. If the intellectual beryl, which possesses both the maximum and the minimum in the same way, is adopted to the intellectual eyes, the indivisible principle of all things is attained."[159] Cusanus understands beryl as a metaphor or an analogy for human and divine "intellectual vision." In looking through the beryl, the human eye enfolds the absolute maximum and absolute minimum of surfaces within its vision, in the same way as God unfolds the absolute maximum and minimum of being within his person. As he elucidates this metaphor, Cusanus shows not only a complete familiarity with contemporary knowledge of optics but also a clear conviction that ideas are not in the world but in our mind, directly present in our vision and in the essential form of our own works. This belief is explicitly articulated in *De beryllo:* "Man measures his own intellect through the power of his works and from this he measures the divine intellect just as truth is measured through an image. And this is enigmatic knowledge. Moreover, he has the most subtle vision through which he sees that the enigma is the enigma of truth so that he knows that this is the truth, which is not imaginable in any other enigma."[160]

Cusanus's notion of enigmatic truth accords with the most characteristic aspect of Renaissance art, its attempt to make the intellectual content of art directly visible. Bringing ideal reality near to its visible manifestation—familiar to us from the architecture of Brunelleschi or from the paintings of Piero della Francesca, for instance—was a unique though rather short-lived achievement, which even today intrigues and fascinates us.

We are still only on the way to understanding and appreciating the coherence of early Renaissance culture and its consistent articulation in a unifying communicative space in which theology, philosophy, humanistic knowledge, and art were closely linked with issues of political and everyday life. The link was mediated and sustained primarily by the visual arts. Cusanus's works illustrate very well both how far the intellectual life of the fifteenth century descended toward visual representation and how far the visual arts ascended to the level of "intellectual" accomplishment. It is in this double movement that the "enigmatic truth" is revealed through the image, as Cusanus himself makes clear: "Truly sensible things are the books of the senses in which the intention of the divine intellect is described in sensible figures, and the intention is the manifestation of God the Creator himself. If therefore you doubt concerning anything, why this should be so or be constituted thus, there is one answer: because the divine intellect wanted to manifest himself to sensitive knowledge so that he would be sensibly known."[161]

If we accept Cusanus's position as a true representation of the fifteenth-century understanding of visual reality, then we must be rather cautious in applying our modern criteria of pure visibility and aesthetic experience to the art of the fifteenth century. The art of the early Renaissance rested in the same tradition as the late medieval art. This continuity was obscured only because of the new mode of perspectival representation, which made the transcendental meaning of art more immanent and implicit, but not absent.

It is somewhat unfortunate that the iconological reevaluation of Renaissance art was concerned primarily with the representational meaning, attending very little, if at all, to the meaning of the process and means of representation. Erwin Panofsky, who contributed more than anybody else to the development of iconology, treated perspective in his influential monograph as a problem of symbolic representation, but the phenomenon of representation only as a formal system.[162] And yet, as we have seen, perspectival construction is intrinsically symbolic. It represents not the neutral appearance of reality but its ontological structure, manifested visibly and directly in the resulting image. This process of visible manifestation is very close to Cusanus's notion of the enigmatic truth, confronting comparable if not identical difficulties of reconciling intellectual intentions with the inexhaustible richness of visible reality.

This brings us back to Ghiberti, whose own effort coincides to a great extent with that of Cusanus,[163] and whose work is an important reminder that the main problem of pictorial perspective is not to demonstrate the correctness of the legitimate construction but rather to reconcile perspectival thinking with the concrete vision of the world. Ghiberti's return to the medieval sources of natural perspective in his third commentary was motivated by his interest in realizing and applying perspective in practice and by an ambition to complement the theoretical work of Alberti.

Such ambition was, it is true, displayed already by Alberti himself in his perspectival interpretation of *historia,* by Piero della Francesca in the perspectivization of the human figure, and by the problematic and inconclusive search for the non-Albertian curvilinear or synthetic perspective.[164] One of Ghiberti's main contributions, reflected in the character of the texts selected for his third commentary, is the articulation of the perspectival space by means of directly visible phenomena such as light and shadows, colors, surfaces, outline, and movements of human bodies showing their remoteness and mutual relationship. Ghiberti discovered behind the geometrical construction of depth a more fundamental depth: the natural spatial relationship of human bodies, their gestures and movements (figure 3.22). This is very clearly spelled out in his own words:

> only moderate distances are certifiable to sight and those by means of continuous and ordered intervening bodies. Indeed, the distance from the observer to the visible object is not perceived by sight, but is determined by reasoning as this philosophy teaches. For if an object that is visible when the eyes are open is not visible when they are closed, it follows and is rightly concluded, that the object is not immediately adjacent to the eye. . . . Therefore I say that perception of the magnitude of a distance derives from the magnitude of the intervening bodies.[165]

If we add to this the passage dealing with the role of light, shadows, and movement, it becomes apparent that Ghiberti formulated a coherent alternative view of the structure of perspectival space that may be described

3.22. Lorenzo Ghiberti, Florence baptistery, the *Gates of Paradise,* the story of Joseph.

as situational. In this structure, spatial distance itself is measured by increments of the intervening space:

> The magnitude of a distance is certified by the evolution of the
> intervening space into magnitudes of exactly known measure. For if
> the intervening bodies are equally uncertain according to whole and
> part, the uncertain distance will never be certified by reference to them.
> Therefore within that distance something certain must be discovered,
> the magnitude of which may be known by experience and in terms
> of which the whole space can be resolved, such as the foot or the length

3.23. Lorenzo Ghiberti, Florence baptistery, the *Gates of Paradise,* the story of Joseph (detail), distribution of grain.

of a measuring body or something that comes readily to the imagination of the measurer.[166] [figure 3.23]

At first it may seem that Ghiberti has returned to the practical perspective of the trecento, but this is not the case. His own version of perspective was deeply informed by the *costruzione legittima* of Alberti, as is evident not only in the explicit use of linear perspective in some of his most important works,[167] but also in his serious concern with the problem of measure and proportion in the unfinished last part of the third commentary. In concentrating on the direct visibility of proportions and their "correctness,"

Ghiberti intended to use vision to resolve the tension between the divine intellect and human understanding.[168] If successful, he would come very close not only to vindicating Cusanus's belief that man can become through his creativity truly godlike but also to instantiating the meaning of the influential Renaissance discourses on the new dignity of man.[169]

What Cusanus shares with those discourses is that both helped to transform the traditional relationship between humanity and divinity into a new relationship contained within and unfolded from the human mind, a relationship in which God is contained not absolutely but "humanely." The unfolding of the world from the human mind corresponds to the essential nature of perspective. We can certainly recognize the presence of perspectival thinking in Cusanus's description of human creativity:

> The active creativity of humanity does not bring about anything new, but discovers that everything that it creates through its unfolding already existed within itself, for we said that all things existed in it in a human way. Just as the power of humanity is essential for humanely (*humaniter*) progressing into all things, so the universe is within itself. Nor is that admirable virtue of proceeding to the illumination of all things anything other than to enfold the universe in itself humanely.[170]

Here we can see the opening of a world from a fixed, introverted position and within the limits of perspectival vision.

That visual knowledge, based on the philosophy of light, might represent the essential nature of reality and might become a legitimate substitute for medieval cosmology was only one of the unattained Renaissance dreams.[171] By the end of the fifteenth century it was already clear that perspective is not a finite universal form of representation but rather an open process akin to a rhetorical discourse in which the success of an argument always depends on the degree of persuasiveness. In this case, the process of persuasion was an inconclusive dialogue between the principles of legitimate construction and the inexhaustible richness of the phenomenal world. As a result, what began as a serious effort to bring the invisible aspects of medieval cosmology into measurable visibility eventually turned into something rather different. Perspective became a reified mode of representation

3.24. Baltimore panel, ideal city with a fountain and statues of the Virtues (late 15th c.), detail.

governed by rules whose original meaning was very often forgotten and by the spectator's personal experience of the world.

In the idealized perspectival setting, the representation and the corresponding experience of the spectator became to a great extent a world itself. In this world, representation acquired a high degree of independence and could even dictate the status of the represented reality. That happened, for instance, in the perspective studies from the end of the fifteenth century known as "Urbinate panels."[172] Much has been written about their ambiguous nature and possible meaning, but even the most recent studies remain inconclusive, acknowledging the panels' enigmatic character. They are variously discussed as ideal pictorial representations, ideal cities, or theatrical settings. Yet such descriptions are beside the point, given that the rigorous use of artificial perspective leads to a creation of settings whose representation is neutral in regard to such distinctions.

We have seen already that linear perspective is closely linked with the geometry of architecture and its elements (*casamenti*) and with the paradigm of an imaginary room. In the perspectival projection of a geometrically structured space, the elements of the space, their configuration, and to a great extent even their physiognomy are subordinated to the rules of perspective, which determine the order of space and its pictorial characteristics. The panels can be seen as an idealized representation of a world articulated by the most sublime humanistic ideas—the cultivation of civic virtues and the creation of ideal society here on earth. These ideas found their fulfillment when perspective was extended from the spatial arrangement of the scenes to their content, a step that can best be described as perspectival interpretation of human history. This is particularly evident in the character of the Baltimore panel, where the individual elements—Roman amphitheater, triumphal arch, baptistery, and palaces—are removed from their original place and time and placed in a new setting organized by the principles of perspective and axial symmetry[173] (figure 3.24). The result is a scene with a strange sense of unreality. What makes the scene unreal and enigmatic is the combination of the ideal vision and its realistic nature. We have reached the threshold of a new era in which representation will be able to emancipate itself from the given conditions of meaning, establishing its own horizon of reference in the internal logic and visual coherence of the individual elements.[174] The emancipated representation can be imposed on reality, thereby transforming the traditional relationship of experience and concept into a new relationship in which concept or conceptual image anticipates experience.

One of the first realizations of such a possibility was Bramante's Cortile del Belvedere. The project in the early stages of its development and Bramante's main intentions are well documented, and I shall therefore concentrate only on those aspects relevant to the main argument here. The Belvedere project represents a turning point in the development of perspective. Unlike architectural settings created earlier, it does not culminate in the perspectival representation of a clearly defined room, but moves further toward constructing an illusionistic setting whose appearance and coherence are that of a picture. The illusionistic construction of the Belvedere setting is in many ways a logical step in the development of the projective possibilities of perspective. Its novelty lay in the close link between the new mode of representation and the artist's own will and intentions. Having gained much control, the artist could more easily move beyond the conditions of primary visibility into an artificial world of a spectacle where a synthesis of many heterogenous elements was less difficult to achieve.

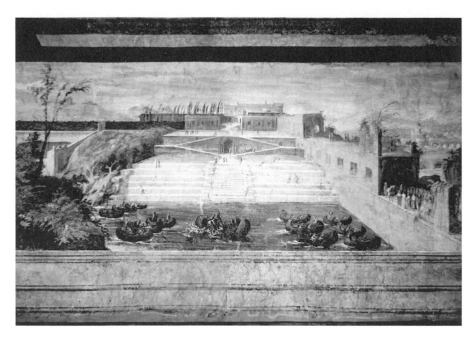

3.25. Perin dal Vaga, naumachia in the Cortile del Belvedere, Vatican Palace.

The notion of a new kind of synthesis is, as I see it, the key to the Belvedere project. Initiated by Pope Julius II, it was realized by Bramante.[175] The main idea was to connect the Vatican Palace with the villa of Innocent VIII (1484–1487), some 300 meters away. The structure of the connecting space, described conventionally as a *cortile,* is in fact a synthesis of *cortile,* theater, garden, and forum, representing together a complex metaphor of a city rather than a monothematic space (figure 3.25). The synthetic nature of the Belvedere project results from an effort to restore the universality of the Roman church, using as a reference the world of imperial Rome.[176]

The space of the Cortile is organized on three levels. The first, the lower court, is described and illustrated in contemporary documents as a place of festivals, tournaments, and theatrical sea battles (*naumachiae*).[177] The lower court is closely linked with the central zone, designed as a theater. This zone, an intricate sequence of spatial arrangements, consists of the sloping auditorium, the central staircase leading to the grotto of the nympheum, and the main diagonal ramps leading to the upper court. The front facade of the nympheum, together with the wall of the diagonal ramps, can be seen as a backdrop (*frons scaenae*) of the theater in the lower court, but it also anticipates the meaning of the upper court. The main feature of the upper court is a regularly planned garden, culminating in the semicircular exedra in front of the most important part of the project: the Belvedere villa with its statue court[178] (figure 3.26).

The meaning of the Belvedere project is usually linked to the Renaissance reconstruction of the classical villa.[179] Though the association is quite convincing, it overlooks the broader context, which shows clearly that the Belvedere project was a critical part of the overall program of the "renovatio Romae."[180] The reference to Rome invokes a wide spectrum of meanings centered on the paradigm of Rome as a second Jerusalem.[181] The juxtaposition of the lower and the upper Belvedere courts illustrates the tension between the ideal and the real city; similarly, the ambigous meaning of the garden of the upper court can be read either as an image of celestial paradise (city) or as a terrestrial paradise.[182]

However, the overall meaning of the Belvedere project cannot be established without taking into account that the visible result, the whole space of the Cortile, was designed for the view from the Stanza della Segnatura, as the inscription "Pulcrum videre pontificis" on Bramante's plan indicates. This viewpoint should be seen not as abstract and geometrically defined by the demands of perspective but as qualified by the content and meaning of this particular space. On the walls of the Stanza, Raphael represented Theology (*Disputa*), Philosophy (the *School of Athens*), Justice (Prudence, flanked by Fortitude and Temperance), and Poetry (*Parnassus*).[183] These four disciplines bring together not only the primary body of contemporary knowledge but also its numinous qualities, manifested most explicitly in the discourse of incarnation in the *Disputa,* where the "knowledge of things divine" (*divinarum rerum notitia*) is represented as coming down to earth in the process and mystery of incarnation. The remaining frescoes share the same ultimate meaning, mediated by the language of poetry. We have to remember that in Renaissance culture, poetry was seen as an anticipation of theology.[184] This is expressed, very clearly, in the inscription "numine afflatur" (divine inspiration) on the ceiling above *Parnassus* (figure 3.27).

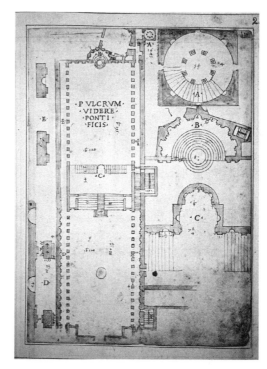

3.26. Donato Bramante, Cortile del Belvedere, Vatican, plan (Codex Coner).

3.27. Raphael, Stanza della Segnatura, Vatican Palace, *Parnassus* and *The School of Athens*.

The location of the frescoes is not arbitrary; each wall is related thematically to one of the great works of Julius II in Rome. The depiction of theology refers to the new building of St. Peter, philosophy to the Vatican Palace (*domus Sapientiae*), justice to the new Palazzo dei Tribunali in Via Giulia, and poetry to the Belvedere.[185] The numinous language of poetry can be thus seen as the key to the understanding of the intricate relations between the classical and Christian meaning of Parnassus, between Apollo and Christ, between the garden of paradise and the ideal city, and between the universality of the Roman Empire and the universality of the Christian church.

What is new in the arrangement of the Cortile is that the whole setting, with its complex meaning, was expressed in a refined visual language and absorbed in a single perspectival view. The new dominant role of perspective is apparent in Bramante's manipulation of the visual appearance of the setting to create a theatrical illusion of indeterminate depth. He made the ground in the upper courtyard slope up fairly steeply toward the end wall. He then placed the pedestals of the Corinthian pilasters of the long buildings on this sloping line, gradually reducing the pilasters' height and gently raising their baseline. At the same time, he made the top of the entablature slope slightly upward toward its end.[186]

The illusionistic effect of depth is enhanced by two instances of optical discontinuity in the Cortile. The first is achieved by the introduction of two massive towers in the area of the theater, the second by the partial screening of the exedra at the end wall of the upper court. In both cases the interrupted continuity of reading is made whole on the level of imagination, which can bridge the gap between the directly and indirectly perceived sequence of architectural elements. The result is an experience of continuity where in fact discontinuity reigns—discontinuity between the directly and indirectly observable phenomena and between two levels of reality: one related to the finite, terrestrial, human reality; the other to the infinite, celestial, divine reality. The association of the ultimate divine order with the infinite and the attempt to treat the infinite as actual set the terms for a new, truly modern problem of continuity and communication between humans and the divine and between the empirical and the intelligible understanding of the world.

Bramante's perspectival representation of contemporary culture as unified was largely successful—but only within the limits of the illusionistic spectacle, with all its problematic consequences, which would be addressed again in the seventeenth century. These are well summarized by a modern writer: "The spectacle obliterates the boundaries between self and world by crushing the self besieged by the presence-absence of the world and it obliterates the boundary between true and false by driving all lived truth below the real presence of illusion ensured by the organization of appearance."[187]

The development of perspective into an illusionistic mode of representation is the main source of modern relativism, beginning the process that led to the emergence of divided representation.

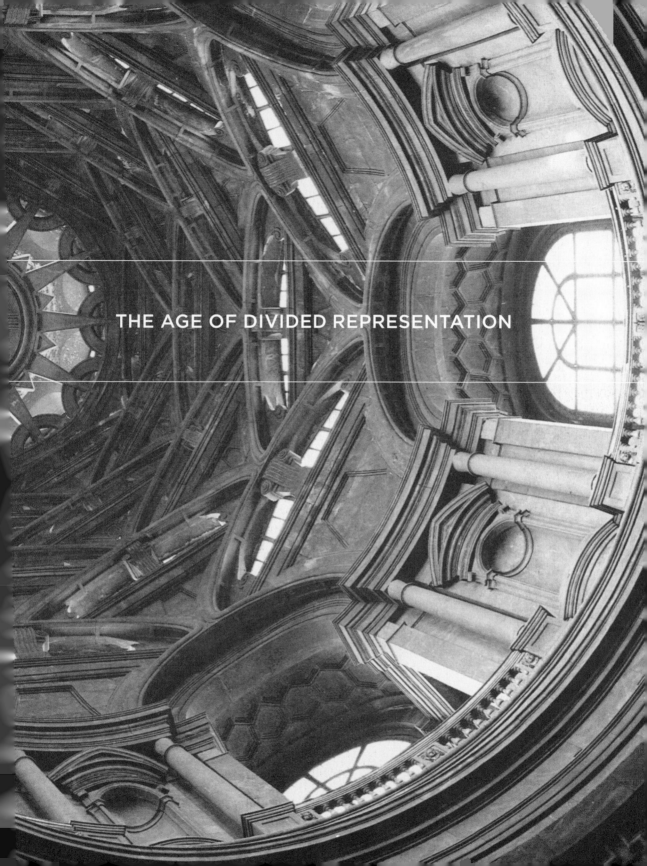

CHAPTER 4

THE AGE OF DIVIDED REPRESENTATION

T HE MOST significant change in the representation of reality took place in the period traditionally associated with the formation and development of modern science and with the beginning of its dominant role in modern culture. Though a connection between the two is plausible, it could be misleading if by "science" we understand the context-free, mathematically structured knowledge that was developed later within new disciplines generally called "natural science." The science of the transitional period between the end of the sixteenth century and the beginning of the eighteenth is instead closely linked with philosophy, metaphysics, theology, and, in a less obvious sense, with the culture as a whole.[1]

The transitional period overlaps significantly with the period generally termed "Baroque," and the science of this era unquestionably shares many of the characteristics of Baroque culture. We don't usually think of prominent figures such as Sir Isaac Newton or Christiaan Huygens as Baroque scientists, yet we would probably agree that Gottfried Wilhelm Leibniz, the great philosopher and mathematician who was involved in a serious metaphysical and theological argument with Newton, is a Baroque thinker par excellence.[2] Architecture was similarly involved in these issues. The works of Christopher Wren, Claude Perrault, and Guarino Guarini represent not only different tendencies in Baroque architecture but also different trends in Baroque science. The affinity between science and Baroque culture hints at deeper dimensions of representation, not yet fully acknowledged.

Because we usually see Baroque science as an independent domain of knowledge, we tend to overlook the fact that science was then an integral part of the general intelligibility of culture and that it becomes autonomous or independent only under particular and more precisely defined conditions (figure 4.1). Indeed, such conditions had never existed before, and their emergence was one of the main characteristics of the transitional period. They were created in unique historical circumstances, by attempts to overcome a deep cultural crisis. I shall say more about that process later. In the meantime, it is important to describe the tendencies that shaped the transitional period as a whole. If we look at the politics, philosophy, literature, visual arts, and everyday life of that time, we find a common search for order and certainty in an environment dominated by fragmentation, relativism of values, skepticism, and pessimism. The radicality of the response, which was based on a dogmatic faith in the mathematical nature of the

4.1. Sebastien Le Clerc, *The Academy of Sciences and Fine Arts,* Paris (1666).

world order, created for the first time in human history a mode of representation that could claim both that it was fully independent and, at the same time, that it could be universally applied.[3] Because any representation, despite its claims to universality, is inevitably partial, there is always a residuum of reality left out, which has to define its own mode of representation. The result is a duplication that may best be described as "divided representation."

A classic example of divided representation is the double standard of truth that has plagued the history of modern science and theology.[4] In architecture, divided representation finds its first clear manifestation in Claude Perrault's distinction between positive and arbitrary beauty,[5] a division that foreshadowed later tensions and conflicts between experience, based on the continuity of tradition, and artificially constructed systems. More recently, divided representation reveals itself as a painful conflict between primary cultural values and technology, which is governed by economic imperatives.

THE NATURE OF DIVIDED REPRESENTATION

We generally think of divided representation as a distorted form of the Cartesian dualism of man and world, of subject and object, formulated originally as a dualism of *res cogitans* and *res extensa*. Cartesian dualism is also responsible, directly or indirectly, for some of the main categories that shape our interpretation of modern history and culture. An obvious example, now a cliché, is the dualism of reason and feeling, classicism and romanticism, rationalism and organicism, and so on. There is probably an element of truth in such oppositions, but they tend to obscure the more fundamental, historically constituted tension between the symbolic-communicative and the instrumental-noncommunicative representations of reality. This tension grew out of a long process in which perspective played a decisive role.

In a perspectival setting it is possible to idealize a whole sphere of reality, to see reality in terms of precisely identifiable elements that are comparable not only in their content but also in their formal qualities and relationships.[6] The given reciprocity of visible reality and vision is here transformed into an idealized representation, with the visible content and its meaning depending more on the nature of vision than on the things represented. That is certainly what the humanists of the sixteenth century believed. "When we say," writes Juan Vives, "that things are or are not, and this or that, are such and so, we base our statement on the judgment of our mind, not on the things themselves. Our mind is the measure, not the things."[7] Such a belief is obviously only a step away from the Cartesianism of the seventeenth century. However, we must remember that we are dealing with representation and not with the phenomenal world; what is described as "mind" is in fact a field of identity in the situational structure of human existence. The tendency to reduce that larger context to a fixed point of view or "mind" and to a "picture" is the most explicit characteristic of perspective representation, and also its chief contribution to the formation of divided representation.

Galileo's well-known distinction between primary and secondary qualities is a good example of this. He understands the qualities of experienced reality as being constituted entirely in human consciousness. "To excite in us tastes, odors and sounds," Galileo writes, "I believe that nothing is required in external bodies except shapes, members and slow or rapid move-

4.2. Hildegard von Bingen, *Liber divinorum operum simplicis hominis,* fol. 6r, microcosmos.

ment. I think that if ears, tongues and noses were removed, shapes, members and movements would remain, but no odors, tastes or sounds[;] . . . hence I think that tastes, odors, colors and so on are no more than names so far as the object in which we place them is concerned and that they reside only in the consciousness."[8]

The tendency to strip the world of things of their qualities, which are then transferred into human consciousness, is a clear reminder that divided representation was not created by an abstract, anonymous mode of representation of the "external reality" of the world alone. Subjective representation and the fixed point of view of perspective are closely linked. Both are already anticipated in the long tradition of microcosmic speculation that sees the human situation and experience as mirroring the larger world (macrocosmos)[9] (figure 4.2).

4.4. Johannes Kepler, *Tabulae Rudolphinae* (1627), frontispiece, the temple of astronomy.

and some of the many contributing factors are rarely taken into account. The most obvious of these is perspective and its role in the perspectivization of reality.[16] Less obvious, but closely linked to the altered view of reality, is the new availability of the printed book, which created conditions for a truly introverted representation of the world—not only through the text but also through illustrations, which became more precise and "realistic"[17] (figure 4.4).

4.5. *Romani Collegii Societatis Jesu Musaeum Celeberrimum* (Museo Kircheriano, 1678), frontispiece.

It is symptomatic of the situation in the late fifteenth century that the old metaphor comparing the world to a book was taken literally, and thus the book became the world—"hic liber est mundus."[18] A similar change affected the sixteenth-century theater, particularly as regards the allegory of the world as a theater or stage.[19] The desire to appropriate reality is manifested most clearly in the creation of spaces that facilitate such a representation. Rooms that were originally used for private reading or study were developed into the elaborate space of the *studiolo,*[20] usually with several temporary literature. It is a place where man can cultivate his humanity and find his salvation. There is a similarity between the solitary life—*vita solitaria*—of the villa and that of monasticism, but also a difference. In the villa, the goal is not asceticism but the ongoing cultivation of one's self.

Such cultivation could not succeed without a corresponding mode of embodiment, which in this case was the setting of the villa itself. The autonomy of one's self can be guaranteed only by a belief, or rather an illusion, that the world as it is represented in the setting of the villa can be truly self-sufficient. This claim is supported by sixteenth-century texts such as Alberto Lollio's *La villa:*

> In our house (villa), music of various sorts is played every day. And we engage in every sort of proper and delightful game. Sometimes we dance for a recreation and to delight the company. Here we read books with pleasure and we discuss various matters. In sum, one has here all those entertainments and diversions that one can decently desire. All in all I have no fear of being thought arrogant in making a comparison, eager as I am to say that as in Athens the house of Isocrates was called the school, the factory of oratorical art, so our house here may be called the armory of diversion.[30]

The attempt to treat the villa as a comprehensive representation of the world is evident in the interior decoration of the more sophisticated villas, such as the Villa Maser (figure 4.9). One of the central spaces—the Sala dell'Olimpo—is decorated with a cosmographical scheme: seven muses, seen as planetary deities on their orbits, together represent the harmonic order of the cosmic spheres.[31] But even the most ambitious and comprehensive representation remains unconvincing, because it cannot be sustained by the narrow confines of the private life of the villa. This was already acknowledged, perhaps unintentionally, at the time; the author of one commentary conceded, "I believe that we should not underestimate the convenience afforded by the city and surrounding places since our villa is, as it were, a center, placed in the midst of many cities and villages in the area around it."[32]

The contradictory belief in both the autonomy of the villa and its dependence on the broader context of culture raises a more fundamental ques-

4.9. Paolo Veronese, Villa Barbaro, Maser, Veneto, Sala dell'Olimpo, ceiling frescoes.

tion about the autonomy of introverted representation as such. Can the dependence of representation on context be ignored? Modern European history has provided no clear answer, in part because the power of explicit representation is difficult to resist, tending to overshadow the loss of implicitly articulated levels of reality. Heidegger convincingly analyzed this tendency as a forgetfulness of Being, but rather than being a process that is accomplished at a particular moment of history it is an ongoing drama, as forgetfulness is repeatedly challenged by the new openness to Being.[33]

Yet introverted representation, where the world appears like a projection on the walls surrounding the narrow confines of each individual private domain, allows room for investigation and contemplation not otherwise possible. It is for these reasons, no doubt, that such representation has contributed decisively to the depth and sometimes even to the authenticity of modern culture. At the same time, however, investigation and contemplation of this type are prone to flawed idealizations and alienated abstractions, particularly concerning the larger world. There is a certain logic to the origination of so many of our intellectual achievements in the relatively small world of the study, workshop, or laboratory, but the conditions of their genesis are also largely responsible for their ambiguous nature and often problematic consequences.

The relation between the apparent autonomy of the introverted world and alienating abstraction is exemplified in Descartes's "discovery" of the primacy of the cogito, described in the second part of his "Discourse" as the most important event in the development of his thoughts. He recalls,

> I was then in Germany, to which country I had been attracted by the wars which are not yet at an end. And as I was returning from the coronation of the Emperor to join the army, the setting in of winter detained me in a quarter where, since I found no society to divert me, while fortunately I had no cares or passions to trouble me, I remained the whole day shut up alone in a stove-heated room, where I had complete leisure to occupy myself with my own thoughts. . . . And then, examining attentively that which I was, I saw that I could conceive that I had no body, and that there was no world nor place where I might be; but yet that I could not for all that conceive that I was not.[34]

It is one thing to describe a possible or imaginary world; it is quite another to build such a world starting from Descartes's position. It is not difficult to see that Cartesian reasoning originated in the development of perspective, where representation became so closely identified with the essence of vision that it was only too easy to substitute one for the other. As a result, it was possible to believe that the world is not only seen but also structured by the spectator's cogito. This belief is clearly illustrated in the sixteenth- and early-seventeenth-century refinements in perspective, known better as anamorphosis[35] (figure 4.10).

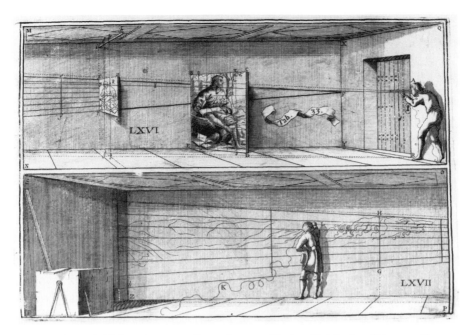

4.10. Jean-François Nicéron, *La perspective curieuse, ou, Magie artificielle des effets merveilleux* (1638), pls. 66, 67.

THE COSMOCENTRIC VISION OF THE WORLD

We may wonder in what kind of world the display of new knowledge did take place. The apparent consistency of the spectator's space does not provide a full answer. Even with the notion of the "world as picture" in mind, we have to look beyond the directly visible setting to understand the structure that holds the scene together and that gives it meaning. In the natural world, such structure is defined by the reciprocity of articulation and embodiment and finds its expression in a particular mode of symbolic representation.

In the age of divided representation, the continuity and wholeness of symbolic representation is undermined, not only because introverted representation has become possible but also because the traditional theocentric world has been transformed into a more abstract cosmocentric "vision" of the world. The best illustration of this change is Kepler's vision of a celestial harmony no longer structured around the earth but centered around the sun, making it necessary to mentally adopt a point of view that is not, as it were, our own. As Kepler put it, "harmony is established but not for man and only as an appearance." This change is inevitable "since speculations on harmony envisage the eccentric motion of the planets as they are seen from the sun."[36]

There is a close analogy between the mental experiment required to achieve the new vision of planetary movements and the nature of projection in anamorphosis. In both cases, traditional relationships are inverted. The new heliocentric thinking seriously undermined the traditional vertical hierarchy of the world, which gave the place of greatest dignity not to the most central but to the highest.[37]

In the heliocentric system, the place of greatest dignity is the center of a perfect sphere. The sun and the sphere are in the static relationship of center and periphery, which together with the intervening space represent in a new manner the traditional mystery of the Trinity.[38] The planets are situated in the intervening space, and their spheres and movements are determined by the proportions of the five Platonic regular solids[39] (figure 4.11). In the Platonic tradition of cosmogonic thinking, the regular solids acted as mathematical models in the dialectical understanding of the formation and transformation of the primary elements of the world.[40] It is both interesting and symptomatic that Kepler associates the regular solids no longer with elements but with planets. This shift illustrates that the ideal domain of celestial phenomena gained importance as it moved closer to the ideal divine order and therefore revealed more literally the true design of the world.[41] The new role of the five solids was associated with the construction of cosmic space, which was, as we have already seen, anticipated in the earlier development of perspective representation.[42]

The geometrization of cosmic space, which closely associated geometry with the divine, was an important step in forming "absolute" space. The process by which space came to be conceived as absolute has its own history, which cannot be repeated here.[43] It will suffice to mention the role of perspective imagination in that history. The conceptual power of perspective imagination was stirred not only by the method of perspective but also by the embodied perspectival reality of the concrete spaces of streets, squares, buildings, and their interiors. In this idealized and highly homogenized world, it became possible to contemplate the ideal existence or nonexistence of anything and everything.

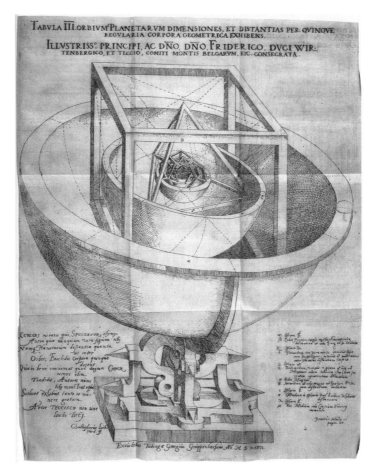

4.11. Johannes Kepler, *Mysterium cosmographicum* (1596), regular solids of planetary model.

Such contemplation was essential for the emergence of Cartesian thought, which became the dominant mode of modern thinking and shaped the modern representation of reality. What is still difficult to comprehend is how this highly abstract mode of representation became a "concrete" and almost natural dimension of our everyday life. Some answers can be found in Cartesianism itself.

The critical assumption on which Cartesianism is built is faith in the mathematical nature of the divine plan of creation. This is a point where late scholastic theology met the challenge of mathematical science. The history of that encounter is a story not, as is sometimes believed, of conflict but of transformation in which theological problems were treated as metaphysical and eventually as physical or natural, culminating in the formation of natural theology.[44]

In Newton's circle, for instance, what came to be known as "physica sacra" evolved. The history of creation in Genesis could be shown, line by line, to be in perfect harmony with the works of Newton.[45] Later, Herder could refer to fifty systems of physical theology (*Physik-theologie*) in all of which God's actions followed mathematical laws.[46] For Descartes and his generation, the link between physics and theology was established through geometry. The unique role of geometry in the formation of natural (physical) theology was conditioned by two beliefs: first, that divine ideas are co-eternal with geometry, second, that divine ideas were present in the human mind.[47] These provided a critical ground for a radical reinterpretation of the traditional world. Descartes was resolved to leave the traditional world behind and speak only of what would happen if God were to create it somewhere in a new imaginary space.[48] The new world—that is, the world of Descartes—was constructed in accordance with principles and rules whose certainty could not be questioned. Such were the principles of geometry and the rules of reasoning "more geometrico." It is important to realize that Descartes's project for the scientific transformation of the natural world represented nothing less than the complete dismantling and rebuilding of the existing world. This was the equivalent of the divine *creatio ex nihilo*, which would have to include not only the world's known reality but also its implicit, prereflective reality. To succeed, such a project had to completely translate history into a transparent representation. Not surprisingly, the project remained only an aim: it was never really a vision of a world in the true sense, but only a program for further research. A well-known historian of science has compared the project to

> intellectual scaffolding within which, from 1687 on, Newton and the other exact scientists constructed modern physics[;] . . . the modern framework was suggestive not directive. The results of the lines of study it suggested cast doubt upon one or another of its members. As a result modern science outgrew its framework with scandalous results and

respectable opinion struggled to maintain the scaffolding intact, while removing its individual timbers one by one.[49]

The early acceptance and strong influence of Cartesianism show that seventeenth-century culture was ready for this kind of articulation.[50] Once the new thinking attained wide currency and familiarity among people who had never read the primary books or understood their meaning, we can assume that the new way of thinking became part of the cultural heritage. The uncritical faith in the universality of geometry created an illusion that there were no limits to its application. Thus Bernard de Fontenelle declared: "the geometrical method is not so rigidly confined to geometry itself that it cannot be applied to other branches of knowledge."[51]

The influential role of Cartesianism benefited the development of modern science, but it was often disastrous in those areas of culture which could not meet the criteria of mathematical truth. As a result, Cartesianism, together with both a general tendency toward abstract mathematical representation and the introverted representation of reality, created a profound discontinuity in European culture that has never been fully remedied. The nature of the discontinuity, which coincides with the nature of divided representation, was made most clear in the language of algebra and the experimental method of modern science.

Algebra is not only a mathematical discipline, as is often believed, but also a new way of thinking. According to a modern mathematician, when letters were first introduced, they "were just representations of numbers and so could be treated as such. The more complicated algebraic technique seemed justified either by geometrical arguments such as Cardan used or by sheer induction on specific cases. Of course, none of these procedures were logically satisfactory."[52] Leibniz characterized the work in algebra as a "melange of good fortune and chance."[53] In algebra the number is removed from the continuum of the articulated world into an imaginary world, where number as structure (*arithmos*) became an abstract symbol, an entity.[54]

With that step, a historian of mathematics points out, the "fundamental (traditional) science of the ancients was replaced by a symbolic discipline whose ontological presuppositions are left unclarified." And yet, it is in this discipline that the things of this world are understood no longer as countable beings but as a "lawfully ordered course of 'events.' The very nature of man's understanding of the world is henceforth governed by the symbolic 'number' concept, which determines the modern idea of science in general."[55]

The influence of the new science on architectural thinking can be illustrated by three groups of architects, who responded to it in different ways. The first tended to follow, rather dogmatically, the inherited tradition, ignoring the fact that the framework that had once made it possible to speak about architecture as reflecting and representing cosmic order was already seriously undermined and to a great extent sterile. This tendency was exhibited most clearly by François Blondel, René Ouvrard, and Charles-Étienne Briseux.[56] The second embraced the possibilities of the new science, and in their number were Claude Perrault, Michel de Fremin, Jean-Louis de Cordemoy, and Carlo Lodoli.[57] The third and most interesting were the architects aware of the new intellectual force of science who were able to reconcile it with a critical and inventive interpretation of tradition. To this group belonged Francesco Borromini, Guarino Guarini, and Bernardo Vittone; more tentatively, we might add Giovanni Santini, Kilian Ignaz Dientzenhofer, and Balthasar Neumann. In order to do justice to their work and to understand better their place in the transformation of Baroque culture, we should look more closely at a concrete example.

THE RECONCILIATION OF THE NEW SCIENCE WITH TRADITION

The building in which the traditional understanding of architectural order was raised to the level of the new emerging science, and where it was possible at the same time to demonstrate the limits of such an attempt, is Guarini's Chapel of the Holy Shroud (Sacra Sindone) (figure 4.12).

Many have offered interpretations of the design of the chapel, particularly the unusual structure of its upper dome, but we still probably do not grasp its real meaning. Because the story of the chapel is well known,[58] I shall refer only to the essentials and concentrate instead on the meaning of the upper dome. The Holy Shroud reached Turin in 1578 from Chambéry; beginning in 1587, it was housed in a small *tempietto* in the presbytery of the Duomo. The first reference to the construction of a chapel in the present position is from 1607, when four black marble columns were supplied

4.12. Guarino Guarini, SS. Sindone, Turin, exterior of the upper dome.

"in conformity with the design of Carlo di Castelamonte for the chapel of the Holy Shroud."[59] The work progressed slowly and eventually came to a standstill that lasted until 1657, when a new plan by Bernardino Quadri was adopted and partly executed on the completed foundations. The new plan established the circular shape of the chapel, its position on the *piano nobile,* and the two lateral staircases, culminating in the small vestibules of the chapel. When Guarini took over the project in 1667, the body of the chapel was completed to the level of the first order of the *piano nobile.* Guarini's prime contribution was constructing the lower and upper dome, as well as completing the lower part of the building. The final configuration of the chapel, which was largely Guarini's own idea, was derived from the circular form and meaning of the Holy Sepulchre.[60]

The symbolic representation of the tomb of Christ was a key to the theme of the Passion, which was to dominate the meaning of the chapel as a whole. The theme is revealed most explicitly in the Passion capitals of the first order and less directly in the elevated position of the chapel. That position was determined, to some extent, by the requirements of access from the Palazzo Reale, but this could have been achieved in other ways. The present arrangement seems rather to refer to the elevated position of Calvary, accessible by steps arranged as an ascent on which the last stage of Christ's journey is reenacted.[61] The thirty-three steps, a reference to the age of Christ, mark a journey toward death; one climbs as if into and out of the tomb, represented by the dark space of the staircase, and toward the light of resurrection, anticipated in the circular vestibules at the top of the stairs. The three main stages of the Passion—death, entombment, and resurrection—are represented in a variety of elements: three pairs of niches on the staircases, the triad of columns and triangular structure of the walls in the vestibules, and the three main arches of the chapel. The principle of the Trinity is extended by multiplication into the hexagons of the upper dome and finally into the twelve rays of light radiating from the sun at the top of the dome. The trinity of elements can be seen as a visual exegesis of the mystery of the Trinity itself, which includes the mystery of incarnation and the presence of the absent Christ—the essential meaning of the shroud.

Guarini interpreted the mystery of the Trinity and incarnation as not only a spatial but also a temporal problem. The temporal transformation from death to resurrection, from darkness to light, was exemplified in the eclipse of light (the sun). There is a reference to an eclipse of the sun in a text of the duke of Savoy, Carlo Emanuele I: "di nambi oscuri il ciclo era turbato."[62] The eclipse of light, the three hours of darkness before death, are followed by three days culminating in resurrection ("after three days I will rise again"; Matthew 27.62). It is no coincidence that Guarini returned to the eclipse in several of his texts, particularly in his astronomical ones, and that he treated the phenomenon of the eclipse in three distinct phases with a beginning, middle, and end.[63]

Guarini's interpretation of the mystery of the Trinity and the incarnation as manifested in the eclipse of light is, in the end, focused on the symbolic role and meaning of the sun. One of the possible keys to its meaning in the program (*concetto*) of the chapel of the Sindone can be found in the il-

4.13. Camillo Balliani, the image of the shroud, *Regionamenti di Santa Sindone* (1616).

lustration of the shroud in an early-seventeenth-century treatise by Camillo Balliani (figure 4.13). We see two angels holding the shroud stretched open, the marks of Christ's body visible in a light radiating from the sun above; the illustration is almost identical with the representation of the sun at the top of the dome of the Chapel. The image is accompanied by a text proclaiming that "l'imagine nella sanctissima sindone contenuta . . . e vivo raggio di Christo Sole."[64]

The association of Christ with the sun has a long history going back to early Christianity. Because the resurrection on the day after the Jewish Sabbath (Hellenistic Saturn) coincided with the day of Helios (Sun-day), Christian theologians used the sun to express the fundamental truths of salvation.[65] According to Isidore of Seville, it is with the sun of Christ that the week begins and with it comes also the memory of the first day of creation. "On the day of Sun-day," writes Justin Martyr in the second century, "the general gathering takes place[:] . . . this being the first day, the day on which God created the world by transforming primal matter and the darkness, and also the day on which our Redeemer Jesus Christ rose from the dead, for on the day before Saturn's day he was crucified, and the day after Saturn's day, which is the day of Helios, he appeared to his apostles."[66]

The Christian interpretation of the sun as Dies Solis or Sol Invictus gained new force in the seventeenth century, when, supported by the spread of heliocentrism,[67] solar symbolism penetrated all domains of Baroque culture. It is against this background that we can appreciate Guarini's contribution. His vision of Christ as sun was still governed by a geometrical structure of the cosmos in which what mattered was not the sun in the center and its relation to the periphery, but the sun situated on high and its relation to that below. This vision preserves the vertical hierarchy of the world and the possibility of differentiating between high and low, because the highest dignity belongs not to that which is most central but to that which is highest. The vertical organization of the chapel clearly reflects this hierarchy.

The meaning of the chapel and its enactment through liturgy and direct participation follow the vertical structure in a sequence that begins with the ascent of the steps and culminates in the contemplation of the upper dome. The tension between the terrestrial zone, where the shroud itself lies, and the upper dome, dominated by the image of the sun, is mediated by the lower dome, consisting of three main arches and three pendentives. The surface of the sail vaults of the pendentives is articulated by squares and crosses, a reference to the crucifixion and incarnation in the terrestrial zone, and by the six-pointed stars and hexagons of the surface defined by the arches, referring to the Trinity and the creative power of the intelligible light in the upper dome.

The dense meaning and unusual spatial arrangement of the chapel invite a different reading from the usual, primarily because Guarini was able to incorporate in his architecture the most advanced knowledge from other disciplines, mainly theology, philosophy, and mathematics. It was in these disciplines that one of the main problems of the Baroque epoch was articulated—how to come to terms with the new mathematical representation of reality while at the same time preserving the ontological continuity of culture. Architecture is the domain where the continuity of culture is explicitly visible. This makes the Sindone a unique full-scale manifestation of Baroque "dilemma."

4.14. Guarino Guarini, SS. Sindone, section.

The upper dome of the chapel has been the subject of numerous interpretations (figure 4.14), some interesting but none convincing.[68] Most fail because they tend to view the structure of the dome either in isolation from the contemporary culture or in a context that is inappropriate or improperly understood. Critics also often tend to underestimate the link between Gaurini's *Architettura civile* and his philosophical and scientific writings.

From a hermeneutical point of view, it would be false to draw a line between a building or architectural treatise and the broader area of knowledge, which in Guarini's case includes philosophy, theology, astronomy, and gnomonics. Such a move is particularly misguided in a period when a broad context for architectural thinking was the norm. Few would doubt that the scientific thought of Claude Perrault or Christopher Wren is reflected in their architectural writings and buildings. To restore the broader context of representations, which have often been reduced to a geometrical level, is not an easy task. However, we have already encountered a similar problem: when examining the development of perspective, we found that perspectival constructions in isolation were meaningless. Context is probably even more significant in the seventeenth century, when symbolization took on forms more introverted, implicit, and dense. In the direct visual experience of the upper dome of the Sindone, several of its characteristics appear unorthodox and original. Most obvious is its treatment of light—how it is interpreted and received in the dome, the relationship between light and the exposed structure of the dome, and the pyramidal sequence of the rotated hexagons. The phenomena of light and the overall geometrical structure of the dome represent a dimension of a complex world articulated in great depth in Guarini's two major written works, his *Placita philosophica* and *Euclides adauctus*.[69]

THE MEDIATING ROLE OF LIGHT

For Guarini light is a universal medium and force that mediates between and binds together terrestrial and celestial reality: "Because light is situated both in the heavens and on the earth and dominates both regions and is, as it were, a chain and in a way binds earthly to celestial things, and may be said to belong as much in the stars as in the elements" (*P.Ph.*, 397). Guarini makes a distinction between celestial light, which is immaterial and infinite, and terrestrial light, which is subject to generation and corruption. However, he also sees continuity between them and at one point writes about the overall homogeneity of light. In principle Guarini accepts the Neoplatonic-Aristotelian notion of light, but is critical of many aspects of it. He attempts to formulate his own understanding, which would preserve the sacrality and qualitative nature of light in an intellectual reality already dominated by mechanistic thinking (that of Galileo, Descartes, Mersenne, and Huygens). The new science derived many of its principles from late scholasticism, which was the main influence on Guarini's own thinking. Thus he shows the same commitment to analytical and mathematical reasoning. For example, Guarini believed in light's divine origin and nature, but could not accept that it is a spiritual quality.[70] Nor could he accept that light is purely corporeal.[71] From a long sequence of arguments it emerges that in Guarini's understanding, light cannot be identified with the luminosity of the world. Light has its own independent reality, which is, understood in its essence, invisible. Visible light and the luminosity of things are only manifestations, or in Guarini's own words "modifications," of light; these modifications include extension, intensity, reflection, refraction, and its fast and slow motion, particularly its velocity.[72]

As a result, visible light is finite and subject to deficiencies.[73] It is by nature finite and corruptible because it "decreases by reason of the space through which it is diffused"; and "given that light is diminished only by reason of space in which it is diffused, as space is solid (*spatium sit solidum*), light also must be diminished according to the proportion of solid space" (*P.Ph.*, 461 Bb, 466 Ca–Ba). However, Guarini is convinced that light in its essential sense has an intrinsic uncorruptibility and therefore, given perfect conditions, can progress to infinity (*posse progredi in infinitum*). Those conditions exist in the perfect diaphaneity of subject (*diaphanum subjectum; P.Ph.*, 461 Ab–Bd).

With the notion of perfect conditions we have moved into an imaginary world of suprasensible intelligible light. To speak about light in this domain is not merely to invoke a metaphor, as we might think. On the contrary, Guarini "sees" light on that level literally as the shining (*relucere*) of divine ideas in human intellect.[74] This understanding of light is based on a tradition that goes back to the thirteenth century, known as "exemplarism." The term refers to an exemplary resemblance between sensible phenomena (the visible world), human concepts, and divine ideas, expressed in terms of illumination and irradiation.[75] Such a relationship preserves the continuity among them all and thus it preserves, by implication, the vital link between the universality of ideas and the particularity of individual things. This issue was discussed above as a problem of articulation and embodiment. What the perspectivists of the thirteenth century defined as a

Guarini's main geometrical treatise, the *Euclides adauctus,* is dominated by the geometrical analogies usually treated as proportions. It is indicative of the direction of his thought that the treatise's first section is devoted to the essence of continuous proportion (*E.A.,* p. 1). Modern thinkers often have difficulty appreciating how critical proportional thinking was in the articulation and eventual development of modern mathematics.[80] Proclus makes the central role and universality of proportion very clear: "mathematics reveals the orderliness of the ratios according to which the universe was constructed and the proportion that links things together in cosmos."[81] It is not surprising that Guarini describes the fifth book of Euclid, which deals with proportion, as a "metaphysics for the philosophers" (*E.A.,* p. 118).

Metaphysics is now seen as providing a new foundation for traditional theoretical disciplines—physics, mathematics, and metaphysics[82]—through one discipline, referred to in the seventeenth century as first philosophy (*prima philosophia*) or universal mathematics (*mathesis universalis*). What has changed is that the Aristotelian universal mathematics has been elevated to a higher level of abstract symbolic thinking (*mathesis universalis*). The mainstream form of universal mathematics was algebra, developed first as calculus and eventually as a method of modern natural sciences. The break that this development created in European culture was briefly forestalled by a tendency, rooted in Aristotelian thinking, to regard *mathesis universalis* as a vehicle of continuity rather than division.[83]

The term "continuity" plays a prominent role in Guarini's writings; that it is most often associated with quantitative proportion and projection to infinity reveals part of its meaning. To understand the full meaning of continuity, we need to take into account the relationship that the Aristotelian tradition maintained between continuity, indivisibility, intelligibility, identity, unity, and divinity. All are characteristics of divine ideas, which stand in contrast to the divisibility, sensibility, difference, and diversity of the material world. Guarini's efforts to come to terms with divine ideas and his skepticism toward the material world may explain why he looked to the indivisible magnitudes of geometry and not the divisible magnitudes of numbers to interpret proportion and to represent the divine ideas (*E.A.,* pp. 132, 444). In the section of his *Euclides* dealing with the continuous quantitative proportion, he writes: "having seen generic proportions, let us descend to particulars according to the diversities of matter to which they are especially applied. For one is the proportion of numbers, the other of continuous quantity. We treat in a true way of the proportion of continuous quantity" (*E.A.*, p. 132).[84] The phenomenon of continuity is closely linked with the nature of the continuum and infinity. There is probably no other concept more important for understanding divided representation in its relation to Baroque culture than infinity.

THE GEOMETRY OF INFINITY

The problem of infinity was not new. It was discussed in antiquity, during the Middle Ages, and throughout the Renaissance, but always with reference to the transcendental nature of divine reality. From the human point of view, infinity could be only potentially present in a world that was by definition finite. This situation had changed by the end of the sixteenth and the beginning of the seventeenth century, when, for the first time, infinity was thought of and experienced as a plausible actuality.[85] The new appreciation of infinity has much to do with developments in mathematics and with the appropriative nature of introverted representation. The contrast between the introverted experience and the indeterminate beyond, which could not be grasped but could no longer be ignored, was probably the main source of the anxiety often expressed in seventeenth-century writing. The contemplation of infinity, Kepler writes, "carries with it I don't know what secret hidden horror; indeed one finds oneself wandering in this immensity to which are denied limits and center and therefore all determinate places."[86] His tone comes close to that of the famous fragment by Pascal: "the eternal silence of these infinite spaces terrifies me."[87]

This fear of the infinite is not shared by Guarini, but it finds its place in his commitment to move beyond the uncertainties and ambiguities of the finite, sensible world and in his elaborate effort to come to terms with the problem of infinity. Guarini's commitment was based on a deep faith in the continuity between the finite human world and the infinity of the divine mind. This faith was combined with an awareness, common in the Aristotelian tradition, that there is not a direct proportion between finite and infinite things or realities.[88] However, if the traditional proportions are raised to the level of universal proportions, the ratios can be generated toward infinity.[89] This possibility is a key to Guarini's universal mathematics and metaphysics (*prima philosophia*), which rests on the assumption that geometrical proportion is both generic and universal in relation to all other proportions.

The important step that Guarini takes is to contemplate approaching the problem of infinity through the continuous progression of ratios in asymptotic approximation. As he himself acknowledges, "the boundary of progression is the end of a series to which no progression can approach, even if it is contained in infinity[,] . . . but it approaches it in perpetuity" (*E.A.,* p. 243).[90] The progression of ratios to infinity closely corresponds to the principle of diminishing proportions in Renaissance perspective. But there is an important difference: the shift from the human to the divine point of view, and from perspective to projection.[91] This shift is readily apparent in the discussion of proportions in the *Euclides adauctus,* which leads to a consideration of the problem of continuity and culminates in the interpretation of the continuous geometrical proportion of surfaces and their projective relationships. Surface plays a unique role in Guarini's thinking, because it is continuous and infinite, and generates geometrical proportions by its very nature—that is, by being a surface.[92] This may explain why Guarini uses the planimetric figure of the hexagon as a primary element in the construction of the Sindone dome. The pyramidal stacking of the hexagons follows the rule of gnomonic difference, which is a proportional difference between individual figures. The sequence may be developed into an infinite series of terms belonging to the same continuous analogy. The key to this idea of the construction of the dome is a relatively little known drawing preserved in the Archivio di Stato in Turin, showing the stereographic pyramidal projection of its triangular elements[93] (figure 4.16).

The Trinitarian meaning of the triangle is preserved in its transformation into a hexagon, as well as in the twelve rays of the sun achieved by the hexagon's rotation. But the hexagon in the dome is open to more than one interpretation. We can see its meaning as a fulfillment of the primary theme of the chapel, the Passion culminating as a resurrection on the first day of the new creation (the day of sun)—in other words, as a new expression of the cosmogonic role and meaning of light in the six days of creation (*hexaemeron*).[94] Supporting this interpretation is another rather interesting, important fact: the dome is composed of six hexagons (six steps in the journey toward the sun; figures 4.17 and 4.18).

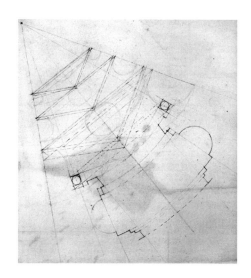

4.16. Guarino Guarini, original drawing for the structure of the upper dome.

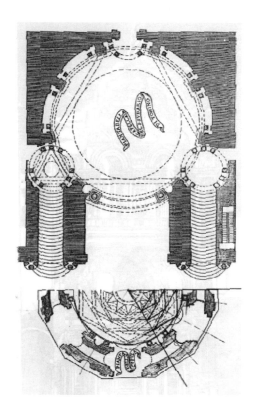

4.17. Guarino Guarini, SS. Sindone, plan.

4.18. Gregory of St. Vincent, *Opus geometricum quadraturae circuli et sectionum coni* (1647), hexagonal diagram.

Guarini's geometrical language becomes comprehensible only in the context of his oeuvre as a whole, which also helps us to enter into the culture of the Baroque in which his architecture was received and understood. Broadly speaking, the Baroque culture of the seventeenth century was still dominated by symbolic thinking, which included mathematical speculation and representation (figure 4.19). More specifically, symbolic representation was sustained by dialectical thinking. It is probably no accident that Guarini titled Expensio V of his *Euclides* "De proportione dialectica."[95] The section treats the dialectical relationship between quantitative entities (magnitudes) and their qualitative meaning. However, the title refers more specifically to the dialectics of geometrical operations in their relation to theological or philosophical discourse. What is new in Guarini's dialectics is its hidden and often enigmatic nature, which must be discerned behind apparently pure geometrical constructions and arguments. This aspect of Guarini's thinking is brought out by his references to Proclus and Nicholas of Cusa, the authors he followed most closely.[96]

Guarini's dialectical interpretation of projective proportions and the problem of infinity is exceptional in attempting to demonstrate the presence of uncorrupted divine light in the hierarchy of beings represented through geometry and the vertical organization of space. His emphasis on reality perceptible only to the intellect may explain the transparent nature of the Sindone's upper dome and its meaning, which can be grasped not

4.19. Gregory of St. Vincent, *Opus geometricum quadraturae circuli et sectionum coni* (1647), frontispiece.

through direct observation but only through intellectual vision. Guarini argues explicitly in *Placita philosophica,* "the truth of being, as it is essential, is not in representation but in being. It would be necessary that creatures be species of God in some other way, for they possess truth according to nature because nature is assigned to all species" (856 Da). The new orientation of vision toward the intelligible structure of reality (Guarini's shining "relucent" ideas) answers the seventeenth-century need to come to terms with the new mathematical understanding of the divine in the form of divine reason.

Though no other architects seem to achieve anything close to Guarini's level of clarity and intention, there is no shortage of those whose works exemplify the principles of Guarini's architecture, with striking similarities to its ontological structure and meaning. The main architectural achievement of the late Baroque, particularly in central Europe, can be understood differently and no doubt better if we keep in mind Guarini's contribution. I am thinking not about stylistic or formal contributions, but rather of the intrinsic structure of space and its specific role in the articulation of intelligible (divine) reality, as embodied in the human world presented in the works of such architects as Johann Lukas von Hildebrandt, Christoph and Kilian Ignaz Dientzenhofer, Balthasar Neumann, and Johann Michael Fischer. All of them tend to organize space by means of geometrical transformations of elementary figures, most often of conic sections or their variations. The hierarchical organization of their spaces is motivated by the tension between the implicit presence of the perfect circle and the explicit presence of its less perfect projections. Its deeper meaning was articulated in the Neoplatonic tradition as a tension between the curve associated with the Creator and the straight line associated with creatures.[97]

That the geometry of Baroque space was not seen as a formal problem is clearly illustrated by Kepler's statement from the dawn of the Baroque era:

> If it were only a question of beauty of the circle, the spirit would decide with good reason for it. . . . But since it was necessary to rely not only on the spirit but also on natural and animal faculties to create motion, these faculties follow their own inclination; and they were accomplished not according to the dictates of spirit, which they did not perceive, but through material necessity. It is therefore not surprising that those faculties mixed together did not fully reach perfection.[98]

The impossibility, owing to material necessity, of reaching perfection refers to the process of creation and to the given conditions of human existence. As Kepler puts it, "To attempt to establish an equivalent between the creator and his creation, God and man, divine judgment and human judg-

4.20. Giovanni Battista Pittoni, *An Allegorical Monument to Sir Isaac Newton* (1729).

ment, is almost as vain as attempting to make the curved line equal to the straight line and the circle to the square."[99]

The tension between the human and the divine levels of reality was expressed and to some extent mediated by conic sections, which participate in both the straight line and the curve of the perfect circle. This may partly explain the role of the curve in Baroque architecture, a phenomenon conventionally described as Baroque "dynamism." It is tempting to follow the argument further and illustrate how the geometrical structure of space reflects a specific program as well as the general content of faith, but such an argument might become one-sided.

Geometry, including the geometry of light, was at the end of the seventeenth century already beginning to play a decisive instrumental role in a new way of thinking in the emerging modern natural science. However, though important, geometry was only one aspect of Baroque representation (figure 4.20); another, equally important, was rhetoric. Understood in its broadest sense, rhetoric represents the whole field of culture as far as it can be directly or indirectly articulated through language. Such articulation includes also the language of geometry.

THE RHETORIC OF THE COMMUNICATIVE SPACE

History shows quite clearly that rhetoric was not only a discipline of persuasion but was in fact the creative soul of Baroque culture. Its foundations in the metaphoricity of language gave it the power to communicate across the most distant levels of reality, from earthly phenomena to concepts and abstract ideas. In the hierarchy of communication, there was always a critical zone of ambiguity and tension between the invisible and the visible sphere of reality. This tension, inherited from the past, became acute between the sixteenth and seventeenth centuries. How critical the tension became in that period is reflected in the considerable literature that grew from the tradition of hieroglyphics and *impresa,* which found its fulfillment in the articulation of emblems, allegories, symbolic images, and iconology.[100] All these modes of expression were motivated by the same questions. Is an idea an image or can it be? Can an image itself be universal? The key to the relation between idea and image is not only historically but also ontologically the *impresa,* a figure of representation that consists of a carefully chosen and structured image together with a short text, both bearing on the same meaning.[101] In a sense, the *impresa* is always a metaphor interpreted visually. What makes it possible is the inherent iconicity of metaphors, which can be seen as a discourse between the invisible meaning of concepts and its manifestation in the properties of things, in human characteristics, in events, and so on. We may conclude that each thought is potentially an *impresa,* because its intuitive content always refers by implication to a corresponding image.

This brings us to a point that must be strongly emphasized. The natural world of the Baroque era was not structured only or even primarily by explicit representations such as emblems and allegories. Tradition was a more important determinant, and it represented a practical and tacit world on which the more articulated level of culture continued to draw, even in its most abstract achievements. Often eloquent ideas were revealed through the primary properties of stones, plants, and elements (water, for instance). The possibility of establishing a link between such distant realities as ideas and the properties of material things rests largely on the metaphorical nature of human experience and communication. However, as already indicated, metaphoricity has its source not in the sphere of poetics or rhetoric but in the tacit world of everyday life. In earlier discussions of the situational structure of the natural world, I noted that the world is articulated primarily on the prereflective level and in the spontaneity of our "communication" with the given phenomenal reality and cosmic conditions.

Communication itself has no identifiable origin. It takes place in a world that is already to some extent articulated, acting as a background for any possible communication or interpretation. Most important, communication is always a dialogue between the new possibilities of representation and the given tacit world, described in modern hermeneutics as an effective history (*Wirkungsgeschichte*).[102] The tacit world is never fully accessible to us. Always to some extent opaque, it can be grasped or represented only through its symbolic manifestations. At the same time, and partly because of its tacit nature, it is a source of identity and relative stability of meaning over time. Meaning is preserved in the continuity of reference to primary symbols, or hierophanies, which are as a result always symbolically present in the tacit world.

Referring to the hierophany of the sky, which happens to be one of the most critical domains in the Baroque vision of the world, Paul Ricoeur observes:

> The figure of the sky supports the symbolism of the Most High and generally of divine transcendence. And to this sky cycle are attached images of ascension, of mountains or ladders, those of flight and of levitation, as well as astral, solar and lunar symbolism, along with celestial epiphanies such as thunder, lightning, storms and meteors.

This symbolism, in turn, refers back to the polarity of divine imma-
nence that, in contrast to divine transcendence, is manifested in the
hierophanies of life.[103]

The process of symbolization follows closely the structure of phenomenal reality and for that reason is also bound to it. This "bound"
character of symbolism—its adherence to reality—makes all the difference in distinguishing between a symbol and a metaphor. A metaphor is
a free invention of discourse, whereas a symbol is bound to the configurations of the cosmos.[104] The symbolic articulation of the tacit level of the
natural world is a precondition of any more elaborate or explicit representation. Paradoxically, only through the more explicit mode of representation can we gain access to and become aware of the natural world.

It is no surprise that the places where the complex Baroque world
is brought to our awareness are themselves rather complex. In a generous but typical meditation on the virtues of Baroque representation,
Leibniz writes:

> the strains of music, the sweet concord of voices, the poetry of the
> hymns, the beauty of the liturgy, the blaze of lights, the fragrant
> perfumes, the rich vestments, the sacred vessels adorned with precious
> stones, the costly offerings, the statues and pictures that awaken holy
> thoughts, the glorious creations of architectural genius with their effect
> of height and distance, the stately splendor of public processions, the
> rich draperies adorning the streets, the music of bells, in a word all the
> gifts and works of honor which the pious instinct of the people prompt
> them to pour forth with lavish hand do not, I trow, excite in God's
> mind the disdain which the stark simplicity of some of our contempo-
> raries would have us believe they do. That at all events is what reason
> and experience alike confirm.[105]

The representations listed by Leibniz often appear simultaneously and are
articulated by the same movement in one communicative space. Because
the nature of a given communication necessarily depends on a particular
mode of embodiment, any proper discussion of communicative representation must focus on a concrete example. I therefore have chosen to analyze

4.21. Zwiefalten, main nave.

the interior of the church in Zwiefalten, where the communicative nature of space was conveyed most convincingly[106] (figure 4.21).

This church, designed by Johann Michael Fischer shortly before the middle of the eighteenth century, consists primarily of one long nave defined by the arrangement of small chapels and galleries along its perimeter with a continuous vault—a characteristic unifying element in the development of the late Baroque space.[107] The iconography of the church—dominated by scenes from the life of Mary, to whom the church is dedicated—can be followed not only in the frescoes and sculpture but also in the stucco decoration. The striking visual unity of the space, which contains many heterogenous elements and yet shows perfect visual continuity in its architecture, stucco, and painting, is very often referred to as an example of Baroque *Gesamtkunstwerk.* Though such an interpretation seems plausible, it is rather misleading. The visual unity of the space is only a secondary manifestation of a deeper unity that cannot be grasped through aesthetic experience. We can comprehend it as we can unfold, while we listen, the meaning of a polyphonic musical composition based on a text.

The key to the iconography and meaning of the church is the large fresco in the nave with the theme of Mary in her mediating role (figure 4.22). Appearing within an uneasily defined frame, the fresco is organized around a large oval separating the lower part from the upper celestial zone. The celestial zone is filled with light that has no obvious source. It is quite clearly treated as intelligible light, which radiates from behind the three figures of the Trinity and descends down toward Mary standing on a cloud supported by an angel. It is at this stage that the light becomes corporeal: it travels down as a visible ray toward a painted image of Mary and child, and moves then toward the founder of the order, St. Benedict, eventually descending as fragmented (refracted) light onto the members of the order and other saints. In the lower part of the fresco, the main centers of the Marian cult in south Germany and elsewhere in Europe are represented.[108]

These main elements of the fresco contain the meaning of the rest and are a good example for our purposes—to understand the nature of Baroque representation and how it is structured in the framework of rhetoric. What is directly visible and recognizable in the fresco tells us a great deal about the implied meaning, though we are also aware that there is more to the coherence and depth of the meaning that cannot be visually apprehended. We obviously have in mind a program, which we assume was in some form available to the artists. In the case of Zwiefalten, we do not know whether a complete program ever existed; only fragments were found.[109] However, even if we had the program, we would soon find that most of it is based on the well-established meaning of the primary scenes and the criteria of possible interpretation.[110]

The meaning of the main themes was widely understood, both in everyday terms and in the sphere of learning—in the liberal arts, history,

4.22. Zwiefalten, main nave, ceiling fresco.

it directs our attention. Emanuele Tesauro describes the *concetto* as the soul of the emblem and the emblem as the body of the *concetto*.[116]

In the emblematic literature of the seventeenth century, the notion of emblem as the body of an idea or concetto was very often extended to the whole visible world, as we can see in the following text: "Before the knowledge of letters, God was known by hieroglyphics, and indeed what are the heavens, the earth, nay every creature but hieroglyphics and emblems of his glory."[117] There is a close affinity but there are also important differences between emblem and allegory. While an emblem is a form of focused visual thinking, an allegory is a fully developed visual discourse. Both are structured by metaphors—but if each metaphor is compared to a star, then allegory must be a constellation. Allegory, perhaps more than any other form of representation, depends on the presence of the articulated, analogically structured world, which constitutes the basic hierarchy of possible meaning as well as a horizon of possible understanding.

The hierarchy of the world in the Zwiefalten fresco is established by the vertical descent and transformation of light that moves from its invisible source in the Trinity to its visible manifestation in the sun, associated in the Christian tradition with Christ. The light of the sun is reflected in the moon, associated with Mary; in the light of stars, associated with saints; and eventually in terrestrial phenomena such as crystals, pearls, water, and so on. This relatively simple sequence of symbolic steps provides the ground and essence of a complex allegory in which Mary plays a central role. She is the most important mediating link (mediatrix) between the celestial and terrestrial zones, between the infinity of the divine and the finitude of humanity.[118]

In the Baroque literature, Mary is very often described as "the fountain and source (*fons et origo*) of life," which is a symbolic reference to the flow of life-giving water, light, and divine knowledge. All three meanings are closely associated in the tradition of symbolic representation. The relation between light and its reflection or embodiment in water is similar to the relation between the intelligibility of knowledge and visible light. The whole sequence is structured as a continuous metaphor, making up an allegory in which the lower element absorbs the meaning of the higher ones. As a result, water, which represents the legion of meanings connected to early cosmogonies, fertility, purification, baptism, and so forth, receives a new meaning from light and eventually from ideas that reveal the unity not only of the divine word but of the world, common good, justice, and so on.[119]

The link between ideas and primary terrestrial elements such as water is articulated metaphorically, but the process does not end there. Metaphors themselves reveal a deeper mode of articulation, which conveys not only the meaning but also the mode of being of the different levels of reality. This ontological sequence has its ultimate embodiment in the body and space of the church. The symbolic relationship between the church as a body and as an ideal community or ecclesia was always associated with the role of Mary as mediatrix. This is clearly expressed in the following seventh-century exegesis:

> In the heavens Helios has a first place and leads the dance. Similarly Christ, who is the spiritual sun, is in heaven placed over all dominions and powers, for he is the door and the chorus leader to the father. On earth, however, whither he descended in humility, taking upon himself the form of a servant, he freely handed over his primacy of place to his body, which is the Church and he did this in the mystery of baptism. Now moon (Selene) gives men light upon earth, by which I mean the Church, for moon has power over all water, and the Church has power over the Holy Ghost whom Christ entrusted and gave to the Church, so that she might bear us in our rebirth.[120]

The allegorical interpretation of the program of the fresco is extended most ingeniously to the body of the church as a whole, using the communicative power of the rocaille ornament[121] (figure 4.23). The main elements of rocaille—acanthus, shells, and rock crystals—preserve the memory of their chthonic origins and their relation to water. In its most developed stage, which we can see in Zwiefalten, rocaille became a highly refined medium capable of imitating not only water but also other elements. It was because of these protean qualities that rocaille took such a universal role in mediating and unifying space. But the part played by rocaille in the unification of space is not pictorial or formal. It is linked directly to the program of the church and its allegorical meaning. The key to the allegorical meaning of rocaille is the historical association of Mary not just with the

4.23. Zwiefalten, detail of the fresco and rocaille decoration.

moon and water, but even more significantly with the virginity of the shell, which creates a pearl without external intervention.[122]

As a result, the allegorical meaning of rocaille is present in the physiognomy of the shell, the acanthus, and the lily or in waterlike appearances; but its actual meaning is in its mediating role, which makes the overall function of the space as allegory possible. As ornament, rocaille is inevitably pictorial, but it is not a picture—it is only like a picture. The same is true of its sculptural and architectural characteristics. It resists becoming a definite art form in order to preserve its metaphorical and creative nature. The best way to appreciate the creative power of rocaille is to follow its development on the wall from the formation of the cartouche. It begins by imitating certain architectural elements such as the lunettes of the vault, while at the same time anticipating and articulating the frame of the fresco and extending into the open, curved sequences of segments and C-curves, in response to the physiognomy of the more specific sculptural and pictorial elements, including finally the fresco itself. The relation between rocaille and the fresco can be most clearly seen in the treatment of the corners of the

4.24. Zwiefalten, the transformations of rocaille.

space, where rocaille invades the surface of the painting and becomes a silhouette imitating elements of the painted architecture and projecting back the transformed shadow of its own three-dimensional presence and physiognomy into the space of the fresco (figure 4.24).

The mediating role of rocaille is clearly communicative, as it participates in the movement and transformation of light radiating from the upper part of the fresco onto the white surfaces of the interior. The distributed light of the space signifies the intelligibility of light, as well as its chthonic equivalent in water and all other elements of the allegorical program. The creative possibilities of rocaille ornament are developed around the similarities, likenesses, and analogies between different visible configurations in the continuum of the space. The text that articulated such possibilities in great detail was Emanuele Tesauro's *Cannocchiale aristotelico* (figure 4.25). For Tesauro, the soul of the communicative movement is metaphor with its capacity to discover similarities between ideas, concepts, images, and meaningful gestures. If we recognize this sequence as a part of the overall architectonics of space, then we can describe the space as a rhetorical

4.25. Emanuele Tesauro, *Il cannocchiale aristotelico* (1670), frontispiece.

space. This is certainly acceptable if we keep in mind that rhetoric has not only its soul in metaphor but also a body in space and that one cannot exist without the other. To describe space as rhetorical is the same as speaking of architectural language, or any other silent language. They are all situated in a space of potential communication.

· CHAPTER 5 ·

THE FOUNDATIONS OF MODERN ARCHITECTURE

T HE UNITY OF Baroque culture, sustained in many places—particularly in north Italy and in central Europe—through to the second half of the eighteenth century, was a relatively isolated phenomenon. England, France, and part of Germany were from the beginning of the eighteenth century involved in a transformation in which divided representation became a reality.[1]

The decisive step in bringing divided representation into the open was the emancipation of the new mathematical science from the context of the natural world and the accompanying creation of a closed system of knowledge based on the Newtonian synthesis and its paradigm of intelligibility. The influence of the Newtonian synthesis on contemporary science is understandable. What is less clear is its influence on other areas of culture, including architecture. The influence has much to do with the demonstrative power and the apparent universality of the mathematical representation of the natural world.

"The order, the clarity, the precision, and the accuracy that have distinguished the worthier kind of books for some time past now," wrote Bernard de Fontenelle in 1699, "may well have been due to the geometrical method that has been continuously gaining ground, which somehow or other has an effect on people who are quite innocent of geometry. It sometimes happens that a great thinker gives the keynote to the whole of the century."[2]

The reception of the Newtonian synthesis and its impact on modern culture cannot be explained by the achievements of science and its applications alone. The synthesis fulfilled an old desire to grasp, or at least to come to terms with, the incomprehensibility of the cosmic movement and the problem of infinity, and thus to understand the mystery of the world order.[3] Strange as it may seem to us, the Newtonian paradigm was not immediately challenged; no doubts about its universal validity lessened its persuasive powers. Yet if we compare one of its most important aspects, the mathematical understanding of movement, to the nature of movement in the living world or in human affairs, it is impossible to ignore the distance between them (which even today is not fully grasped and appreciated).

Such an example illustrates the extent to which the Newtonian paradigm of knowledge is simply a method for explaining certain aspects of reality—a method that may later be improved and completed. The possibility of making final any kind of understanding in the future, together with the cumulative nature of mathematical knowledge, decisively influenced the orientation of modern culture toward progress, toward a new sense of time and history, and toward an unlimited faith in the perfectibility of human nature.[4] And yet the question "What is progress, history, or human nature?" was never addressed on the level of Newtonian intelligibility, which was taken for granted as a possible answer in the period of enlightenment and modern positivism. It was long before anyone could convincingly argue that human affairs cannot be adequately understood within the framework of natural science.

The duality of natural and human phenomena was present in modern natural science from its very beginning, as Alexandre Koyré has noted:

> There is something for which Newton—or better to say not Newton alone, but modern science in general—can still be made responsible: it is the splitting of our world in two. . . . It did this by substituting for our world of quality and sense perception, the world in which we live and love and die, another world—the world of quantity, of reified geometry, a world in which though there is a place for everything, there is no place for man. This, the world of science—the real world—became estranged and utterly divorced from the world of life which science has been unable to explain—not even to explain away by calling it subjective. . . . True, these worlds are everyday—and even more and more conceited by the praxis. Yet for theory they are divided by an abyss. Two worlds, this means two truths. Or no truth at all. This is a tragedy of modern life which solved the riddle of the universe but only to replace it by another riddle, the riddle of itself.[5]

The consolidation and the gradual expansion of the Newtonian model introduced new criteria of intelligibility, truth, and relevance that have transformed and silenced whole areas of creativity and culture as outdated or irrelevant. The most significant consequence of this change has been the disintegration of the communicative structure and unity of the common world. The belief in the autonomy of the new representation of reality—based on the assumption that its identity and meaning can be established, as long as one follows the rules of formal logic, respects the principle of noncontradiction, and uses sufficient reason as the main criterion of truth—has many problematic consequences[6] (figure 5.1).

The first is the separation of ideas and concepts from the body of language, followed by a separation of language itself from the practical world. We have seen how critical the structuring power of the practical world and of language is for the orientation and meaning of all creative endeavors. One can readily grasp how difficult it is for an architect in such a situation to decide what references, principles, or rules to follow in his or her work. Only dogmatic faith could justify an attempt to follow the principles inherited from earlier tradition, transformed by the new scientific thinking into a set of formal or aesthetic rules. A more penetrating approach, noted in the case of Guarini and at Zwiefalten, was to accept the historical possibilities preserved in symbolic representation and in the rhetorical tradition. However, such possibilities were not available in all parts of Europe. In some countries, they had already been overtaken by new ideas, which mainly originated in France in the late seventeenth century.

The occasion for these new ideas to surface and receive a coherent formulation was the "querelle" of the ancients and the moderns.[7] Originally a literary dispute, the *querelle* eventually involved all the arts, including architecture. The main issue, the possibility of emulating or surpassing the ancients, was not new; it was taken up first in the Renaissance. But it was formulated with new clarity and confidence by Charles Perrault in 1687 in his *Age of Louis the Great.*[8] The new confidence of the moderns had much to do with Cartesian certainty, with the encouraging results of experimental sciences, and with the political and cultural supremacy of France at the end of the seventeenth century. The argument for regarding the modern French as equal or superior to those living in any other epoch in European history was strengthened by a new sense of time and history. This new sense of time was expressed most clearly by Pascal in one of his *Pensées:* "The whole sequence of mankind during so many centuries should be considered as a single man continually existing and continually learning. At each stage of his life this universal man profited by the knowledge he had acquired in the preceding stages, and he is now in his old age."[9]

This notion of accumulating the "experience of the ages" is applicable only to that experience which can be appropriated and taught as *mathēma*— that is, as mathematically oriented knowledge.[10] In making their case, the

5.1. Jacques de Lajoue, *Le cabinet physique de M. Bonnier de la Mosson* (1752), detail.

moderns used advances in this type of knowledge to gauge progress in culture as a whole.[11] Not surprisingly, the most influential document of the *querelle*, Charles Perrault's *Parallèle,* situates the dispute in Versailles, the most explicit cultural achievement of the age of Louis the Great.[12] The choice of setting together with the pro-modern bias of the dialogue illustrates the tendentious nature of the arguments of the moderns. The dialogue closely resembles experimental investigations conducted with clear a priori knowledge of what the results should be (figure 5.2).

5.2. Claude Perrault, *Memoires pour servir à l'histoire naturelle des animaux* (1671), frontispiece.

The second dialogue of the first book of the *Parallèle* is devoted to architecture, and its argument largely echoes that expressed earlier in the writings of Charles's brother, Claude Perrault.[13] In both cases, architecture is seen as the most important contribution to the greatness of the Grand Siècle. That greatness, the moderns believed, was accomplished not simply by imitating ancient architecture, but by striving to perfect and surpass it. The ancients themselves had not achieved perfection. The moderns, for whom Claude Perrault speaks, were convinced that the works that survived from antiquity are like "books from which we must learn the proportions of architecture"; however, they "are not the originals created by the first true authors, but simply copies at variance with one another."[14] Such an argument assumes that surviving works are copies of some true original based on true proportions and that it is therefore "necessary to search through these different copies, which, as approved works must each contain something correct and concrete."[15]

The search for true proportions, correct and accurate, may seem at first incomprehensible, pedantic, and irrelevant. However, we must remember that between the fifteenth and the eighteenth century, proportional treatment of orders became the dominant mode for representing architectural order in all its wholeness. This compact, and to some extent abstract, representation was entirely dependent on an articulation of the world in which proportionality was cultivated and understood.[16] We have seen examples of such articulation above in the discussions of proportionality in perspective, projective proportionality in Guarini, and the role of proportional metaphor (analogy) in the rhetorical tradition. In the new position developed by Perrault and the moderns, the rich world represented through proportions was reduced to an introverted experience described as taste (*bon goût*), which is based on prejudice and custom.

To see architecture in this light, according to Charles Perrault, is to experience its arbitrary beauty, which, "like the fashions and the patterns of speech . . . have in themselves nothing positively likeable, since after a time they offend us without their having undergone any inherent change." Its counterpart is the beauty described by Perrault as positive and natural, which is "bound to please everyone" because it is based on inherent, convincing reasons. These include "the richness of materials, the size and magnificence of the buildings, the precision and cleanness of the execution and symmetry."[17]

The difference between arbitrary and positive beauty, which modern interpreters consider to be Perrault's main contribution to the new architectural thinking, is to a great extent illusory. Richness of materials or the size of a building is judged in accordance with prejudice, custom, and taste in the same way as are visible proportions. If there is a dichotomy in Perrault's approach, it is not between the two kinds of beauty but between the arbitrariness of taste and the numerical representation of true order.[18] There is, no doubt, a dichotomy between Perrault's effort to transform the history of interpretation into arbitrary taste and a system of correlations whose careful calculations inevitably lead to relative results (figure 5.3). By giving the orders of architecture a new precision and perfection, Perrault attempted to preserve something essential and immutable from tradition, which could justify such relativity of experience and inventiveness. His own explanation seems to point to that interpretation: "I maintain, that one of the first principles of architecture as in all the other arts, should be, that no single principle has ever been completely perfected, even if perfection itself is unattainable, one may at least approach it more closely by reaching for it."[19]

However, in his demand for the perfect principles, we hear the voice of someone who either does not know the history of the problem or does not appreciate it; he speaks like a scientist for whom the inherited world has become a distant background and the principles themselves a vision of mute, isolated representations. The potential emptiness and formal nature of the results anticipated a new epoch in the development of architecture; and although Claude Perrault himself was not responsible for it, he was one of the first to formulate its main assumptions.

In the new epoch, architecture was treated as a discipline emancipated from the cosmology and metaphysics of the European tradition. It became an introverted domain, with buildings designed either according to criteria of personal judgment and taste or as anonymous constructions fulfilling only the most elementary requirements or strict technical specifications. No longer connected to the cosmic and metaphysical structure of the world, architecture participated in a transformation in which the cosmic paradigm of order was gradually replaced by a historical one. As a result, the vertical articulation of the world was subordinated to a horizontal articulation. The question of origins, speculation about the role of primitive precedents, historical styles, and the realization of utopia began to dominate architectural thinking.[20]

The main characteristic of the new epoch is a growing reliance on theoretical knowledge. The traditional guilds and lodges were replaced by academies and eventually by special centers of learning where architecture was taught together with other disciplines such as civil engineering, surveying, mechanics, and the like.[21] The combination of theoretical knowledge and the new modes of representation—made possible by the develop-

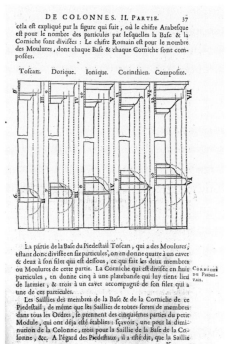

5.3. Claude Perrault, *Ordonnance des cinq espèces des colonnes selon la méthode des anciens* (1683), new simplified version of orders.

ment of technical drawing, as well as new projective and descriptive geometries—transformed architecture into a highly formalized discipline. It is scarcely surprising that form and formalization came to dominate modern architecture, as the debates that accompanied its development made clear. The nature of formalization is closely linked to the history and meaning of form—itself a very elusive term. On the one hand, form partakes of sensibles and may appear as the very essence of reality; on the other hand, it is also something invisible. The oscillation between the real and the possible, the imaginative and the imaginary, the concrete and the abstract is what makes form such a powerful concept, and at the same time so elusive and difficult.

The notion has its origin in the Aristotelian understanding of creativity (*poiēsis*) in terms of matter and form. Matter (*hylē*) is everything that can be formed, while form was originally seen as an idea (*eidos*), which in the sphere of visual reality appears as an icon (*eikon*). Throughout most of the history of the visual arts, form played hardly any role in criticism. Attempts to reduce the diversity and richness of the visual world to "visual form" began only in the late eighteenth century. Until then a wide range of terms—including paradigm, typos, symbol, allegory, emblem, *impresa,* schema, and *figura*—were used to grasp the meaning that was later ascribed simply to "form." Each revealed an aspect of a primary transcendental reality (divine order, the world of ideas, etc.), and only in that sense were they also revelations of the invisible forms (ideas) and their particular visible manifestations and embodiments. What matters here is that all these terms participate—in one way or another—in the formative power of invisible reality by a property that we may describe as structural or morphological, which becomes visible as a recognizable and meaningful representation. This in turn may be described as their physiognomic or iconic aspect.

The critical element in the development of the physiognomy of representation, particularly in architecture, was a tendency toward idealization. As visible representation moved closer to ideal forms, they seemed to acquire a new tangibility. For obvious reasons, the most important influence on the idealization of architectural physiognomy was the emergence of modern science. Paradoxically, it was architecture and the other visual arts that contributed to this development during the fifteenth and sixteenth centuries, only to become later an insignificant appendage of the newly created science.

Key to this paradox was the belief, shared by both artists and scientists during the critical period of transition, that the true order of reality was mathematical and that mathematical language thus provided the most adequate representation of reality. At this stage, not only art and architecture but science as well were part of the same cosmic vision of reality. Kepler's cosmology was viewed as an attempt to represent and, through representation, to participate in the hidden order of the universe. It was religious zeal together with the possibility of treating both ideal and empirical reality as mathematical that brought representation to a point of deep ambiguity and confusion (figure 5.4).

As modern instrumental thinking began to overtake traditional, symbolic representation based on cosmology, the illusion arose that it could

5.4. Versailles, Chasses du Roi, the geometrization of the landscape.

and should act as a perfect substitute: what was indeterminate and vague could be replaced by an unambiguous and precise mathematical equivalent. This desire is evident in Descartes, who writes, "I have observed certain laws which God has established so firmly in Nature, and which he has imprinted so steadfastly in our souls, that after reflecting on them long enough, we can no longer doubt that they are precisely observed in everything that happens in the world."[22] The novelty and audacity of this statement are astonishing. It reduces the distance between the divine and the human, the ideal and the real, which was always seen as insurmountable, to the hypothetical identity of "everything that happens in the world" and its mathematical representation. Here we see that modern science is essentially both experimental and hypothetical. The richness of symbolic mediation between the ideal and the real nature of things was replaced by a hypothetical experiment in which the distinction between the possible and the actual lost its meaning.

THE CHALLENGE OF INSTRUMENTAL REPRESENTATION

To understand how the complexity of symbolic mediation might be replaced by the relative simplicity of an experiment, we must consider the nature of the experiment itself. In modern scientific thinking, the experiment rests on the assumption that reality is essentially mathematical. This initial hypothesis is the point of departure for interpreting and projecting reality in such a way that it can be described mathematically. Such projection then determines the facts of the given reality, and the facts in turn support the projection as warranted. This process of mutual confirmation is the very essence of the experiment.[23] As Husserl observes, "What in truth is merely a method and the results of that method [are] now taken for 'real nature'; nature is reduced to a mathematical manifold."[24]

This step introduces a profound ontological disorientation from which we have not recovered. In the expanding domain of experimentally established knowledge, it becomes difficult to see how far modern science genuinely represents reality and truth, and how far it is only a partial representation, identical with the know-how of modern technology. There is little doubt that both technology and modern science are motivated by the same interest—the domination of reality and the will to power. They also share the same construction of reality that leads to "productive" knowledge.

The level of formalization achieved in science and technology throws an interesting light on the problem of representation. If modern science is oriented toward not demonstrative or representative but rather productive knowledge, and if its main interest is the domination and control of reality, what role, if any, is left for representation? Nevertheless, representation remains a problem in even the most abstract of sciences. The pure autonomy of science is a fiction which any genuine scientist would dismiss. Thus Max Planck declares "that a complete elimination of sense impressions is quite impossible—since we cannot shut off the acknowledged source of all our experience—in other words that direct knowledge of the absolute is out of the question."[25] That the relation of science to actual reality may be highly abstract and distorted does not change the fact that science must represent something, for otherwise it is an empty construction. What science represents is obviously determined both by the nature of scientific knowledge and by hermeneutical conditions—that is, the cultural context in which it is received and understood. The dogmatic belief that the scientific "world-picture is at last commanding general recognition, independently of the good will of the individual researcher, independently of nationalities and of centuries—indeed independently of the human race itself"[26] is one of the most profound misconceptions of modern times.

According to more critical scientists, such as Werner Heisenberg, "contemporary thought is endangered by the picture of nature drawn by science. This danger lies in the fact that the picture is now regarded as an exhaustive account of nature itself so that science forgets that in its study of nature it is merely studying its own picture."[27] Such an understanding is consistent with my own line of argument, which attempts to show that science is only a partial representation of reality: that is, it takes account only of that which is susceptible to mathematical understanding. Ultimately, the instrumental representation of reality is part of the essence of modern technology. For that reason, symbolic and instrumental representation are inevitably deeply opposed. While the former is reconciliatory and serves as a vehicle of participation, understanding, and global meaning, the latter is aggressive and serves as an instrument of autonomy, domination, and control.

It is unfortunate that this fundamental conflict has not been recognized as the main source of the contemporary crisis of meaning and of the general crisis in contemporary culture. In disciplines such as architecture, most believe, even today, that instrumentality can be brought into harmony with symbolism, that a balance can be established between them, that instrumentality can produce its own symbolism, or that the two can exist independently. The absurdity of such a belief becomes clear in view of an earlier tradition which understood precisely that *instrumentality* (*technē*) must always be subordinated to symbolic representation (*poiēsis*), because *technē* refers to only a small segment of reality, while *poiēsis* refers to reality as a whole.[28]

The elevation of *technē* to a universal, self-sufficient instrumentality coincides with the growing influence of modern science on architecture. I have already referred to Claude Perrault and the role played by scientific thinking in his interpretation of architectural order. The problematic influence of science on the rest of architectural knowledge—that is, on experience, tradition, and the primary conditions of design—is characteristic of the eighteenth century. Apart from the specific influence of geometry, stereotomy, mechanics, theory of materials, and so on, a less visible but even more powerful influence was exercised by the new style of thinking—which appeared in the fascination with encyclopedism, taxonomies, comparative studies, different kinds of measured observations, and the like. This fascination with everything supporting the desire for autonomy, certainty, and power is a key to a deeper understanding of the growing sway of modern science at the end of the eighteenth century.

During the Napoleonic period, particularly in institutions such as the École Polytechnique, architecture was taught—probably for the first time—as a science. The science that it was then fashionable to emulate was experimental physics. The model for applying that approach to the whole field of culture was established most forcefully by the group of intellectuals known as the group of Auteuil,[29] whose famous "idéologie" became the methodological base of any possible science. The notion of *idéologie* was derived from the abstract interpretation of sensations; the word meant literally a science of ideas, which included not only conceptual thinking but also the rest of human experience.[30] The method of physics, it was believed, was suitable for any area of culture. So abstract and ambitious a program was a logical

ÉLÉVATION DU CIMETIÈRE DE LA VILLE DE CHAUX.

5.5. Claude-Nicolas Ledoux, elevation of the cemetery of the town of Chaux (1804).

culmination of the Newtonian vision of reality. It was also an anticipation of things to come in the twentieth century. This high degree of confidence—one might also say naivete—was created by the persuasive power of mathematical representation and its promise of universality[31] (figure 5.5).

The belief in the universal intelligence to which each individual found access, an experience so characteristic of the period of the French Revolution, was articulated succinctly by Laplace:

> Given for one instant an intelligence which could comprehend all the forces by which nature is animated and the respective situation of the beings who compose it—an intelligence sufficiently vast to submit these data to analysis—it would embrace in the same formula the movement of the greatest bodies of the universe and those of the lightest atom; for it, nothing would be uncertain and the future, as the past, would be present to its eyes. The human mind offers in the perfection which it has been able to give to astronomy, a feeble idea of this intelligence. Applying the same method to some other objects of its knowledge, it has

succeeded in referring to general laws of observed phenomena and in foreseeing those which given circumstances ought to produce. All these efforts in the search for truth tends to lead it back continually to the vast intelligence, which we have just mentioned.[32]

Ignoring the intellectual hubris of this vision, we can see clearly the fulfillment of the seventeenth-century dream of representing the world as *mathēsis universalis,* as a closed system that is in no need of an explicit reference to the natural world.

Similar results were attained in the work of the so-called revolutionary architects, especially that of Jean-Nicolas-Louis Durand. It is generally accepted that Durand was the first to lay the foundation of an architectural order without directly referring to existing tradition, referring instead to a state of architectural autonomy. If we study the pages of his *Recueil,* what unfolds before us is not a history of architecture but a collection of systematically selected examples, organized into a comparative survey similar to the comparative studies and taxonomies of contemporary science[33] (figure 5.6). However, the set of images, drawn carefully to the same scale, were only a point of departure for the real task—the analysis of comparative material and the definition of principles and primary elements that would enable him to create a universal "mécanisme de la composition."

The process of design is discussed in Durand's second and better-known treatise, the *Précis*[34] (figure 5.7). In the first three sections he deals with architectural elements such as walls, columns, and vaults; with composition; and with genres—public buildings, temples, triumphal arches, town halls, and so on. The critical aspect of the treatise is composition, which is like a grammar of a new language. It is Durand's chief concern:

> We shall see how architectural elements should be combined with one another, how they are assembled each in relation to the whole, horizontally as well as vertically; and in the second place how, through these combinations, a formation of such different parts of the building as porticoes, atriums, vestibules, interior and exterior stairs, rooms of every kind, courts, grottoes, and fountains is achieved. Once we have noted this part well, we shall then see how they combine in turn in the composition of the entire building.[35]

5.6. Jean-Nicolas-Louis Durand, *Recueil et parallèle des édifices en tout genre anciens et modernes* (1801), frontispiece.

This new method of design, which was supposed to be the foundation of a new architectural order, was based on several assumptions that, while not made obvious, can be identified and disputed. The first is that history had run its course and come to a standstill at the end of the eighteenth century. History therefore could be transformed into a new form of understanding: as a theory, it would be a recapitulation and consummation of its past as well as the ground on which the new architecture would take shape. A second and even more curious assumption is that the new order could be based on formal principles situated outside history. How might it be possible to create a system which claimed to be self-referential, but which could at the same time provide a framework for historical criticism and design? This contradiction was quietly absorbed, without being addressed, into the new ways of thinking inspired by the continuing success of the natural sciences; those ways of thinking thus became a new, sophisticated form of self-deception.

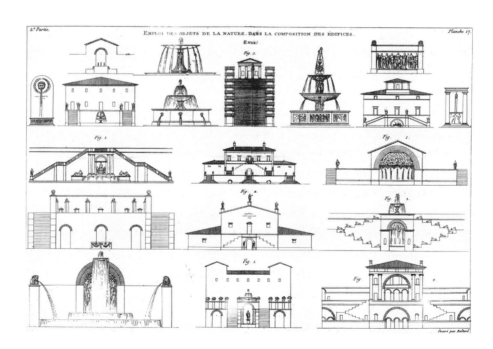

5.7. Jean-Nicolas-Louis Durand, *Précis des leçons d'architecture données à l'École Royale Polytechnique* (1819), pls. 11, 17.

Durand's attempt to create a universal method of design had a surprisingly broad influence, and in that sense enjoyed relative success; but in practice his approach was limited and naive. It could succeed only in a culture that had forgotten its own tradition and history. An ideal vehicle for eclecticism, it was nevertheless useless in the face of a living history, which, of course, did not stop. The main weakness of Durand's method was his belief that historical time could be arrested and encapsulated in a theory that would have a permanent validity. The limits of Durand's achievement were recognized in the following generation, particularly by Gottfried Semper, who had a similar ambition. "The Frenchman Durand," he writes, "in his *Parallels* and other works on architecture came closer to the task [i.e., scientific architectural theory] than anybody else. But even he lost his aim. . . . He lost himself in tables and formulae, organized everything into series, and brought individual elements together in a mechanical way without demonstrating the organic law that establishes their relationship."[36] Semper was better equipped and more sophisticated; he seemed also to be aware (unlike Durand) that his goal was nothing less than a complex science of architectural design, as one of his earlier statements makes plain:

> When I was a student in Paris I went often to the Jardin des Plantes, and I was always attracted, as it were by a magical force, from the sunny garden into those rooms where the fossil remains of the primeval world stand in long series ranged together with the skeletons and shells of the present creation. In this magnificent collection, the work of Baron Cuvier, we perceive the types for all the most complicated forms of the animal empire; we see progressing nature, with all its variety and immense richness most sparing and economical in its fundamental forms and motives. . . . A method, analogous to that which Baron Cuvier followed, applied to art and especially to architecture would at least contribute toward getting a clear insight over its whole province; and perhaps also it would form the base of a doctrine of style and of a sort of topic or method of how to invent.[37]

I have quoted this passage at length because it illustrates very clearly the inspiration and main intentions behind Semper's own system. What such a system might be was determined by his admiration of science—particularly biology, a science that could deal with change and purpose. Moreover, he was influenced by the contemporary belief that art is an expression of mysterious and still unknown powers in nature, no less than his personal conviction that architecture should also refer to its own past. This last led Semper to choose the primitive hut as a generative matrix of architectural order; he saw it, however, not only as a symbol but also as a formal structure constituted by material and technical elements. Central to Semper's system was a vision of architecture as "a conformity of artistic form with the history of its origin, with all the conditions and circumstances of its creation."[38] Such conformity, or harmony, was conceived as directly analogous to a mathematical structure: the artwork was meant to derive from a functional relationship among the individual conditions (material, technical, religious, political, etc.), including individual talent and freedom.[39]

Semper's impressive but impossible task was never completed. Its completion would have required transforming the whole culture to which architecture inevitably belongs into a transparent and verifiable understanding to make it part of an all-encompassing functional system. The difficulty of such an enterprise was probably recognized by Semper himself. However, what he did not recognize (and neither did his followers) was its self-defeating nature. Its success would have meant turning architecture into an instrumental discipline with a formal purpose but no explicit meaning, making it an instrument of pure *ars inveniendi*.

Only a small part of Semper's doctrine influenced H. P. Berlage, Otto Wagner, Adolf Loos, the German Werkbund, or the Bauhaus. The rest was abandoned as an unfulfilled dream. But circumstances have changed. The influence of scientific doctrines has been replaced by a more powerful influence—that of technology. Architecture has been confronted with the possibility of design based on no more than an understanding of form, formal purpose, material, and technique, whose simplicity and intrinsic poverty are complemented by an unprecedented complexity of personal intentions and formalizations. We have moved deep into the instrumental realm of production.

What remains of architecture in this new context? Clearly, the question cannot be resolved within the domain of technology, yet it must be pursued because even the most abstract technological structures are in the end visible, serve a particular purpose, and have a latent meaning. We appreciate and are aware of the beauty of incomprehensible or enigmatic structures in aesthetic experience. The aesthetic appreciation of architecture is one of the most critical focuses of modern architectural debate.

THE NEW REALM OF AESTHETIC REPRESENTATION

In the current understanding, aesthetics covers the appreciation of beauty in everything from nature to art. Often it is simply identified with art, whose function par excellence is seen as the production of aesthetic objects. During the past hundred years, aesthetics has also taken on role oppositional to science and technology. This, as we shall see, is a misconception, and in fact a contradiction. Science, technology, and aesthetics belong together. The development of scientific objectivity depends, as we have already seen, on the subject responsible for the project of science. In other words, the more objective reality becomes, the more subjective must be the position of the individual who encounters in modern science by definition, as it were, only his or her own projection of reality. One might conclude that objectivity in science is in fact the product of human subjectivity.

The transformation of the traditional relationship of humans to the world did not affect only science, but became the basis for the gradual split of the whole of European culture into artificial domains of objectivity and subjectivity. With the first we are already familiar. The second contains everything that resists mathematization—qualities, perception, imagination, feeling, and fantasy. It was in this ambiguous domain of qualities that cannot be precisely determined, but at the same time cannot be completely suppressed or ignored, that aesthetics came into existence. It grew slowly out of repeated attempts to establish some kind of logic or order in the qualitative world, aided as well by what could later be labeled a general aestheticization of culture (figure 5.8).

The critical turning point in the formation of modern aesthetics was the contribution of Leibniz, who opposed the Cartesian autonomy of clear and distinct ideas that deprived human senses of any claim to understanding and truth. He firmly believed that our senses do, in their own way, reveal the nature and truth of the world. Unlike ideas, however, the senses are not clear and distinct but only clear and confused, and for that reason inferior. Somewhat poetically he compares them to the murmur of the sea:

5.8. Pierre Patel, perspective view of the chateau and the gardens of Versailles (1668).

"Although our senses relate to everything, it is not possible for our soul to attend to all individually, and that is why our confused sensations are the result of a variety, altogether infinite, of perceptions. It is almost like the confused murmur heard by those approaching the shores of the sea that arises from the accumulation of the reverberations of the innumerable waves."[40]

Leibniz's understanding of the senses is still based on the integrity of the scholastic world in which the sensible or visible is a manifestation of the universal order. This manifestation is also our main encounter with beauty, in which the perfection of the order is revealed. What is new in Leibniz is the shift toward individualizing such experiences, which coincides with his notion of the individual soul as monad. As he sees it,

the beauty of the universe could be learned in each soul, could one unravel all its folds which develop perceptibly only with time. But as each distinct perception of the soul includes an infinity of confused perceptions which embrace all the universe, the soul itself does not know the things which it perceives, except in so far as it has perceptions of them which are distinct and heightened and it has perceptions in proportion to its distinct form. Each soul knows the infinite, knows everything, but confusedly.[41]

Such confusion arose, Leibniz and his contemporaries thought, because perceptions could not account for their own reason, because their origins and meaning remained hidden. For Leibniz himself and others who believed in providence, this obscurity was not a significant problem, because the unknown, inexplicable, and mysterious was seen as part of the divine plan of things. However, for those who believed in the transparency of the world, in reason, the inexplicable was very troubling. It was difficult to accept that whole areas of reality, such as works of art or the landscape, stirred strong feelings and a sense of beauty that could not be ignored yet could not be explained. This experience was described already in the seventeenth century as the "*je ne sais quoi*—I know not what."

Dominique Bouhours, who devoted a whole treatise to the issue, declares: "One can say with certainty that 'je ne sais quoi' is one of the greatest wonders and one of the greatest mysteries of nature." Montesquieu, some eighty years later, writes: "There is something in people and in things, an invisible charm, a natural grace, which cannot be defined and which one is forced to name 'je ne sais quoi.' It seems to me that this is an effect based primarily on surprise."[42] The self-sufficiency of the Leibnizian monad was what brought the inexplicable into the domain of subjectivity, "each mind being as it were a little divinity in its own department."[43]

With Leibniz, we stand on the threshold of a new epoch, in which the harmony and beauty of the world, revealed gradually in a dialectical process, became a field of aesthetic experience dependent on the cultivation of taste and on the role of the genius. The new experience created a distance from things and events, thereby contributing to the formation of modern aestheticism and historicism. Aestheticization itself is closely linked with the relativity of taste and the formalization of experience. We might turn here yet again to Perrault, who was one of the first to acknowledge that architectural order and the new phenomena, such as conventional beauty or

Der Macedonische Berg Athos in Gestalt eines Riesen, wie der
Dinocrates, des großen Alexanders Architect, solchen Bau
angegeben. Vitruv. Præfat: La: Strabo Lo

Le Colosse du mont Athos en Macedoine selon le dessein
qu'en forma Dinocrate Architecte du grand Alexandre.
Vitruv. Præfat: La: Strabo Lo

5.9. Johann Bernhard Fischer von Erlach, *Entwurff einer historischen Architectur* (1721), Dinocrates.

taste, are not absolutes. The work of Johann Bernhard Fischer von Erlach exemplifies this shift even more explicitly.

In his *Entwurff einer historischen Architectur,* published in Vienna in 1721, Fischer von Erlach assembled the first history of architecture. It was a personal interpretation, based on historical and archaeological reconstructions and, to a great extent, on invention (figure 5.9). His main intention—to legitimize and deepen the meaning of his own work by drawing historical links between contemporary building and the Temple of Jerusalem and the sequence of empires—is not important here. What is important for my argument is the unprecedented survey of history, represented in a series of panoramic pictures; the fascination with knowledge and its translation into concrete images; and, most important of all, the invention of an architectural order that is both syncretic and pictorial.

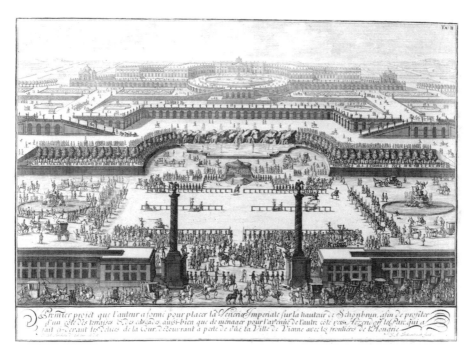

5.10. Johann Bernhard Fischer von Erlach, *Entwurff einer historischen Architectur* (1721), first project for Schloss Schönbrunn.

Fischer von Erlach's emphasis on *inventio*, which entails freedom and choice, stands in sharp contrast to the traditional *imitatio naturae*, which stresses the direct and implicit continuity of architectural precedents. He himself seems to draw this contrast in his preface: "The author's intention has been more to furnish admirers of this art with designs in sundry species of architecture and to lay down plans for those who make a profession of this art to raise new inventions upon, than to instruct the learned"; further, "this essay of diverse architecture will not only please the eye of the curious and those of good taste, but will embellish their minds. . . . Artists will here see, that nations dissent no less in their taste for architecture, than in food and raiment, and, comparing one with the other, they themselves may make a judicious choice"[44] (figure 5.10). The pictorial and scenographic qualities intended to "please the eye of the curious" were developed to a high level of perfection in late Baroque illusionistic painting, and perhaps even more explicitly in Baroque theater design.

The nature of illusionism and its role in the scenography of the Baroque theater are still much discussed.[45] There is no doubt that illusionism can make representation so ambiguous that its function in the positive and imaginative transcendence of everyday reality—as we have seen, for instance, in Zwiefalten—becomes unsustainable and it begins to live its own life. This change can be described as a transition from participatory to emancipatory representation. What is manifested and experienced in emancipated representation is a world transformed into a reified picture with a high degree of autonomy and self-referential meaning. The picture's capacity for emancipation and autonomy is closely linked with the emancipation of the logical structures of language and their role in the formation of a priori knowledge. The deep reciprocity between image and language makes it possible to use pictures as freely as we use abstract concepts.[46]

Under such conditions, the reference to the represented world is only indirect and formal—the picture loses connection with its grounding and becomes predominantly a visual phenomenon. We can assign no particular dates to this process; it is rather a tendency fulfilled in stages. The most important is the emancipation of aesthetic representation, which was followed by stylistic representation in the period of historical revivals, conceptual representation in the modern movement, and simulated or virtual representation today. The individual stages are differentiated by changes in the density, scope, and meaning of the visible results. These results obviously depend on changing historical circumstances, but it is worth noting that the role of perspective continued to be crucial throughout these developments. We have seen already how critical the influence of anamorphosis and the new proportional projections was in shaping Baroque representation.

In the early eighteenth century, Ferdinando Galli da Bibiena invented a new form of diagonal perspective that he described as "veduta per angolo" (figure 5.11). Unlike stage sets that relied on traditional perspective, which were structured as illusionistic extensions of the auditorium, the diagonal arrangement fostered discontinuity. The architecture of the stage presents a world that looks like ours but does not belong to it; it is only a picture of something similar. As one modern scholar declares, this "flight into the unreality of the picture declared to be 'only' art destroys the

5.11. Ferdinando Galli da Bibiena, *L'architettura civile* (1711), pl. 23, *perspectiva per angolo.*

unity of Baroque illusion."[47] We may also add that the separation of Baroque illusion from its context destroys the continuity on which symbolic representation depends. The illusion may still represent something, but the representation itself is merely aesthetic.[48]

The transformation of symbolic representation into aesthetic representation was clearly shaped by seventeenth- and eighteenth-century culture; more specifically, it was conditioned by a desire to use inventive interpretation to dominate visible reality. We can see an indication of this

5.12. Giovanni Battista Piranesi, *Opere varie* (1750), *capriccio.*

new order in the ideal projects for the Concorsi Clementini, in the drawings of the young architects in Rome in the early eighteenth century, and, most important, in the work of Piranesi. Some of his cycles, especially the *capricci,* display historical erudition and a polemical intention that conceptually are still fully in accord with the continuity of the classical tradition. But visually, the same context is represented as a discontinuous field of elements; though sometimes they have a precise symbolic meaning, most often they are only metaphorical allusions (figure 5.12). The unity of the scenes is established through standard pictorial devices derived from theater set design—gradation of light, contrasts of foreground and background, dramatic juxtaposition of elements, and so on—but it has very little to do with the content, which remains a cipher even for those versed in classical iconography and iconology. The relationship between the content of the picture and its order, dependent on the viewers' imagination, is very similar to the relationship between empirical phenomena and the ordering mind in scientific experiments.[49] In that sense, Piranesi's *capricci* and *invenzioni* are also experimental projects. Only slightly later would the experimental nature of the artistic project be "discovered" as a power that could produce its own reality—the aesthetic reality of "pure" art.

Because of its subjective nature, aesthetic reality is inevitably identical with subjective experience. The work of art becomes a world in itself, removed from almost all connection with practical reality; it is to be experienced only as a beautiful form. Such an understanding of art was codified at the end of the eighteenth century in the principle of artistic disinterestedness,[50] which separates art not only from science but also from any specific purpose. As Gadamer says, "for now art, as the art of beautiful appearance, was contrasted with practical reality and understood in terms of this contrast. Instead of art and nature complementing each other, as had always seemed to be the case, they were contrasted as appearance and reality."[51] The consequences of this change are profound. First, through "aesthetic differentiation," the work of art loses its place in the world, insofar as it belongs to aesthetic consciousness. At the same time, artists also lose their place in the world.[52] Second, in the aesthetic experience nothing needs to be known about the objects that are judged as beautiful. And because their nature and meaning do not affect the essence of aesthetic judgment, the work of art has nothing to do with truth. It is only a beautiful form, a "mere nodal point in the possible variety of aesthetic experiences,"[53] which exists for the purpose of pleasure.

The separation of art from the practical sphere of life, from everything that is not just useful but also true and good, has its source in a false and misleading interpretation of necessity and freedom. In modern culture, necessity is linked to the objectivity of nature and therefore to the domain of science; freedom is seen as a primary attribute of the subject and therefore belongs entirely to the domain of subjectivity. Because only that which is necessary can be useful, art, which falls into the domain of freedom, must be useless.

In architecture, however, it is impossible to separate the fine arts and the practical arts, and therefore many have searched for a form of architectural representation that could be common to both art and science. Étienne-Louis Boullée's designs represent one of the first attempts to produce this

5.13. Étienne-Louis Boullée, project for the Temple of Reason, section.

kind of representation explicitly (figure 5.13). In his introduction to *Architecture, essai sur l'art* (1778–1788), a treatise unpublished in his lifetime, he asserts that "art in the true sense of the word [i.e., art understood aesthetically] and science, these we believe have their place in architecture." However, "it must be admitted that the beauty of art cannot be demonstrated like a mathematical truth; although this beauty is derived from nature, to sense it and apply it fruitfully, certain qualities are necessary and nature is not very generous with them."[54] Boullée hints elsewhere in his essay at what these qualities are: "It is impossible to create architectural imagery without a profound knowledge of nature: the Poetry of architecture lies in natural effects. That is what makes architecture an art and that art sublime. Architectural imagery is created when a project has a specific character which generates the required impact" (p. 88). The notion of a "required impact" is borrowed from contemporary sensationalist philosophy (especially that of Condillac), whose influence he acknowledges: "Let us listen to a modern Philosopher who tells us, 'All our ideas, all our perceptions come to us via external objects. External objects make different impressions on us according to whether they are more or less analogous with the human organism'" (p. 86).

Boullée more specifically describes the relationship between architecture reduced to the status of an object and our experience of it: "Let us consider an object. Our first reaction is, of course the result of how the object affects us. And what I call character is the effect of the object, which makes some kind of impression on us" (p. 89). But if the poetry of architecture lies in natural effects, in what does this poetry consist? He explains, "it lies in the art of creating perspectives through the effect of volumes. What causes the effects of volumes? It is their mass. And so it is the mass of these volumes that gives rise to our sensations. Without doubt. And it is the effect that they have on our senses that has enabled us to give them appropriate names and to distinguish massive forms from delicate ones, etc., etc." (p. 115). Even more interesting, for the purposes of my argument, is Boullée's description of the development of his thought:

> Weary of the mute sterility of irregular volumes, I proceeded to study regular volumes. What I first noted was their regularity, their symmetry and their variety; and I perceived that that was what constituted their shape and their form. What is more, I realized that regularity alone had given man a clear conception of the shape of volumes, and so he gave them a definition which, as we shall see, resulted not only from their regularity and symmetry but also from their variety. (p. 86)

If architecture can be reduced to the configuration of volumes and their perception, then architectural order can be established merely by regularizing the relationships between particular shapes and our experience of them (figure 5.14). Such a method may be described as a self-reinforcing process of self-consciousness. Architecture here becomes a source of positive sensations, which in turn create a regular order of architectural forms. In this vicious circle, sensationalist psychology and its experimental possibilities are identical with aesthetics and could apparently serve as the foundation for a self-referential architectural order. However, the process is fundamentally flawed—but Boullée himself was not aware of its flaw. The most important element and source of meaningful regularity is found not inside but rather outside the vicious circle. Any meaningful order primarily depends not on our experience but on the complex history of architecture, which has evolved and taken its form in a particular tradition. In Boullée's

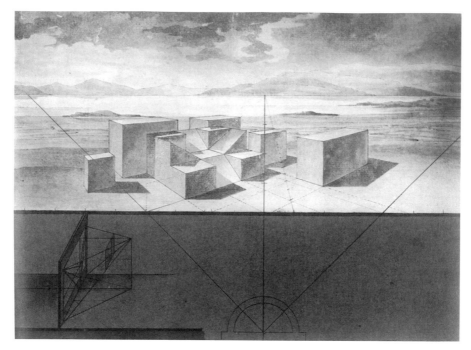

5.14. Friedrich Gilly, perspective study with landscape scene (1799).

system, the role of tradition is obscured by the apparent autonomy of his method, by his inventive vocabulary, and most of all by the illusion that nature dominates all—the insistence that "architecture derives from volumes and that since all its effects have the same source, it inevitably derives from nature," and "that it is through nature that we can grasp the poetry of architecture, that this is what constitutes art" (p. 111).

The attempt to eliminate any dependence on tradition was characteristic of the late eighteenth century, and it was inevitably accompanied by an effort to find some substitute for the normative role of tradition. In Boullée's architecture the normative role of tradition is replaced by the normative role of character—not derived entirely from nature, as Boullée claimed, but also from historical precedent.[55]

Character had a very ambiguous position in late-eighteenth-century architectural thinking. On the one hand, it was related to earlier tradition as a primary mode of architecture's order; on the other, it was seen as an abstract physiognomy that could be manipulated with great freedom. In the latter sense, it came close to the newly emerging meaning of style. "Style" is a term borrowed originally from rhetoric, and initially it was synonymous with *maniera, ordine,* and genre. Only during the eighteenth century was it elevated to a new status as a formal characteristic of a work, epoch, or whole tradition. Its new meaning reflects the shift from tradition, which was transcendental and given, to a human idea—an abstract concept that is immanent and invented.

In 1801, August Wilhelm Schlegel, lecturing in Berlin about the relation of architecture to tradition, declared that since architectural works appear to manifest none of the great and eternal ideas that nature instills into its creations, it follows that they must be governed by a human idea.[56] This opinion is typical of the time, as critics recognized the end of the classical tradition. Marie-Joseph Peyre, for example, could state quite openly, "We read Vitruvius without understanding him." Charles F. Viel de Saint-Maux made an even more radical claim: "This book of Vitruvius would be useful only on the island of Robinson Crusoe."[57] Yet an awareness seemed to persist that style could not be just an arbitrary human notion but must possess at least some of the powers intrinsic to tradition. The generation of Friedrich Gilly, Karl Friedrich Schinkel, and Leo von Klenze still felt strongly that a contemporary style should relate architecture to its past, should be a guiding principle for future development, and should therefore be normative. To fulfill such conditions became ever more difficult in a culture increasingly dominated by a new sense of history, known as "historicism."

For historicists, history is a field of unique events and epochs; the only continuity remaining is of change, not of principles or ideas. Each epoch is seen as having its individual character or style, which has the same value as that of any other epoch or style. The growth of historicism was spurred by a desire for autonomy, independent judgment, and a critical approach to the past. Its lodestar was a vision of the future as the fulfillment of a lost perfection. More generally historicism belongs to the tradition of the quarrel between the ancients and moderns. Historicism in architecture was a theoretical bent concerned with the present and future rather than the past, though we currently (and erroneously) tend to associate historicism with nostalgia and revival of the past.

The problem of architectural historicism corresponds to the problem of style.[58] We have seen that style represents a conflict between the normative idea and historicity, between the idea as an ahistorical representation of tradition and the individuality and wholeness of an epoch. The only way that historicism can resolve this conflict is by eliminating the normative idea altogether and proclaiming its own historical relativity as the norm. As a result, the architect alone becomes the source of reference, of continuity, and of meaning—in fact the sole legislator of his art. This position was predicated in the eighteenth century by the notion of genius. In its original sense, genius was a power of inspiration, invention, and creativity derived either from the divine or from nature and known as *ingenium*—hence *ingenium* loci.[59] It was through the appropriation of the *ingenium,* which then became identified with the qualities of exceptional individuals, that the modern notion of genius came into existence.[60]

To emancipate architecture from the fetters of tradition was the task of the late eighteenth and early nineteenth centuries, and the architect-genius was to achieve nothing less. The architect's own view at the beginning of the nineteenth century is expressed by Schinkel: "Classicism appears as a 'style of lies,' for men are only regarded as serving truth or as being sincere when they are creating something new; wherever they feel wholly sure of themselves their condition must be regarded as suspect, for then they know something absolutely, which means that something that is already there is only being re-exploited, and repetitively re-applied."[61]

The creation of a new style was seen from the very beginning as an analytical and theoretical problem and not as a reverie about some past, ideal world. In a little pamphlet provocatively called *In welchem Style sollen wir bauen?* (*In What Style Should We Build?*), Heinrich Hübsch, the disciple of Friedrich Weinbrenner, says quite explicitly, "Style in architecture should be created through reflection." And, he further explains, this is a sign of maturity and a step toward the full emancipation of architecture, which must "result not from the past but from the present condition of genuine building elements."[62]

The logic of historical development underscored the importance of reflection and a theoretical foundation for creating a new style; in the words of the program for a competition to invent an appropriate style, "We no longer live in the age of unconscious and spontaneous creation through which earlier architectural orders came into existence, but in the age of thinking, research, and self-conscious reflection. For the solution of the mentioned task, it would be appropriate to understand the conditions which did and still do influence the architecture of different countries."[63] Sponsored by Maximilian II, the king of Bavaria, this competition was the result of a long discussion and correspondence with such illustrious personalities as Schinkel, Klenze, the philosopher Friedrich Wilhelm Joseph von Schelling, and the historian Leopold von Ranke. Some of the comments make the intention of the program very clear. The king himself says, "It is important for me to have the best possible knowledge of the future, toward which I can aim in the present." His second comment has more specific architectural implications: "We live in the age of inventions. Why shouldn't an architect also sit down and invent a new architectural style?"[64] The very odd idea of competing to create a new style grows even odder once we realize that the program was based almost entirely on the recommendations of Schinkel, and in fact on the core of his own architectural philosophy.

Schinkel believed style to be directly related to creative invention, or, as he preferred to call it, to a "gradual development" (*stuffenreihe Entwicklung*). The architecture of the past was, in his view, a "closed historical" (*abgeschlossenes historisches*) reality. The past can be recovered only through radical reinterpretation, providing that its intention is to create a "true historical work" (*ein wahrhaft historisches Werk*)—that is, a work truly belonging to one's own time: "The architecture of paganism is from our point of view totally meaningless; we cannot use the Greek and the Roman directly but must, for that purpose, create for ourselves what is meaningful." Schinkel found his inspiration and justification for such a step in the early Christian interpretation of Roman architecture: "For the new orientation of architecture of this kind, the Middle Ages give us a hint. At that time the life of Christian religion was generally more powerful and this power was also expressed in art. We must take up this power of former times and, under the influence of the principles of beauty, which we have inherited from pagan antiquity, we must develop it further and bring it to fulfillment."[65]

5.15. Karl Friedrich Schinkel, Schloss Charlottenhof, Potsdam.

The polarity of classical (Greek) and medieval (Gothic) styles was an important theme around 1800, but it had never before been regarded as generating something new. Schinkel was probably the first to accept the classical style as a thesis, the Gothic as an antithesis, and the present as a synthesis—principles well known to all German Romantics—and to develop these as a consistent dialectic of invention that could be extended to the whole of history:

> If one could reserve the spiritual principle of Greek architecture, bring it to terms with the conditions of our own epoch—which also includes the harmonious synthesis of the best from all the periods in between— then one could find perhaps the most genuine answer to our task. This, however, requires genius, which no one can attain to by striving, but

5.16. Karl Friedrich Schinkel, project of the mausoleum for Queen Luise, Schloss Charlottenhof park (1810–1812).

which heaven imparts to the fortunate without their being aware of it[66] (figure 5.15).

The genius, blessed with inspiration and abilities, is now considered a sufficient substitute for a historical process—and perhaps even an improvement, for in the view of genius all historical epochs become contemporary. Formulations such as "die harmonische Verschmelzung des Besten aus allen Zwischenzeiten" (the harmonious synthesis of the best from all the periods in between) bring Schinkel's dialectical thinking close to that of Legrand and Durand, yet a fundamental difference remains: Schinkel's vision of architectural style is an accomplished synthesis situated in the future, at the end of a long period of historical development. In the text accompanying his project for a mausoleum for Queen Luise (figure 5.16), he wrote,

"Everyone should be inspired to create for himself an image of the future, by virtue of which his being will be elevated to a higher plane and move toward a perfect state."[67]

Once the normative idea of architecture was placed in the future, the transcendental meaning of tradition was transformed into an immanent form of eschatology—in other words, into a project that depended entirely on human memory and will. Nothing illustrates this dependence better than the importance given to the architectural monument. In the new cultural context, the monument was viewed as recalling the past and establishing a reminder for the future; in that sense, it contained the residuum of the historical continuity of architectural meaning. But its meaning had no historical basis: the monument was no more than a work of art understood aesthetically. In Schinkel's own words, "the monument belongs to all times and therefore should be established in the sphere of the fine arts."[68] In a different context, he declared: "the work of art, if it is not in some way a monument, is not a work of art at all."[69]

The subtlety of Schinkel's reasoning illustrates well the agonizing struggle to preserve the specificity, order, and meaning of architecture—its poetic qualities—in a milieu dominated more and more by science. Unlike Boullée and others, for whom the scientific and aesthetic sides of architecture were already separate domains, Schinkel saw them as one: he hoped to design useful and truthful buildings and, at same time, to make them beautiful. What rendered the aspiration difficult to achieve was the separation of aesthetic reality from anything that is useful, and the monopoly of science over everything that belonged to the sphere of necessity—mostly function, materials, and construction. In one of his more forthright statements, Schinkel claimed that "architecture is construction. In architecture everything must be true, any disguise or concealment of construction is an error. The proper task is to create every part of construction beautifully and in accordance with its character. In the word 'beautiful' is the whole history, whole nature, and whole sense of relationship."[70]

This last sentence brings us back to the notion of monumentality. Through monumentality, Schinkel believed, it was possible to transcend the relativity of useful and material tasks in achieving beauty, which was then capable of representing the whole of history, all of nature, and the sense of relationships. This is the beauty of monuments, highly refined and remote;

5.17. Karl Friedrich Schinkel, mausoleum for Queen Luise, Schloss Charlottenhof park.

it represents not a normative tradition, as before, but only an aesthetic idea—which becomes a normative idea in the experience and memory of a genius (figure 5.17). Schinkel himself described the beauty of monumental architecture as conveying "a higher form of beauty, which does not excite sensuality inappropriate to human dignity, but shows a sensuality of a higher order penetrated by intellect, in which the divine aspect of earthly form can and must share."[71]

The ambiguity we so often feel in front of late neoclassical or early historicist buildings can be largely attributed, I believe, to the transformation of architectural physiognomy and meaning into an abstract form of spirituality which, in the end, has become identical with the results of scientific formalization. What is most disturbing in this whole process is not just its potential for confusing spiritual with instrumental meaning but the possibility that architectural reality as a whole may be replaced by aesthetic or scientific fiction and that when we manipulate that fiction, we may believe we are manipulating or even creating reality itself. This manipulation is described very aptly by Eric Voegelin as "magic operations in a dream world."[72]

Such a transformation is characteristic not only of eclecticism but also of all modern forms of classicism, which, despite all claims to the contrary, are distant recollections and pale echoes of early-nineteenth-century monumentalism. Schinkel himself never reached such a level of freedom in his buildings or in his projects. However, at times he anticipated quite clearly the development of architectural thinking, and in particular the close relationship that would be established between aesthetics and science (technology). In one of his later texts he wrote that he had "arrived at the point in architecture where the genuine artistic element occupies a place in this art which otherwise is, and remains, a scientific craft; that at this point, as always in the fine arts, the nature of the real doctrine is difficult and must, in the end, be reduced to the cultivation of feelings."[73]

This statement illustrates the strength of the belief, in the early nineteenth century, in the omnipotence of art, and equally the difficulty of seeing the difference between art and a purely aesthetic appreciation of form. For Semper, who stood halfway between German Idealism and Positivism, the art, "das Künstliche," of architecture was the result of the emancipation of form from material necessity. In his famous "stoffwechsel" thesis, Semper formulated a theory of architectural symbolism in which the symbol appears as a sublimation and formal representation of both material conditions and the conditions of necessity. If the building or a work of art is aesthetically successful, then it represents only itself, as a pure form.[74]

REPRESENTATION AS THE WILL TO POWER AND NIHILISM

The identity of art, aesthetics, and pure form created an illusion that the conflict between art and science (technology) had been resolved. It was taken for granted that aesthetic representation was the essence of art and had a universal validity. Works of engineering—the Eiffel Tower and the Delage automobile, which Le Corbusier compared with the Parthenon (figure 5.18), as well as Duchamp's readymades and the structures of Mies van der Rohe—are even today discussed, without qualification, as works of art.

faire mieux que l'adversaire *dans toutes les parties*, dans la ligne d'ensemble et dans tous les détails. C'est alors l'étude poussée des parties. Progrès.

Le standart est une nécessité d'ordre apporté dans le travail humain.

Le standart s'établit sur des bases certaines, non pas arbi-

5.18. Le Corbusier, *Vers une architecture,* Parthenon and Delage automobile.

The purpose of my argument so far has been to show how confusing and deceptive the modern situation is; how art, a revelation of the truth of reality preserved in symbolic representation, differs from aesthetic representation, created and experienced as a source of pleasing sensation; and finally, how similar aesthetic reality is to the reality of science and modern technology. The affinity between science, technology, and aesthetics is of particular importance because it was in their confluence that modern architecture emerged. Whole movements have been formed around programs based on ambiguous and often confused aesthetic ideas that obscure rather than clarify questions about the goal of architecture and the nature of function, form, beauty, or meaning.[75]

The state of architecture was more complex in the twentieth than in the early nineteenth century. Despite the apparent richness of individual ideas and experiences, the ground on which a normative idea or principle can be established became narrower. Apart from a few abstract principles, often borrowed from contemporary science or technology, the ground consisted largely of that experience which the avant-garde preferred to describe as "inner necessity." A typical declaration, by August Endell, a leading member of the German Art Nouveau, illustrates what such a necessity was: "we are not only at the beginning of a new stylistic phase, but at the same time on the threshold of the development of a completely new art. An art with forms which signify nothing, represent nothing and remind us of nothing, which arouse our souls as deeply and as strongly as music has always been able to do."[76]

The appearance of the notion of architectural form as emancipated from all explicit references coincides, not altogether surprisingly, with the development of modern music and of nonfigurative painting. We do not need to follow the arguments that sustained the works of Malevich, Kandinsky, or Mondrian to understand the nature of the new visual order and to recognize the characteristics of aesthetic representation in the following judgment by J. J. P. Oud:

> The idea of inner balance and perfection is much more meaningful
> when applied to the art of painting, for instance, than when applied to
> architecture which is prevented from achieving this inner balance
> by its dependence on the dualism of necessity and beauty. Architecture
> is a balancing of purely architectural and utilitarian factors, and
> any evaluation of it from an aesthetic point of view must presuppose
> this compromise. . . . Purity of expression in architecture can only be
> increased when the aesthetic and utilitarian factors come to resemble
> each other as closely as possible, thus making it less necessary to
> adjust them in relation to the other.[77]

The "adjustment" Oud has in mind is a creative process in which the aesthetic and technological concerns become identical. We have been too influenced by the Romantic distinction between usefulness and beauty to realize that modern architecture, like most modern art, is moving in the same direction as modern technology. Nietzsche was among the few who understood that this movement is in fact the most significant aspect of modern art. Writing at a time when architecture and art had achieved almost complete autonomy, Nietzsche had no difficulty in identifying them with the free creative will of the artist, most notably in the notebooks published as *The Will to Power*. Will was for him a natural force that penetrated the world at large but was most intimately related to our own existence, and was therefore an innermost nerve of life: "Becoming more beautiful is the expression of a *victorious* will, of increased co-ordination, of a harmonizing of all the strong desires, of an infallibly perpendicular stress. Logical and geometrical simplification is a consequence of enhancement of strength."[78]

Nietzsche challenged the established dogma of aesthetics as pleasure when he stated, "Pleasure and displeasure are mere consequences, mere epiphenomena—what man wants . . . is an increase of power. Pleasure or displeasure follow from the striving after that" (sec. 702). In a section on the grand style, which he considered to be the highest possible achievement in modern art and the nearest equivalent to the classical style of the past, Nietzsche had this to say about the relation of the artist's will to power and grand style: "This style has this in common with great passion, that it disdains to please; that it forgets to persuade; that it commands; that it *wills*— To become master of the chaos one is; to compel one's chaos to become form: to become logical, simple, unambiguous, mathematics, *law*—that is the grand ambition here" (sec. 842). In Nietzsche's understanding, the intrinsic quality of style is beauty—not an objective beauty that belongs to the work of art, but a subjective experience of harmony, reconciliation, and power. Here he touches on the deep motives beneath the process of adjustment of aesthetics and technology, as well as what sustains modern art in general. "'Beauty' is for the artist something outside all orders of rank, because in beauty opposites are tamed; the highest sign of power, namely power over opposites; moreover, without tension:—that violence is no longer needed; that everything follows, obeys, so easily and so pleasantly— that is what delights the artist's will to power" (sec. 803).

The affinity between aesthetics and technology and their common ground in the will to power may explain, or at least help us to better understand, the nature of many modern phenomena that otherwise seem incomprehensible. An example that comes to mind at once is the so-called classical architecture of totalitarian regimes (figure 5.19). This is an explicitly aesthetic phenomenon, yet it makes serious and sometimes persuasive

5.19. Paul Ludwig Troost, House of German Art, Munich (1933–1937).

claims to symbolic meaning; at the same time, it can be used as an instrument for manipulating history. I am obviously not referring here to an external manipulation—in that sense almost anything can be manipulated—but to the effect of the intrinsic quality of the architecture itself, its constituent principles.

Before we turn to contemporary architecture and to postmodernism, which is the latest and so far the most accomplished example of the formalization of architectural meaning, I should mention the problem concerning the content of aesthetic representation. In previous references to aesthetic phenomena, I have called them "formal." And yet we have often encountered examples that quite clearly do have content. What kind of content? This is the most difficult as well as the most complicated question facing modern art. Nietzsche understood the depth of the question, observing, "One is an artist at the cost of regarding that which all non-artists call 'form' as content, as 'the matter itself.' To be sure, then one belongs to a topsy-turvy world: for henceforth content becomes something merely formal—our life included" (sec. 818).

Transforming content into "formal content" is the equivalent of transforming transcendental into immanent meaning. Transcendental meaning is embodied in symbolic representation, in which we can participate, while immanent meaning is embodied in formal representation, which we can experience and possess. As a result, "formal content" is the aesthetic equivalent of the original transcendental meaning. Rather than making a long excursion into philosophy, I use an explicit example of such a transformation. After the death of his wife, Camille, in 1879, Claude Monet told a friend:

> When I contemplated Camille at daybreak on her deathbed, I noticed—in spite of all my grief—that my eyes perceived more than anything else the different colorations of her young face. Even before I decided to record her likeness for the last time, my painter's instinct had seen the blue, yellow, and gray tonalities cast by death. With horror I felt myself a prisoner of my visual experiences and compared my lot to an animal that turns a millstone.[79]

The dissolution of content in aesthetic experience is not a simple event. There is a residuum of transcendental meaning in each person's background experience that can endow even abstract forms with a semblance of symbolic meaning, and thus encourage the belief that what is merely an aesthetic representation is also a symbolic one. Such beliefs have played an important role in European architecture from the beginning of historicism, and they have changed only in degree and not in kind. Here I should perhaps emphasize that what today are still erroneously described as periods of historicism, "modernity," and "postmodernity" are only phases of the same way of thinking, more or less explicitly articulated in their different iconographies.

From an ontological point of view, the difference between particular iconographies is less important than the overall meaning of architectural order. In my earlier discussion, I tried to demonstrate that the order of modern architecture had been established on a deep and cultivated sense of identity between the creative will of the individual artist and the accepted relativity of history, in a process which had thus far gone uninterrupted and did not change in principle. The conventional understanding of modernity as a rejection of historicism is therefore erroneous. Modernity is only a step toward a more radical form of historicism. What appears to be a pronounced difference in architectural style is only a difference in how the argument is couched, as varying degrees of confidence determine to what extent history and historical "material" is accepted or ignored.

Today, phenomena such as "postmodernism" illustrate a new level of confidence that can be explained as an uncritical acceptance of false assumptions, regarded as truth and used as such with indiscriminate freedom. It is sufficient for the purpose of my argument to identify only the most important of these: historicism taken for history, aestheticism taken for symbolic meaning, individual style taken for participation in tradition, and individual creativity taken for architectural order. It is typical that most of these assumptions appear in the form of instruments and "materials"— as reified order, historical quotations, iconic signs, or stylistic features. When this occurs, the contemporary architect becomes the ideal artist, described by Nietzsche as a man who "has once again become master of 'material'—master of truth!—And whenever man rejoices, he is always the same in his rejoicing: he rejoices as an artist, he enjoys himself as power, he enjoys the lie as his form of power" (sec. 853).

In calling the lie a form of power, Nietzsche points to an important aspect of the reality of modern art, which became a form of "truth" in itself, and also of the world—"The world as a work of art that gives birth to itself" (sec. 796). This kind of artistic "truth" is a new phenomenon. We know that when art was emancipated from the normative power of tradition, its truth was seriously undermined. The truth of the historical styles of the nineteenth century could not, in the end, survive, even defended by the most elaborate of arguments. However, as art moved away from tradition, it also moved closer to the world of science and technology and their truth, which, as we may recall, is instrumental and closely linked to the nature of power. This alliance of art with instrumental truth is manifested in the orientation of modern art toward invention, experiment, construction, originality, and novelty. As a result, the new artistic truth has become a truth created in defiance of tradition. It has become a product of inventive will, which, having no particular boundaries, can be imposed on reality without discrimination.[80]

The impossibility of reconciling such a vision of art with the cultural reality of the twentieth and twenty-first century has left modern art in a curious position, halfway between truth and fiction (lie). This dilemma is exemplified in Picasso's famous remark: "We all know that art is not truth. Art is a lie that makes us realize truth, at least the truth that is given us to understand. The artist must know how to convince others of the truthfulness of his lies. From the point of view of art, there are no concrete or abstract forms, but only forms which are more or less convincing lies. That those lies are necessary to our mental selves is beyond any doubt, as it is through them that we form our aesthetic view of life."[81]

The uncertainty that surrounds the nature of truth,[82] and by implication the normative value of modern art, is clearly felt in the current architectural debate. It has become impossible to grasp the truth of that architecture produced under the name of "rationalism," "postmodernism," "radical eclecticism," or "deconstruction," to say nothing of their normative value. Can anyone be blamed? During the past decades, serious and often impressive attempts have been made to understand at least the conditions of truth—that is, the foundation and possible meaning of design (figures 5.20 and 5.21). What has been achieved? Nostalgia for the preindustrial city, a vernacular vision of eighteenth-century classicism, a reversion to late-eighteenth-century monumentalism, a typological version of character, and, on a different plane, indiscriminate faith in the iconicity of technology. This list of achievements could be extended, but the result would be no different; its entries would remain, in most cases, problematic. What makes them problematic is their reliance on the belief that the renewal of architecture is possible through an arbitrary and instrumental manipulation of iconography, or through principles borrowed from a period of history already in the throes of crisis and riddled with contradictions from which we ourselves have not yet emerged.[83] The uncritical acceptance of this state of affairs creates an ideal ground for dogmatism, because it is in the nature of uncritical thinking to refuse a genuine dialogue with the past or with the present. Under such conditions, the truth of architecture is a matter of its instrumental power and of private opinion.

The possibility of interpreting not only the nature but also the truth of architectural representation instrumentally brings my argument to its conclusion, and at the same time to its beginning—to the comment on the

5.20. James Stirling, Stuttgart Gallery, entrance to the lower galleries.

paradoxical relation between the production of architecture and our real intentions. The essence of this paradox is our inability to see that an uncritical faith in symbolism, historical reference, meaning, and so on could be, and very often is, only a disguised form of technical rationality. If this is not recognized, the paradox is likely to take the form of a vicious circle in which only immanent values are taken into account.[84] As a consequence, anything that transcends the circle and might support our critical understanding is

5.21. James Stirling, Stuttgart Gallery, detail of the main facade.

considered to be either irrelevant or dubious. This is a typical modern stance, identified already at the end of the nineteenth century as nihilism.[85]

In Nietzsche's interpretation, nihilism is directly linked to the nature of immanent values, to the fact "*that the highest values devaluate themselves*" (sec. 2) and that

> All the values by means of which we have tried so far to render the
> world estimable for ourselves and which then proved inapplicable and

5.22. Terry Farell, television studios, Camden Town, London, entry courtyard.

therefore devalued the world—all these values are, psychologically considered, the results of certain perspectives of utility, designed to maintain and increase human constructs of domination—and they have been falsely *projected* into the essence of things. What we find here is still the *hyperbolic naiveté* of man: positing himself as the meaning and measure of the value of things. (sec. 12B)

That nihilism is a critical dimension of modern culture is recognized only indirectly, through secondary phenomena such as alienation, meaninglessness, inauthenticity, and the like. Our difficulty in understanding the nature of modern nihilism is directly related to the general uncertainty about the nature of a technologically oriented culture. In the sphere of architecture, this uncertainty is manifested in the ambiguous relationship between architecture, technology, and aesthetics, which has obscured the primary conflict of modern culture—that between symbolic and instrumental representation (figure 5.22). This conflict between two fundamentally different forms of representation is the main source of our contemporary confusion and nihilism. It is difficult to believe that scientific and technological rationalities, or individual talent, experience, and intuition, can suffice for practicing architecture as architecture and not as a branch of technology or aesthetics. That conditions to make possible such practice do exist, at least potentially, is a belief that I explore in the final chapter.

· CHAPTER 6 ·

CREATIVITY IN THE SHADOW
OF MODERN TECHNOLOGY

T HE TENSE RELATIONSHIP between architecture and technology is a relatively new phenomenon. In the previous chapter we saw that instrumental representation, the main characteristic of modern technology, did not seriously influence architecture before the eighteenth century, though divided representation, which made possible such influence, appeared almost a century earlier. It is of course true that certain aspects of instrumental thinking emerged even earlier, for instance, in the development of Renaissance perspective, but they did not in any significant way alter the primary nature of making (*techne, ars*).[1]

The most accomplished technical devices and machines used in constructing buildings and animating gardens, as well as scientific instruments or surveying techniques, were in the sixteenth and early seventeenth century still considered part of the mechanical arts[2] (figure 6.1). Theoretical knowledge of the liberal arts—particularly the mathematical arts of the quadrivium, which were always closely associated with architecture—played an important role in the formation of architectural order, mainly in the *ars fabricandi,* the execution of buildings. The process of making remained a practical problem, as is clearly expressed in the well-known maxim "ars sine scientia nihil est," advanced in the late-fourteenth-century controversy about the role of theoretical knowledge in the project and construction of Milan's cathedral.[3] This controversy demonstrated that art engages with the sciences in the fulfillment of its meaning but is not transformed by science in the process.

The possibilities of such a transformation first arose in the seventeenth century, when the practical nature of arts—*technai*—was absorbed by the theoretical project of instrumental thinking.[4] The theoretical basis of technology reveals the radical discontinuity between the modern and traditional way of making. It distances itself from practical knowledge, spontaneous creativity, and skill in a process dominated by new goals of economy, efficiency, and perfection of performance—and, on a deeper level, by the acquisition of power and the desire to achieve the highest possible level of emancipation and autonomy. There is a feeling today that the traditional forms of creativity are slowly being absorbed into one dominant way of making and thinking. This process of homogenization is not new, but today has reached unprecedented levels. To grasp the novelty of our contemporary situation, it is enough to recall the nature and the intensity of

6.1. Sebastian Le Clerc, representation of the machines used to raise the large stones in the construction of the Louvre fronton (1677).

discussions about creativity in different domains of culture; about the relation between art, science, and technology; and about the nature and status of the applied arts, industrial design, and so on in the early decades of the twentieth century—in periodicals and movements such as the Werkbund, *L'Esprit Nouveau, L'Architecture Vivante,* Futurism, and Constructivism. While some awareness of the distinction between invention, creativity, and pure production remains, it is no longer clear how this distinction should be established. This fundamental lack of clarity, may be one of the reasons why the current debate is so confusing and frustrating.

The subject of this debate, to which most other questions are considered subordinate, is the merit of technical efficiency versus that of aesthetics. Even issues of cultural meaning or social and political relevance, or issues that directly affect the long-term well-being of our society, are often reduced to such simplistic terms. This oversimplification has its roots in the belief in the universality of technical thinking. As a result, a technical way of making has become the standard against which any kind of making is measured, reflecting what is usually referred to as the technical or technological imperative. We often hear of the inevitability of technological development and progress, of technology's historical destiny and even "mission." Yet despite the growing number of skeptical voices and despite the quantity of literature devoted to examining the technological transformation of modern culture, our understanding of the nature of technology remains surprisingly limited.

One of the main obstacles to a better understanding is our inability to discuss technological problems from a noninstrumental point of view. In current scientific parlance, the latter stance is often considered to be nonscientific—a verdict that seals the issue and encloses it hermetically in a vicious circle of understanding/nonunderstanding. Thus, for example, we find recent research on the problems of ecology that extends existing technological knowledge into wider fields while leaving the primary criteria and goals of research unchanged. Such studies are misleading and inevitably limited, as Werner Heisenberg's incisive analogy makes clear: "With its seemingly unlimited growth of material power, mankind finds itself in the situation of a skipper who has his boat built of such a heavy concentration of iron and steel, that the boat's compass points constantly at herself and not north. With a boat of that kind, no destination can be reached; she will go around in a circle, exposed to the hazards of the winds and the waves."[5]

Instrumental thinking tends to impose its hegemony by creating a world it can control. Control of this sort requires not only a special kind of knowledge but also a particular kind of will. And the knowledge that meets the conditions of the will to control is the "knowledge of power."[6] Because it must be subordinated to the will, we can speak here simply of a "will to power," which as a consequence becomes a "will to will." It is well known that knowledge as power represents the essence of modern science—its metaphysical foundation; but it is also the essence of modern technology.[7] By recognizing the nature of modern technology, we gain a deeper insight into the hegemony of technical reason and into the nature of the vicious circle of our "understanding" of technology. The difficulty in breaking that hegemony—and in understanding that technology as the fulfillment of the will to power is not unconditional—is well summarized by Martin Heidegger:

Because the will to will absolutely denies every goal and only admits goals as means to outwit itself wilfully and to make room for its game, the will to will may not appear as that anarchy of catastrophes that it really is. However, if it wants to assert itself in beings, it must legitimate itself. The will to will invents here the talk about "mission." Mission is not sought with regard to anything original and its preservation, but rather as the goal assigned from the standpoint of fate, thus justifying the will to will.[8]

TECHNOLOGY AS WILL AND HISTORICAL DESTINY

The need of the will to justify its role and its fulfillment reveals that the will itself is not absolute, that it is always situated and cannot completely disguise its own "situatedness."[9] References to mission and fate clearly manifest a deeper intentionality and deeper historical conditions in which the will appears as a historical possibility, but always in contrast with other possibilities. While the will represents a movement toward the appropriation of power, culminating in modern technology, the other possibilities represent a movement toward participation that has been most consistently preserved in the domain of the arts (figure 6.2). The existence of other possibilities—and their replacement by simple will—must be taken as a point of departure for any understanding of the apparent fatality of technological progress and of the belief that this kind of progress is our historical destiny. It is true, as we have seen, that such a belief belongs to the essence of modern technology; but it is also true that there is nothing technological in this kind of belief itself: "Because the essence of technology is nothing technological, essential reflection on technology and decisive coming to terms with it must happen in a realm that is, on the one hand, akin to the essence of technology and, on the other, fundamentally different from it. Such a realm is art."[10]

The arts today are akin to but at the same time fundamentally different from technology, because of how these two domains that originally shared a common ground have developed through history. Art originates in *technē*, which in its Greek sense is knowledge related to making and is always known in its final sense as *technē poiētikē*. *Technē*, once known, superseded spontaneous knowledge and intuitive skills, which required a close contact with tasks and objects but could lead to the discovery of what was common and permanent in all of them. This emancipated knowledge teaches us a general lesson about things and can be used without direct

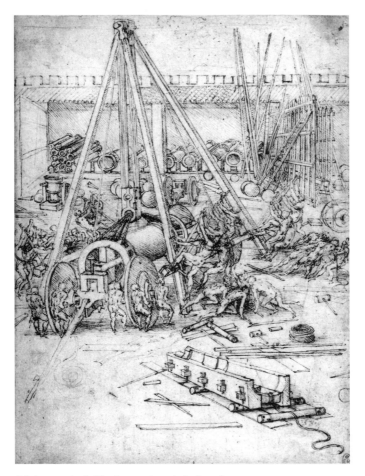

6.2. Leonardo da Vinci, a courtyard of a foundry.

reference to the things themselves. As a project of what can be known, *technē* relies on accumulated experience but elevates it to a priori knowledge that can be taught.

What exists a priori and can be taught was for the Greeks a *mathēma*—hence mathematics emerges as a special form of such knowledge. In *mathēma*/mathematics we find the true origin of the transformation of *technē* into technique and finally into modern technology. For the Greeks, however, such changes lay far in the future. They situated *technē* between the new possibilities of knowledge and the intimate understanding of the inner possibilities of nature (*physis*). *Technē* was not yet seen as a human possession: it was instead a power of nature, which humans could possess only to a limited extent. This may explain why, according to Aristotle, "the first man who invented art [*technē*] beyond common sense was looked upon by his fellow man as a wonder, not only because there was something useful in this discovery, but also because he was thought wise and superior to others."[11]

That *technē* is only a transition to technique is reflected in its relation to making (*poiēsis*). Broadly speaking, "making" means to bring into being something that did not previously exist. *Poiēsis,* Aristotle tells us, can be found not only in human effort but also in nature: "All things that come into being are generated, some by nature (*physis*), others by art (*technē*)." Art originally received its legitimacy and meaning from the universal divine order, which was seen as the product of the ultimate craftsmanship. "When a thing is produced by nature, the earlier stages in every case lead to the final development in the same way as in the operation of art, and vice-versa."[12] In this rather dense formulation, all the future definitions of art are already present—it is skill and knowledge that complement nature, a completion and fulfillment of nature's inner possibilities, or an imitation of nature. Imitation is a creative process that contains a large residuum of mystery, of which the Greeks were very much aware: they called it "chance" (*tychē*). Thus Aristotle declared in a well-known passage: "Art dwells with the same objects as chance[;] . . . chance is beloved of art and art of chance."[13] Elsewhere he wrote: "Some hold that chance is the genuine cause of things, but one that has something divine and mysterious about it that makes it inscrutable to the human intelligence."[14]

Making is based on productive knowledge, but such knowledge is never complete. It always depends on a prior understanding that has its origin in the spontaneity of making. The inscrutable element in making which is tied to chance has its main source in *mimēsis,* which is therefore equally inscrutable to our intelligence. In principle, it is possible to say that mimesis is a creative imitation in which something with the potential to exist is recognized and reenacted as a significant gesture; it may be sound, as song or music; visible reality, as image or picture; or ideas, as an articulated and structured experience. In its earliest sense, Gadamer observes, mimesis is a reenactment of elementary order: "Testifying to order, *mimesis* seems as valid now as it was in the past, insofar as every work of art, even in our own increasingly standardized world of mass production, still testifies to that deep ordering energy that makes our life what it is. The work of art provides a perfect example of that universal characteristic of human existence—the never-ending process of building a world"[15] (figure 6.3). In making, mimesis reveals the mystery of order as a tension between its potential and actual existence, which ultimately always points toward the ultimate order—the cosmos. It is in this sense that the reenactment of cosmic order can be seen as the primordial form of making.[16]

Mimetic making, which precedes the formation of *technē,* takes place most often in the domain of ritual. This mode is apparent not only in such rituals as dance or music but also in the rhythm and movement of the process of making itself, which demonstrate that the making of order and the making of things belong together. In both cases, the result of the mimetic action becomes a vehicle for participation in the overall order of things. The participatory meaning of mimesis and ritual—the need to come to terms with the universal order of reality—is challenged and largely displaced by the growing appropriation and manipulation of order-creating powers. This tendency has its origin in the efficacy of traditional rituals, often misidentified as magic. It is wrong to see magic where we are dealing only with the instrumental aspect of such rituals.[17] That certain gestures or objects used in rituals may have the power to produce certain desirable results does not justify their being described as magic or as primitive techniques. The power to influence the order of things in a culture that does not yet recognize the difference between the natural and the supernatural always depends on a reference to reality as a whole, which cannot itself be manipulated. A modern scholar notes, "there is an important difference between two kinds of actions, actions done by man and actions done by man in the belief that their efficacy is not human in any reducible sense, but proceeds from elsewhere. Only the second kind of action can be called any sort of a religious rite."[18] Magic by definition differs from ritual and other forms of religion, for the desire to dominate reality is essential to its nature.

Unlike ritual and other participatory actions, magic—with its emancipatory, appropriative tendency—arises only under particular circumstances. A historian of religion explains, "the domination by will has one

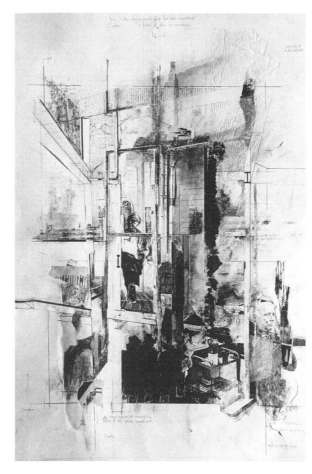

6.3. David Weston-Thomas, political building, preliminary study of the main entry space.

essential condition: before the world can be thus controlled it must be transferred inward and man must take it into himself. He can actually dominate
it only when it has in this way become an inner realm. For this reason all
magic is autism, or living within oneself."[19] Historically, this condition first
appeared during Hellenistic times, when the disintegration of the cultural
and political institutions of the polis led to the disintegration of traditional
corporate rituals, leaving individuals to their own resources and in relative
isolation. As the classicist E. R. Dodds says succinctly, "Magic is commonly

the last resort of the personally desperate, of those whom man and God have alike failed."[20] The release of magic was closely linked to the growing interest in other esoteric disciplines (such as astrology, alchemy, and theurgy), as well as to new interest in mechanics and technical skills.

In the introduction to his book on mechanics, Pappus of Alexandria recognized the link between mechanics and magic: "The ancients also describe as mechanicians (*mechanikos*) the wonder-workers or the magicians (*thaumasiourgos*) of whom some work with air as Heron in his *Pneumatica*."[21] Under such circumstances, *technē* emerged as technique in its most elementary form. J. P. Vernant acknowledges as much, as he concludes a long study on the possibilities and limits of technical thinking in ancient Greece: "Only in the work of the Alexandrian engineers, especially Heron, is there any evidence of interest in the instruments and machines as such, and only here was their construction undertaken with an attitude that we can describe as truly technical."[22] The technical attitude was marked not only by a new type of knowledge, but by a new interest and will. For example, a typical Hellenistic definition of a machine tells us that a "machine is a continuous material system . . . moved by appropriate revolutions of circles which by the Greeks is called 'cyclicen cinesin.'"[23] Circular movement is not a purely mechanical phenomenon, however; the text points to its origin in the regularity of the celestial movement, which is imitated in ritual and dance but can be represented more tangibly by a machine.

The incomprehensibility of the movement of nature, most explicitly manifest in the movement of the celestial bodies, has been identified by modern anthropology as the deepest motif of technicity and called a "fascination with automatism"[24] (figure 6.4). This fascination is seen in the unending attempts to grasp what is incomprehensible in terms that we can understand, construct, and manipulate. These attempts might be described as a "technization" of the original mimetic reenactment. Because the machine is a tangible model of such a process, it is also a model of the inscrutable cosmic order. A model is comprehensible because we have constructed it. Hellenistic authors themselves came to this understanding; Vitruvius declares:

All machinery is generated by Nature and the revolution of the universe guides and controls it. For first indeed, unless we could observe and

6.4. William Cuningham, *The Cosmographical Glasse* (1559), Atlas bearing the heavens.

contemplate the continuous motion of the sun, moon and the five planets; unless these revolved by the device of Nature, we should not have known their light in due season nor the ripening of the harvest. Since then our fathers have observed this to be so, they took precedence from Nature; imitating them, and led on by what is divine, they developed the necessities of life by their inventions.[25]

At this stage, technique became, at least potentially, methodical—it could be pursued to a predictable end. Unlike *technē*, which is always rooted in the concrete life of the polis, magic and technique are largely emancipated from any political and cultural context. Ethically, they represent individual or group egocentrism, rooted in acquiring power and in domination. The emancipation of magic and technique from the ethically oriented life of the polis leads to a freedom that allows no room for good or evil and for the sense of guilt or sin. Under such conditions, practical achievement substitutes for truth. Because this applies to both magic and technique, it is very difficult to draw a clear line between them. Yet we can say that in modern times magic recedes into the background, leaving a certain residuum of its original power in the more rationalized forms of technique. For this reason, as we analyze the development of modern technique, it is more appropriate to speak of an element of magic than about magic itself. And it is also more appropriate to speak about a technical tendency in the existing arts (*technai*) than about technique when we refer to the act of making. Greater care in terminology would certainly simplify today's confusing and often misleading discussions about the role of magic in the shaping of modern technology.[26] We must keep in mind that the traditional understanding of art includes every kind of making—from the making of shoes or tools to arithmetics and geometry. They were distinguished by their degree of involvement with matter and manual labor and were placed in broad categories, which were most often expressed only by adjectives— the mechanical arts (*artes mechanicae*), usually situated at the bottom of the hierarchy because of the labor involved; the liberal arts (*artes liberales*), which include the trivium (grammar, rhetoric, and logic) and the quadrivium (arithmetic, music, geometry, and astronomy); and, finally, the theoretical arts, sometimes known as *scientiae,* consisting of theology, mathematics, and physics.[27] That the arts represented not only experience and skills but also an important mode of knowledge is reflected in the ambiguity of their relation to science.[28]

THE ORIGINS OF MODERN TECHNOLOGY

The sciences that contributed to the formation of modern technique and eventually to technology were astronomy, harmonics, optics, and mechanics, known as *scientiae mediae* (the "middle sciences"). The reason for this designation was not their "mixed" nature, as is sometimes thought, but their position halfway between metaphysics and physics.[29] The *scientiae mediae* should be seen as a branch of mathematics—physical mathematics—preparing the way for the development of mathematical physics though radically different from it in principle. This fundamental distinction is important to bear in mind, particularly because many scholars today treat medieval optics, Renaissance perspective, and early mechanics as if they were already modern sciences. These interpretations do not seem to recognize the novelty of the new stage in the "mathematization" of reality.

In Renaissance art, mathematics serves to approximate, mediate, and symbolize. It still represents, on the one hand, the essential, intelligible structure of reality, and, on the other hand, the visible manifestation of such structures. The mediating and symbolic role of mathematics, and not just its precision, gives it a prestigious place in early modern thinking. The indirect mathematization of reality—the process that is the main characteristic of the middle sciences—can be seen in the nature of medieval optics, in the development of perspective, and in the mechanical inventions of the sixteenth century. Attempts to bring the physical reality of vision and movement under the purview of mathematical reasoning long faced a paradox of apparent success and real failure. Each successful step forward revealed a new area of reality that resisted the completion of mathematization. Sixteenth-century artisan-"engineers" were only too aware of the gap separating speculative mathematics from concrete reality. The concepts with which the mathematician works, they acknowledged in frustration, "are not subject to those impediments, which by nature are always conjoined to the matter which is worked on by the artisan"[30] (figure 6.5). For these reasons, Renaissance perspective and mechanics, like the arts, can be called "sciences" only by analogy. True sciences in the modern sense are concerned with universal reality and require explicit proof. Perspective and artisan mechanics, in contrast, are concerned with particular situations, with human works and operations, and with contingent things.

If we take into account the actual practice of Renaissance perspective and mechanics, rather than stressing how they are presented in textbooks, we see them as arts, deeply influenced and informed by science. But unlike science or emancipated technique, art deals with direct experience and with the probable. It belongs to the primary mode of embodiment—to the visible world, to which it ultimately refers for its meaning, relevance, and success. That indirect or partial mathematization did not alter this focus shows the limits of the mathematization and technization of the traditional arts.[31] As long as the arts were situated in the life of society, they could not become a subject of mathematical understanding and control, and to that extent their

6.5. Agostino Ramelli, *Le diverse et artificiose machine* (1588), pl. 9, water-raising machine.

technicization remained partial and limited (figure 6.6). Only the direct mathematization of reality could remove these limits.

It was in the second half of the sixteenth century that such a project became, for the first time, a genuine possibility. The initial inspiration came from the middle sciences, when the old and jealously guarded boundaries between mathematics and physics were crossed.[32] However, the most decisive change took place within mathematics itself, particularly in the sphere of algebra, which had developed into a "universal mathematics."[33] This change was complemented by similar changes within metaphysics, where the *prima philosophia* became a "universal science." Universal mathematics became the mathematical equivalent of traditional logic. Because universal mathematics operates with the pure essences of things, which are taken for simple magnitudes, formal essence becomes identical with pure mathematical essence/magnitude.

6.6. Hendrik Bleu (Bles), *Landscape with the Ironworks* (1544).

Under these conditions, universal mathematics could lay claim to the same area of knowledge as traditional logic—in other words, to all possible knowledge.[34] But in its mathematical form, the idea of all possible knowledge is very different from traditional dialectical or demonstrative knowledge. It aims to explain things only in terms of order and measure, regardless of their material and qualitative nature. Because of the universality of such a claim, universal mathematics already in the sixteenth century had earned the name "queen of sciences" (*regina scientiarum*), sometimes elevated to *scientia divina* or *ars divina*.[35] These lofty titles could not convince without supporting evidence from the physical world. As in mathematics, the development of knowledge in sixteenth-century physics underwent a radical change. The traditional distinction between divine and human knowledge was weakened to such an extent that it became possible to speak of physics and metaphysics in the same terms.[36] The affinity between the metaphysical interpretation of physics and universal mathematics was reflected in the new understanding and use of the *scientiae mediae,* particularly mechanics. Contrary to a widely held opinion, the usefulness of mechanics was secondary to its primary meaning—the understanding and representation of movement in the created world.

The continuity of movement between the celestial and terrestrial domains played a critical role, first in Aristotelianism and later in scholastic metaphysics; the latter was decisive in the formation of modern mechanics.[37] Only with great effort can we now comprehend the complexity and importance of movement in the seventeenth-century vision of reality. The enigma of creation, the manifestation of the divine order in the terrestrial world, and the continuity of this order were all related to the phenomenon of movement. Movement was seen not only as a universal principle of reality but also as the efficient cause of everything persisting in life. The divine origin of movement was not yet in doubt, nor was the long-standing view that divine reality manifested itself as an eternal truth that could eventually be grasped as mathematical truth. Descartes wrote: "Mathematical truths which you call eternal were established by God and depend on him entirely like all other created beings. Do not hesitate to assert and proclaim it everywhere that it is God who set up these laws in nature as the king sets up laws in his kingdom."[38] Attempts at understanding these laws were strongly influenced, if not determined, by the new idea of knowledge—knowing by making. In other words, universal reality could be known by the art by which it was made. In Descartes's own words, "God's will, understanding and creation are one and the same thing; none is prior to another, even conceptually."[39] The identity of understanding and creation was the final condition needed to make mechanics the critical discipline in shaping modern science and technology.

A metaphysical quest, not utilitarian or technical interests, gave mechanics its privileged position. It was in the domain of mechanics that the mathematization of physical movement was explored and finally accomplished. The tendency to treat physical reality and movement as predictable and potentially mathematical was motivated by the growing desire to discover more tangible links between human and divine reality—which, in Galileo's time, meant more tangible links between physical and mathematical reality. In Galileo's *Dialogue,* we find the following exchange: "I still say, with Aristotle, that in physical (*naturali*) matters one need not always require a mathematical demonstration." "Granted, where none is to be had; but when there is one at hand, why do you not wish to use it?" Galileo himself answers the possible objections: "As to heaven, it is in vain that you fear for that which you yourself hold to be inalterable and invariant. As for the earth, we seek rather to ennoble and perfect it when we strive to make it like the celestial bodies, and, as it were, place it in heaven, from which your philosophers have banished it. Philosophy itself cannot but benefit from our disputes, for if our conceptions prove true, new achievements will be made; if false, their rebuttal will further confirm the original doctrines."[40]

The key to Galileo's achievement is that he performed a mathematical demonstration in a domain that had traditionally been considered to be only contingent. This demonstration, which was radically new, can best be described as a dialogue between an a priori mathematical formula and idealized physical reality. In this dialogue, the mathematical formula, used as a hypothesis (as an argument *ex suppositione*), is followed by an approximation and anticipation of the physical result.[41] On the physical side of the experimental dialogue, phenomena are simplified through abstraction until the approximate mathematical form is free of all difficult material impediments and circumstances. For example, Galileo describes how he approaches the conditions of free fall: "A more considerable disturbance arises from the impediment of the medium; by reason of its multiple varieties, this is impossible to subject to firm rules, understood, and made into science. . . . No firm science can be given of such events as heaviness, speed, and shape which are variable in infinitely many ways. Hence, to deal with such matters scientifically, it is necessary to abstract from them."[42]

Galileo's experimental method and its potential rigor confront a deep ambiguity that can be eliminated only when physical impediments can be successfully abstracted. But such abstraction is not always possible—certainly not to a sufficient degree. To that extent, Galileo's mechanics remains a promise and, even in its best moments, a rigorous hypothetical discipline rather than a rigorous science. It contains an enigmatic element that cannot be completely eliminated. The enigma has much to do with the process of mathematization, specifically with the nature of the experimental dialogue. Experimental reasoning replaces an explicit with an implicit demonstration, in which one need not take into account or know all the circumstances, conditions, and causes of a particular phenomenon or event (for example, irregular movement). What need not be known remains hidden, because this omission also remains unknown to the understanding—and therefore an enigma.

For these reasons, the experimental dialogue is better viewed as the result of intellectual craftsmanship than of a rigorous philosophy or science. Thus the *topos* of the workshop or laboratory is a more appropriate vehicle for understanding the nature of modern science and technology than the *topos* of the study (figure 6.7). The laboratory is a place where nature is systematically transformed into idealized models. In a world that has been transformed into a laboratory, construction and making become the privileged form of knowing.

As ideal places for conducting experimental dialogue, the workshop and the laboratory represent a new, secondary mode of reality where new rules of knowledge can be developed. Unlike traditional knowledge, which was cultivated in a dialogue with the phenomenal reality, the new rules are articulated in a relatively closed world of the experimental dialogue. The imaginary nature of this new world is emphasized by Descartes himself: "For a short time, therefore, allow your thought to leave this world in order to come to see a wholly new one, which I shall cause to be born in the presence of your thought in imaginary spaces." As for the nature of knowledge or science that can be developed in these new "imaginary spaces," Descartes again tells us what is possible and what is anticipated: "By science I understand skill at resolving all questions and in inventing by one's own industry everything in that science that can be invented by human ingenuity (*ars inveniendi*). Whoever has this science does not desire much else foreign to it, and indeed is quite properly called *autarches*—self-sufficient."[43] The science invented by human ingenuity is a construct. It is productive, motivated by an ambition to be nothing less than a *creatio ex nihilo,* a status traditionally linked only with divine creativity. However, what is traditionally true for the divine is now considered to be also true, or at least possible, for humans. In other words, we know and can create, at least in principle, as God knows and creates.

This new level of confidence has its origins in a deep metaphysical faith in the mathematical nature of reality sanctioned by divine presence. Without such faith, a drastically simplified vision and representation of re-

6.7. Pieter Bruegel the Elder, *Alchemist* (1558).

ality would not have been possible. It resulted, somewhat unintentionally, in a new method of producing knowledge, relying on experimental reasoning that perceived no bounds. The simplified vision of reality was identified already by Descartes and his contemporaries as the idea. "Idea," he writes, "was the term I used because it was the familiar philosophical term for the forms of which the divine Mind is aware (*'formas perceptionum mentis divinae'*)."[44]

In my own interpretation, the Cartesian "idea" not only represents a new vision of reality and a new type of knowledge but also stands at the origin of modern technology. The unlimited possibilities of invention opened by experimental dialogue have their source in the infinity of will, which for Descartes is a direct analogy of the human and the divine. Its full meaning, according to a twentieth-century philosopher, is "most visibly displayed in the programmatically anticipated infinity of artifices through which the new sciences are to prove their credentials."[45]

An openness to future possibilities was the foundation of the idea of progress and, on a deeper level, of the intramundane eschatology of modern technology.[46] The convergence of the infinity of will and the infinity of artifices enabled thinkers to fulfill their ambition to understand given reality as a priori and whole, and from a clearly defined position. A modern historian observes, "Applying knowledge-through-construction to the whole world was an inevitable as it was dangerous. It was dangerous because it makes mankind be 'like God, knowing good and evil.' Many seventeenth century philosophers shunned its inevitable consequences, but only the Occasionalists had the courage to deny categorically that this kind of knowledge reveals reality."[47] In a sense, we have not progressed beyond the seventeenth-century philosophers. We do not yet understand the real nature of the experimental knowledge on which modern technology is based, because we have difficulty following the transformation of reality and the nature of its representation in a picture (model) from which all but efficient causes have been eliminated and in which the qualitative diversity of phenomena has been reduced to a mathematical interpretation of matter in motion. There is a gap between the domain of situated knowledge and that of productive knowledge. This gap, which represents a radical discontinuity with the natural world, reduces the cognitive value of productive knowledge and makes it merely a technical tool. To be sure, such a tool can lead to the most sophisticated achievements imaginable: consider, for example, nuclear research, or the current breakthroughs in genetics or electronics. However, productive knowledge has its overwhelming success only when dealing with phenomena susceptible to mathematical treatment.

The limits of productive knowledge are reflected in the uneven development of individual disciplines, especially in their different degrees of the mathematization of reality and thus their disparate reliance on technology. Architecture itself can serve as a good example here.

ARCHITECTURAL SITUATIONS AND ENGINEERING SYSTEMS

The individual aspects of architecture belong to a very heterogenous spectrum of knowledge and to technologies with very different degrees of sophistication. Under such conditions, the extension of instrumental thinking into the whole field of architecture took place slowly. Only in very specialized areas did the process of technization have initial success. These successes included factories, railway stations, exhibition halls, and structures that can be treated as engineering problems. Other areas of the field—mostly those of greater complexity, or dominated by values more deeply rooted in the cultural tradition—cannot be treated in the same way. The disparity can be seen in the development of modern cities, where traditional culture is to a greater extent introverted and confined to the private domain, leaving public space problematic and often meaningless in its anonymity. Because technology approves of anonymity, it could be applied more easily in the public domain. As a result, the anonymous areas of modern cities better reveal the impact of technological thinking and development than do residential areas or private buildings. The transformations of cities during the nineteenth century—unlike their earlier improvements, which were slower and partial—were for the first time systematic and truly comprehensive. The fundamental difference lay in the new possibility of interpreting urban space in terms of self-referential structures, ensembles, and systems. As they form, modern systems follow the paradigm of the laboratory experiment, based on the principle of transparent knowledge; the paradigm of the laboratory applies insofar as reality can be represented as a system. And yet only the actual conditions of particular cases can determine how far a system can be extended and to what extent the given reality can be incorporated in a convincing representation.

Consider the development of railways in the nineteenth century, and in particular their extension into the cities; railways stand in sharp contrast not only to earlier forms of transport, such as roads or canals, but also to the traditional character of the surrounding landscape and the urban fabric that it confronts (figure 6.8). Unlike roads or canals, built in a close dialogue with given conditions and the landscape, railways were designed as comprehensive systems. Designing such a system requires a plan that determines everything beforehand such that the project follows its a priori logic. Nothing from outside the chosen system can interfere with its coherence and with its workings. For railways, this amounted to creating an autonomous world in which the network of tracks, rolling stock, stations, yards, and signaling devices might be synchronized and made totally

6.8. Railway viaducts in Southwark, London, aerial view.

predictable and reliable. Under such conditions, together with a specially trained staff, trains could operate any time of the day, every day of the year, in all kinds of weather and to a precise timetable. Nothing so perfect could be achieved in the day-to-day world. Not surprisingly railways became a paradigm for the development of many areas of modern technology. Examples of similar undertakings include large-scale water and sewage systems, public transportation, telegraph and telephone networks, and large corporations.

The self-sufficiency and perfection of individual systems is one thing, but how they are mutually related and can be situated in the real world is another. The modern city exemplifies the problem. If we look at the parts of cities where railways were built more than century ago, we discover that the rational clarity of the original intentions has led to urban landscapes of great complexity, difficult to comprehend. These are far from the terrestrial paradise envisioned by the technicians and planners of the nineteenth

6.9. Railway bridge in Camden Town, London.

century. There is likewise an element of surreality in the spaces developed against arbitrarily introduced viaducts, built into an already-existing city fabric (figure 6.9). However, the complexity of these spaces, their arbitrary and chaotic nature, reveals a certain logic: the logic of the intersection of two different horizons of order and rationality. One represents the rationality of the disengaged autonomous world, the other the rationality of everyday life.

If we extend what is true for the railways to technological systems in general, we see a key problem of technology. Its dual productive and creative nature is revealed in its complexity. We have noted that complexity is often the result of an attempt to reconcile different spheres of reality. If the reconciliation is successful, the whole situation may be enriched; if it is not, complexity remains as only an unfulfilled promise of richness. Complexity can be produced, but richness must be created. The history of the Eiffel Tower illustrates how difficult and rare is the creative reconciliation of an

6.10. Eiffel Tower, the first elevator section, detail.

autonomous abstract structure within the cultural context of a city (figure 6.10). As we know, the tower was seen at the time of its construction and immediately after as an alien and intrusive object on the Parisian landscape. Yet only a few decades later, the same tower was hailed as a symbol of Paris. How did this happen? The change certainly cannot be explained as part of some automatic process of adaptation, as many similar structures have remained alien, with little likelihood of being accepted (television towers in many European cities are as good an example as any). In the case of the

6.11. Robert Delaunay, *The Eiffel Tower* (1910–1911).

Eiffel Tower, the distance between its abstract appearance and the richness of the Parisian culture was articulated in incremental stages by the life that developed in relation to the tower; in paintings, films, literature, poetry, and music; and to some extent even in philosophy.[48] As the original gap closed, the isolated structure took its place in the communicative space of the city. Blaise Cendrars commented on the famous series of paintings by Robert Delaunay, "Delaunay wanted to show not only the tower but to situate it in Paris"[49] (figure 6.11). This comment may be reinforced by Le Corbusier's appraisal in 1925: "The Eiffel Tower has entered the domain of architecture. In 1889 it was the aggressive expression of calculation. In 1900 the aesthetes wanted to demolish it. In 1925 it dominates the Art Deco exhibition. Rising above the plaster palaces with their twisted decor it looks pure as a crystal."[50]

The history of the Eiffel Tower is obviously not typical, but it nonetheless illustrates the deep and very often intricate relationship between technology and culture, which in most cases remains hidden. We forget that in both the design and the appreciation of engineering structures we are dealing not with isolated realities but with a whole spectrum of structural possibilities situated in the framework of a particular technological system of thought, which is itself situated in the broader field of culture. Each design begins in the phenomenal world, because that is the only place where communication is possible and where memory, imagination, and thought have their source.[51]

Engineering disciplines enjoy the privilege of ignoring the phenomenal world to concentrate only on elements relevant to their narrow viewpoint. These are mainly the structural and material parameters of the envisaged structures and the criteria of performance. The contemporary engineering approach to design grows out of a process that has lasted at least two hundred years, in which the concreteness of the primary human situation was transformed through idealization and abstraction into its schematic equivalent. The openness of modern architecture to such a development reinforced the illusion not only that an abstract instrumental representation of architectural problems might offer a plausible solution but that such a solution might be unconditional and self-sufficient.[52]

The limits of this illusion are revealed when we compare the instrumental and architectural approaches to the design of a particular space. Architectural interpretation always begins with some vision of how to structure the anticipated space in its context and takes into account the brief, the site conditions, and the possible form of structure and materials—all factors simultaneously and reciprocally pertaining to the quality and purpose of the space. Architectural design also remains an open dialogue between the initial conditions and the space's emerging configuration. The process is in many ways similar to acts of interpretation in other areas of culture, particularly in the humanities, where dialogue and deliberation are fundamental.

The instrumental advantage of the engineering approach, by contrast, quite clearly becomes a disadvantage in the context of a real space. There are no techniques for grasping its concreteness and simultaneity. Only two options seem to be available. One is an instrumental representation of space, which focuses on its diagrammatical or geometrical configuration; the second is to reduce space to its elements, as far as they can be defined and then recomposed. In both cases the original situational structure of space is transformed into a system. It is only on that level of abstraction that an engineering approach can be useful. And yet, even the most abstract engineering structures depend on a dialogue with the initial conditions characteristic of the architectural approach, which despite everything retains a certain validity in the domain of engineering. Any good engineer would almost instinctively transcend the requirements of a given brief by taking into account the unquantifiable conditions of the site, as well as the social and cultural implications of the proposed structure. However, his or her broader thought would probably dwell most on the side of professional responsibility, measured by the criteria of cost, performance, and perhaps also aesthetics—that is, by the criteria of efficient, closed systems. The tendency to bring all considerations, regardless of how unquantifiable, into the framework of the defined system illustrates the limitation of engineering thinking.

A deeper understanding of the relationship between architecture and engineering is particularly rewarding, because, in Heidegger's words again, it illustrates how "the essential reflection upon technology and decisive coming to terms with it must happen in a realm which is on the one hand akin to the essence of technology, and on the other fundamentally different from it"; he adds, "such a realm is art."[53] If by "art" is meant not only fine art, then architecture should be included in its domain. But why should architecture come to terms with technology when most believe that architecture and technology are already identical, or will be in the future?

We have seen that the structure of space depends on the embodied spatiality of the natural world, that meaning depends on the spontaneity of communication and generally on a high level of articulation and the continuity of embodiment. It is one of the paradoxes of our time that as a large number of architects ascend the steps of emancipation toward the zone of purer technological possibilities, they meet a large number of engineers moving in the opposite direction in order to grasp the deeper ground and broader context of their own field and operations. It is no coincidence that architects are proud to act like engineers while many engineers are proud to call themselves architects. We have reached a point at which it does not much matter what we call ourselves and who does what, as long as we understand that the higher we want to build the deeper the foundations must be, that the notion of technological autonomy is only an idea, and that coming to terms with technology is possible only by coming to terms with the conditions of our earthbound cultural existence.

This understanding will be particularly important and useful in the coming years, which are likely to be dominated by new dreams of emancipation boosted by the electronic revolution. The new generation of dreams is allied to new possibilities of instrumental representation, in which not only the formal structure but also the physiognomy of reality can be manipulated through reproduction and simulation (figure 6.12). The "realistic" appearance of the results unintentionally promotes a misleading belief in the adequacy of representation, based on an illusion of the representational adequacy and unity of abstract simulations. In the new generation of illusions and dreams, the traditional unity of representation and what is represented is seen no longer as resulting from a dialectical process of revelation, but as indicating the direct presence of reality. This is a logical fulfillment of the experimental productive mentality, which assumes that we can understand only what we can make. Therefore only what can be produced is real.[54]

Against this background we can better grasp the visions of the immediate future, as produced not by writers of science fiction but by researchers in the most respectable and influential institutions in the field. The following is a good example:

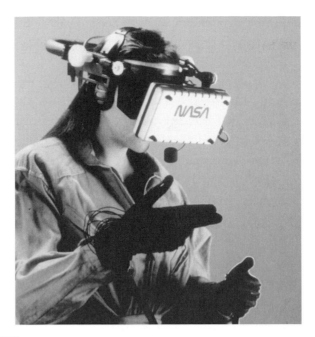

6.12. Virtual reality simulation, NASA.

We are entering an era of electronically extended bodies living at the intersection points of the physical and virtual worlds, of occupation and interaction through telepresence as well as through physical presence of mutant architectural forms that emerge from the telecommunications-induced fragmentation and re-combination of traditional architectural types and of new, soft cities that parallel, complement and sometimes compete with our existing urban concentration of brick, concrete and steel.[55]

The critical term in this vision is "telepresence," which understood onto-logically marks a transformation of the traditional fabric of architecture, including our own corporeal involvement, into a "new" kind of reality struc-tured by electronic media in which "computers will weld seamlessly into the fabric of buildings and buildings themselves will become computers—the outcome of a long evolution. It will become meaningless to ask where the smart electronics end and the dumb construction begins. Architects will increasingly confront practical choices between providing for bodily presence and relying on telepresence."[56]

Such a vision need not be taken too seriously, but it would be naive to ignore it. Regardless of its consequences, this form of instrumental representation already plays an important role in current design and planning. The question that needs to be addressed, and is not very easy to answer, is how the new electronic representations differ from the traditional ones; to what extent are they only more sophisticated tools, or do they rather represent something altogether different? There is no doubt that even the most advanced forms of representation are ultimately only tools, because they contribute to the representation of the given reality and only indirectly to its transformation. They are certainly not independent. They are more involved with, and reflect more clearly the conditions and limits of, our imagination and thinking than any earlier modes of representation. The belief that concrete involvement can be replaced by skillful imitation of our intellectual abilities depends entirely on the high degree of knowledge and understanding that makes such imitation possible.

This brings the assumptions of instrumental representation, and indirectly of technology, to a real test. The critical understanding of these assumptions has its own history, particularly in the domain of philosophy, but this seems to have been ignored by the proponents of digital representation. In the domain of productive knowledge, philosophical understanding usually doesn't count for much.[57] There, the only convincing argument seems to be an experimental demonstration, but thus far such demonstration have not proven very successful. Unsuccessful results are nevertheless useful in showing how intricate are human perception, orientation in space, and intelligence. We see that intricacy in architecture, when architects attempt to design intelligent buildings and experiment with the virtual reality of space. In both instances the results depend on the knowledge of our experience of space, the precondition of design.

Virtual reality in its more ambitious forms follows the principles of artificial intelligence, and to that extent shares its limits. Producing a complete and authentic simulation of human intelligence—adequate perception, recognition of meaning, orientation in space, and knowledge of the world—is proving to be more difficult than was once thought. The basic difficulty is the discrepancy between human knowledge of reality, which is mostly implicit, and its explicit representation.[58] In digital simulation, discrete data or complete data structures, simulated perspective, color, texture, edge quality, illumination, light, haze, and movement are commonly represented as clearly defined, and integrated in a program structured by explicit rules. What is impossible to simulate is the context in which the defined data and elements are situated. To appreciate just how complicated the explicit representation of the context is, we should recall the discussion in chapter 2 of the transformation of space in inverted vision, where only a small part of the process could be explicitly articulated and understood. The main part, as we have seen, was hidden to our view and could take place only through slow adaptation and learning. The logic of the transformation is still a mystery that resists clear description.

A similar situation, which illustrates even better the problematic nature of virtual reality, is the recovery of sight after an operation (also discussed in chapter 2). We have seen that recovery of the retinal image is not sufficient for proper vision. Such vision can be acquired only through a process of adaptation in which visual, kinesthetic, and tactile experiences are coordinated in a long and very often painful learning process. This evidences the depth and plasticity of normal vision—as well as its fundamental difference from the visual experience in virtual reality, which consists of context-free information and images produced following the principles of retinal photo images. In order to be plausible, the simulated experience of reality must be initiated and completed in the domain of a situated human experience and existence. These are the conditions that any electronic device will have to reproduce in order to claim autonomy. To achieve full autonomy, notes a critic of artificial intelligence, the electronic device would have to be "a learning device that shares human concerns and human structure to learn, to generalize the way human beings do. And as improbable as it was that one could build a device that could capture our humanity in a physical symbol system, it seems at least as unlikely that one could build a device sufficiently like us to act and learn in our world."[59]

To perceive, to move, and to learn in the human world is possible only because of our corporeal involvement. The disembodied nature of computer programs is the main reason for their inability to match human intelligence. This is acknowledged, though only indirectly, in the attempts to simulate larger segments of the environment. Because "it turned out to be very difficult to reproduce in an internal representation for a computer the necessary richness of environment," the researchers concluded that "it is easier and cheaper to build a hardware robot to extract what information it needs from the real world than to organize and store a useful model." This led inevitably to the further conclusion "that the most economic and efficient store of information about the real world is the real world itself."[60] Despite its problems and limited relevance, artificial intelligence is an important turning point in the development of modern technology. It is the last sphere of reality that has not yet been directly technicized, a sphere where technology finds its ideal fulfillment but also its limits. "The recent difficulties in artificial intelligence," the same critic writes, "rather than reflecting technological limitations, may reveal the limitations of technology."[61]

The awareness demonstrated in his conclusion is rare. Society today is dominated by faith in the unlimited possibilities of technology, including artificial intelligence. The monopoly of the computer paradigm presents as fundamental a danger of dogmaticism and naive optimism as that of the Newtonian paradigm at the beginning of the eighteenth century. In both cases, one-sided and overoptimistic expectations tend to override any other avenue to truth, with much the same consequences—a painful weakening and impoverishment of culture. In other words, to quote the critic again, "if a computer paradigm becomes so strong that people begin to think of themselves as digital devices on the model of work in artificial intelligence, then, since machines cannot be like human beings, human beings may become progressively like machines. Our risk is not the advent of super-intelligent computers, but of sub-intelligent human beings."[62] The potential for this danger is present in all areas of modern technology, though in more or less explicit and conclusive forms. Most often it manifests itself as a monologue of instrumental thinking, accepted as a universal approach to all possible questions and problems that may be encountered.

The belief in the universal power of instrumental reasoning is accompanied both by a search for originality and by a desire for the competitive advantages of new inventions. It is taken for granted that what is new and original must be the best and most appropriate. This assumption creates a strange situation, particularly in fields like architecture, where only certain areas are susceptible to radical technological change while others remain relatively stable. Technology tends to develop in areas that can be more easily rationalized, that are technically more interesting, and that offer a better market return. Architecture has only a very limited influence on what is produced—somewhat paradoxically, in view of the difficulties and the time it takes to make new materials and new structures architecturally relevant. To understand how difficult, intricate, and controversial this process of transformation and adaptation is, consider the phenomenon of transparency.

Since the beginning of the twentieth century, transparency has been hailed as a main characteristic of truly modern buildings. However, it is doubtful that architectural conditions or requirements played any important role in initiating this development; it was determined rather by new ways of using concrete and steel in frame structures, by the resulting redundancy of load-bearing walls, and by a growing indifference to the physiognomy of buildings (figure 6.13). From an architectural point of view, transparency is certainly welcome in situations where a high level of unobstructed visibility or light is required, but this is not true everywhere. In many parts of buildings, larger areas of surface and solid enclosures are equally desirable. However, once the process of making, as determined by material and structural reasons, is established, transparency turns into a predictable aim. It becomes an aspect of a value-free style and eventually an emancipated symbolic representation of modernity.

The present tendency to use ingenious and complex structures to perform relatively banal tasks, or to use elaborate lightweight structures where they are not needed, can only be explained by pointing not to technical or architectural motives, but to deeper reasons. One, I believe, is the desire for emancipation and autonomy, mentioned earlier. The emancipation from history and from the implicit, unquantifiable conditions of design finds its fulfillment in the transformation of buildings into structures approaching the transparency of pure concepts.

Such transparency of concepts expresses the will to eliminate from design everything that cannot be calculated or controlled. This brings us to one of the more mysterious characteristics of contemporary architecture—its fascination with those aspects of design that can be treated like disengaged problems of construction and its tendency to suppress, almost

6.13. Bryan Avery, IMAX cinema, Waterloo, London.

instinctively, everything that is beyond our control, namely the material and spatial reality of the results.

The tendency toward idealization and disembodiment, so prevalent among contemporary architects and designers, may be compared with the most recent developments in artificial intelligence and the attempts of contemporary technology to simulate the conditions of embodiment. Technological thinking has to examine itself in order to understand the conditions of its own inner possibilities—mainly the limits of emancipation and disembodiment and, by implication, the ambiguous nature of the technologically constructed illusion of wholeness. As the philosopher Jacques Ellul declares,

> The wholes established by technology do not make us feel complete or satisfied, they are still experienced as splintered wholes. Here and there, man recognizes and greets a fragment of his former universe, integrated in a functional but alien and anonymous whole, in which he nevertheless must live. There is no other. Against that feeling and splintering, modern man feels a keen desire for all-inclusiveness, for synthesis. But, alas, any synthesis produced by technology fails and comes to naught.[63]

• CHAPTER 7 •

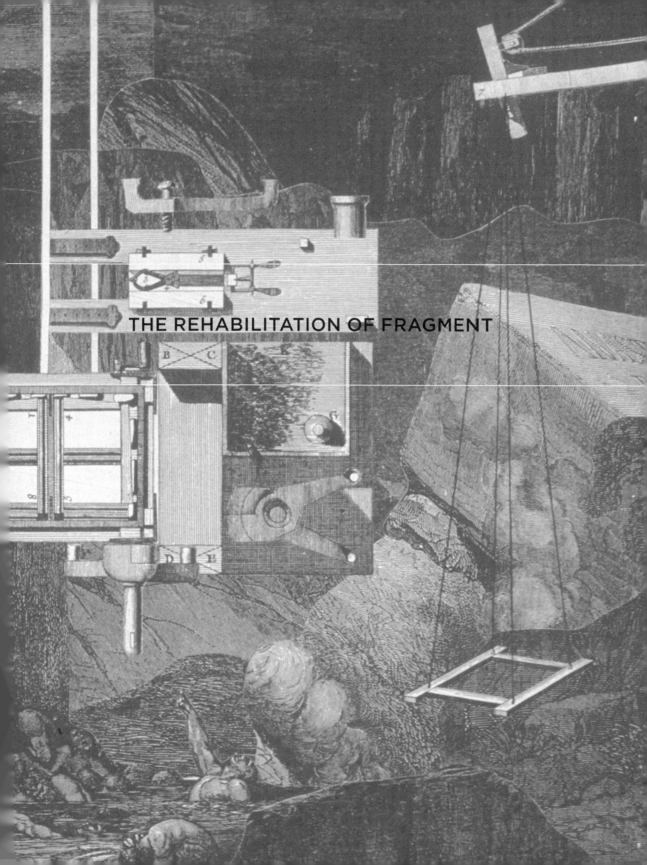

THE REHABILITATION OF FRAGMENT

C ONSIDERATION OF the fragment is today usually assimilated into the more universal question of fragmentation. It is not difficult to recognize that fragmentation is one of the main characteristics of our modern predicament. There is a tendency to see fragmentation as a result of isolation and disintegration and thus as potential chaos. Yet we must also account for the fact that in so many areas of culture apparent fragmentation has played the opposite role, contributing to the formation of meaning and a sense of wholeness. We need think only of the works of Synthetic Cubism, Surrealism, and the art of collage or of similar tendencies and achievements in contemporary literature, poetry, music, and to some extent architecture. All these illustrate that the phenomenon of fragmentation has more than one meaning and that mere appearance is not a sufficient criterion by which to judge which of them is before us.

Thus, for instance, a collage can under some circumstances be seen as arbitrary, chaotic, and rather meaningless, while under different conditions of understanding it can represent a meaningful configuration (figure 7.1). The ambiguous meaning of elements or fragments is a manifestation of a much deeper ambiguity, which is related to a more authentic notion of the meaning of an object or artwork. The ambiguity of objects was called by André Breton a "crisis of the object." Breton takes as his point of departure the positivistic state of the object, which has been reduced to an unsituated, quantifiable entity, without particular qualities or particular meaning. As a first step, he expresses his strong reservations about the hegemony of the cogito by revealing that the recognition of the marvelous characteristics of the object is not limited, in his understanding, to the domain of dreams and poetic experience, but extends to the realm of science: "One cannot fail to be struck by the fact that it was in 1870 that mathematicians elaborated a generalized geometry which included Euclidean geometry as part of a comprehensive system and so retrieved it from its contemporary eclipse. This involved the same kind of transcended contradiction which Lautrémont and Rimbaud used, in a different field, as a means of achieving a total disruption of existing sensibility."[1]

This disruption of sensibility is well illustrated in the early work of Giorgio de Chirico, whose art is dreamlike but never coincides with the main intention of a dream. Its mysterious meaning has its source in the intriguing construction, a "metaphysical" geometry that, at a certain point,

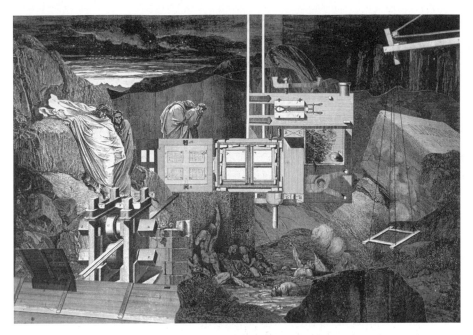

7.1. Robert Wood, preparatory metaphorical study for the project of an ecological research center.

collapses into ambiguity. Based on a systematic exploration of traditional perspective, the world of his paintings and drawings is disturbing in its precise definition of the space that separates individual elements or fragments, establishing, in de Chirico's own words, "a new astronomy of objects, attached to the planet only by the fatal law of gravity."[2]

What Breton termed the "shock wave" of this art, its resonance, can be discerned in recent architectural projects and proposals. The drawings consist very often of no more than fragments of potential objects, which come to exist only through the process of transformation and projection—or, to use one architect's words, "deconstructive constructions."[3] It is not surprising that the approach used in such drawings derives quite often from the tradition of perspective anamorphosis, from projective geometry, and more recently from digital simulation, making it possible to follow visually the intentionality of thought far into imagined realities. What we are witnessing are the same stirrings of thought rebelling against established habits of thinking seen in Breton's "crisis of the object." In both instances, "the object ceases to be fixed permanently on the near side of thought and re-creates itself on the further side as far as the eye can reach."[4] The conventional meaning of individual elements in the drawings is subordinated to their transformational and potentially metaphorical meaning. The close links between the metaphorical meanings of individual elements in the process of rational construction are surprising. Such ambiguity can serve as a point of departure for a clearer understanding of the nature and meaning of the fragment.

THE ORIGINS OF FRAGMENTATION

The emergence of the fragment as a significant phenomenon can be traced back to the origins of perspective. We have already examined some of the stages in the development of perspective that eventually extended the possibilities of the new representation into all areas of culture. In this process, the reality represented appears as a "picture" that can be treated as an object experienced by a single subject. The apparent objectivity of the picture is guaranteed not by reference to represented reality, but only by the objectivity of the representation. This is a source of a modern illusion that the world as a whole can be reduced to a picturelike representation, fully accessible to a disengaged subject—seen in the seventeenth century as an isolated monad, and by the Romantics as a self-sufficient fragment. The close relationship between the new mode of representation and the disengaged subject demonstrates that the fragment cannot in fact be seen as an isolated thing or object but can be seen only in relation to the experiencing person: in other words, the fragment always has a situational structure. This situatedness is acknowledged in one of the first treatises on projective geometry, where we find a page illustrating the newly emerging meaning of the fragment (figure 7.2).

The contrast between the identity of experience and the silence of the isolated figures serves as a paradigm of the new vision of the world. However, to make this vision a genuine form of knowledge and understanding, the seventeenth century relied on faith. This faith was most clearly expressed in the concept of the monad. Each monad was seen as a spiritual universe, an isolated and perfectly self-sufficient world; each was a different

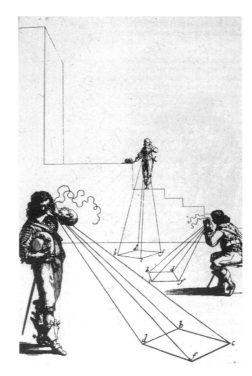

7.2. Abraham Bosse, *Manière universelle de Monsieur Desargues* (1648), pl. 2.

expression of the same universe. Everything in the monad was determined internally and therefore required no direct experience. As Leibniz remarks, "monads have no windows, by which anything could come in or go out."[5] The law that relates monads to one another, known as "preestablished harmony," was grounded in the belief that God has acted on the being of monads in such a way as to make their perceptions correspond to one another. The difference between individual monads is directly related to the point of view from which the universe is seen.

The loss of faith in the original meaning of preestablished harmony left behind no more than mathematical laws of reality, the promise of universal knowledge, and isolated perceptions. The result, as we know too well, is modern pluralism, the fragmentation of scientific knowledge and human experience. The reality of the modern world is divided into isolated areas of specialized knowledge and the specialized production of fragmented realities. But such specialization and fragmentation are not intentional; they are inevitably produced by modern knowledge, a paradoxical outcome of the ideal of mathematical universality, which can be achieved only piecemeal. The process of fragmentation is thus like an unwanted guest, a by-product of an underlying tendency in the evolution of modernity. As such it must be accepted as destiny.

Fragmentation is a distinctly modern phenomenon. Today, it appears almost everywhere, even where we are unaware of it. Its manifestations can be misleading and obscure; a fragment can appear as an object, as a structure, or as a complete and coherent system (figure 7.3). A building or large development, for instance, may appear complete, well-integrated, and unified, while in reality it is only a large fragment, unsituated and empty of any particular meaning. Simulated situations often have an effect contrary to that intended. The simulated integrity of an artificial setting (Disneyland, for instance) creates a fragment rather than a theatrical stage set. That simulated integrity increases fragmentation is not always recognized as detrimental, partly because it is difficult to assess its true nature and partly because the original situation from which the fragment was abstracted is always present, at least potentially, in a latent form. The memory of the original situation can only be suppressed, as happens in science, or restored, as happens in poetry, art, or in genuine interpretation (hermeneutics). While science has discovered the instrumental analytical meaning of the fragment, it is to poetry that we have to turn to "discover" its restorative and symbolic meaning. Even though the analytical and synthetic (instrumental and symbolic) meanings of fragment belong together, their history is different—at least up to the end of the eighteenth century. The restorative or symbolic meaning of the fragment can be discerned already in the *spoglia* (spoils) so frequently used in the Middle Ages—equally in the collections of curiosities of the late Renaissance, or in the cult and poetics of ruins, which reached a peak in the eighteenth century.

What is common to all is the reference to the original context to which they belonged and which they represent. The fragment of a building, the torso of a sculpture, an object taken out of its context, and an artificial ruin often initiate symbolic meaning and reference more powerfully than does the piece intact in its original setting. Their power was recognized by

7.3. Houston, commercial center, view from Buffalo Bayou.

Diderot, who wrote, "one must ruin a palace in order to make it interesting."[6] Before the eighteenth century such a statement would not have been necessary, because each fragment was experienced as part of a whole (figure 7.4). What made such experience possible and interesting was the presence of a highly articulated world in which even the smallest element could send reverberations through the continuum of preexisting references. Under such conditions it would be perhaps more appropriate to speak of elements or parts rather than of fragments. The isolated column traditionally belongs to a particular order, the isolated keystone belongs to an arch or to a vault, and the same is true of other architectural elements.

7.4. Louis Carrogis (Carmontelle), Park Monceau, panoramic view.

Our current way of thinking, which seizes on isolated elements that can be combined at will, has its origin in the late eighteenth century, when the elements were treated for the first time as real fragments able to generate their own context. Today, the term "fragment" is used with reference to elements of any period. It is true that in the past, architectural elements were very often treated as independent; for instance, they were sometimes identified with individual letters of the alphabet.[7] This identification is interesting, for it shows that the apparently isolated nature of elements or letters is an illusion. The purpose of letters is not to speak for themselves but to constitute words, sentences, and discourse.[8] The same is true for the elements, but not for the modern fragment. The formation of the modern fragment is a historical process that cannot be identified with some mysterious qualities of objects or with our attitudes. It depends on possibilities of representation in which a part can be a believable equivalent of the whole, or at least a promise of the whole.

It was in the art of aphorism that the restorative meaning of fragment was first recognized as an intentional and creative possibility. The aphorism is a mode of symbolic representation that belongs to an era dominated by highly individualized and introverted experience, atomistic thought and feelings, an absence of commonly accepted religious beliefs and moral standards, and the general disintegration of traditional culture.[9] The modern cultural situation and the aphorism are strikingly parallel in nature. In both cases, fragments are endowed with meanings and values formerly resident in the whole. It is by virtue of an immanent—that is, self-conscious—interpretation that they cease to be fragments rather than by virtue of a belief in a transcendent whole. The aphorism is not just a figure of speech: it is a configuration of discourse, usually a short statement in which the primary topic is confronted by a secondary one. In the tension thus created, the commonsense meaning of the original topic is challenged—a challenge that makes possible a new imaginative interpretation and reading. The new reading can be metaphorical or reflective, and often it cannot be precisely identified or labeled. The truth revealed in an aphorism is primarily a truth of suggestion and sudden illumination. But the integration and wholeness that can be achieved through the fragmentary nature of the aphorism can be sustained only briefly. The real virtue of the aphorism is its heuristic quality, that is, its ability to discover a new relation and new insight into a personal world that may eventually become a common world.[10]

The difference between an aphorism and a fragment is in their means of articulation. While aphorisms are primarily literary or philosophical, fragments can be pictorial, musical, or architectural as well. But because the highest degree of articulation can be achieved in an aphorism, it remains for all fragments the measure of possible expression and of their latent meaning.[11] With this relationship between the aphorism and the fragment in mind, we recognize the real difference between the positive and negative meanings of fragments and can assess their restorative or reductive roles. Such assessment is particularly important in the visual domain, where the role of the fragment is much more difficult to judge because visual experience has a less explicit meaning than verbal experience (figure 7.5). In language, particularly in the language of everyday communication, sentences expect completion, and meaning is judged by the depth of the completed

7.5. Park Monceau, naumachia, current state.

reference. The period in which the fragment reached its full emancipation coincides, broadly speaking, with European Romanticism.

ROMANTICISM AND THE NEW SENSE OF FRAGMENT

The Romantic notion of the fragment is a logical culmination of Leibnizian monadology, and in a sense also a culmination of a long tradition of microcosmic speculation.[12] However, in the late eighteenth century, the monad and the microcosm are no longer regarded as analogous to the macrocosm but have become identical with it. This anthropocentric, emancipated mode of representation is the very essence of the modern fragment. In Friedrich Schlegel's words, "Many of the works of the ancients have become fragments. Many modern works are fragments as soon as they are written."[13]

The autonomy of the fragment is a result of a gradual transformation of the natural world into an immanent representation in which "a fragment like a miniature work of art has to be entirely isolated from the surrounding world and be complete in itself like a hedgehog."[14] We may wonder how the isolated fragment could be accepted as a miniature work of art and could substitute for the primary representation of the natural world. In poetry, which the Romantics considered to be the very essence of culture, "every whole can be a part and every part really a whole."[15] Most important among the conditions that made such a belief possible was the secularization of the idea of divine creativity. Already in the Renaissance, creativity could make man godlike; in the seventeenth century, man could play a god; now, at the end of the eighteenth century, man was for the first time treated as if he were a god.[16]

The new sense of creative freedom may explain why artists of the late eighteenth century moved away from the traditional imitation of cultural precedents and instead established a direct communication with nature or what was considered to be natural. With this change, the articulated continuum of the natural world was gradually replaced by individual experience, memory, and the ability to grasp the world through one's own resources. This new freedom was already identified by contemporaries as potential nihilism. Jean Paul Richter's diagnosis, in his *School of Aesthetics,* is so explicit that it is worth quoting in full:

It follows from the lawless capricious spirit of the present age, which would egoistically annihilate the world and the universe in order to clear a space merely for free play in the void and which tears off the bandage of its wounds as a bond, that this age must speak scornfully of the imitation and study of nature. When the history of an age gradually becomes unimportant to the historian and religion and patriotism are lost, then the arbitrariness of egotism must stumble at least on the hard, sharp commandments of reality. Then egotism prefers to flee into the desert of fantasy, where it finds no law to follow except its own narrower and pettier ones for the construction of rhyme and assonance. In our age, when God has set like the sun soon afterwards the world too passes into darkness. He who scorns the universe respects nothing more than himself and at night fears only his own creations.[17]

It is not surprising that the appropriate spatial setting for the self-centered mode of existence was the prison—not so much because it was feared but because it was conducive to dreams and expressive of a problematic search for identity.[18] Jean-Jacques Rousseau describes the ideal place to live as an island. "I could have desired that this place of refuge be made my life-long prison, that I be shut up here for the rest of my days," he writes, and then he asks the critical question: "What is the source of our happiness in such a state? Nothing external to us, nothing apart from ourselves and our own existence; as long as this state lasts we are self-sufficient like God."[19]

To be self-sufficient means to be able to appropriate the whole of history and culture and make them part of one's own world and to remain open to unlimited inventiveness—in other words, to be a true genius.[20] The concept of genius marks the transition from a long tradition of creative imitation to self-expression. In this transition the unity of representation, sustained by the communicative space of culture, was replaced by fragmentary individual achievements appearing to represent the world in its wholeness. The deep contradiction between the partiality and universality of representation is the main characteristic of the modern fragment.

We may understand these characteristics more clearly by comparing the unity of Baroque space with the state of its disintegration. The unity of Baroque space, as we have seen, was sustained by close communication between the word, the image, and the body, usually instantiated in a textual program, painting, sculpture, and architecture. In the process of communication, the decisive role was played by decor (ornament), which was akin to each of the arts but did not identify with any one of them. The fragile neutrality of decor exemplified in the creative role of late Baroque rocaille began to change with its secularization and naturalization. Both tendencies undermined the communicative and mediative role of rocaille by reducing it to the representation of primary natural powers.[21] Emancipated from the need to communicate, rocaille became a paradigm of creativity which manifested itself as quasi-painting, sculpture, or architecture (figure 7.6). This step marks the separation of the individual arts from one another and from their histories.[22]

In its different manifestations, rocaille could be identified as a protean element and universal creative power that could turn into anything

Die Erde.

N.16

La Terre.

I. W. Baumgartner, del.

Joh. Georg Hertel excud. A.V.

7.6. Johann Wolfgang Baumgartner, Earth rocaille.

from rocks, plants, and trees to living creatures. There is a close affinity between the manifestation of the creative powers of nature and the genius, who eventually becomes their sole expression. In the Romantic understanding, later taken up by the Expressionists and Surrealists, a modern scholar observes, "the creativity which brought forth independent and organically evolved works of art was given to the artist by 'great creative nature,' the productive force or originating spirit of the center of life. The artist could create *like* nature, because, being a force of this creative nature, he possessed in his soul an unconscious formative power which enabled him to identify himself with the formative energies of the world."[23]

Every work of art generated by rocaille appears to be unfinished, more like a fragment or ruin than a complete creation.[24] However, this unfinished nature is intentional, for it expresses the possibility of completion in the future in the same way that an organism attains fulfillment, wholeness, and perfection through growth.[25] The late-eighteenth-century fascination with fragments, torsos, and ruins cannot be explained simply as reflecting nostalgia for the past; rather, it is the discovery of a creative power that determines the rise and fall of civilizations, a power with which humans can identify.

The intentionally unfinished character of the fragment marks the distinction between the mimeticism and completeness of the artwork and the new sense of creativity based on the assumption that every artist is a representative of all humanity, and that every artwork is a representation of the universe in the process of becoming. As Paul Klee wrote of modern art in general, "our work is given form in order that it may be a functioning organism. To achieve the same as nature, though only in parallel. Not to compete with nature, but to produce something that says it *is as in* nature. There is no copying or reproducing, but rather transformation and new creation."[26]

The conviction that art and architecture give shape to an autonomous self-organizing process is a key source of the modern crisis of representation. This crisis is already apparent in the Romantic understanding of architecture. The Romantics saw architecture primarily as a response to natural conditions, needs, and an overall useful goal, but they also acknowledged that architecture was an art. Because art was viewed as indifferent to utility or purpose, the notion of architecture as an art posed an inherent self-contradiction.[27] To resolve it the Romantics had to invent an ingenious fiction about the sublimation of the original purpose and natural necessity reflected in the process of building as a higher form of representation, which Goethe named the poetic part of architecture. "Architecture," he declares, "is not an art of imitation, but rather an autonomous art; yet at the highest level it cannot do without imitation. It carries over the qualities of appearance of one material into another: every order of columns, for example, imitates building in wood; it carries over the characteristics of one building into another."[28]

In this mode of thought, architecture was treated as a self-sufficient organism which in the process of self-articulation imitated only itself. Regarded as an organism, architecture became a complex fragment in the process of becoming. This, I believe, is the historical origin of all later discussions concerning the autonomy of architecture as well as of the problematic tradition of organic architecture. The term "organic" remains ambiguous. In its earlier contrast to mechanism, it reflected the spontaneity and naturelike characteristics of artistic creativity. In Romantic interpretation, however, the organism became rather an abstract concept, closely linked to notions of organic totality and system. In Schlegel's words, "the more organic, the more systematic—though system is not some kind of form but the essence of the work itself."[29] Paradoxically, the sense of wholeness—without which the fragment could not be a fragment—was found in organic totality, seen as a construct and system.[30]

This is a point of departure for a better understanding of modern attempts to restore a sense of wholeness, particularly in the sphere of architecture. The failure of these attempts is manifested in the repeated effort to establish a collaboration between architecture, sculpture, painting, and other arts in the form of *Gesamtkunstwerk* and in the more recent effort to simulate a concrete human situation in the context of virtual space. This failure is grounded in the impossibility of substituting a system for the unity of culture—which is always situational and dependent on the continuity of communication. A good illustration of the problem is the limited success in preserving the unity of communicative space in the post-Baroque period. The unity that had been sustained by the continuity between conceptual representation and reality was seriously challenged by system-oriented thinking. As a result, astronomy first replaced traditional cosmology, and similar steps in other areas of culture followed. The ensuing fragmentation was more obvious in larger systems, in large structures, and in cities. The complexity and the scale of a system do not guarantee wholeness, because, as Schlegel writes, "even the largest system is after all only a fragment."[31]

It therefore follows that the fragment is not a goal but rather an incomplete project that aims for completion on a higher level of synthesis and

7.7. Karl Friedrich Schinkel, *Gothic Cathedral on a River* (1813) (copy by Wilhelm Ahlborn, 1823).

perfection, as part of an organic totality and system. Yet even systems, because we create them ourselves, are incomplete and finite. The desire to reach a level of absolute wholeness has led to the identification of fragments with ideas, seen by the Romantics as concepts of reason.[32]

Though concepts are created by humans, the Romantics believed that "ideas are infinite, independent, unceasingly moving in themselves, god-like thoughts," and that "only someone who has his own original way of looking at infinity can be an artist."[33] This original way of looking at infinity reveals a deep discrepancy between the desired and actual infinity and between the wholeness of the natural world and human concepts. That discrepancy is apparent already in eighteenth-century gardens in the contrast between the transparency of the artificial order and the incomprehensibility of the order of landscape and nature. The contrast reveals the gap between our ability to form concepts of totality, wholeness, and infinity and our incapacity to experience them on the level of the finite and sensible. At the end of the eighteenth century, this gap was considered to be a source of fascination and creativity—a space where it might be possible to come to terms with the infinite through the experience of the sublime[34] (figure 7.7).

THE SUBLIME AND THE SENSE OF WHOLENESS

The notion of the sublime is a secularized version of the earlier theocentric understanding of infinity. In a certain sense, the sublime represents an experiential vacuum created by the disintegration and transformation of the hierarchically structured world in which infinity was the natural culmination of an implied sense of identity and unity. The result is an introverted world, in which the search for infinity coincides with the ability of creative individuals to invent order without limits out of formless chaos.[35] As Schelling notes, "The fundamental intuition of chaos itself lies within the vision or intuition of the absolute. The inner essence of the absolute, that in which all resides as one, and one as all, is primal chaos itself."[36] In that sense, chaos is a basic intuition of the sublime. This intuition, in spite of its kinship with elements of the ideal and the ethical, is aesthetic.[37] We find the sublime in our experience of infinity, Richter observes, "which the senses and the imagination despair of grasping and representing, while the reason creates and holds it fast."[38] The tension between the potential presence of the infinite and the finitude of our sensible experience is, I believe, the key to the sublime's enigmatic nature. It is tempting, though virtually impossible, to identify beforehand situations in which it arises.

In the Romantic period, the sublime was generally associated with high mountains, waterfalls, atmospheric phenomena, the sky, the sea, the light, and the greatness of cathedrals and churches—the list can obviously be extended much further. We might still share some of these experiences today, but probably not most of them. Their place has been taken by new forms of the sublime tied to the contemporary conditions of life. For example, the order discovered in recent chaos theories, experiences related to new technologies of communication, and new extremes of movement, speed, and distance all contain significant elements of the sublime.[39] This shift may not be of great import, but it does demonstrate the continuity of the search for wholeness and infinity and the extent to which the results of the present search are confined to the domain of aesthetic experience. The presence of the sublime in contemporary culture is sustained by the latent structure of our world, which is a constant reminder of a wholeness that stands in sharp contrast to the transitory and fragmentary nature of our experience.

Thus far we have been concerned with the fragment in its historical manifestation. The Romantic vision of the fragment exercised great influence on the art of Art Nouveau and Expressionism and on repeated attempts to achieve a unity of arts in the form of the *Gesamtkunstwerk*. Even today, the fragment is usually seen either in a Romantic light or as the destructive fragmentation of reality into isolated facts, data, and systems.

Yet the fragment also has a second, altogether different, meaning, briefly described at the beginning of this chapter as positive, restorative, and symbolic. The positive meaning of the fragment has its source not in personal experience but in a dialogue with the latent content and structure of our world. It cannot be grasped in a single intuition; it relies on a sequence of stages bringing together individual phenomena and the universal ground in a process that may be described as the restorative mapping and articulation of the world.

The restorative nature of the fragment contributed significantly to the heuristic power of the aphorism and was also closely linked with the origins of modern hermeneutics—a new mode of interpretation based on the dialectics of part and whole.[40] One of the main virtues of modern hermeneutics is that it enables us to see and understand the richness of linguistic articulation in other areas of culture. This is a first condition for a genuine restoration of meaning and wholeness in the field of architecture and the visual arts. Its importance for the understanding of the restorative role of the fragment is evident in the development of modern painting, particularly during the period between late Impressionism and Synthetic Cubism. The emancipation of color from its direct material reference (local color) in the pointillist period of Impressionism, the discovery and use of simultaneous contrast, the simulation of the effects of light: these are some of the steps that challenged the homogeneity of the traditional perspective representation, particularly the illusionistic treatment of separate volumes. Pointillist technique substituted fragments of color, acting on one another and thus restoring some of the situational conditions of the depicted objects, in an il-

7.8. Paul Cézanne, *La route tournante* (ca. 1881).

lusionistic vision of reality framed like a trompe l'oeil. As a result, objects and their setting became more integrated. However, the Impressionists did not change the principles of perspectivity, and their quasi-scientific method of ordering color fragments did not lead to a real restoration. Their work was no more than a new method of representation in a traditional framework.

The restorative role of the fragment was understood very differently by Paul Cézanne (figure 7.8). In his paintings, color is not an isolated element; it always belongs to the fundamental nature of things, to their primordial situatedness and thus to the plenitude of their thingness. It is because of this plenitude that we see not only the depth but also the hardness of things, their softness, and, as Cézanne claimed, their odor. In the words of Merleau-Ponty, "If the painter is to express the world, the arrangement of his colors must carry with it this indivisible whole, or else his picture will only hint at things and will not give them the unity, the presence, the unsurpassable plenitude which is for us the definition of the real."[41] For this reason, each separate brush stroke (fragment) needs to satisfy a number of conditions. It must contain, Cézanne explains, "the air, the light, the object, the composition, the character, the outline and the style."[42] The fragmented patches of color, across which the receding perspective, outlines, angles, and curves are inscribed like lines of force, create a spatial structure that vibrates as it is formed. We can see objects appearing and organizing themselves before our eyes. What motivated Cézanne was not perspectival space, geometry, or laws governing color, but the still life, portrait, or landscape in its totality. This is what Cézanne himself referred to as the "motif," which can also be described as the "theme."

The organizing power of a theme is not always apparent and can be easily confused with the purely formal configuration of a painting. This confusion occurs not only in the prevailing interpretations of Cézanne but also in interpretations of Cubism, where the formal problems of space, volume, and the fragmentation of objects into geometric elements are considered to be the main characteristics of the movement. The absence of explicit reference to the visible world is no good reason to believe that its aim is formal, however. The standard belief that content can be identified only with the advent of Synthetic Cubism is incorrect; it clearly originates in the nonperspectival space and the content of Analytic Cubism. Traditional perspective was indeed replaced by a notion of space that was, as a rule, more complex and abstract, and early Cubism may appear to be a formal endeavor; but the configuration of geometrical lines and fragments characteristic of that period was only a transition to something else: to the world slowly revealed in the process of construction, after which the resulting configuration remained only a mediating, symbolic representation (figure 7.9).

It is important to realize that mediating representation has always been the primary purpose of any authentic art, insofar as it is a means of participation in the world and not a goal in itself—as it seemed to become in the late development of perspective. The rigidity of late perspectival space and illusionistic representation stirred modern art's revolt. Surprisingly, the revolt did not have a deeper effect on our understanding of the nature of representation in Cubism. There is still a tendency to read the works too literally, too much like aesthetic objects, or simply like a differently

7.9. Georges Braque, *Still Life with Clarinet and Violin* (1912).

structured trompe l'oeil. In such a reading, the nature of the fragment remains enigmatic and potentially negative. That the role of fragments can be
also positive, not only potentially but actually, is demonstrated in the context of the world to which each fragment directly or indirectly refers.

The dissolution of the object in Analytic Cubism creates an ambiguous situation in which fragments always preserve some reference to the
original objects as they situate those objects in a radically new structure of
space. Hence objects lose their rigid definition and become part of the newly

articulated world. Georges Braque describes this phenomenon very clearly: "It seems to me just as difficult to paint the spaces *'between'* as the things themselves. The space *'between'* seems to me to be as essential an element as what they call the object. The subject matter consists precisely of the relationship between these objects and between the object and the intervening spaces. How can I say what the picture is *of* when relationships are always things that change? What counts is this transformation."[43]

The relationship between the object and the intervening spaces is not formal; it is always rooted in the context of a particular setting. The nature of the relationship is thus determined by the logic of the situation and by the meaning of individual elements. "The subject, for instance a lemon next to an orange, ceases to be a lemon and an orange—they become fruit."[44] What we see at work here is a metaphor that has the capacity to establish the similarity between different objects, and as a consequence the capacity to reveal on a deeper level what is common to them. The metaphorical vision of the given reality depends on productive imagination and on the existence of a latent world that is always present, waiting for articulation.[45]

The notion of a latent world waiting for articulation is a strange phenomenon and in some sense a paradox. On the one hand, our existence depends on its availability and coherence; on the other, we are hardly aware of it and find it difficult to see its universal presence and role. The latent world is constantly articulated in our everyday speech, but we rarely notice it. Our ability to see the link between language and world—to see how language is situated in our everyday life and to recognize that language is not only an articulation of verbal or visual meanings but also the articulation of the world itself—is directly related to our ability to see the limits of the positivistic understanding of reality, of perspectivism and illusionistism.

The fragmentation that is taking place in Analytic Cubism, or through the use of an isolated fragment in Synthetic Cubism, coincides with the articulation of the world. What is apparent even in the first stage of Cubism (1908–1910) is the elementary nonperspectival structure of a world represented through the particular settings of the still lifes, portraits, or landscapes. These settings are radically nonperspectival because they are situational, and that is neither arbitrary nor a result of a pure construction. The setting follows instead the deep logic of a particular structure into which each object or fragment is placed in accordance with its "situational meaning." This can be compared with how we organize our familiar living or working space. It is in the situational structure of Cubist space that the topography of familiar settings meets the fragment in its metaphorical role, as Braque's description of his method makes apparent: "I started by painting a space and then by furnishing it. The object is a dead thing. It only comes alive when it is activated. Find the common ground between things. That is what poetry is, don't you see?"[46] If the common ground of things is space, it is a space that can be understood not through geometry or as a formal structure, but as a living structure in which the metaphorical power of fragment plays a decisive role. This becomes clear in Synthetic Cubism, in the art of collage, and later in Surrealism.

The formation of space in Synthetic Cubism and in the early development of collage is almost entirely determined by the situational meaning of individual fragments. The creative process can be compared to a visual discourse that depends on a few critical points of reference (*points de repère*), usually fragments of a familiar reality that are developed through a sequence of metaphorical steps into a more complex configuration. The complexity consists in the references generated by the metaphorical possibilities, which enable viewers to recognize sameness and difference in the context of a world opened up by the main theme and represented initially by the chosen fragments. There is no obvious intention to restore the unity of some object in the process. On the contrary, the fragmentary presence of a particular object should be seen as a thing in its thingness—as it would be, for example, in contemporary hermeneutics. In the hermeneutical understanding, the thingness of a thing is its purpose and serviceability (human attitudes, dreams, aspirations, and so on); taken together, they represent a world to which a thing belongs and which in turn belongs to it. The world to which a particular thing belongs is inexhaustible, and it is for this reason that the creation (as well as the reading) of a Cubist painting is always open to further revelations. That seems to be the message of Braque's statement: "You can always invert the facts. There are relationships between objects that sometimes give us the feeling of infinity in painting. The objects themselves fade next to these relationships. Life is revealed in all its nakedness as if outside of our thoughts. I'm not searching for definition, I tend toward infinition."[47]

Is it reasonable or relevant to ask what the possible goal of "infinition" is, and where may it lead? Anybody who works with the metaphoricity and restorative possibilities of fragments is like the author of an aphorism, who, as one modern scholar writes, "holds in his hands the potsherds of a vessel so large and so shattered that from its thousand fragments he finds it almost impossible to tell what shape the vessel once had. He makes it his task to contemplate each and try to fit them together as best he can. Sometimes he is helped by their shape, sometimes he works by bright ideas, sometimes a dim memory stirs in him."[48] Such is the position of any genuine artist in the twentieth and twenty-first century. Situated in the heart of a culture that has become introverted and fragmented, the artist is faced with a deep dilemma, knowing that the relevance of his or her art is closely linked not only with its cultural authenticity but also with public recognition and thus its shared universal validity. The artist could simply accept the current notion of universality, which is mostly formal, based on instrumental reason, and empty of any particular content. This is the line followed by Constructivism or neo-Plasticism, for instance. But art can also overcome the limits of its isolation through a restorative work, by recognizing the presence of the latent world waiting for articulation.[49] While the first approach has produced art with a certain level of universality but without a particular content (only formal content), the second has created art that has a rich content, but its universality is not yet fully visible and recognized. We still tend to see the achievements of Cubism, the art of collage, and Surrealism as private constructions or as a regress to the realm of private dreams. What we do not grasp clearly enough is how close these movements—which were part of a long tradition—came to the genuine creative nucleus of modern culture.

THE CREATIVE ROLE OF FRAGMENT

The metaphoricity of fragment not only pertains to the domain of the arts but is also a germ of a new universal restorative power, relevant to our culture as a whole. This potential was recognized by the Surrealists and, on a broader scale, by modern hermeneutics.[50] In the thinking of the Surrealists, the restorative power of fragment was closely linked with the notion of poetic analogy. In Breton's own words, "poetic analogy transgresses the

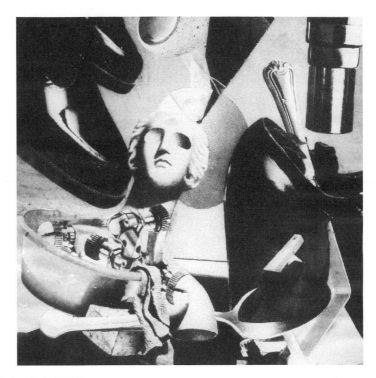

7.10. Daniel Libeskind, collage (1980).

deductive laws in order to make the mind apprehend the interdependence of two objects of thought situated on different planes, between which the logical functioning of the mind is unlikely to throw a bridge, in fact opposes a priori any bridge that might be thrown."[51] "Poetic analogy" here refers primarily to the art of collage. Though collage itself originated in the early stages of Synthetic Cubism (1911–1912), it was the Dadaists and later the Surrealists who made it a medium in its own right (figure 7.10). In the peak period of its development, collage became a visual text not unlike a poetic text, with which it was always closely linked. The metaphorical and often aphoristic nature of collage can be recognized in Max Ernst's comment on the "mechanism" of collage: "I'm tempted to see in collage the chance meeting of two distant realities on an unfamiliar plane, or to use a shorter term, the culture of systematic displacement and its effect."[52] The "culture of systematic displacement" is only a more explicit version of the sequence (passage) of metaphorical steps that structured the situational space of early Cubism.

The continuity between Cubism and Surrealism is nowhere more apparent than in the metaphorical nature and role of the fragment and the role of the analogical or metaphorical image. The analogical image that illuminates partial similarities cannot be seen as a simple equation; it moves and mediates between the two realities (fragments) present in a way that is never reversible. "The greater and truer the distance between two juxtaposed realities, the stronger will be the image and the greater will be its emotive power and reality."[53] It is interesting to compare this statement by Pierre Reverdy, which refers to poetry and possibly to late Cubist paintings, with Breton's comment on Ernst's collages on the occasion of their first Paris exhibition in 1920: "The marvelous faculty of reaching two distant realities without leaving the field of our experience and their coming together, of drawing out a spark, of putting within reach of our senses figures carrying the same intensity, the same relief as the other figures, and in depriving ourselves of a system of reference, of displacing ourselves in our own memory—that is what provisionally holds us."[54]

The movement away from the established system of references creates in collage the potential for forming a situational space whose controversial identity is more explicit than was the case in Cubism. The strange, enigmatic reality of the Surrealist space often includes not only elements of illusionism but also explicit architectural references. This is a logical outcome of a development that became in Surrealism a more complete encounter with the reality of everyday life. In this encounter, the work of art was extended into the work of life, where different circumstances are in play and where the "latent world waiting for articulation" can be activated more globally. I am thinking here of the Surrealist activities which took place outside the walls of studios—on the streets of Paris, in the theaters, films, exhibitions, and so on. The unpredictability of the encounters in these environments had its source in the anonymity of circumstances much richer and more rewarding than the limited realm of personal experience and memory. It was their concreteness, their spatial and corporeal nature, that brought the poetic interpretation of reality into the domain of architecture.

In spatial and corporeal phenomena, the Surrealists discovered the source of primary creativity, embodied in the image of the crystal. Breton declared, "The great secret of the environment of things can be discovered in this way: the crystal possesses the key to every liberty."[55] In another context, he partly clarified this enigmatic statement: "I have never stopped advocating creation, spontaneous action, insofar as the crystal, nonperfectible by definition, is the perfect example of it. . . . Here the inanimate is so close to the animate that the imagination is free to play infinitely with these apparently mineral forms."[56] The crystal became for the Surrealists a supreme metaphor of spontaneity, imagination, and creativity. It also became a principle of order more primordial than the order provided by reason. The facets of a crystal, in their way as anonymous as the fragments of a city, appear as a forest of symbols, a world like a "cryptogram which remains indecipherable only so long as one is not thoroughly familiar with the tool that permits one to pass at will from one piece of reality to another."[57] The tool that permits us to move through the forest of symbols and indices is analogy. Analogy can reveal the deep relation between distant realities which we cannot link together in logical thought. In exploring analogies, the Surrealists discovered the anonymity of natural creativity and also, without being fully aware of it, of the latent world, where our imagination and its organizing power have their source.[58] In the narrative journey through Paris, the poetic experience of particular places opened a sequence of analogical readings that led eventually to the formation of a coherent poetics of analogies.

The history of Surrealism shows interesting similarities with the history of the positive fragment, which began with the discovery of the restorative power of the word, followed by the discovery of the same power in the image and, finally, in the space of the city. It is a strange irony that the achievements of the Surrealists are seen, even today, as subjective and arbitrary—merely as interesting readings of reality. Such a view fails to recognize that Surrealism represents the most admirable effort to date to bring the latent world of our common existence into our awareness, not only in the domain of art but also in everyday life. That we have not understood this message may partly explain why the restorative role of fragment was recognized in architecture much later than it was in literature or painting. The articulation of the latent world, which became deeply introverted and very personal, was difficult to follow in areas of culture much more open to external constraints, public scrutiny, and a shared understanding.

The movement toward a situational understanding of space was also hampered by the perspectival and object-oriented thinking that dominated most of twentieth-century architecture. It is true that many modern architects moved away from traditional perspectivism and that many also used fragments in their work, but in most cases the effort was offhand, limited, and without a clear restorative intention. The first consistent use of fragment as part of a positive vision can be found in the work of Le Corbusier. His use of fragment was first labeled phenomenal transparency,[59] however, it is clear that phenomenal transparency, described as a result of the overlapping of figures or elements, as a simultaneous perception of elements in various spatial locations, and as a dialectic of visual facts and their implications, is only a different name for the role of fragment. In the discussion of phenomenal transparency, the structure of pictorial and architectural space is seen as a formal problem, but we know that in the Cubist tradition each element of space is related to the others through its situational characteristics and meaning. Such relations are certainly apparent in Le Corbusier's interiors, where the juxtaposition of elements and the overall layering of space are motivated by situational criteria. A good example is the solarium on the roof terrace of the Beistegui apartment (figure 7.11), which is treated simultaneously as an open space and a closed interior. The carpet of grass on the ground and the openness of the space to the sky refer to the first of these meanings, while the furniture and the fireplace in the back wall refer to the second. As a whole, the solarium is open to a series of readings in which individual elements play the role of metaphorical fragments, revealing the situational character of the dwelling in the context of a room, a city, and nature.[60]

The movement away from the rigid conditions of perspectivity and functionality of space and the attempts to recover meaning through the use of fragments represent a tendency that has gone almost out of control in recent years, mostly because they are rarely based on a proper understanding of what is involved. In too many cases, fragments are used purely as formal devices or only as a source of experimental possibilities, which may produce interesting solutions but not necessarily a meaningful work. But how can we judge what is "meaningful"?

7.11. Le Corbusier, Beistegui apartment, solarium.

Meaning depends on the continuity of communicative movement between individual elements and on their relation (reference) to the preexisting latent world. The continuity of communicative movement manifests itself in the legibility of concrete architectural space in the same way as it does in a poem or a collage. In that sense, the meaning of a work can be judged by how legible and comprehensible it is. The communicative movement between individual elements of architectural space (its legibility) creates a communicative space, ruled by the situational structure of typical elements and their metaphorical meaning. Yet the creation of a communicative space requires more than good intentions: it depends to a great extent on a more profound understanding of the given cultural conditions and their interpretation. Architecture, perhaps more than any other discipline, is deeply rooted in tradition and in the continuity of latent culture. Under such conditions the radicality of creative achievement cannot be measured by its tendency to use clear-cut solutions or something wholly new. It is important to remember that even Surrealism in its effort to overthrow conventional modes of representation did not completely abolish traditional illusionism and perspectivity, and that this sense of continuity was probably part of its strength rather than a weakness.

We have already seen that one of the main conditions of a well-articulated culture is the communicative continuity of space, where the meaning of positive fragments is ultimately established. It was mainly for these reasons that the creation of a new communicative space became the theme of a project for Spitalfields in London. The point of departure was a vision of a space not as we would like to see it, but as it is given to us today in a typical form represented by highly abstract programs, environmental analysis, calculations and diagrams, formal plans, sections, axonometrics, and other geometrical approximations. It is deeply ironic that these abstract and partial representations are so often presented as complete and self-sufficient. This is no doubt the main source of the confusion and the detrimental fragmentation within current architecture. What makes this scene most confusing is the difficulty of identifying the true fragmentary nature of particular representations.

The best way to reveal the fragmentary nature of a representation is through dialogue with the concrete reality of space. In such a dialogue, even the most abstract and fragmentary vision of the project can be identified as potentially positive fragment and engaged in a genuine communicative process. The project for the alternative development of the area of Spitalfields Market in London illustrates how this can be done[61] (figure 7.12). The market is situated on the edge of the city, where the city's most recent commercial expansion has taken place; on its other side it borders a community whose population has tried repeatedly over several hundred years to establish there its own urban identity.

The clash between commercial interests and civic interests is typical of most contemporary cities, and there is no obvious way to reconcile them. Their incompatibility is a manifestation of a more fundamental problem: the incompatibility of the fragmentation characteristic of many urban structures and systems with the situated nature of urban life. The Spitalfields project illustrates how such difficulties may be reduced and even eliminated if the current city of isolated fragments is seen in the light of the restorative potential of the fragments and with the awareness that such a new

7.12. Spitalfields project (London), model.

7.13. Spitalfields project, civic area.

vision cannot be realized instantly. Time is a key to addressing the difficulty and complexity of the problem.

In place of a short-term solution, which may favor one side of the conflict, the project suggests allowing the commercial development to take place on the western part of the site and the civic on the eastern leaving the central area temporarily free as a garden. The space of the garden can be used as territory on which the slow process of reconciliation of the commercial and civic interests can occur. This goal can be achieved by the creation of new institutions and structures, such as research and cultural establishments, hotels, clubs and restaurants, department stores, language schools, and so on (figure 7.13). As the process takes place, its unpredictability and generous time scale can help those involved to discover the common ground of the isolated parts of the city and situate them as positive fragments in a larger space of meaningful communication. On a small scale, this process can be illustrated by a project for a shadow theater (figure 7.14). Here the spatial organization of the performance space is represented in its first stage by conventional axonometrics.

However, what could be seen as a complete representation is taken as a point of departure for an imaginative dialogue with the deeper structure and content of the space. It is at the limits of geometrical representation that we discover a world in which geometry itself is situated. In the case of the shadow theater, it is a world where the performance and its visibility are not yet reduced to a predictable representation, stereotype, or cliché. The movement of figures and their shadows create their own space, which follows not the rules of geometry but only the rules of communicative space. The final structure of the space is the result of a process whereby the relations between the figures, lights, audience, and projection screens create a series of possible settings that may eventually be translated into a plausible configuration. Unlike conventional perspectival space, communicative space generated by positive fragments has the capacity to hold together a plausible solution and a series of possible ones. This power depends almost entirely on the metaphorical articulation of the space. It is for this reason that the metaphorical exploration of each particular space has been used as an important heuristic stage for the final design.

In a proposal for a museum of Surrealist art, which could be treated as a collection of neutral fragments, each part of the museum is handled instead as a segment of a situation linked metaphorically with other segments (figure 7.15). The process of metaphorical interpretation begins in the workshop for metal plating located in the lower part of the museum, exploiting a deep analogy between the transformation of materials and the poetic metamorphosis in the artworks.[62] How preliminary metaphorical studies contribute to the richness, quality, and meaning of the ultimate solution can be seen in a project for a center for experimental music (figure 7.16). In one of the final drawings we can see the attempt to establish communication

7.14. Adam Robarts, Spitalfields project, shadow theater, composite study.

between the physiognomy of the room, the light, and the sound, and at last between the room and the outside world (garden). The most interesting discovery was the mediating role of light. In the final arrangement, light penetrates into the room through an aviary situated behind a large window. Animated and articulated by the movement of the vegetation and the movement and sound of the birds, it provides a medium by which we can better see the link between the visual and acoustic articulation of the room.

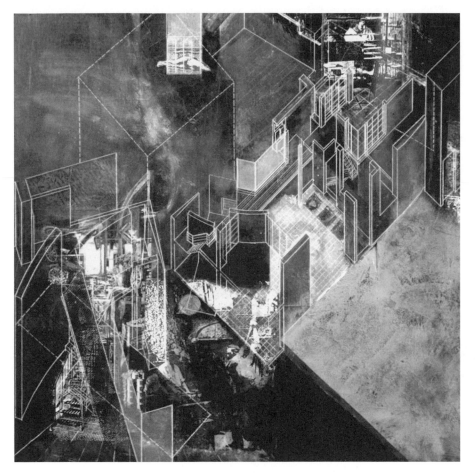

7.15. Christian Frost, Spitalfields project, museum of Surrealist art, composite study.

The metaphorical links established between the individual elements of the space reveal their deeper common ground, which is the key to understanding and restoring communicative space. It is encouraging to see that behind the silence of mutually isolated negative fragments there is a potential world of communication that can be, under certain conditions, articulated and revived. The role of architecture and visual arts in the restoration of the communicative space illustrates how it is possible to overcome

7.16. Elspeth Latimer, center for experimental music, interior.

the current state of fragmentation—not only in the sphere of the arts but in culture as a whole.

It is perhaps not necessary to emphasize that other media and means also contribute to the formation of the practical world of communication. But at the same time it is clear that the process of fragmentation is more complex, subtle, and contradictory.

• CHAPTER 8 •

TOWARD A POETICS OF ARCHITECTURE

T HE PRESENT understanding of architectural representation is rather confined and ambiguous. There is no clear notion as to what architecture should represent or whether in fact it should represent anything other than itself. However, there is also a strong belief that architecture cannot be confined entirely to its immanent existence in the form of some absolute presence. Inevitably buildings have an appearance and a physiognomy. Our natural, spontaneous reaction is to articulate experience thematically and thus physiognomically, even in situations in which we are concerned only with the conceptual character of the visible. This tendency is particularly evident in current interest in "autonomous" or "self-referential" architecture. The twentieth century witnessed many attempts to treat architecture as a culturally emancipated discipline, free of all references to the natural world.[1] Such attempts parallel key developments in nonfigurative, minimal, and conceptual art (figure 8.1). However, the main formative influence in the development of autonomous architecture has been technological determinism, producing structures that in their universality and anonymity are heedless of particular physiognomy. And yet even the most abstract structures have a certain physiognomy that cannot be ignored. This has to do not so much with the appearance of the structures themselves as with the context in which they are situated. The distance that separates the appearance of structures from their cultural context is probably the main source of the vexed and problematic nature of representation today.

The difficulties we face in relation to the question of representation, very often referred to as a "crisis of representation," should be characterized as revealing not a lack of meaning but rather a displacement of meaning. Displacement points to a contradiction between the monotony and sterility of buildings and the complexity of our life, experienced in situations very often associated with the same or similar buildings.[2] Displacement raises a question of appropriateness that has always been integral to architectural thinking, with its emphasis on the tangibility of experience and knowledge. The cultural consequences of modern thinking can be observed, most of all, in the transformation of symbolic representation into instrumental representation. Symbolic and instrumental representation, as we have already seen, stand very often in conflict. While the former is reconciliatory and serves as a vehicle of participatory understanding and all-encompassing

8.1. Coop Himmelblau, Factory Funder 3, St. Veit/Glan, Austria (1988–1989).

meaning, the latter is aggressive and serves as an instrument of autonomy, domination, and control.

In instrumental thinking, the problem of representation tends to be reduced to the overt relationship between an instance of representation and the process of its genesis. This reduction inevitably leads to a tautology. The belief that a building represents by referring to something that is not present takes no account of the simple fact that the only way we can experience any reference is through the situation of which not only the building but we also are a part. Gadamer is particularly clear on this point: "it is an objectivist prejudice of astonishing naiveté for our first question to be, 'what does this picture represent?' Of course, that is a part of our understanding of a picture. Insofar as we are able to recognize what is represented, that recognition is a moment of our perception of it." In symbolic representation, "the symbolic does not simply point toward a meaning, but rather allows that meaning to present itself." In other words, "what is represented is itself present in the only way available to it."[3]

In our current understanding of representation, we are generally unaware of such distinctions and their consequences. This ignorance is confirmed by the widespread belief among architects that instrumentality can be reconciled with symbolism, that a balance between them can be established, or that instrumentality can simply produce its own form of symbolic representation. As a consequence, we have not grasped that there is still one domain of experience that contains a residuum of authentic representation. This is the domain to which we refer when we use the word "character."

THE RESIDUAL MEANING OF CHARACTER AND STYLE

The significance and deep-seated meaning of character are apparent only indirectly—for instance, in our concern to maintain a proper relationship between the purpose of a building and its appearance, or in our care to choose the right materials and structures for the overall nature of a particular building or space. What the "presence of representation" really means in connection with character is obscured and partly lost in the introverted and highly personalized version of character accepted today. Nonetheless, we cannot ignore the fact that it is the prime, if not the only, link still preserved with a more authentic tradition of representation. Character explicitly belongs to that tradition, though it radically changed in the eighteenth century when it first became the dominant concept in architectural thinking.

Among those categorically emphasizing the role of character was Germain Boffrand, who wrote, "A man who does not know these different characters, and who does not make them felt in his works, is no architect."[4] The eighteenth-century notion was derived largely from contemporary rhetoric and treatises on painting[5] (figure 8.2). This renewed interest in individual expression and physiognomy evidenced in the treatises was prob-

8.2. Jean Charles Delafosse, *Nouvelle iconologie historique* (1768), *Spring and Summer.*

ably one of the main motives behind the study of character, which, for more than a millennium, had been treated as a secondary issue.

The introduction of character into architectural thinking was not without difficulty. A notion that emerged from a vast cultural field encompassing not only architecture and painting but also rhetoric, poetry, and philosophy was loaded with a range of meanings that architecture on its own could not readily absorb. The simplification of the earlier modes of representation was the first consequence; the aestheticization of character was the second. This is clear from Boffrand's statement, which may even be taken as a definition of character:

> Architecture, although its object may seem to be no more than the use of material, is capable of number of genres that bring its component parts to life, so to speak, through the different characters that it conveys to us. Through its composition a building expresses, as if on the stage, that the scene is pastoral or tragic; that this is a temple or a palace, a public building destined for a particular purpose or a private house. . . . The same is true of poetry: this, too, has its different genres; and the style of one does not suit another. In this respect, Horace has left us some excellent principles in his *Art of Poetry*.[6]

The ambition to subsume the traditional order and poetics of architecture into the aesthetics of character created an illusion of order, but in the long run it proved to support relativism, arbitrariness, and confusion. The general aestheticization of character made it vulnerable to the operations of taxonomy, which made possible the isolation of individual manifestations of character from the context of tradition and from the culturally established norms. This was already evident to Jacques-François Blondel, who observes, "after all, it matters little whether our monuments resemble former architecture, ancient, Gothic, or modern, provided that they have a satisfactory effect and a character suited to each genre of edifice."[7]

Character eventually lost its deep relation to the inherited culture, and as a result it could be manipulated with a much greater degree of freedom and persuasive power. As Blondel admits, "a building can by its appearance (aspect) take away, move, and so to speak raise the soul of the spectator, carrying it to a contemplative admiration which he himself would not be able to explain at first sight (*coup d'oeil*) even though he were sufficiently instructed in a profound knowledge of art."[8]

The emancipation and formalization of character required a more focused and precise definition of appearances, a demand fulfilled by the notion of style. Blondel was one of the first to use this term in its modern sense. The history of character can be seen as culminating in style, as he conceives it. "We have tried," Blondel writes, "to present a precise idea of what is to be understood by an architecture whose ordered arrangement (*ordonnance*) distinctly presents a style, an expression, a particular character."[9] In this context, style clearly is only a partial representation of the deeper structure and richer content of architecture, which is inherently situational. Style, as a self-sufficient notion, may be instrumentally useful but remains culturally problematic. How problematic the instrumentality of style became, particularly in the period of historicism, we have seen in the earlier discussion. It is interesting to note that the main features of historicism are already present in Blondel's idea of style: "There is no doubt that one can arrive, aided by rules, by reason and by the taste for the art, at the true style that assigns to each building the character that is proper for it and it is by that alone that one can sense masterpieces."[10] The history of the nineteenth century shows what the expected masterpieces were like.

There is a close and rather unfortunate relationship between the narrow, formalized notion of style and the shape of the modern history of art and architecture, pervaded even today by the stifling influence of stylistic thinking.[11] The current obsession with substituting a personal style for the richness and complexity of design demonstrates just how stifling this influence is. "The word 'style,'" declares Kurt Schwitters, "is worn out but still it signifies better than anything else the type of artistic striving that is characteristic of our age."[12] As creative effort concentrates on style, style takes precedence over truth and thus is seen to carry within itself the proof of its own sufficiency. This attitude, according to Ernst Jünger, seems to be based on the belief "that in the cultivation of a new style is concealed the only sublime possibility of making life bearable."[13]

In the contemporary attempts to liberate individual creativity from cultural and historical conditions—a tendency evident in recent architecture associated with the notion of deconstruction—we find a clear echo of the stylistic aspects of late Expressionism. Among the possible forerunners, Schwitters stands out as particularly relevant. Schwitters ranked with the artists who pursued a program of "style instead truth" to its logical conclusion. In some of his works he successfully eliminated all relations to the natural world for the sake of formal stylistic relationships between the individual visual elements. This is particularly clear in the art form named by him "merz" that he aimed at a utopian life conceived as pure style (figure 8.3). "Merz," Schwitters concludes, "produces sketches for a collective reorganization of the world, for a universal style."[14]

8.3. Kurt Schwitters, Merzbau (Hannover), view of the Gold Grotto, Big Group, and movable column (1930).

The vision of a universal style is in many ways linked with the attempt to create, or at least to identify, an international architectural style in the early 1930s. In both cases the goal was to articulate a paradigm of one dominant style. In their influential monograph on the International Style, Henry-Russell Hitchcock and Philip Johnson write: "The problem of establishing one dominant style, which the nineteenth century set itself in terms of alternative revivals, is coming to a solution." They elucidate what they mean here by "style": "Style is character, style is expression; but even character must be displayed and expression may be conscious and clear or muddled and deceptive. The architect who builds in the international style seeks to display the true character of his construction and to express clearly his provision for function."[15]

The attempt to make visible and express that which is visible only as an appearance, such as rationalized construction or function, reveals the deep predicament of the modern notion of style and also explains why the term has practically disappeared from recent architectural debates. However, the problem of visibility in architecture has not disappeared. All would probably agree that even the most neutral or abstract structure nevertheless displays a physiognomy through which the structure points beyond itself.

The dilemma at the heart of the modern notion of style is ultimately a problem of representation. Its source is the gray zone between symbolic and instrumental representation and the persistence, even in instrumental representation, of a certain residuum of a derivative symbolism. This residuum can be traced back to the history of character and the transformation of its symbolic content into formal aesthetic appearance.

The symbolic content of character that was overridden in the late eighteenth century by the aesthetic autonomy of specific characters— *tableaux*—was explicit in the earlier notions of *convenance* and *bienséance*. Both terms belong to a tradition that originated in classical decorum, of which they are simply later equivalents. In one of his earlier texts, Blondel mentions this correspondence: "suitability (*convenance*) ought to be regarded as the most essential aspect of building; by means of it the architect ensures the dignity and character of the edifice. What we mean here by *convenance* is called by Vitruvius *bienséance* (decor)."[16]

The difference between *convenance* and *bienséance* is not as important for my argument as the distance that separates them both from character.[17] When eighteenth-century texts are read inattentively, character, *convenance*, and *bienséance* very often appear to be synonymous. However, they are different—and the difference is fundamental. In character we clearly see a tendency to move toward the surface of a building, interior, or garden, toward the experience of appearances; in *convenance* and *bienséance* there is a tendency to move into the depth of architectural reality, toward an order still understood in terms of a certain ethos.

The shift toward ethos brings architecture into the realm of humanistic culture, from which it was indivisible until the seventeenth century. Architecture's close relationship with humanistic culture can be seen in its emphasis on the ethos of representation, but even more clearly in its emphasis on the communication with other areas of knowledge and skills—painting, poetry, rhetoric, music, mathematics, and so on. Under such circumstances, the problem of representation could not be discussed with the same ease as became possible in the case of character and was, to a limited degree, already possible in the case of *convenance* and *bienséance.*

In the humanistic tradition, the ethical understanding of representation was based on the notion of decorum. The original meaning of the term was to a great extent lost in that of its architectural equivalent—decor. In turn, the notion of decor, historically the older equivalent of *bienséance,*[18] was so dependent on contributions from nonarchitectural sources (mainly poetics and rhetoric) that its treatment in most architectural treatises imparts only a fraction of its full meaning.[19] This was true already in the first discussion of the notion by Vitruvius. The account of decor, the only part of his text that refers explicitly to the representative content of architecture, remains problematic. Decor is defined in the treatise promisingly as a "faultless ensemble of a work composed in accordance with precedent (*auctoritas*) of approved details" and is described as based on convention (*statio*), custom (*consuetudo*), and natural circumstances (*natura*).[20] But the connection between decor and the other architectural principles mentioned in the text (*ordinatio, dispositio, eurhythmia, symmetria, distributio*) is obscure, if it can be established at all. Even when such relationships are discussed more explicitly, the qualitative meaning of decor is always subordinated either to its quantitative equivalent or to another category, most often to symmetry, eurhythmy, and distribution.[21]

The inadequacy of the Vitruvian definition becomes apparent when it is compared with contemporary philosophical and rhetorical treatments of decorum. The comparison is legitimate because we know that it was from such sources that Vitruvius borrowed most of his theoretical terms.[22] The term that captures most lucidly the classical view of decorum (propriety) is the Greek *prepon.*[23] Cicero comments on *decorum,* "Such is its essential nature, that it is inseparable from moral goodness, for what is proper is morally right, and what is morally right is proper. The nature of the differ-

8.4. Aegina, temple of Aphaia (5th c. B.C.E.).

ence between morality and propriety can be more easily felt than expressed. For whatever propriety may be, it is manifested only when there is pre-existing moral rectitude."[24]

As we move back from decor and decorum to *prepon,* we come close to the essence of classical Greek culture as well as to the essence of the problem of representation. The tension between the ethical and aesthetic meaning of representation that we have seen in character and decor does not exist in *prepon.* Only that which is good can be proper; in that sense, a twentieth-century scholar explains, "the morally good is nothing else than a harmonious fulfillment of human nature, which becomes part of the beautiful, manifested in the particular as *prepon.*"[25] In its primary sense, *prepon* belongs to the domain of appearances and means simply "to be seen clearly, to be conspicuous" (figure 8.4). In its fully articulated sense, it means a harmonious participation in the order of reality, as well as the outward expression of that order.[26]

"Outward expression" does not refer to mere imitation of order, which is already familiar to us. It implies rather that order is represented in such a way that it becomes conspicuous and actually present in sensuous abundance. It is obvious that this type of representation is the same as mimesis. *Prepon* (appropriateness) itself is not a representation, but it is a decisive criterion of the ethos and truth of representation. This particular meaning of *prepon* was largely preserved in the tradition of decorum in poetics and rhetoric, but it was lost in the Vitruvian tradition of decor. It is not difficult to demonstrate that most of the possibilities of representation between the classical era and the end of the Baroque were developed around the principles of decorum rather than decor. Indeed, very little could have been built on the notion of decor itself. And this observation brings us to the uncomfortable but inevitable conclusion that the Vitruvian doctrine of decor is more of an obstacle than a help for any genuine understanding of representation.

THE MIMETIC NATURE OF ARCHITECTURE

A second obstacle, more formidable than Vitruvius's doctrine, is the distorted and partial presentation of mimesis in modern tradition. This is an impediment that we have still to overcome. The original relationship between *prepon* and mimetic representation reveals how close architectural representation is to mimesis. And yet we do not as a rule think about architecture as being a mimetic art. This disinclination has partly to do with the well-established tradition in which architectural mimesis was reduced to the imitation of reified precedents, such as the primitive hut, the Solomonic Temple, exemplary buildings, and so on, or to such generalized notions as the "imitation of nature." Mimesis is not the same as imitation; classical thinkers saw it as a particular form of *poiēsis*. The affinity between architecture and the arts, with *poiēsis* as their potential common ground, is questioned in a thought-provoking way in Plato's *Symposium:*

> You will agree that there is more than one kind of poetry (*poiēsis*)
> in the true sense of the word—that is to say, calling something into
> existence that was not there before, so that every kind of artistic
> creation is poetry, and every artist is a poet.

True.

But all the same, we don't call them all poets, do we? We give various names to the various arts, and only call the one particular art that deals with music and meter by the name that should be given to them all. And that's the only art that we call poetry, while those who practice it are known as poets.[27]

The ambiguous nature of *poiēsis*, clearly apparent in this text, reflects a deep ambiguity characteristic of the age in which a traditional oral culture became literate and for the first time also philosophical. Some of the traditional notions, such as *poiēsis* and mimesis, became the subject of new philosophical interpretations, which produced invaluable insights but also some problematic and one-sided conclusions. Particularly unfortunate was the distinction drawn between mimetic and nonmimetic arts, partly because it was formulated in a polemic against the Sophists and was therefore partisan; as a result, it had a most fateful influence on the later understanding of mimesis and representation generally.[28] These are some of the reasons why I have chosen to concentrate on the analysis not of Plato but of Aristotle, whose interpretation of mimesis in the *Poetics* is less partial and, more important, is still based on a pre-philosophical tradition.

That architecture is not explicitly mentioned in the *Poetics* is of no significance. Aristotle's treatment of the role of mimesis and human praxis, the formation of poetic mythos, and the nature of representation related to art generally sufficiently corroborates my argument. In the *prepon*-based understanding of representation, architecture—apart from being an art (*technē*) in its own right—is deeply embedded in the ethos of life and is also closely linked with the other arts, particularly with painting and poetry.[29] Both painting and poetry are discussed explicitly in the text, which, as Aristotle remarks in its first sentence, is concerned not with individual arts but with *poiēsis* itself (*peri poiētikēs autēs*).[30] *Poiēsis*, which finds its fulfillment in mimesis, also grounds Aristotle's well-known definition of the work of art as "mimesis of praxis": "It is mainly because a play is a representation (*mimēsis*) of action (*praxis*) that it also for that reason represents people as doing something or experiencing something (*prattontes*)."[31]

What is praxis? Generally speaking, it is living and acting in accordance with ethical principles. More specifically, it is best to see praxis as a situation that includes not only people doing or experiencing something but also things that contribute to the fulfillment of human life.[32] Situations represent the most complete way of understanding our experience of the surrounding world and the human qualities of the world (figure 8.5). They also endow experience with durability in relation to which other experiences can acquire meaning and can form our memory and history. The temporal dimension makes the process of differing and stabilizing situations more comprehensible. The deeper we move into history, the more situations have in common until we reach the level of myth, which is their ultimate comprehensible foundation. Myth is the dimension of culture that opens the way to the unity of our experience and to the unity of our world. In its essence, myth is an interpretation of primary symbols that form spontaneously and that preserve the memory of our first encounters with the cosmic condition of our existence. The persistence of primary symbols, especially in the field of architecture, contributes decisively to the formation of secondary symbols and finally to the formation of paradigmatic situations. Paradigmatic situations are similar in nature to institutions, deep structures, and archetypes.

The role of the paradigmatic structure of a spatial situation is comparable to the role of poetic mythos in a poem or play. Both have the power to organize individual events and elements of praxis into a synthesis and give them a higher and more universal meaning. The formation of a poetic mythos or paradigm represents the first half of the creative cycle whose second half is the innovative interpretation of that poetic mythos or paradigm. This is quite clearly what Aristotle means when he declares that "the poet must be a 'maker' not of verses but of stories [mythos], since he is a poet in virtue of his 'representation' [mimesis], and what he represents [imitates] is action [praxis]."[33] The prominence given to poetic mythos illustrates how important the concept of representation is in the creative process and to what extent the poetic mythos "is the first principle and as it were the soul of tragedy: character comes second. It is much the same also in painting."[34] Is it not also the same in architecture? If it is not, how could architecture, painting, and practical life ever meet?

For instance, in Mannerist and Baroque spaces, the relationship between painting and architecture is based so strongly on content, decor, and

8.5. David Weston-Thomas, political building, metaphorical study of the museum and exhibition space.

the overall meaning that formal criteria such as perspective, optical illusion, or overall composition contribute little to our understanding. What then is the ground on which architecture, art, and practical life can meet in such a way that they constitute a meaningful unity? In my earlier discussion on the nature of situations, I emphasized their synthetic role and their capacity to structure our experience. But situations act also as receptacles of experience and of those events that endow them with meaning—not just as survivals and residues, but as the invitation to a sequence of future experiences.

This receptivity of situations is mostly prereflective and synesthetic. Visual, auditive, and tactile phenomena are closely related, and their affinity constitutes an important condition for the life of metaphors. It is mostly owing to the metaphorical structure of situations and more specifically to the mimetic nature of metaphor that paradigms are formed, paradigms that play not only a synthetic but also a receptive role. The unity of Baroque space is established by the metaphorical structure of space, which has the capacity to hold together different arts and at the same time meet all the important conditions of practical life, decorum, and ethos.

That the synthesis of a situation is accomplished mostly through the metaphoricity of language needs no emphasis. What should be emphasized is the role of metaphor in significant gestures, rituals, drama, and most of all in spatial imagination as it functions in sculpture, painting, or literature as a complement to the synthetic role of language. The nature of the relationship that exists between language, metaphor, and spatial situation can best be illustrated in the development of ancient drama.

The language of drama had its origin in the song of the chorus, and the chorus in turn emerged from the ritual unity of event and place. The word "chorus" refers to the group of dancers and actors, as well as to the dancing floor, and both have a common root in the archaic word for place—*chōra*. Apart from a common etymology, both chorus and *chōra* refer to the same symbolic situation of becoming, creating, and rebirth.[35] The meaning of place in the mimetic dance becomes more apparent if we remember that mimetic dance refers not only to the dance of the dancers but also to the dance of the stars, which represent the mathematical regularities and proportions of the celestial order.

The metaphoricity of language also made it possible to relate the experience of simple movements and rituals to the experience of rhythms, regularities, and concepts. Language became the medium in which more abstract paradigms of the creative process (*poiēsis*) could be formed. The conceptual paradigms later became a source of tension and conflict with traditional poetic mythos. The poetic role of mythos was first challenged, as I have mentioned above, when the culture took on a philosophical orientation, particularly during the Greek enlightenment of the fifth century B.C.E. This move, which was to have a lasting effect, was expressed in Plato's philosophy of *poiēsis*, formulated in response to a new development and in full awareness "that there is from of old a quarrel between philosophy and poetry."[36] Plato's own contribution was the most decisive in transforming the traditional poetic myth to a sophisticated paradigm capable of preserving not only the truth of poetry but also the truth of traditional myth in its encounter with philosophy. The confidence with which he addresses the traditional poets from his new position was not unjustified:

> Respected visitors, we are ourselves authors of a tragedy, and that the
> finest and best we know how to make. In fact, our whole polity has been
> constructed as a dramatization of a noble and perfect life; that is what
> we hold to be in truth the most real of tragedies. Thus you are poets, and
> we also are poets in the same style, rival artists and rival actors, and
> that in the finest of all dramas, one which indeed can be produced only
> by a code of true law—or at least that is our faith.[37]

This passage from the *Laws* represents the climax of the arguments in one of Plato's last dialogues; it shows how the conflict between poetry and philosophy was established and how it can be resolved within the context of the city (polis), the most accomplished spatial situation known to us. What is the difference here between the situational paradigm and the poetic mythos? In content and means of representation, each particular art obviously has specific distinguishing characteristics. But the difference in their nature is negligible, so that we can speak about poetic mythos as the soul of all the creative arts, including architecture.

It follows from this conclusion that architecture, like any other art, is a representation of human praxis and not a direct representation of nature or abstract ideas. Praxis, situated between ideas and nature, serves as a vehicle of their unity. It was not until much later that the poetic paradigm was replaced by the conceptual idea, and, as a consequence, the imitation of ideas in idealism was complemented by the imitation of nature in naturalism. Such a dichotomy was characteristic of Hellenism, Mannerism, and the eighteenth century, but it was not a critical issue before the end of the Baroque.

The nature of the poetic paradigm was newly interpreted in the eighteenth century in an attempt to formulate a rational equivalent of traditional poetics. This rather self-defeating enterprise was lucidly described by

Alexander Gottlieb Baumgarten in a set of simple definitions in his *Reflections on Poetry:* "by poem we mean a perfect sensate discourse; by poetics, the body of rules to which a poem conforms; by philosophical poetics, the science of poetics." At the end of this work, he defined the nature of the new science of poetics as a science of perception: "Things known are to be known by the superior faculty as the object of logic; things perceived are to be known by the inferior faculty as the object of the science of perception or aesthetic."[38] The word "aesthetic," which was here used for the first time with reference to a discipline of knowledge, belongs, as I argued in chapter 5, to the domain of instrumental representation. There art not only is subjected to the criteria of science but, as a consequence, is isolated from practical life and from ethics. This, as we have seen, is the basis of the "crisis of representation." While the confrontation of poetry and philosophy resulted in reconciliation, the confrontation of poetry and science resulted in subordination: poetry and poetics became already for Leibniz an inferior form of knowledge (*gnoseologia inferior*), best known as aesthetics. However, this is not the end of the story. The poetic paradigm of art is present still in the depths of our culture. Its persistence is evident in movements such as Romanticism, Symbolism, and Surrealism; as Gadamer puts it, "every work of art still resembles a thing as it once was insofar as its existence illuminates and testifies to order as a whole. Perhaps this order is not one that we can harmonize with our own conceptions of order, but that which once united the familiar things of a familiar world."[39]

THE POETIC PARADIGM OF DESIGN

The presence of the poetic paradigm is recognized not only by humanists and artists, but also by contemporary scientists. Werner Heisenberg refers to it when he speaks of language still related to phenomena, or when he speaks of the "one," which is only a different name for the unifying role of praxis. "In the last resort," he writes, "even science must rely upon ordinary language, since it is the only language in which we can be sure of really grasping the phenomena[;] . . . the language of images and likenesses is probably the only way of approaching the 'one' from more general domains. If the harmony in a society rests on a common interpretation of the 'one,' the unitary principle behind the phenomena, then the language of poetry may be more important here than the language of science."[40]

The poetic paradigm lingering in the depths of our culture has been overshadowed by the contemporary version of poetics often reduced to technical innovation and aesthetics. Yet we should not therefore conclude that the creative power of the poetic paradigm is lost or dead. It is still alive in many areas of culture, including architecture, and most strongly in the creative conditions and possibilities of practical life, traditionally seen as a domain of human praxis.[41]

The classical notion of praxis belongs to the fundamental constitution of human beings and their situation in the world; for that reason, it should not be confused with its modern equivalent, seen merely as an application of theoretical knowledge. Praxis does not depend exclusively on the abstract knowledge of norms but is always concretely (i.e., practically) motivated. Gadamer notes, "In every culture a series of things is taken for granted and lies fully beyond the explicit consciousness of anyone, and even in the greatest dissolution of traditional forms, mores and customs, the degree to which things held in common still determine everyone is only more concealed."[42]

The concreteness of praxis is apparent to anyone taking seriously the creative possibilities of a project, its program or brief, which defines not only the content but also the fulfillment of the project. Its close affinity with typical situations indicates that praxis always belongs to a world it articulates and thus brings about. Conversely, each situation, no matter how specifically or abstractly defined, is always practical. That practical nature is revealed not only in how people act or in what they do in a particular setting but also in the nature of the setting itself (figure 8.6). We need to remember that, as stated above, the practical situation "includes not only people doing or experiencing something but also things that contribute to the fulfillment of human life." The latter category embraces everything associated with human activity: for instance, the table on which we take our daily meal, or the walls that protect the intimacy of our conversation within a room.

Restoring the practical nature of situations as a primary vehicle of design enables us to move away from inconclusive play with abstract forms and functions. Once divorced from the unity of practical life and cultivated separately, forms and their functions can never be satisfactorily integrated

8.6. Adela Askandar, Vienna project, media center, composite drawing of a reading space.

with the concrete reality of architecture. The tendency to express the richness of life through transparent, clearly defined functions grows out of the replacement of the traditional understanding of creativity, based on the creative imitation of praxis and poetic knowledge (*technē poiētikē*), by the imitation of rationally formulated standards and theoretical knowledge (*technē theōrētikē*). This replacement has led to the degeneration of practice to technique and to a serious impoverishment of culture.

But despite this change, Gadamer observes,

the normative character of practice and hence the efficacy of practical reason is "in practice" still a lot greater than theory thinks it is. It certainly looks at first as if we are being overwhelmed in one economic and social system by a rationalization of all relations of life that follows an immanent structural compulsion so that we are always making new inventions and we are always increasing the range of our technical activity without being able to see our way out of this vicious circle. Far-seeing people already consider this a fatal path down which humanity is heading.[43]

The fatality of this path is apparent in some developments in contemporary architecture in which the broader purpose of space is reduced to clearly defined functions closely related to the abstract organization of space.

The acme of this tendency is comprehensive coordination that makes the purpose of a particular space identical with its quantifiable characteristics. Once this has been achieved, the identity of the function and structure of space can be extended into the domain of purely conceptual configurations, eventually reaching a point at which the sequence can be inverted—and the structure of space itself can generate its own purpose. This dynamic further supports my earlier argument that formalization is the ideal vehicle for cultivating the will to power. Acquiring power over the complexities of life may be technically exciting, but it is not necessarily practical. In fact, technical success very often heightens the tension between a newly created environment and our day-to-day life.

While technical development advances rapidly, the deeper levels of our lives and the natural world tend to be stable and change relatively slowly. Practical situations are usually formed spontaneously. On the deeper level, they are shaped not only by our exploration of new situational possibilities, individual preferences, intentions, and desires but also by the given conditions of everyday life. These conditions tend to challenge our creative freedom; thus we should speak not of freedom but of the spontaneity of creative movement in which there is no clear distinction between our own creativity and the creative power of nature (the natural world).

It was probably this spontaneity that the Surrealists had in mind when they used such terms as "automatism" and "objective chance" or emphasized the metaphor of the crystal to express the mystery of the creative process in its ultimate anonymity. However, this is only one aspect of a more fundamental problem in the history of European architecture—the formation and the role of the creative paradigms.

The most obvious example is the classical paradigm, which preserved its authority well into the eighteenth century and in some instances even beyond. The deep continuity of the classical tradition is clearly visible, particularly in periods of radical transformation—for instance, in the Middle Ages or in the Baroque period, when the classical paradigm was challenged by other traditions and tendencies that included Christianization, secularization, and modernization. The assertive power of paradigms established in a particular tradition is a mystery that cannot be fully explained but can be appreciated, especially if we better understand the conditions under which the cultural paradigms exert their dominating influence.

The best place to start is in the sphere of typical situations close to everyday existence. Because we always live somewhere, the situations most familiar to us are those related to the place of our dwelling (figure 8.7). These have changed very little in comparison to situations related to other spheres of life—places of work and places of commercial and public life, such as schools, hospitals, theaters, and museums. The most radical experimental interpretations of dwelling during the twentieth century resulted in interesting proposals and formal solutions that nonetheless did not much alter the substance of the dwelling itself. I have in mind projects for the collective form of living in the 1920s, Buckminster Fuller's Dymaxion House, Frederick Kiesler's Endless House, and similar, more recent projects. There is a sharp contrast between the inventiveness and novelty of the projects and their surprisingly limited effect on the primary nature of the dwelling. An extreme example occurs in the dining arrangements in the module of the Sky Laboratory, an environment discussed in chapter 2. The arrangement of sitting around a fixed table, preferred by the astronauts, stands in striking contrast to the freedom of other solutions possible in zero gravity and suggested by the NASA designers. Are we now in a better position to understand the nature of dwelling?

Dining is obviously not an isolated phenomenon. It is rooted in a broader context that includes conversation, direct and indirect relations with other people, specific settings, time, and so on. What gives such situations a very high degree of stability is their repetitive nature originating in the daily cycle of human life, which has its ultimate source in primary cosmic conditions and movements. It is on this level that the identity (sameness) of morning, of evening, and of the seasons is most conspicuously

8.7. Ladislav Žák, Villa Frič, Prague (1934–1935).

manifested. In the communicative structure of the natural world, the anonymous cosmic movement becomes a communicative movement that, in different degrees, penetrates and determines all areas of culture. We can recognize its presence in the dialectical play of sameness and difference in the structure of metaphor, imagination, and reasoning. The question of how highly differentiated human experience, expressed in language, can be related to more elementary forms of identity revealed on the level of imagination and visual experience, and ultimately on the level of primary corporeality, is connected with chapter 2's discussion of the continuity of articulation and embodiment, summarized in the problem of reference.

We already know that the reference at issue is not to some clearly defined origin but rather to an identifiable symbolic structure and its link to a primordial situation, which may also be described as a primary paradigm. Primary paradigms come into existence spontaneously in the anonymity of the historical process. Their nature is established in the reciprocity between prereflective creativity and given natural conditions. Examining this reciprocity is probably the best way to understand the nature and role of the primary architectural paradigms of European culture, which can be traced back to the broader Mediterranean world. The earliest paradigms are derived from the annual movements of the sun and the moon, the division of time into seasons, and the separation of the world into four zones. A clear sense of center and periphery, a notion of horizontal and vertical axes, the origins of geometry and its creative application—these are only some of the characteristics of the early paradigms.[44]

The decisive stage in the development of early paradigms was the formation of classical cosmology (mainly rooted in the Platonic tradition). For more than two millennia, architectural thinking was based on changing interpretations of this cosmology. Having analyzed its characteristics in its later stages, in the period of the Renaissance and the Baroque and in its disintegration during the eighteenth century, we can appreciate how important the cosmological framework was as a focus and foundation for architectural thinking, for the unity of culture, and for the role of architecture in sustaining this unity.[45] Indeed, it was the disintegration of that frame of reference, its replacement by the genealogy of historical precedents, and their eventual overthrow at the beginning of the twentieth century that has left us with ambiguity, arbitrariness, and disorientation. However, it would be premature to believe that our condition is permanent. Regardless of how problematic and difficult our situation is, we still have access to cultural memory and history and, in principle, to the cosmological foundations of our culture.

There are many areas of contemporary culture that are not directly affected by instrumental thinking. This is certainly true for the large part of poetry, literature, philosophy, music, and other arts, as well as for the deeper strata of everyday life. It is in these areas that we encounter the continuum of the latent world, which we all share without being fully aware of it.

ARCHITECTURE AND THE LATENT WORLD

I am using the term "latent world" in an attempt to describe the silent background of the natural world. The phrase brings together number of our earlier investigations into the prereflective levels of reality, which showed that the prereflective world is not amorphous or chaotic but well structured, with a clear sense of meaning, unity, and wholeness. That the latent world lacks explicit articulation, and thus the capacity to be openly and publicly

8.8. Jemal Badrashi, Prague project, institute of medical ethics, demonstration theater, composite drawing.

shared, does not, of course, mean that it is only personal or subjective. To the contrary, because it is constituted spontaneously in a direct response to the natural conditions mediated by cultural tradition, the latent world is the primary source and measure of objectivity.

In contemporary design we don't follow many objective rules, principles, and norms based on a living cultural content. Instead, most of our decisions are guided by formal principles and geometries of space and by personal experience. Current progressive design is based on the assumption that formal principles and geometry are neutral tools, subordinated entirely to the working of our minds. This illusion disappears, however, when we remember that they originate in the deep structures of reality and that their objectivity is therefore not a result of our choice. The complex status of such principles becomes apparent if we take into account the whole body of the available geometries, including chaos and self-organizing systems, and look at their ability to represent real space (figure 8.8).

The impossibility of representing real space mathematically was acknowledged already by Carl Friedrich Gauss in 1830, when, as we may recall, he wrote: "The theory of space has an entirely different place in knowledge from that occupied by mathematics[;] . . . space has a reality outside our mind and we cannot completely prescribe its laws."[46] Gauss is pointing, quite obviously, to the deeper structure of space, which geometry can approximate but cannot grasp. The limits of these approximations are apparent in geometry's inability to reveal its own foundations. The geometrical representation of architectural space, structured as a real human situation, ultimately depends on the primary, historically determined horizontal and vertical structure of reference.

The horizontal reference has its origins in the archaic experience of the imaginary line at which the earth meets the sky. The mysterious nature of this imaginary horizon line is revealed in its power to define the boundary of our visible world, as well as in its invitation to transcend that boundary (figure 8.9). The association of the horizon with the surface of the earth, so conspicuous on plains, in the desert, and on lakes and seas, is a fundamental measure for everything that is above and below, far and near.

It is not surprising that the horizon played a decisive role in forming our world, our language, and our thought. By defining the limits of what we can see, receding with our movement, but not disappearing, it became a vehicle integrating reference and continuity for everything in the visible world. Horizon belongs to the human way of seeing the world: it holds the human situation together and gives it coherence and meaning. "We define the concept of 'situation,'" Gadamer writes, "by saying that it represents a standpoint that limits the possibility of vision. Hence an essential part of the concept of situation is the concept of 'horizon.' Horizon is the range of vision that includes everything that can be seen from a particular vantage point. Applying this to the thinking mind, we speak of narrowness of horizon, of the possible expansion of horizon, of the opening up of new horizons, etc." The continuity between the archaeology and the hermeneutics of horizon shows that horizon reflects not only the spatiality but also the temporality and history of human situations. "In the sphere of human understanding we also like to speak of horizons, especially when referring to the

8.9. Jacob van Ruysdael, *View of Amsterdam and the Harbor* (1665).

claim of historical consciousness to see the past in terms of its own being, not in terms of our contemporary criteria and prejudices."[47]

Given this background, we can better understand the power of horizon in the experience of the architectural space. We are familiar with the surprising effect of changing the floor levels of a room, raising a chair or table on a podium, seeing the same space from a balcony, and entering a room or building by steps that take us up or down. The role of the horizon is even more explicit when the context is broader, such as in gardens, where a part of the space is very often leveled, thereby serving as a reference and measure for the rest of the garden. The relation of the visual organization of space to the horizon is most clearly demonstrated in perspective, where the horizon not only holds together but also generates the structure of the visual field.

It is important to remember that perspective originated in the radical transformation of the visible world, a transformation not just formal but qualitative. As we follow the later stages of the transformation, we see clearly that the original content of the visible world was never completely lost: it became part of the silent background of our culture and thus can be, with some effort, rediscovered and articulated. We are aware of its presence particularly when, in designing more complex spaces, we discover that the richness of the content and our intentions cannot be adequately represented by conventional plans and sections. In such cases we tend to put ourselves into a horizon of a situation in order to better grasp the true potential of the intended spatial configurations. That horizon, taken literally, opens up the possibility of exploring potential space in its most concrete manifestation. It also enables us to follow more closely the imaginative transformations of space achieved by defining the boundary of direct visibility and transparency.

In a more subtle sense, horizon contributes to the identity of a situation, while at the same time serving as a key to exploring its inexhaustible richness. The most important aspect of horizon is, no doubt, its ability to bring to our awareness what is in our experience but is not yet visible or known. In that sense it is a constant reminder that every situation can be defined, up to a point, but never completely, in positive terms. The relative constancy and incompleteness of all human situations has its source in the wholeness of the latent world, the silently structured continuum in which we live and act spontaneously and which we all share.[48]

This brings us closer to understanding situational identity and its continuity in time, an issue discussed in chapter 2 by examining the example of the French café. The surprising degree of integrity in the character of well-established situations, preserved under changing conditions and in different places, resists full explanation. The reasons for that resistance are not difficult to find, as Gadamer points out: "The very idea of a situation means that we are not standing outside it and hence are unable to have any objective knowledge of it. We are always within the situation, and to throw

8.10. Alberto Giacometti, sculptures in the atelier (1945–1947).

light on it is a task that is never entirely completed. This is true also of the situation in which we find ourselves with regard to the tradition that we are trying to understand."[49] In our first attempt to understand the essential character of typical situations (dining, study, place of work, etc.)—to determine what gives them their richness and relative stability and how they belong to the broader context of culture—we have discovered the importance of communicative movement and the continuity of reference.[50] With the notion of horizon we can take the argument one step further, as we can suggest that it is not only an imaginary line but also a structure that holds together the individual elements of a particular situation by the continuity of reference to the horizon of the latent world. This understanding is consistent with the approach of contemporary hermeneutics.[51]

The structure of space generated by horizon would be incomprehensible without reference to its verticality. Every horizon establishes a clear distinction between above and below. Erwin Straus explains, "The direction upward, against gravity, inscribes into space world-regions to which we attach values, such as those expressed by high and low, rise and decline, climbing and falling, superior and inferior, elevated and downcast, looking up to and despising." The phenomenon of verticality, closely associated with an upright posture, gives situations their true human qualities (figure 8.10). "With upright posture counteracting gravity, the vertical, pointing upward and away from the center of gravity, becomes a natural determinant."[52] As a natural determinant, the phenomenon of verticality dominated the history of architecture until the end of the eighteenth century. An obvious example is the long tradition of architectural orders, exemplified in the vertical structure of the column, which stands on its foot (base) and culminates in the head (capital), while the body plays the role of the mediating link between the celestial and terrestrial levels of reality. The verticality of upright posture removes us from the ground and thus contributes to development, which requires freedom; at the same time, it points toward the earth that pulls us downward to the ground that carries and gives support to everything achieved in the fulfillment of our freedom.

The reference to the horizontality and verticality of typical human situations should be taken as only an incomplete approximation of the given natural conditions. There is obviously no limit as to the depth and number of the world dimensions manifested in particular situations; they include temporality (the main source of rhythm), regularity of movement and proportionality, and the question of centrality and periphery. Any attempt to name all the primary dimensions would be futile, because they always arise from a dialogue rooted in a particular historical context. It is also in such situations that the primary conditions and dimensions of the world assert themselves and predetermine its nature. As noted many times before, to do justice to the richness of real situations, it is best to examine a concrete example. I have deliberately selected a commercial building to show that even under apparently unfavorable conditions it is sometimes possible to open a dialogue with the given natural conditions of the project.

The example chosen is an office building at Stockley Park outside London[53] (figure 8.11). The building takes advantage of being situated at the

8.11. Eric Parry Architects (EPA), Stockley Park (Heathrow), office building.

edge of a newly created lake, which represents, together with the ground, its first horizon. In the original proposal the lake is connected with the atrium in the heart of the building by a channel of water parallel with the axis of the entry into the vestibule (figure 8.12). The channel of water is complemented by a skylight of the same size and orientation. The link between the channel and the skylight represents a cut through the building, but at the same time it also connects horizons of the ground and the first floor.

In its nature and arrangement, the space on the first floor is particularly typical of the thinking of the architects. The character of the open plan office space is defined by the translucent glass block walls and continuous narrow ribbon windows (figure 8.13). The contrast between the semitransparency of the walls and the full transparency of the windows creates a strong sense of horizon and of the building's engagement with its

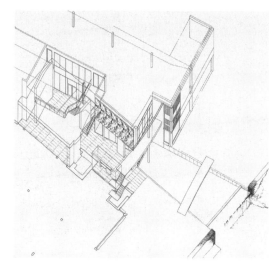

8.12. EPA, Stockley Park, initial proposal.

surroundings. To appreciate horizon's engaging and integrative role, we must recall the discussion earlier in this chapter.

The meaning of the building culminates in the atrium, where the relation between the different horizons is established not only by the source and orientation of light but also by the reflective qualities of water transferred into different materials—slate on the floor and marble on the vertical wall of the vestibule (figure 8.14). The link between the light reflected on the floor and that entering through the skylight is reinforced by the position and orientation of the staircase, which transforms the higher meaning of light into a prosaic everyday reality. This transformation is the best criterion for judging any potential meaning of the building. The meaning either survives such a test or disappears as a wishful dream of the designer or the critic.

This brings us to the critical question—what is the nature of architectural poetics? The first part of the answer is already present in the discussion of the nature of communicative movement and space (in chapter 2), and the discussion of the restorative power of fragments (in chapter 7). In its original sense, poetics refers to a way of making (*poiēsis*) in which the

8.13. EPA, Stockley Park, horizontal window of the first floor (winter landscape).

result preserves continuity with the conditions of its origin. In other words, what characterizes a way of making as poetic is the situatedness of the results in the communicative space of culture. The phenomenon of situatedness stands in clear contrast to instrumental thinking and to the subjective experience of aesthetics. It represents deep respect for the given reality of the natural world, manifested in the rich articulation of typical situations.

The use of typical situations as a primary vehicle of design is a new departure toward an approach that may best be described as situational or as a new poetics of architecture (figure 8.15). The aim of the new poetics is not to become a new theory but to formulate a limited set of creative principles, articulate in the fullest possible way the content and structure of the typical situations, and establish the basic orientation of design. The articulation of content may include contributions from nonarchitectural areas, such as theater, painting, literature, or poetry, where we very often find a surprisingly rich understanding of architectural space. The individual contributions from different areas of culture throw their own light on the same topic—for instance, a living room, library, concert hall, garden, or street—and can thus grasp its essential nature with greater precision and richness

8.14. EPA, Stockley Park, view of the atrium and foyer.

than is possible in conventional causal thinking. Because architecture is in essence a visual discipline, causal thinking can never fully grasp its true reality. We can better achieve such a grasp by accepting the role of similarities, analogies, and metaphors in understanding the visible world. It is mostly owing to the metaphorical structure of the visible world that we can identify and use the contributions from different levels of reality, bringing them into the sphere of architecture much as one can perform a melody in another key.

8.15. Adela Askandar, Vienna project, media center, library interior.

I wonder if it is necessary to argue any further that poetics is not a discipline based on dreams or improvisations and that it could be, as far as architecture is concerned, more rigorous than an analytical or causal approach. We have reached a point where it is probably clear that the new architectural poetics cannot be articulated by one person making a single effort. As a discipline situated in the broad context of culture, poetics can be articulated only in a broad collaboration and over time. To outline the nature of the task was one of my main intentions in writing this book.

- NOTES -

1. M. L. Stackhouse, *Ethics and the Urban Ethos: An Essay in Social Theory and Theological Reconstruction* (Boston: Beacon Press, 1972), p. 3.

2. H. L. Dreyfus, "Misrepresenting Human Intelligence," in *Artificial Intelligence,* ed. R. Born (London: Croom Helm, 1987), pp. 41–55.

3. H. G. Gadamer, *The Relevance of the Beautiful and Other Essays,* trans. N. Walker, ed. R. Bernasconi (Cambridge: Cambridge University Press, 1986), p. 35.

4. Ibid., pp. 92–115. See Aristotle, *Poetics* 1448b2–1450a8; E. Grassi, *Die Theorie des Schönen in der Antike* (Cologne: DuMont, 1962), p. 118.

5. E. H. Gombrich, *Art and Illusion,* Bollingen Series, 35; A. W. Mellon Lectures in the Fine Arts, no. 5 (New York: Pantheon, 1960), pp. 203–212. On a deeper level, unity of representation has a close affinity with the articulation of the world in the Heideggerian tradition; see M. Heidegger, *Being and Time,* trans. J. MacQuarrie and E. Robinson (Oxford: Basil Blackwell, 1967), pp. 91–149; H. G. Gadamer, *Truth and Method,* [trans. W. Glen-Doepel, trans. ed. G. Barden and J. Cumming], 2nd ed. (London: Sheed & Ward, 1975), pp. 397–449.

6. "Congress of International Progressive Artists," in *The Tradition of Constructivism,* ed. S. Bann, Documents of Twentieth-Century Art (London: Thames & Hudson, 1974), p. 59.

7. G. Platz, "Elements in the Creation of a New Style," in *Form and Function: A Source Book for the History of Architecture and Design, 1890–1939,* ed. T. and C. Benton, with D. Sharp (London: Crosby Lockwood Staples, 1975), p. 161.

8. Mies van der Rohe, quoted in F. Neumeyer, *The Artless Word: Mies van der Rohe on the Building Art,* trans. M. Jarzombek (Cambridge, Mass.: MIT Press, 1991), p. 324.

9. Ibid., p. 332.

10. Ibid., p. 324.

11. Ibid.

12. H. Bauer, "Architektur als Kunst," in *Kunstgeschichte und Kunsttheorie im 19. Jahrhundert* (Berlin: W. de Gruyter, 1963), pp. 138–147; A. Horn-Oncken, *Über das Schickliche: Studien zur Geschichte der Architekturtheorie* (Gottingen: Vandenhoeck & Ruprecht, 1967), pp. 9–29.

13. Mies van der Rohe, quoted in Neumeyer, *The Artless Word,* p. 324.

14. Ibid.

15. Ibid., p. 332.

16. The history of the problem of emancipatory representation is outlined in R. Poggioli, *The Theory of the Avant-Garde,* trans. G. Fitzgerald (Cambridge, Mass.: Harvard University Press, 1968); Marc Le Bot, *Francis Picabia et la crise des valeurs figuratives* (Paris: Klincksieck, 1968); H. Osborne, *Abstraction and Artifice in Twentieth-Century Art* (Oxford: Clarendon Press, 1979).

17. T. van Doesburg, *Art Concret,* no. 1 (April 1931): 1; trans. in Osborne, *Abstraction and Artifice in Twentieth-Century Art,* p. 128.

18. D. Libeskind, *End Space: An Exhibition at the Architectural Association* (London: The Association, 1980), pp. 12, 22.

19. Ibid., p. 20.

20. J. Ladrière, "Mathématiques et formalisme," in *Revue des Questions Scientifiques,* October 1955, pp. 538–573; trans. as "Mathematics and Formalism," in *Phenomenology and the Natural Sciences,* ed. J. J. Kockelmans and T. J. Kisel (Evanston, Ill.: Northwestern University Press, 1970), pp. 481–483.

21. M. Seuphor, *Cercle et carré,* Collections Art—Action—Architecture (Paris: P. Belfond, 1971), p. 38.

22. R. Dubos, *Man Adapting* (New Haven: Yale University Press, 1965), p. 42.

23. See G. Gusdorf, *Naissance de la conscience romantique au siècle des lumières,* vol. 7 of *Les sciences humaines et la pensée occidentale* (Paris: Payot, 1976); M. H. Abrams, *The Mirror and the Lamp: Romantic Theory and the Critical Tradition* (Oxford: Oxford University Press, 1953); E. Behler and J. Hörisch, eds., *Die Aktualität der Frühromantik* (Paderborn: Schöningh, 1987).

24. The attitude of the Romantics is exemplified in Goethe's view of Newtonian science; see H. B. Nisbet, *Goethe and the Scientific Tradition* (London: Institute of Germanic Studies, University of London, 1972). For a general history and assessment of Romantic science, see W. Lepenies, *Das Ende der Naturgeschichte: Wandel kultureller Selbstverständlichkeiten in den Wissenschaften des 18. und 19. Jahrhunderts* ([Frankfurt am Main]: Suhrkamp, 1978).

25. Scharoun, quoted in E. Janofske, *Architektur-Räume: Idee und Gestalt bei Hans Scharoun* (Braunschweig: F. Vieweg & Sohn, 1984), p. 22.

26. Ibid., p. 17.

27. Scharoun, quoted in P. Blundell-Jones, *Hans Scharoun* (London: Phaidon, 1995), p. 178.

28. Janofske, *Architektur-Räume*, p. 35.

29. See S. Honey, *Mies van der Rohe: European Works* (London: Academy Editions, 1986); W. Tegethoff, "From Obscurity to Maturity," in *Mies van der Rohe: Critical Essays*, ed. F. Schulze (New York: Museum of Modern Art, 1989), pp. 28–94; B. Colomina, "Mies Not," in *The Presence of Mies*, ed. D. Mertins (New York: Princeton Architectural Press, 1994), pp. 193–223.

30. Tegethoff, "From Obscurity to Maturity," p. 43.

31. H. Scharoun, "Bauen und Leben," *Bauwelt* 58 (1967): 157.

32. Mies van der Rohe, "Architektur und Zeit," *Der Querschnitt* (1924), quoted in P. Johnson, *Mies van der Rohe* (New York: Museum of Modern Art, 1947), p. 186; Scharoun, quoted in Janofske, *Architektur-Räume*, pp. 137–138.

33. See P. Ricoeur, "Universal Civilization and National Cultures," in *History and Truth*, trans. C. A. Kelbley (Evanston, Ill.: Northwestern University Press, 1965), pp. 271–287; C. H. Taylor, *The Sources of the Self: The Making of the Modern Identity* (Cambridge: Cambridge University Press, 1989); G. Vattimo, *The End of Modernity*, trans. J. Snyder (Cambridge: Polity Press, 1988).

34. Mies van der Rohe, quoted in Neumeyer, *The Artless Word*, p. 326.

35. K. Teige, "Konstruktivismus a likvidace 'umění'" (Constructivism and the liquidation of 'art') in *Disk* 2 (1925): 4–8; reprinted in K. Teige, *Svět stavby a básně* (The world of building and poetry) (Prague: Československý Spisovatel, 1966), pp. 129–144 (quotation, 142).

36. Conversation between Alvin Boyarsky and the members of the Coop partnership (Wolf Prix, Helmut Swiczinsky), in Coop Himmelblau, *Blau Box* (London: Architectural Association, 1988), pp. 12, 16.

37. L. Aragon, *Treatise on Style*, trans. A. Waters (Lincoln: University of Nebraska Press, 1991), p. 96.

38. J. Habermas, introduction to *Observations on "the Spiritual Situation of the Age": Contemporary German Perspectives*, ed. Habermas, trans. A. Buchwalter (Cambridge, Mass.: MIT Press, 1985), p. 23.

39. M. Merleau-Ponty, *Phenomenology of Perception*, trans. C. Smith (London: Routledge & Kegan Paul, 1962), p. 340.

40. Ibid., p. 291.

41. The communicative space of traditional culture was articulated in a dialectical process known as the Great Chain of Being; see A. O. Lovejoy, *The Great Chain of Being* (1936; reprint, Cambridge, Mass.: Harvard University Press, 1974).

CHAPTER 2 **THE NATURE OF COMMUNICATIVE SPACE**

1. I have discussed the problem of representation on many occasions with Hans-Georg Gadamer, whose influence on my own understanding was very profound. In the field of architecture and visual arts I have learned much from similar discussions with a number of friends and colleagues—most of all with Colin St. John Wilson, whose knowledge of modern architecture, art, and humanities, as well as support of my work, were particularly stimulating. It is for that reason that I dedicate this chapter to him.

2. The vision is inverted by a set of lenses that turn the visual field upside down and flip it from left to right. For a detailed description of the experiment, see P. Schilder, *The Image and Appearance of the Human Body: Studies in the Constructive Energies of the Psyche* (1935; reprint, New York: Science Editions, J. Wiley & Sons, 1950), pp. 106–114.

3. M. Merleau-Ponty, *Phenomenology of Perception,* trans. C. Smith (London: Routledge & Kegan Paul, 1962), pp. 248–254.

4. Ibid., p. 250.

5. Ibid., p. 253.

6. Schilder, *The Image and Appearance of the Human Body,* p. 109.

7. See Merleau-Ponty, *Phenomenology of Perception,* pp. 222–225; M. Thomson, "The Nature of Space and the Blind" (dipl. diss., University of Cambridge, 1996); J. V. Weelden, *On Being Blind: An Ontological Approach to the Problem of Blindness* (Amsterdam: Netherlands Society for the Blind, 1967); W. P. Roland, *Being Blind in-the-World: A Phenomenological Analysis of Blindness* (Pretoria, South Africa: National Council for the Blind, 1985).

8. See David Katz, "Der Aufbau der Tastwelt," *Zeitschrift für Psychologie* 2 (1925): 104–145; G. Révész, *Psychology and Art of the Blind,* trans. H. A. Wolff (London: Longmans, Green 1950).

9. Merleau-Ponty, *Phenomenology of Perception,* p. 223.

10. The long and very often painful process of adaptation to the "new" world of vision is discussed, using clinical case studies, in M. von Senden, *Space and Sight: The Perception of Space and Shape in the Congenitally Blind Before and After Operation,* trans. P. Heath (London: Methuen, 1960).

11. Patient quoted in ibid., p. 62.

12. Von Senden, *Space and Sight,* p. 129.

13. Ibid., p. 199.

14. The first long-term experience in zero gravity was acquired in the Sky Laboratory (launched on 13 May 1973), as described by H. S. F. Cooper, Jr., in *A House in Space* (New York: Holt, Rinehart, & Winston, 1977). The space station consisted of two sections. The command module had a clear floor and ceiling arrangement; it was connected by the docking adaptor, designed radially as a tunnel, to the long cylindrical workshop divided into two parts: the larger open upper deck and the smaller lower deck, situated at the very end of the station and used both for working and as living quarters, with an oriented floor and ceiling. The lower deck was designed as if it were a room on earth, and included a dining table and seats. It is instructive to see that for inhabitants of the station, the main problem in most of its spaces was the same as that experienced on earth in cases of disturbed orientation.

15. Ibid., pp. 72, 111.

16. Ibid., p. 111.

17. Ibid., p. 72.

18. See K. Goldstein, "L'analyse de l'aphasie et l'essence du langage," *Journal de Psychologie* 28 (1933): 430–496; *Selected Papers—Ausgewählte Schriften,* ed. A. Gurwitsch, E. Haudek, and W. E. Haudek (The Hague: Nijhoff, 1971); T. Kisiel, "Aphasiology, Phenomenology, Structuralism," in *Language and Language Disturbances,* ed. E. W. Straus, Fifth Lexington Conference on Pure and Applied Phenomenology (Pittsburgh: Duquesne University Press, 1974), pp. 201–234.

19. Kisiel, "Aphasiology, Phenomenology, Structuralism," p. 217.

20. Merleau-Ponty, *Phenomenology of Perception,* p. 136.

21. Goldstein and, following him, Merleau-Ponty and others use the terms "concrete" and "abstract." On the other hand, Kisiel uses the term "categorial" instead of "abstract" and replaces "concrete" with "de-differentiation of the categorial background." For a summary of the debate, see Kisiel, "Aphasiology, Phenomenology, Structuralism," pp. 201–203.

22. K. Goldstein, "Autobiography," in *A History of Psychology in Autobiography,* vol. 5, ed. E. G. Boring and G. Lindzey (New York: Russell & Russell, 1967), p. 162.

23. O. Sacks, *A Leg to Stand On* (New York: Summit Books, 1984), pp. 144–150.

24. See the discussion of aphasia and language disturbances in K. Goldstein, *Language and Language Disturbances* (New York: Grune & Stratton, 1948), and also Kisiel, "Aphasiology, Phenomenology, Structuralism."

25. For a survey of the main tendencies in ecological research, see A. Bramwell, *Ecology in the Twentieth Century: A History* (New Haven: Yale University Press, 1989).

26. I am referring to the notion of world that was introduced into modern thinking by Edmund Husserl, developed further by Martin Heidegger and in more recent hermeneutical phenomenology by Hans-Georg Gadamer; see Gadamer, "The Science of the Life World," in *Philosophical Hermeneutics,* trans. and ed. D. E. Linge (Berkeley: University of California Press, 1976), pp. 182–198; W. Biemel, *Le concept de monde chez Heidegger* (Paris: J. Brin, 1950).

27. See J-P. Sartre, *Imagination,* trans. F. Williams (Ann Arbor: University of Michigan Press, 1962); E. Minkowski, "Imagination," in *Readings in Existential Phenomenology,* ed. N. Lawrence and D. O'Connor (Englewood Cliffs, N.J.: Prentice-Hall, 1967), pp. 75–93.

28. A. Gehlen, *Man, His Nature and Place in the World,* trans. C. Macmillan and K. Pilliner (New York: Columbia University Press, 1988), p. 54.

29. Ibid., p. 55.

30. Ibid., p. 56.

31. Ibid., p. 61.

32. For a detailed description of the windows, see M. Y. Delaporte, *Les vitraux de la cathédrale de Chartres* (Chartres: E. Houvet, 1926).

33. H. Rahner, "The Christian Mystery of Sun and Moon," in *Greek Myths and Christian Mystery* (1963; reprint, New York: Biblo & Tannen, 1971), pp. 89–179.

34. The separation of individual arts, which gained theoretical legitimacy at the end of the eighteenth century (see, e.g., Lessing's *Laokoön*), was accepted by modern scholarship; it has remained a major obstacle for a genuine understanding of individual arts ever since.

35. Exceptions include G. Bandmann, "Ikonologie der Architektur," in *Politische Architektur in Europa (vom Mittelalter bis heute),* ed. M. Warnke (Cologne: DuMont, 1984), pp. 19–72; E. Forssman, "Ikonologie und Allgemeine Kunstgeschichte," in *Ikonographie und Ikonologie,* ed. E. Kaemmerling (Cologne: DuMont, 1979), pp. 257–301; H. Sedlmayr, *Kunst und Wahrheit: Zur Theorie und Methode der Kunstgeschichte* Rowohlts deutsche Enzyklopädie (Hamburg: Rowohlt, [1958]).

36. See M. Baxandall, *Painting and Experience in Fifteenth Century Italy: A Primer in the Social History of Pictorial Style*, 2nd ed. (Oxford: Oxford University Press, 1988); E. Kris and O. Kurz, *Legend, Myth, and Magic in the Image of the Artist: A Historical Experiment* (New Haven: Yale University Press, 1979); R. Wittkower and M. Wittkower, *Born under Saturn; The Character and Conduct of Artists: A Documented History from Antiquity to the French Revolution* (New York: Random House, 1963); C. Smith, *Architecture in the Culture of Early Humanism: Ethics, Aesthetics, and Eloquence, 1400–1470* (New York: Oxford University Press, 1992); M. Wackernagel, *The World of the Florentine Renaissance Artist*, trans. A. Luchs (Princeton: Princeton University Press, 1981).

37. Goldstein, *Language and Language Disturbances*, p. 357.

38. Ibid., p. 327.

39. Merleau-Ponty, *Phenomenology of Perception*, p. 191. Categories have their foundation in perception, where they are "seen" not as categories but as perceptions anticipating categorial apprehension. Categorial intuition is intuition of that which is then conceptually grasped as a category. A good illustration of categorial intuition is the ability of a child who does not speak yet to identify a dog—not just a particular animal but dog as such, as a species. See M. Heidegger, "Categorial Intuition," in *A History of the Concept of Time*, trans. T. Kisiel (Bloomington: Indiana University Press, 1985), pp. 47–72.

40. See Gehlen, *Man, His Nature and Place in the World*, pp. 167–181; P. Lersch, *Aufbau der Person*, 10th ed. (Munich: J. A. Barth, 1966), pp. 121–215; M. Polanyi, *The Tacit Dimension* (New York: Doubleday, 1967), pp. 1–27.

41. Merleau-Ponty, *Phenomenology of Perception*, pp. 174–203. See also his *Consciousness and the Acquisition of Language*, trans. H. J. Silverman (Evanston, Ill.: Northwestern University Press), 1973.

42. Albert Einstein, answering the question about the working method of a mathematician; quoted in J. Hadamard, *The Psychology of Invention in the Mathematical Field* (1945; reprint, New York: Dover, 1954), pp. 142–143.

43. L. S. Vygotsky, *Thought and Language*, ed. and trans. E. Hanfmann and G. Vakar (1962; reprint, Cambridge, Mass.: MIT Press, 1981), p. 115.

44. O. Sacks, *Seeing Voices* (London: Picador, 1991), pp. 62–70; "If all the trajectories of all the sign actions—direction and direction—change of all upper arms, forearms, wrist, hand, and finger movement, all the nuances of all the eye and face and head actions— could be described, we would have a description of the phenomena into which thought is transformed by a sign language" (p. 90).

45. This affinity can be illustrated by the development of hieroglyphs; see E. Iversen, *The Myth of Egypt and Its Hieroglyphs in European Tradition* (1961; reprint, Princeton: Princeton University Press, 1993).

46. Merleau-Ponty, *Phenomenology of Perception,* p. 183.

47. The following lines from the anonymous manuscript "Stein-Mezbuechlein" typify the stonemasons' rhymes:

> Was in Stainkunst zu sehen ist,
> das kein irr—noch Abweg ist
> sondern schnurrecht ein Linial,
> durchzogen den Cirkel überall,
> so findest du drey in viere stehn,
> und also durch eins ins Centrum gehn.
> (C. Heideloff, *Die Bauhütte des Mittelalters in Deutschland* [Nuremberg: Johann Adam Stein, 1844], p. 15)

48. E. Husserl, *The Crisis of European Sciences and Transcendental Phenomenology,* trans. D. Carr (Evanston, Ill.: Northwestern University Press, 1970), pp. 363–364.

49. Proclus, *A Commentary on the First Book of Euclid's Elements,* trans. G. R. Morrow (1970; reprint, Princeton: Princeton University Press, 1992), p. 50.

50. The relation between geometry and dialectics is discussed in Plato's *Republic* 511d, 526e, 533c; the relation between geometry and the logic of language, in Aristotle's *Posterior Analytics* 75b12, 79a9.

51. H. Keller, *The Story of My Life* (1903; reprint, New York: Bantam, 1990), p. 16.

52. Though some argue that the term "sensory deprivation" is not appropriate, the nature of the experiments is clear—they study human experience under conditions of the most extreme possible isolation from the influences of the surrounding world. See J. A. Vernon, *Inside the Black Room* (1963; reprint, Harmondsworth: Penguin, 1966), pp. 82–88.

53. A. R. Luria, *The Man with a Shattered World,* trans. L. Solotaroff (Cambridge, Mass.: Harvard University Press, 1972), pp. xv, 43, 159.

54. The domain of the natural world extends the domain of the life world in the direction of natural conditions of cultural existence. The term "natural world" was introduced in this context by the Czech philosopher Jan Patočka in *Přirozený svět jako filosofický problém* (The natural world as a philosophical problem) (Prague, 1936), published in French as *Le monde naturel comme problème philosophique,* trans. J. Danek and H. Declève (The Hague: Martin Nijhoff, 1976), and in English (short selections) as "The Natural World and Phenomenology," in E. Kohák, *Jan Patocka: Philosophy and Selected Writings* (Chicago: University of Chicago Press, 1989), pp. 239–274.

55. See G. Brand, *Die Lebenswelt* (Berlin: W. de Gruyter, 1971); H. Hohl, *Lebenswelt und Geschichte* (Freiberg: Karl Alher, 1962).

56. Speaking of language in areas outside the domain of the verbal depends on our ability to see these individual languages as different modes of articulation in a corresponding mode of embodiment, which can be expressed in words only indirectly and metaphorically. Some authors hold a position very close to my own: See N. Goodman, *Languages of Art*, 2nd ed. (Indianapolis: Hackett Publishing, 1976); W. Weidle, *Gestalt und Sprache des Kunstwerkes* (Mittenwald: Mäander, 1981); H. G. Gadamer, *The Relevance of the Beautiful and Other Essays,* trans. N. Walker, ed. R. Bernasconi (Cambridge: Cambridge University Press, 1986); C. Braegger, ed., *Architektur und Sprache: Gedenkschrift für Richard Zürcher* (Munich: Prestel-Verlag, 1982).

57. It is possible to see an analogy between the Greek notion that *physis* is articulated through *logos* and the contemporary notion that Being (world) is articulated through language. Otto Pöggeler calls this possibility the "topology of Being" in *Martin Heidegger's Path of Thinking,* trans. D. Magurshak and S. Barber (Atlantic Highlands, N.J.: Humanities Press International, 1989), pp. 227–243.

58. M. Heidegger, *Being and Time*, trans. J. MacQuarrie and E. Robinson (Oxford: Basil Blackwell, 1967), pp. 102–122; H. G. Gadamer, *Truth and Method,* [trans. W. Glen-Doepel, trans. ed. G. Barden and J. Cumming], 2nd ed. (London: Sheed & Ward, 1975), pp. 397–414.

59. The nature and structure of preunderstanding is discussed by Heidegger in "Being-there as Understanding" and "Understanding and Interpretation," in *Being and Time,* pp. 182–195.

60. M. F. Boyer, *The French Café* (London: Thames & Hudson, 1994).

61. Gehlen, *Man, His Nature and Place in the World,* p. 125.

62. Ibid., p. 120.

63. See J. L'Hermitte, *L'image de notre corps* (Paris: Nouvelle Revue Critique, 1939); Schilder, *The Image and Appearance of the Human Body;* E. Straus, "Born to See, Bound to Behold: Reflections on the Function of Upright Posture in the Aesthetic Attitude," in *The Philosophy of the Body: Rejections of Cartesian Dualism,* ed. S. F. Spicker (Chicago: Quadrangle Books, 1970), pp. 334–363.

64. Merleau-Ponty, *Phenomenology of Perception*, p. 146.

65. E. Straus, "Aesthesiology and Hallucinations," in *Existence: A New Dimension in Psychiatry and Psychology,* ed. R. May, E. Angel, and H. F. Ellenberger (1958; reprint, New York: Simon & Schuster, 1967), p. 165.

66. Ibid., p. 160.

67. H. Jonas, *The Phenomenon of Life: Toward a Philosophical Biology* (New York: Harper & Row, 1966), p. 141.

68. Gehlen, *Man, His Nature and Place in the World,* p. 173.

69. The problem of constancy has been studied for some time by psychologists, mostly by those of the Gestalt orientation; see W. Köhler, *The Gestalt Psychology* (London: G. Bell, 1930). Some have assimilated constancy to archetypes, without appreciating fully that the source of constancy is not in individual phenomena but in the structure of the situation as a whole; see H. Frankfort, "The Archetype in Analytical Psychology and the History of Religion," *Journal of the Warburg and Courtauld Institutes* 21 (1958): 166–178.

70. The primacy of perception was first discussed at length by Merleau-Ponty in a lecture delivered in 1946 and published in 1949; see "The Primacy of Perception and Its Philosophical Consequences," trans. J. M. Edie, in *Primacy of Perception and Other Essays,* ed. Edie (1964; reprint, Evanston, Ill.: Northwestern University Press, 1971), pp. 12–42.

The unique place of vision in the field of perception is discussed by H. Jonas, "The Nobility of Sight: A Study in the Phenomenology of Senses," in *The Phenomenon of Life,* pp. 135–157, and by Straus, "Born to See, Bound to Behold."

71. The extent to which visible reality has lost its primacy and meaning can be seen in current developments in architecture and the visual arts dominated by the conceptual imagination and conceptual structures. And yet the visible remains the matrix of cultural continuity across the spectrum, from texts to our corporeal existence. The visible world is also the indisputable source of our imagination, fantasies, invention, and creativity. See M. Thomson, "Architecture and the Depth of Visibility" (dipl. diss., University of Cambridge, 1999); J. V. Weelden, *On Being Blind: An Ontological Approach to the Problem of Blindness* (Amsterdam: Netherlands Society for the Blind, 1967); R. V. Hine, *Second Sight* (Berkeley: University of California Press, 1993); J. Zimler and J. M. Keenan, "Imagery in the Congenitally Blind: How Visual Are Visual Images?" *Journal of Experimental Psychology: Learning, Memory and Cognition* 9, pt. 1 (1983): 269–282.

72. The term *per visibilia* refers to the sensible world—associated in the history of European thinking with corporeality, human finitude, and terrestrial existence. The relationship of *visibilia* to *invisibilia,* of the concrete phenomena to concepts or ideas, constitutes the main axis of European culture and its unity.

73. The delicate relationship between individual modes of representation is very often overshadowed by such global terms as "symbolic image"; and yet we are able to see without great difficulty the difference between the literary, pictorial, and architectural symbol. See Goodman, *The Languages of Art.*

74. The hierarchy of representation exemplifies the Great Chain of Being, an idea that dominated European culture from antiquity until modernity; see A. O. Lovejoy, *The Great Chain of Being* (1936; reprint, Cambridge, Mass.: Harvard University Press, 1974).

75. See R. Sedlmaier and R. Pfister, *Die fürstbischöfliche Residenz zu Würzburg*, 2 vols. in 1 (Munich: G. Müller, 1923); M. H. von Freeden and C. Lamb, *Das Meisterwerk des Giovanni Battista Tiepolo: Die Fresken der Würzburger Residenz* (Munich: Hirmer, 1956).

76. See S. K. Heninger, Jr., *The Cosmographical Glass: Renaissance Diagrams of the Universe* (San Marino, Calif.: Huntington Library, 1977), pp. 177–178; George Hersey, *The Lost Meaning of Classical Architecture* (Cambridge, Mass.: MIT Press, 1988), pp. 69–77.

77. G. Bachelard, *Air et songes* (Paris: Corti, 1962), pp. 14–15; trans. C. Gaudin in *On Poetic Imagination and Reverie* (Indianapolis: Bobbs-Merrill, 1971), p. 37.

78. Merleau-Ponty, *Phenomenology of Perception,* p. 144. For an investigation of the relation of movement and experience see V. von Weizsäcker, *Der Gestaltkreis: Theorie der Einheit von Wahrnehmen und Bewegen* (Frankfurt am Main: Suhrkamp, 1973).

79. E. Minkowski, *Vers une cosmologie* (Paris: Aubier-Montaigne, 1936), pp. 101–102; English translation in Bachelard, *On Poetic Imagination,* pp. 71–72 (quotation, p. 72).

80. The metaphorical nature of analogy anticipates the notion of order (expressed as a geometrical proportion) in Plato's *Gorgias* 508a and the notion of just practice (similarly expressed) in Aristotle's *Nicomachean Ethics* V.4, 1131b25–1132b20. For a further discussion of the nature of proportion, see U. Eco, *The Aesthetics of Thomas Aquinas,* trans. H. Bredin (London: Radius, 1988), pp. 71–98.

81. Architecture was not related to tectonics before the nineteenth century. The recent revival of tectonics as an essential aspect of architectural order is a sign of intellectual confusion that leads critics to seriously misunderstand the true nature of architecture. For a critical assessment of the problem of tectonics, see H. Bauer, "Schopenhauer und Botticher: Tektonik als Symbol," in *Kunstgeschichte und Kunsttheorie im 19. Jahrhundert* (Berlin: W. de Gruyter, 1963), pp. 147–152, and most recently M. Hvattum, "Poetics and Practical Aesthetics in the Writing of Gottfried Semper" (Ph.D. diss., University of Cambridge, 1999), pp. 88–98.

82. The use of the term "architectonics" in other areas of culture, mainly in philosophy, is discussed in D. Payot, *Le philosophe et l'architecte* (Paris: Aubier-Montaigne, 1982).

83. See M. Ashton, "Allegory, Fact, and Meaning in Giambattista Tiepolo's Four Continents in Wurzburg," *Art Bulletin,* March 1982; M. Levey, *Giambattista Tiepolo: His Life and Art* (New Haven: Yale University Press, 1986), pp. 167–213.

84. Gadamer, *Truth and Method,* p. 140.

85. Ibid., p. 141.

86. The dominance of architectural setting in the art of memory can be explained by natural locations (*locationae naturae*) of memory. The notion of topics (commonplaces) and their role in our use of language illustrate this point. In the art of memory, images are retained more easily than abstract thoughts, for they "require an abode" for "the embodied cannot be known without a place (*corpus intelligi sine loco non potest*)" (M. J. Carruthers, *The Book of Memory: A Study of Memory in Medieval Culture* [Cambridge: Cambridge University Press, 1990], p. 73; see also pp. 74–79).

87. F. Yates, *The Art of Memory* (1966; reprint, Harmondsworth: Penguin, 1969), pp. 97–98; Yates is quoting a commentary by Bartolomeo de San Concordio (1262–1347) on Aristotle's *On Memory and Reminiscence.*

88. Merleau-Ponty, *Phenomenology of Perception,* p. 291.

89. E. Straus, "Remembering and Infantile Amnesia," in *Phenomenological Psychology: The Selected Papers of Erwin W. Straus,* trans. E. Eng (London: Tavistock, 1966), p. 63.

90. See W. Ong, "Oral Memorisation," in *Orality and Literacy* (New York: Methuen, 1982), pp. 57–68; E. A. Havelock, *The Muse Learns to Write: Reflections on Orality and Literacy from Antiquity to the Present* (New Haven: Yale University Press, 1986), pp. 29, 42, 75.

91. Merleau-Ponty, *Phenomenology of Perception,* p. 19.

92. At a certain depth, situations are not part of personal memory; hence the saying that "we know always more than we remember." An interesting exploration of the impersonal, tacit reality of memory was undertaken by the Surrealists; see M. Carrouges, *André Breton and the Concepts of Surrealism,* trans. M. Prendergast (Tuscaloosa: University of Alabama Press, 1974), pp. 179–220.

93. H. L. Dreyfus, "Misrepresenting Human Intelligence," in *Artificial intelligence* (London: Croom Helm, 1987), p. 44.

94. H. L. Dreyfus, *What Computers Still Can't Do: A Critique of Artificial Reason* (Cambridge, Mass.: MIT Press, 1992), p. 300.

95. A. Maurois, *The Quest for Proust,* trans. G. Hopkins (London: Cape, 1968), p. 178.

96. "And in all the stone's veins and bones and flame-like stainings, and broken and disconnected lines, they write various legends, never untrue, of the former political state of the mountain kingdom to which they belonged, of its infirmities and fortitudes, convulsions and consolidations, from the beginning of Time" (Proust, in E. E. Frank, *Liter-*

ary Architecture: Essays toward a Tradition [1979; reprint, Berkeley: University of California Press, 1983], p. 124).

97. M. Proust, *À la recherche du temps perdu* (1914–1927; reprint, Paris: Gallimard, 1964), 1:4, 5.

98. M. Heidegger, *The Metaphysical Foundations of Logic,* trans. M. Heim (Bloomington: Indiana University Press, 1984), pp. 123–128.

99. E. Straus, "Norm and Pathology of I-World Relations," in *Phenomenological Psychology,* p. 268.

100. The relation between play (game) and architecture is not only analogical. There is a close link between play, theater, and architecture, as the history of theater and the tradition of the art of memory make clear. For the deeper, ontological understanding of play and its relevance for comprehending architecture and art, see H. G. Gadamer, "The Concept of Play," in *Truth and Method,* p. 91.

101. M. Heidegger, "The Origin of the Work of Art," in *Poetry, Language, Thought,* trans. A. Hofstadter (New York: Harper & Row, 1971), p. 46.

CHAPTER 3 **THE PERSPECTIVAL TRANSFORMATION OF THE MEDIEVAL WORLD**

1. Unfortunately, the narrow and dogmatic assessment of Renaissance perspective persists, as the following statement illustrates: "A particular work of art is never an inevitable outcome of social and intellectual factors: there is no supreme principle of necessity in artistic causation. Whatever conditions we may believe to have been conducive to the formulation and consolidation of linear perspective in early fifteenth-century Florence, they are not 'causes' in a scientific sense. The only direct cause in the invention of perspective was Brunelleschi himself" (M. Kemp, "Science, Non-Science, and Nonsense: Brunelleschi's Perspective," *Art History* 1, no. 2 [1978]: 135).

2. The first important work on optics in the West was that of R. Grosseteste, and the first center of optical studies was the Papal Palace in Viterbo, closely linked with the changes in visual art in Assisi; see P. Hills, *The Light of Early Italian Painting* (New Haven: Yale University Press, 1987), p. 64.

3. In painting, this new sense of space was primarily the work of Cavallini and his circle in Rome, of Cimabue and Giotto and their circles in the church of San Francesco in Assisi, and Giotto and his disciples in the church of Santa Croce in Florence; see J. White, *The Birth and Rebirth of Pictorial Space,* 3rd ed. (London: Faber & Faber, 1987), p. 47; J. White, "Cavallini and the Last Frescoes in San Paolo," *Journal of the Warburg and Courtauld Institutes* 19 (1956): 84–95; H. Belting, *Die Oberkirche von San Francesco in Assisi* (Berlin: Mann, 1977). For architecture around 1300, see W. Gross, *Die* *abendländische Architektur um 1300* (Stuttgart: W. Kohlhammer, 1948); W. Braunfels, *Mittelalterliche Stadtbaukunst in der Toskana* (Berlin: Mann 1953); H. Bauer, *Kunst und Utopie: Studien über das Kunst- und Staadtsdenken in der Renaissance* (Berlin: de Gruyter, 1965). Among the examples of the new sense of space, the most conspicuous is the choir of Santa Croce (see Gross) and, on the urban level, the thirteenth-century transformation of the Campo in Siena (see Braunfels, p. 35).

4. E. Konigson, *L'espace théâtral médiéval* (Paris: Éditions du CNRS, 1975).

5. Braunfels, *Mittelalterliche Stadtbaukunst in der Toskana,* p. 85.

6. In the period around 1300, contemporary documents compare some European cities (particularly in Italy) with the perfection of the celestial paradise—"quod civitates factae sunt ad similitudinem paradisi" is a typical phrase. This new phenomenon is discussed by Bauer in *Kunst und Utopie,* pp. 1–17.

7. White, *The Birth and Rebirth of Pictorial Space,* p. 125.

8. On 9 April 1830, Gauss wrote to Friedrich Wilhelm Bessel, "According to my most sincere conviction the theory of space has an entirely different place in knowledge from that occupied by pure mathematics. There is lacking throughout our knowledge of it the complete persuasion of necessity which is common to the latter; we must add in humility that if number is exclusively the product of our mind, space has a reality outside our mind and we cannot completely prescribe its laws" (quoted in M. Kline, *Mathematics: The Loss of Certainty* [Oxford: Oxford University Press, 1980], p. 87).

9. Kline, *Mathematics,* p. 88.

10. D. R. Lachterman, *The Ethics of Geometry: A Genealogy of Modernity* (New York: Routledge, 1989), p. 80 n. 88.

11. R. Grosseteste, *On Light (De Luce),* trans. C. C. Riedl (Milwaukee: Marquette University Press, 1978), p. 10. On the nature of light, Grosseteste declares: "The form cannot desert matter, because it is inseparable from it, and matter itself cannot be deprived of form, but I have proposed that it is light which possesses of its very nature the function of multiplying itself and diffusing itself instantaneously in all directions. Whatever performs this operation is either light or some other agent that acts in virtue of its participation in light to which this operation belongs essentially. Corporeity, therefore, is either light itself or the agent, which performs the aforementioned operation and introduces dimensions into matter in virtue of its participation in light, and acts through the power of this same light. But the first form cannot introduce dimensions into matter through the power of a subsequent form. Therefore light is not a form subsequent to corporeity, but it is corporeity itself" (p. 11).

12. Grosseteste's precedents for the philosophical interpretation of creation can be found in St. Basil's *Hexaemeron,* St. Augustine's *De trinitate,* and in John Scotus Erigena's *De divisione naturae.*

13. G. Duby, *The Age of the Cathedrals: Art and Society, 980–1420,* trans. E. Levieux and B. Thompson (Chicago: University of Chicago Press, 1981), pp. 148–149.

14. Plotinus, *Enneads* VI.4.8.; trans. A. H. Armstrong as *Plotinus,* 7 vols., Loeb Classical Library (Cambridge, Mass: Harvard University Press; London: Heinemann, 1966–1988), 6:297.

15. Plotinus, *Enneads* II.4.5; trans. Armstrong, 2:115.

16. For the nature of the intelligible world (*noētos kosmos*), see Philo, *De opificio mundi* 16, discussed in J. Dillon, *The Middle Platonists* (London: Duckworth, 1977), pp. 158–159; also see St. Augustine's *De Genesi ad litteram* 11.9.17.

17. See K. Hedwig, *Sphaera Lucis: Studien zur Intelligibilität des Seienden in Kontext der Mittelalterlichen Lichtspekulation* (Münster: Aschendorff, 1980); M. T. d'Alverny, "Le cosmos symbolique du XIIème siècle," *AHDLMA [Archives d'histoire doctrinale et littéraire du Moyen Age]* 20 (1953): 31–81.

18. F. Ohly, "Deus Geometra," in *Interdisziplinäre Forschungen zur Geschichte des frühen Mittelalters,* ed. N. Kamp (Berlin: de Gruyter, 1982), p. 142.

19. The term *perspectiva* was associated with medieval mathematical optics (*perspectiva naturalis*). Roger Bacon introduced the term as a title of Part V of his *Opus maius,* thus originating the tradition of *perspectiva* in the West. Bacon had a strong influence on his fellow Franciscan John Peckham, later archbishop of Canterbury, who wrote a popular treatise, *Perspectiva communis* (1279), and on the Silesian scholar Witelo and his long and equally influential treatise *Perspectiva* (1273). The perspectivist tradition persisted through the fourteenth century. The most influential treatise of that period was Biagio (Pelacani) da Parma, *Quaestiones perspectivae* (ca. 1390).

20. See, e.g., D. Lindberg, *Theories of Vision from al-Kindi to Kepler* (Chicago: University of Chicago Press, 1976).

21. Aristotle, *Physics* 194a10, 26; trans. P. H. Wicksteed and F. M. Cornford, 2 vols., Loeb Classical Library (1929–1934; reprint, Cambridge, Mass.: Harvard University Press; London: W. Heinemann, 1957–1960), 1:121, 123.

22. See W. R. Theisen, ed. and trans., "The Mediaeval Tradition of Euclid's Optics" (Ph.D. diss., University of Wisconsin, 1972); Euclid, *L'optique et la catoptrique,* trans. P. Ver Eecke, new ed. (Paris: A. Blanchard, 1959); H. E. Burton, trans., "The Optics of Euclid," *Journal of the Optical Society of America* 35 (1945): 357–372; A. Lejeune, *Euclide et*

Ptolémée: Deux stades de l'optique geométrique grecque (Louvain: Bibliothèque de l'Université, Bureaux du "Recueil," 1948).

23. Proclus, *A Commentary on the First Book of Euclid's Elements,* trans. G. R. Morrow (1970; reprint, Princeton: Princeton University Press, 1992), p. 58; F. M. Cornford, introduction to *Plato and Parmenides,* trans. Cornford (1939; reprint, London: Routledge & Kegan Paul, 1980), p. 15. For the meaning of cosmic figures and the dialectical reasoning in Plato's cosmology (*Timaeus*), see H. G. Gadamer, *Dialogue and Dialectic: Eight Hermeneutical Studies on Plato,* trans. P. C. Smith (New Haven: Yale University Press, 1980), pp. 156–194; see also Aristotle, *De anima* 404b.

24. Geometry has a capacity to "facilitate the apprehension of the idea of the good" and to "force the soul to turn its vision round to the region where dwells the most blessed part of reality, which it is imperative that it should behold." It is for these reasons that geometry "is the knowledge of that which always is, and not of a something which at some time comes into being and passes away"; it "is the knowledge of the eternally existent." Plato, *Republic* 526e, 527b; trans. P. Shorey, Loeb Classical Library (1930–1935; reprint, Cambridge, Mass.: Harvard University Press; London: W. Heinemann, 1980), 2: 169–170.

25. "Geometry and the studies that accompany it are as we see dreaming about being, but the clear waking vision of it is impossible for them as long as they leave the assumptions which they employ undisturbed and cannot give any account of them" (ibid., 533c; trans. Shorey, 2: 203).

26. Proclus, *Commentary on Euclid,* p. 26.

27. Aristotle, *De anima* 429a5.

28. The intuitive character of geometry is very precisely described by Aristotle in *De memoria* 449b30. For dialectical interpretation of optical phenomena, see G. F. Vescovini, *Studi sulla prospettiva medievale* (Turin: G. Giappichelli, 1965), p. 233.

29. Following the same line of thought, he adds, "One science is the mistress of the others, namely, theology, to which the remaining sciences are vitally necessary, and without which it cannot reach its end." R. Bacon, *Opus maius,* trans. R. G. Burke (Philadelphia: University of Pennsylvania Press, 1928), 1:36.

30. Ibid., p. 195.

31. Ibid., pp. 171, 233–234. In appraising the role of geometry in the understanding of the true reality of the world, Bacon concludes: "For without doubt the whole truth of things in the world lies in the literal sense, as has been said, and especially of things relating to geometry, because we can understand nothing fully unless its form is presented before our eyes, and therefore in the Scripture of God the whole knowledge of things to be defined by geometrical forms is contained, and far better than mere philosophy could express it" (p. 234).

32. See L. Baur, *Die philosophischen Werke des Robert Grosseteste Bishofs von Lincoln,* Beiträge zur Geschichte der Philosophie des Mittelalters, vol. 9 (Münster: Aschendorff, 1912); L. Baur, *Das philosophische Lebenswerk des Robert Grosseteste Bishofs von Lincoln* (Cologne: J. P. Bachem, 1910); J. McEvoy, *The Philosophy of Robert Grosseteste* (Oxford: Clarendon Press, 1986).

33. In Grosseteste's definition, light "significat enim substantiam corpoream subtilissimam et incorporalitati proximam naturaliter sui ipsius generativam" (*Hexaemeron,* MS fol. 203c; quoted in McEvoy, *The Philosophy of Robert Grosseteste,* p. 392).

34. Among the perspectivists, a special role was played by the Franciscans of Oxford. See A. G. Little, "The Franciscan School at Oxford in the Thirteenth Century," *Archivum Franciscanum Historicum* 19 (1926): 803–874.

35. His early access to the new translations of Aristotle from Arabic made Grosseteste one of the first thinkers who contributed to the Aristotelian revival. See D. C. Lindberg, "The Transmission of Greek and Arabic Learning to the West," in *Science in the Middle Ages,* ed. Lindberg (Chicago: University of Chicago Press, 1978), pp. 52–91; B. G. Dodd, "Aristoteles Latinus," in *The Cambridge History of Later Medieval Philosophy: From the Rediscovery of Aristotle to the Disintegration of Scholasticism, 1100–1600,* ed. N. Kretzmann, A. Kenny, and J. Pinborg (Cambridge: Cambridge University Press, 1982), pp. 45–80; McEvoy, *The Philosophy of Robert Grosseteste,* pp. 149–167.

36. The philosophical (theological) interpretation of Genesis has a tradition that goes back to St. Basil's *Homilies in Hexaemeron.* Grosseteste's *Hexaemeron* contributed fundamentally to the understanding of the role of light in his cosmology; see J. T. Muckle, "The *Hexaemeron* of Robert Grosseteste," *Medieval Studies,* no. 6 (1944): 151–174; McEvoy, *The Philosophy of Robert Grosseteste,* p. 486. Grosseteste's seminal text on light is *De luce.*

37. St. Augustine, *De trinitate* II.7–11. The firmament represents a boundary—a sphere—where the capacity of matter to expand is realized and reaches its finite limits.

38. The source of this hierarchy, cultivated through the Middle Ages, can be found in Aristotelian tradition; see Aristotle, *De caelo et mundo.*

39. The number of spheres structuring the space between the center and circumference of the firmament was never well established. Already at this time, the number was related to other phenomena and symbolic meanings such as number of the angelic choirs, etc. Grosseteste himself ends on a skeptical note: "There can be but one conclusion: no-one can profess to have the truth about the nature, number, motion or matters of the heavens. The philosophers of this world are foolish boasters if they think they possess the truth, for their fine-spun reasonings are more fragile than spiders" (quoted in McEvoy, *The Philosophy of Robert Grosseteste,* p. 194).

40. The elimination of the difference between celestial and terrestrial matter anticipates a development that will culminate in the mechanics of Galileo. See Galileo Galilei, *Dialogue Concerning the Two Chief World Systems, Ptolemaic and Copernican,* trans. S. Drake, 2nd ed. (Berkeley: University of California Press, 1967), pp. 106–107.

41. Grosseteste, quoted in McEvoy, *The Philosophy of Robert Grosseteste,* p. 185.

42. The homogenization of the universe could have been inspired by Grosseteste's understanding of the role of light in the formation (materialization) of space through the continuous expansion of light.

43. J. McEvoy, "The Sun as Res and Signum: Grosseteste's Commentary on Ecclesiasticus, chap. 43, vv. 1–5," *Recherches de Théologie Ancienne et Médiévale* 41 (1974): 38–91. See also *De motu corporali et luce,* where Grosseteste defines the link between light and corporeal movement: "Et in hoc patet, quod motio corporalis est vis multiplicativa lucis. Et hoc idem est appetitus corporalis et naturalis" (Baur, *Philosophische Werke des Grosseteste,* p. 92). This statement establishes a close affinity between optics and mechanics and thus anticipates the future identity of both disciplines.

44. McEvoy, *The Philosophy of Robert Grosseteste,* p. 202.

45. This ability of the soul can be seen as an argument against determinism and astrology; see R. C. Dales, "Robert Grosseteste's Views on Astrology," *Medieval Studies* 29 (1967): 357–363.

46. "Vision is the privileged one among the senses, because it is through the eyes that pure, unmixed light is diffused, shining forth in rays to perceive objects. Mixed first with the pure, higher air, it acts in the organ of hearing, then with thicker, misty air in the sense of smell, which requires qualities of heat to produce evaporation, and moisture to prevent the steamy substance dissipating through volatility. When light combines with earthy dampness, the mixture of both forms taste; when light reaches down through the thicker air right to the grosser dampness, it produces the activity that is smell; when finally it penetrates through to earth, with its passive heaviness it forms the sense of touch" (Grosseteste, *Hexaemeron,* fol. 203b–c, quoted in McEvoy, *The Philosophy of Robert Grosseteste,* p. 287).

47. The sequence of illuminations that share the same source of light corresponds to Grosseteste's understanding that God, who is light (*lux*), shines on every intellect in order to reveal all truths, thereby activating light not only in things but also in human sight. For a more detailed discussion, see R. Grosseteste, "Com. in Hier. Cael.," ed. J. McEvoy (MA thesis, Queen's University, Belfast, 1967); "In hoc autem quod illuminationes est quis gerit typum divinitatis, que radians indistanter super omnem veritatem et omnem occulem intellectualem oculo intellectuali veritatem manifestat" (p. 145).

48. See Bacon, *Opus maius*, 1:46; McEvoy, *The Philosophy of Robert Grosseteste*, p. 397.

49. S. G. Nicholls, Jr., *Romanesque Signs: Early Medieval Narrative and Iconography* (New Haven: Yale University Press, 1983), p. 101. See also M. M. Davy, *Initiation à la symbolique romane, XIIe siècle* (Paris: Flammarion, 1964).

50. R. Bacon, *Roger Bacon's Philosophy of Nature; A Critical Edition*, ed. and trans. D. C. Lindberg (Oxford: Clarendon Press, 1983), p. 5.

51. Ibid., p. 5. Bacon continues: "It is called 'form' by Alhazen, author of the widely-known *Perspectiva*. It is called 'intention' by the multitude of naturalists because of the weakness of its being in comparison to that of the being itself, for they say that it is not truly a thing but rather the intuition that is the similitude of a thing."

52. Ibid., p. 7; see also Aristotle, *De anima* 424a17. In the last important reference, Bacon calls the species "the shadow of philosophers," "since they are not clearly visible except in the instances namely of a ray falling through a window and of a strongly coloured species, and the expression 'of the philosophers' is employed because only skilful philosophers know the nature and operation of this shadow, as this treatise will make clear" (Bacon's *Philosophy of Nature*, p. 5).

53. Bacon, *Bacon's Philosophy of Nature*, p. 7; see also Aristotle, *De generatione et corruptione* 323b30.

54. The continuity between the first agent and the last recipient is further underscored by the unity that Bacon saw between celestial and terrestrial matters. "Celestial nature is assimilated to terrestrial, for the sake of well-being and greater unity of the universe and to meet the needs of sense, especially sight, the species of which comes to the stars and to which the species of the stars come in order to produce vision" (*Bacon's Philosophy of Nature*, p. 75).

55. Ibid., p. 93.

56. D' Alverny, "Le cosmos symbolique"; B. Stock, *Myth and Science in the Twelfth Century* (Princeton: Princeton University Press, 1972).

57. Signifying the rehabilitation of nature in the medieval world are Grosseteste's translations and commentaries on Aristotelian texts (*Posterior Analytics, Physics*, etc.), as well as the introduction of Aristotelian studies at the University of Paris after 1220. Grosseteste is aware of the limits of the Aristotelian approach, using it mainly in relation to physical phenomena; for the higher realities he reserves a Neoplatonic approach. Both Aristotelian and Neoplatonic interpretations are parts of one single art of understanding. The unity of higher and lower realities is best described by Grosseteste himself: "Earth is [contains] all the higher bodies because all higher lights come together in it. . . . The intermediate bodies have a two-fold relationship. Toward lower bodies they have the same relation as the first heaven has to all other things, and they are related to the higher bodies as earth is related to all other things. And thus in a certain sense each thing contains all other things" (*On Light,* p. 15).

58. H. Blumenberg, *Die Lesbarkeit der Welt,* Suhrkamp Taschenbuch Wissenschaft, 592 (Frankfurt am Main: Suhrkamp, 1986); also O. Pöggeler, "The Topology of Being," in *Martin Heidegger's Path of Thinking,* trans. D. Magurshak and S. Barber (Atlantic Highlands, N.J.: Humanities Press International, 1989), pp. 222–243.

59. Grosseteste produced the most coherent and original cosmology of the High Middle Ages. See McEvoy, *The Philosophy of Robert Grosseteste,* pp. 155, 371.

60. I am using the term "philosophy of light" to express the synthetic nature of light and its treatment by the perspectivists. It is true, of course, that individual thinkers put different emphasis on the physical, theological, or optical aspects of light, but there is no evidence that these aspects could be separated and treated as independent disciplines.

61. The perspectival and other optical works of Bacon had a strong influence on John Peckham and Witelo, mostly via the papal court in Viterbo—the main center of optical studies in the thirteenth century. Bacon sent his *Opus maius* there to Pope Clement IV (1265–1268) while Witelo traveled personally to Viterbo, arriving probably around 1270. It was in Viterbo that he wrote his treatise on perspective, between 1270 and 1273. John Peckham was there from 1277 to 1279, the period when he most probably wrote his influential *Perspectiva communis*—a widely circulated text on perspective, used in university curricula and disseminated further by the writers of the fourteenth century. The most important writer from our point of view was Biagio da Parma (d. 1416), whose *Quaestiones perspectivae,* written around 1390 (influenced mostly by Peckham's *Perspectiva communis*), was brought to Florence by Paolo Toscanelli in 1424. See Lindberg, *Theories of Vision,* pp. 116–132.

62. The following assessment of Bacon's optical works typifies such scientistic illusion: "Bacon," D. C. Lindberg claims, "simply lifts Grosseteste's physics of light out of its metaphysical and cosmogonical context and develops it into a comprehensive doctrine of physical causation" (Lindberg, introduction to *Bacon's Philosophy of Nature,* p. liv). Such a verdict is difficult to reconcile with the historical position of Bacon, who, as Lindberg acknowledges, "did not possess a seventeenth-century or twentieth-century mind, but a very good thirteenth-century one and there is no possibility for understanding his achievement unless we view it in the medieval context" (p. liii).

63. Aristotle, *Metaphysics* 1026a10.

64. R. Grosseteste, *De lineis, angulis et figuris seu de fractionibus et reflexionibus radiorum*, in Baur, *Die philosophischen Werke des Grosseteste*, pp. 59–65; trans. in E. Grant, ed., *A Source Book in Medieval Science* (Cambridge, Mass.: Harvard University Press, 1974), p. 385. Baur identifies the works of Grosseteste dealing with the "things that pertain to the whole universe" as *De sphaera, De motu corporale et luce,* and *De motu supercelestium.*

65. Bacon's *On the Multiplication of Species* is illustrated by optical diagrams, but they serve only as a reference for a text that is partly independent (like any other philosophical text) and partly structured by optical language. Its contents are based on references to Aristotle, Avicenna, Averroes, Al-Kindi, Euclid, Apollonius, and Grosseteste but draw most heavily on Ptolemy's *De aspectibus (optica)* and Alhazen's *De aspectibus (perspectiva)*. See C. A. R. do Nascimento, "Une théorie des opérations naturelles fondée sur l'optique: Le *De multiplicatione specierum* de Roger Bacon" (Ph.D. diss., Université de Montréal, 1975).

66. "It is to be understood that the lines along which multiplication occurs do not consist of length alone, extended between two points, but all of them have width and depth, as the authors of books on optics determine. Alhazen demonstrates in his fourth book that every ray coming from a part of a body necessarily has width and depth, as well as length[;] . . . the impressing body has three dimensions, and therefore the ray has the same corporeal property. And he adds that rays do not consist of straight lines between which are intervals but that multiplication is continuous, and therefore it does not lack width. And, in the third place, he says that whatever lacks width, depth and length is not perceived by sight, therefore a ray if it were to lack width and depth would be unseen, which it is not. And we know that a ray must pass through some part of the medium; but every part of the medium has three dimensions" (Bacon, *Bacon's Philosophy of Nature*, p. 95).

67. Bacon's text can help us to understand the rather obscure meaning of the geometrical optical language of Alberti's treatise on painting. The optics of Alberti is practically all contained in John Peckham's *Perspectiva communis*, which is in turn based on the works of Bacon.

68. Bacon, *Bacon's Philosophy of Nature*, pp. 97, 99–101, 101.

69. Ibid., pp. 157, 161, 247.

70. "The other figure required for natural action is the pyramid. [Grosseteste uses the term 'pyramid' to denote all figures having a plane or curved base and straight lines extending from every point on the base to a common apex; the base need not be a regular polygon.] For if power should issue from one part of an agent and terminate at one part of the recipient, and if this should be true of all powers so that power always comes from one part of the agent to a single part of the recipient, no action will ever be strong or good. But action is complete when the power of the agent comes to every point of the recipient from all points of the agent or from its entire surface. But this is possible only by means of a pyramidal figure, since powers issuing from the single parts of the agent [which constitutes the base of the pyramid] converge and unite at the apex of the pyramid; and therefore all are able to act strongly on the part of the recipient encountered" (Grosseteste, *De lineis, angulis et figuris,* in Grant, ed., *A Source Book in Medieval Science,* p. 388).

71. Bacon, *Bacon's Philosophy of Nature,* p. 199.

72. It should be emphasized that the mixing of species is the inevitable condition of the differentiation and unity of the experienced world; more precisely, it is an ontological ground of all visual experience.

73. Bacon, *Bacon's Philosophy of Nature,* p. 199.

74. A. Manetti, *The Life of Brunelleschi,* trans. C. Enggass (University Park: Pennsylvania State University Press, 1970), pp. 42–46; Filarete, *Treatise on Architecture,* trans. J. R. Spencer (New Haven: Yale University Press, 1965), book 23, fol. 179r, p. 305; G. Vasari, "Brunelleschi," in *The Lives of the Artists: A Selection,* trans. G. Bull (Harmondsworth: Penguin, 1965), p. 136. The important modern contributions to the debate can be found in R. Klein, *Form and Meaning: Essays on the Renaissance and Modern Art,* trans. M. Jay and L. Wieseltier (New York: Viking Press, 1979), pp. 129–143; A. Parronchi, *Studi su la dolce prospettiva* (Milan: A. Martello, 1964); White, *The Birth and Rebirth of Pictorial Space,* pp. 113–121; R. Beltrani, "Gli esperimenti prospettichi del Brunelleschi," in *Rendiconti delle Sedute dell'Accademia Nazionale dei Lincei, classe di Scienze morali, storiche e filologiche,* ser. 28 (Rome: Accademia Nazionale dei Lincei, 1974), pp. 417–468; S. Y. Edgerton, *The Renaissance Rediscovery of Linear Perspective* (New York: Harper & Row, 1975), pp. 143–153.

75. The few exceptions are the contributions of Alessandro Parronchi, Samuel Y. Edgerton, Federici Vescovini, and to some extent John White.

76. There is a fundamental difference between the role of geometry in medieval or Renaissance science and in modern science, where it ceases to be part of dialectical reasoning and becomes a pure tool (instrument) of experimental research. See Lachterman, *The Ethics of Geometry.*

77. See the writings of White, Parronchi, Vescovini, and Edgerton.

78. The association of Renaissance with individualism and naturalism goes back to Jakob Burckhardt's *Civilization of the Renaissance in Italy* (1860), and dominates art historical writing even today. The problem is discussed in a new and revealing way in C. H. Taylor, *The Sources of the Self: The Making of the Modern Identity* (Cambridge: Cambridge University Press, 1989), and D. Summers, *The Judgment of Sense: Renais-*

sance Naturalism and the Rise of Aesthetics (Cambridge: Cambridge University Press, 1987).

79. L. B. Alberti, *On the Art of Building in Ten Books,* trans. J. Rykwert, N. Leach, and R. Tavernor (Cambridge, Mass.: MIT Press, 1988), chap. I.4–4v, p. 7.

80. Compare Alberti's position with Grosseteste's in *De lineis, angulis et figures:* "All causes of natural effects must be expressed by means of lines, angles and figures for otherwise it is impossible to grasp their explanation" (in Grant, ed., *A Source Book in Medieval Science,* p. 385). On *disegno interno,* see F. Zuccaro, *L'idea de' pittori, scultori e architetti* (Turin, 1607), discussed in Summers, *The Judgment of Sense,* pp. 283–308.

81. See O. G. von Simson, "Measure and Light," in *The Gothic Cathedral: Origins of Gothic Architecture and the Medieval Concept of Order,* Bollingen Series, 48 (1956; reprint, New York: Pantheon, 1965), pp. 21–61. In the late medieval treatise "Concerning Pinnacle Correctitude," Mathias Roriczer describes the construction of the pinnacle, which some medieval authors associated with the pyramidal multiplication of light, preserving on each level the similarity (*simile*) of light to its source (*lux*); see Hedwig, *Sphaera Lucis,* p. 177. In the individual steps of his construction, Roriczer seems to observe the same principle of similarity, which he describes as "correct proportion" (*rechtem Mass*): "since each art has its own matter form and measure, I have tried, with the help of God, to make clear this aforesaid art of geometry, and for the first time, to explain the beginning of drawn-out stonework—how and in what measure it arises out of the fundamentals of geometry through manipulation of the dividers, and how it should be brought into the correct proportions" (L. R. Shelby, ed. and trans., *Gothic Design Techniques: The Fifteenth-Century Design Booklets of Mathes Roriczer and Hanns Schmuttermayer* [Carbondale: Southern Illinois University Press, 1977], pp. 82–83). There is a close affinity between the proportional sequence in the pyramid of the pinnacle (*simile-proportio*) and the proportional foreshortening in the perspectival pyramid.

82. Zuccaro, quoted in Summers, *The Judgment of Sense,* p. 292. See also E. Panofsky, *Idea: A Concept in Art Theory,* trans. J. J. S. Peake (Columbia: University of South Carolina Press, 1968), pp. 85–93.

83. See Ohly, "Deus Geometra."

84. E. Gilson, *The Philosophy of St. Bonaventura,* trans. I. Trethowan and F. J. Sheed (Paterson, N.J.: St. Anthony's Guild Press, 1965), p. 209.

85. Grosseteste, *On Light,* p. 12.

86. R. Wittkower, "Brunelleschi and 'Proportion in Perspective,'" *Journal of the Warburg and Courtauld Institutes* 16 (1953): 275–291; quotation, p. 275.

87. See E. Panofsky, "Die Perspektive als symbolische Form," *Vorträge der Bibliothek Warburg* 4 (1924–1925): 258–330 (trans. C. S. Wood as *Perspective as Symbolic Form* [New York: Zone Books, 1991]); E. Cassirer, *Philosophie der symbolischen Formen,* 3 vols., 2nd ed. (Darmstadt: Wissenschaftliche Buchgesellschaft, 1953). For critical assessments of the concept "symbolic form," see G. Boehm, *Studien zur Perspektivität: Philosophie und Kunst in der frühen Neuzeit* (Heidelberg: C. Winter, 1969), pp. 13–15; Davos Disputation between Ernst Cassirer and Martin Heidegger, in M. Heidegger, *Kant and the Problem of Metaphysics,* trans. R. Taft, 4th ed. (Bloomington: Indiana University Press, 1989), appendixes, pp. 264–268.

88. For the Devotio Moderna movement, see R. R. Post, *The Modern Devotion: Confrontation with Reformation and Humanism* (Leiden: E. J. Brill, 1968), p. 33; *Devotio Moderna: Basic Writings,* trans. J. Van Engen (New York: Paulist Press, 1988); F. Heer, *The Intellectual History of Europe,* trans. J. Steinberg (London: Weidenfeld & Nicolson, 1966), pp. 158–172.

89. Aristotle, *De anima* 425b. There is a close affinity between "common sensibles" and Heidegger's categorial intution; see M. Heidegger, *History of the Concept of Time: Prolegomena,* trans. T. Kisiel (Bloomington: Indiana University Press, 1985), pp. 47–75.

90. Leonardo similarly defines common sensibles for painting: "Painting is concerned with all the ten attributes of sight which are—darkness, light, solidity and colour, form and position, distance and propinquity, motion and rest" (*The Notebooks of Leonardo da Vinci,* ed. J. P. Richter [(New York: Dover, 1970], 1:19).

91. Summers, *The Judgment of Sense,* pp. 153, 83.

92. See G. F. Vescovini, "La prospettiva del Brunelleschi, Alhazen e Biaggio Pellacani a Firenze," in *Filippo Brunelleschi: La sua opera e il suo tempo,* [ed. P. Ragionieri] (Florence: Centro Di, 1980), 2:333–348.

93. Biagio's *Quaestiones perspectivae* may have been known in Florence already before the end of the fourteenth century; the text was certainly available after Paolo Toscanelli's return to Florence in 1424; see G. F. Vescovini, "Biaggio Pelacani da Parma," *Rivista di Filosofia* 51 (1960): 179–185, and "Biaggio da Parma e la perspectiva," in *Studi sulla prospettiva medievale,* pp. 239–272; E. Garin, "Ritratto di Paolo del Pozzo Toscanelli," in *Ritratti di umanisti* (Florence: Sansoni, 1967), pp. 41–67.

94. M. Merleau-Ponty, *Phenomenology of Perception,* trans. C. Smith (London: Routledge & Kegan Paul, 1962), p. 254.

95. I am using the term "workshop" (*botegha*) in the broadest sense, as a place of work that includes not only the studio but also a building site and the spaces in which large commissions are created.

96. The adjustment of figures to their setting can be compared with the architectural structures (*casamenti*) in the figurative scenes of Donatello or Ghiberti; for instance, see R. Krautheimer, *Lorenzo Ghiberti* (1956; reprint, Princeton: Princeton University Press, 1970), 1:231–233.

97. See H. Sedlmayr, "Über eine mittelalterliche Art des Abbildens," in *Epochen und Werke: Gesammelte Schriften zur Kunstgeschichte* (Vienna: Herold, 1959), 1:140–155; G. Bandmann, *Mittelalterliche Architektur als Bedeutungsträger,* 5th ed. (Berlin: Mann, 1978).

98. Until the seventeenth century, infinity was discussed as "potential" and "actual," and in the human world, only potential infinity was conceivable. How to actualize infinity is a modern problem that remains unsolved. See J. E. Murdoch, "Infinity and Continuity," in Kretzmann, Kenny, and Pinborg, eds., *The Cambridge History of Later Medieval Philosophy,* pp. 564–594; see also A. Koyré, "L'infini et le contenu," in *Études d'histoire de la pensée philosophique* (Paris: Gallimard, 1971), pp. 29–31.

99. Merleau-Ponty, *Phenomenology of Perception,* p. 261.

100. For a recent discussion, see H. Damish, *The Origin of Perspective,* trans. J. Goodman (Cambridge, Mass.: MIT Press, 1994), pp. 74–88.

101. Nicholas of Cusa (1401–1464), in a symbolic representation of truth, used mathematics as a vehicle in an interpretation situated halfway between Nominalism and Neoplatonic mysticism. See P. M. Watts, *Nicolaus Cusanus, a Fifteenth-Century Vision of Man* (Leiden: Brill, 1982), pp. 68–72, 93–101.

102. The picture could be seen in the mirror through a hole in the panel. Brunelleschi claims "that whoever wanted to look at it should place his eye on the reverse side, where the hole was large and while bringing the hole up to his eye with one hand to hold a flat mirror with the other hand in such a way that the painting would be reflected in it. The mirror was extended by the other hand a distance that more or less approximated in small braccia the distance in regular braccia from the place he appears to have been when he painted it up to the church of San Giovanni" (Manetti, *The Life of Brunelleschi,* p. 44).

For critical assessments of Brunelleschi's inconclusive experiments, see A. Parronchi, "Le due tavole prospettiche del Brunelleschi," *Paragone,* no. 107 (1958): 3–32; no. 109 (1959): 3–31; P. Sanpaolesi, *Brunelleschi* ([Florence]: G. Barbèra, 1962), pp. 41–53; R. Klein, "Studies on Perspective in the Renassance," in *Form and Meaning,* pp. 129–143.

103. Avicenna describes sight as a formation of images in a mirror, and thus sees the eye as a mirror: "The eye is like a mirror and the visible object is like the thing reflected in the mirror by the mediation of air or another transparent body; when light falls on the visible object, it projects the image of the object onto the eye. If a mirror should possess a soul, it would see the image that is formed in it" (*Compendium on the Soul;* trans. in Lindberg, *Theories of Vision,* p. 49).

The role of mirror in the formation of perspective can be also illustrated by Filarete's argument: "If you should desire to portray something in an easier way, take a mirror and hold it in front of the thing you want to do. Look in it and you will see the outlines of the thing more easily. Whatever is closer or further will appear foreshortened to you. Truly I think that Pippo di ser Brunellesco discovered perspective in this way. It was not used by the ancients, for even though their intellects were very subtle and sharp, still they never used or understood perspective. Even though they exercised good judgment in their works, they did not locate things on the plane in this way and with these rules. You can say that it is false, for it shows you a thing that is not. This is true; nevertheless it is true in drawing, for drawing itself is not true but a demonstration of the thing you are drawing or what you wish to show" (*Treatise on Architecture*, book 23, fols. 178v–179r; p. 305).

104. Richter, ed., *The Notebooks of Leonardo da Vinci*, 1:45. Leonardo's rules appear already in Alhazen's *De aspectibus* and later in Witelo's *Perspectiva*.

105. Leonardo, quoted in Lindberg, *Theories of Vision*, p. 159.

106. Richter, ed., *The Notebooks of Leonardo da Vinci*, p. 56.

107. It is most likely that Alberti became familiar with the primary texts on perspective during his studies in Bologna (1421–1428); he certainly knew them after his return to Florence in 1434. His treatise on painting shows clear indebtedness to John Peckham's *Perspectiva communis*, Witelo's *Perspectiva*, and probably also Paolo Toscanelli's treatise on perspective. For discussion of the text and its possible attribution to Toscanelli, see Parronchi, *Studi su la dolce prospettiva*, p. 583.

On Masaccio, see C. Dempsey, "Masaccio's Trinity: Altarpiece or Tomb?" *Art Bulletin* 54 (1972): 279–281; J. Polzer, "The Anatomy of Masaccio's Holy Trinity," *Jahrbuch der Berliner Museen* 93 (1971): 18–59; R. Gotten, ed., *Masaccio's Trinity* (Cambridge: Cambridge University Press, 1998).

108. Alberti's arguments resemble Euclidean geometrical demonstrations, as they lead to axiomatic conclusions. Rather misleadingly, he writes in the first book of his *De pictura* that "I earnestly wish it be borne in mind that I speak in these matters not as a mathematician but as a painter" (*On Painting*, trans. C. Grayson [London: Penguin, 1991], p. 37). In truth, he speaks like a mathematician trying to be comprehensible to the painters.

109. The foreshortening in perspective is based on the proportionality of similar triangles, well known from the theorem in book 6 of Euclid's *Elements*. It was used in triangulation and in surveying tall, distant buildings and objects. Alberti refers to this method in his *Ludi mathematici;* see *Opere volgari*, ed. C. Grayson (Bari: G. Laterza, 1973), vol. 3.

110. Wittkower, "Brunelleschi and 'Proportion in Perspective'"; see also K. H. Veltman, "Proportionality and Perspective," in *Linear Perspective and the Visual Dimensions of Science and Art* (Munich: Deutscher Kunstverlag, 1986), p. 241.

111. Alberti, *On Painting*, p. 53.

112. See E. Cassirer, *The Individual and the Cosmos in Renaissance Philosophy*, trans. M. Dolmandi (1963; reprint, Philadelphia: University of Pennsylvania Press, 1972); B. Groethuysen, *Anthropologie philosophique* (Paris: Gallimard, 1953); Taylor, *The Sources of Self*.

113. Alberti, *On Painting*, p. 6.

114. Alberti's own paintings did not survive, and we cannot draw even on indirect evidence to learn their nature; but he provides a plausible description of a device he constructed in the form of an optical chamber (*camera ottica*) for the demonstration of perspective construction. "By looking into a box through a little hole one might see great planes and immense expanse of a sea spread out till the eye lost itself in the distance. Learned and unlearned agreed that these images were not like painted things but like nature herself" (Alberti, *Vita anonima*, in *Opere volgari de Leon Battista Alberti*, ed. B. Anicio ([Florence: Tipografia Galileiana 1843], 1: cii–civ; trans. K. Clark in "Leon Battista Alberti," *Proceedings of the British Academy* 30 [1944]: 284).

115. Alberti, *On Painting*, p. 93.

116. Ibid, p. 88.

117. Alberti understood composition as being directly linked with the principles of perspectival construction: "This method of dividing up the pavement pertains especially to that part of painting which, when we come to it, we shall call composition" (ibid., p. 58).

118. Ibid., p. 38.

119. Interest in the Platonic solids was instigated by the circle of artists and humanists around Luca Pacioli, and it is in his treatise *De divina proportione* (1509) that the first set of primary solids and their transformation is illustrated. The drawings were produced specially for the treatise by Leonardo da Vinci. Probably the most complete is the treatise *Perspectiva corporum regularium* by Wenzel Jamnitzer (1568). The primary solids play also an important role in treatises of Augustin Hirschvogel (1543), Jean Cousin (1560), Daniele Barbaro (1569), and Hans Lencker (1571).

120. These treatises are *Trattato d'abaco* and *Libellus de quinque corporibus regularibus*. Both are discussed in M. Daly-Davis, *Piero della Francesca's Mathematical Treatises* (Ravenna: Longo, 1977).

121. The request appears in the dedication of the *Libellus* to Guidobaldo da Montefeltro. The treatise, Piero asks, should stand "next to our little work on perspective, which I gave you a previous year" ("penes aliud nostrum *de Prospectiva* opusculum, quod superioribus annis edidimus"); in *L'opere "De corporibus regularibus,"* ed. G. Mancini (Rome: n.p., 1916), p. 488 (see also M. Daly-Davis, *Piero della Francesca,* p. 45). In his request Piero emphasizes the unity of content in the *Libellus* and the *De prospectiva pingendi.*

122. Piero della Francesca, *De prospectiva pingendi,* ed. G. Nicco-Fasola (1942; reprint, Florence: Casa Editrice Lettera, 1989), 17v, p. 100.

123. Pacioli formed a close relationship with Leonardo and acknowledged that Leonardo illustrated the stereometric bodies in his *De divina proportione;* see the dedication and fols. 22r, 28v, and 30v.

124. Leonardo, quoted in Veltman, *Linear Perspective,* p. 199.

125. L. Pacioli, *Divina proportione* (Venice, 1509); all citations are from the French translation by G. Duchesne and M. Giraud, *Divine proportion* (Paris: Librairie de Compagnonnage, 1980), 1:55.

126. Piero della Francesca, *De prospectiva pingendi,* book 3, introduction; trans. in *Documentary History of Art,* ed. E. G. Holt, 2nd ed. (Garden City, N.Y.: Doubleday, 1957), 1:265.

127. Daly-Davis, *Piero della Francesca,* p. 97.

128. Pacioli, quoted in ibid., p. 65.

129. Pacioli, *Divine proportion,* I.55, p. 111; The commentary on Plato's *Timaeus* by Calcidius (fourth century C.E.) became influential again in the twelfth century and soon was circulating in a large number of manuscripts; see Calcidius's translation of *Timaeus,* with commentary, ed. J. H. Waszink (London: Warburg Institute; Leiden: E. J. Brill, 1962). Macrobius (late fourth century C.E.) wrote a famous commentary on the dream of Scipio that was printed for the first time in 1472 in Venice; see Macrobius, *Commentary on the Dream of Scipio,* trans. W. H. Stahl (1952; reprint, New York: Columbia University Press, 1990).

130. Apart from the explicit references to Platonic authors in the text of *Divina proportione* there is also a close link between the Renaissance Platonism and the revival of classical mathematics; see P. L. Rose, *The Italian Renaissance and Mathematics: Studies on Humanists and Mathematicians from Petrarch to Galileo* (Geneva: Droz, 1975).

131. Pacioli, *Divine proportion,* 23, 6, pp. 74, 60.

132. Ibid., 5, p. 59.

133. The primary body of Euclid's *Elements* was formed in the old Athenian Academy, where it played the role of a paradigm for the ontological and cosmological speculation of Plato's followers about the link between ideas and sensible reality. The paradigm was expressed genetically as a transition from point through line and surface to sensible body. In that sense the *Elements* can be seen as a propaedeutic to Platonic cosmology. See Plato, *Plato's Cosmology: The Timaeus of Plato*, trans. F. M. Cornford (London: Routledge & Kegan Paul, 1937), p. 210; Proclus, *A Commentary on Euclid*, p. 58; Gadamer, *Dialogue and Dialectics*, p. 176.

134. "Das ist, ein fleyssige Furweysung, wie die Fünff Regulirten Cörper, darvon Plato inn Timaeo, unnd Euclides inn sein Elementis schreibt, etc. Durch einen sonderlichen, newen . . . weg . . . inn die Perspectiua gebracht, Und darzu ein schöne Anleytung, wie auss denselbigen Fünff Cörpern one Endt gar viel andere Cörper mancherley Art und gestalt, gemacht . . . werden mügen" (W. Jamnitzer, *Perspectiva corporum regularium* [Nuremberg, 1568], preface).

135. H. Lencker, *Perspectiva literaria* (Nuremberg, 1567).

136. The culmination of the relation between geometrical figures and language (letters), declared as early as Pacioli's *Divina proportione*, was Galileo's understanding of the language of nature (*alphabeta rerum*): "Philosophy is written in this grand book, the universe, which stands continually open to our gaze. But the book cannot be understood unless one first learns to comprehend the language and read the letters in which it is composed. It is written in the language of mathematics, and its characters are triangles, circles and other geometric figures, without which it is humanly impossible to understand a single word of it, without these one wanders about in a dark labyrinth" ("The Assayer" [*Il saggiatore*], in *Discoveries and Opinions of Galileo*, trans. D. Stillman [Garden City, N.Y.: Doubleday, 1957], pp. 237–238).

137. See Boehm, *Studien zur Perspektivität*, pp. 137–172.

138. See E. Hempel, "Nikolaus von Cues in Seinen Betziehungen zur Bildenden Kunst," *Berichte über die Verhandlungen der Sächsischen Akademie der Wissenschaften zu Leipzig* 100, no. 3 (1953): 3–42; C. N. Santinello, "Cusano e L. B. Alberti: Pensieri sul bello e sull'arte," in *Nicolò da Cusa, Relazioni tenute al convegno interuniversitario di Bressanone nel 1960* (Florence: G. C. Sansoni, 1962), pp. 147–182.

139. E. Panofsky, "Facies illa Rogeri Maximi Pictoris," in *Late Classical and Mediaeval Studies in Honor of Albert Mathias Friend, Jr.*, ed. K. Weitzmann (Princeton: Princeton University Press, 1955), pp. 392–400.

140. Nicholas of Cusa, *De visione Dei* VIII.30; trans. H. L. Bond in *Selected Spiritual Writings* (New York: Paulist Press, 1997), p. 249.

141. Ibid., IX.35, X.40; trans. Bond, pp. 250, 253.

142. The equivalence of light and vision is fully acknowledged by Leonardo da Vinci, who wrote: "Il lume nel ufitio della prospettiva non a alcuna differeza coll' ochio" (In the practice of perspective, the same rules apply to light as they do to the eye) (Richter, ed., *The Notebooks of Leonardo da Vinci*, p. 45).

143. Nicholas of Cusa, *De coniecturis,* in *Opera omnia,* vol. 1 (Paris 1514), fol. 46. All subsequent references to *De coniecturis* are from the critical Heidelberg edition, ed. J. Koch, C. Bormann, and I. G. Senger, vol. 3 of *Nicolai de Cusa Opera Omnia* (Hamburg: Felix Meiner, 1972) (here, p. 46).

144. Richter, ed., *The Notebooks of Leonardo da Vinci,* p. 56.

145. Vision has for Cusanus the same creative (cosmogonic) meaning as light, as he declares: "God, you are visible by all creatures and you see all. In that you see all, you are seen by all. For otherwise, creatures cannot exist since they exist by your vision. If they did not see you who see, they would not receive being from you. The being of a creature is equally your seeing and your being seen" (*De visione dei,* X.40; trans. Bond, in *Selected Spiritual Writings,* p. 253).

146. Nicholas of Cusa, *De coniecturis,* p. 14.

147. Cusanus's understanding of perspective is of a piece with his understanding of the communication between God and man. The unfolding of the visible world corresponds to the meaning of the vanishing point, the unity of things, and the notion of the "one": "The manner in which the numerical world is unfolded from the number 'one' through endless multiplication, division and proportion is analogous to the manner in which the divine mind unfolded the creation from itself and to the way in which the human mind unfolds the conjectural world from itself" (ibid.).

148. *Der dritte Kommentar Lorenzo Ghibertis: Naturwissenschaften und Medizin in der Kunsttheorie der Frührenaissance,* ed. and trans. K. Bergdolt (Weinheim: VCH, 1988), pp. xxiii–xxvii.

149. The uniqueness of Ghiberti's treatise has been discussed by many authors, most recently by Krautheimer, *Lorenzo Ghiberti,* pp. 229–254, 306–315; White, *The Birth and Rebirth of Pictorial Space,* pp. 126–130; K. Bloom, "Ghiberti's Space in Relief: Method and Theory," *Art Bulletin* 51 (1969): 164–169; and C. Maltese, "Ghiberti teorico, i problemi ottico-prospettichi," in *Lorenzo Ghiberti nel suo tempo* (Florence: L. S. Olschki, 1980), 2:407–421.

150. Ghiberti's personal relations with the humanists, particularly with Ambrogio Traversari and Niccolò Niccoli, were discussed by P. Castelli, "Ghiberti e gli umanisti," in *Lorenzo Ghiberti, materia e ragionamenti,* exhib. cat. (Florence: Centro Di, 1978), pp. 523–540; Vespasiano da Bisticci (1421–1498), *Vite di uomini illustri del secolo XV*

(Rome, 1839), trans. W. George and E. Waters as *The Vespasiano Memoirs: Lives of Illustrious Men of the Fifteenth Century* (London: Routledge & Sons, 1926), p. 401.

151. See S. Bellandi, *Luigi Marsili degli Agostiniani: Apostolo ed anima del rinascimento letterario in Firenze, An. 1342–1394* (Florence: Tip. Arcivescovile, 1911); Vespasiano, *Lives,* pp. 208–213; E. Garin, *Italian Humanism: Philosophy and Civic Life in the Renaissance,* trans. P. Munz (Westport, Conn.: Greenwood Press, 1965), p. 56.

152. "But in everything we shall say I earnestly wish it to be borne in mind that I speak in these matters not as a mathematician but as a painter. Mathematicians measure the shapes and forms of things in the mind alone and divorced entirely from matter. We on the other hand, who wish to talk of things that are visible, will express ourselves in cruder terms" (Alberti, *On Painting,* p. 37).

153. Summers, *The Judgment of Sense,* pp. 151–182; A. Parronchi, "Le misure dell'occhio secondo il Ghiberti," in *Studi su la dolce Prospettiva,* pp. 313–348.

154. For instance, Kemp claims that there is no direct relationship between medieval optics and Renaissance perspective and that the character of Ghiberti's *Third Commentary* is therefore entirely retrospective (see his "Science, Non-Science, and Nonsense").

155. R. Klein, "Judgment and Taste in Cinquecento Art Theory," in *Form and Meaning,* pp. 161–172.

156. Of the 568 pages of Bergdolt's edition of Ghiberti's treatise, only 16 are Ghiberti's own words.

157. "Lo terzo modo e lo corpo diafano: l'aria, l'acqua, il vetro, il cristallo, il calcedonia il berillo" (Ghiberti, *Der dritte Kommentar,* p. 6).

158. *Berillus* is in the Middle Ages a name for a glass or crystal, as well as for a semiprecious stone (of Indian origin) often used to decorate reliquaries and monstrances. Sometimes it is also associated with prisms or lenses. Nicholas of Cusa's treatise *De beryllo* was completed in 1458. The text is devoted to the question of truth—both visible and invisible—attainable through intellectual vision (*visio intellectualis*); in *Opera Omnia,* II.1, ed. L. Baur (Hamburg: F. Meiner, 1940).

159. "Beryllus lapis est lucidus, albus et transparent, cui datur forma concava pariter et convexa et per ipsum videns attingit prius invisibile intellectualibus occulis si intellectualis beryllus, qui formam habeat maximam pariter et minimam adaptatur per eius medium attingitur indivisibile omnium principium" (ibid., pp. 4–5).

160. Ibid., p. 7.

161. Ibid., p. 49.

162. Panofsky, *Perspective as Symbolic Form;* see Boehm, *Studien zur Perspektivität,* pp. 13–15; M. A. Holly, *Panofsky and the Foundations of Art History* (Ithaca: Cornell University Press, 1984), pp. 130–157.

163. The evidence for Ghiberti's personal acquaintance with Cusanus is rather scanty, but they shared a number of very close friends—among them, Niccoli, Traversari, Alberti, and Toscanelli. See Castelli, "Ghiberti e gli umanisti," pp. 512–515; Watts, *Nicolaus Cusanus,* pp. 21–22.

164. See Panofsky, *Perspective as Symbolic Form,* and White, *The Birth and Rebirth of Pictorial Space;* but see also the critique in D. Gioseffi, *Perspectiva artificialis per la storia della prospettiva spigolature e appunti* (Trieste: Facoltà di Lettere e Filosofia, 1957), and Klein, *Form and Meaning,* pp. 133–140.

165. Ghiberti, *Der dritte Kommentar,* p. 234. "This philosophy" in this passage probably refers to the philosophy of Alhazen. The role of reasoning in the visual process is consistent with the preunderstanding of the visible phenomena and of their context. Ghiberti himself quotes the text of John Peckham: "Only the discriminative faculty (*virtus distinctiva*) discerns between light and colour acting on the eye simultaneously. Since light and color touch the pupil and act on the same part, they are received in the sense commingled and cannot be distinguished by the sense. Therefore they can be distinguished only by previous experience of light and color and by acquired knowledge" (ibid.; see John Peckham, *Perspectiva communis,* translated and edited by D. C. Lindberg as *John Peckham and the Science of Optics: Perspectiva communis* [Madison: University of Wisconsin Press, 1970], p. 138; all subsequent citations of the work are to this edition).

166. Ghiberti, *Der dritte Kommentar,* p. 238; John Peckham, *Perspectiva communis,* pp. 140–142.

167. Ghiberti used linear perspective on the Cassa di S. Zenobio in Florence cathedral and on the *Isaac, Joseph,* and *Solomon* panels of the *Gates of Paradise.* See Krautheimer, *Lorenzo Ghiberti,* vol. 2, plates 78A, 94, 98, and 116.

168. Parronchi, *Studi su la dolce prospettiva,* pp. 313–348; Summers, *The Judgment of Sense,* pp. 167–170.

169. Giovanni Pico della Mirandola, *"De hominis dignitate," "Heptaplus," "De ente et uno," e scritti vari,* ed. E. Garin (Florence: Vallechi, 1942); Gianozzo Manetti, *De dignitate et excellentia hominis* (Florence, 1452); Cassirer, *The Individual and the Cosmos;* Groethuysen, *Anthropologie philosophique.* For Cusanus's claim, see *De coniecturis,* pp. 143–144.

170. Nicholas of Cusa, *De coniecturis,* p. 144.

171. The belief that painting as an epitome of visual knowledge can become the foundation of natural science was most emphatically held by Leonardo, who in the introduction to his *Treatise on Painting* has this to say: "Whoever disparages painting loves neither philosophy or nature. If you disparage painting which alone is the imitation of all the works to be seen in nature, you most surely will disparage an invention which, with philosophical and subtle speculations, examines all qualities of forms, the sea, lands, animals, plants, flowers, which are surrounded by shadows and light. This is truly science and the legitimate daughter of nature, because painting is born of nature herself or, to put it more correctly, let us say the granddaughter of nature, because all things we sense are born of nature and painting is born of all those things" (*Leonardo on Painting*, ed. M. Kemp [New Haven: Yale University Press, 1989], p. 13).

172. See F. Kimball, "Luciano Laurana and the High Renaissance," *Art Bulletin* 10 (1927): 124–151, G. R. Kernodle, *From Art to Theatre: Form and Convention in the Renaissance* (Chicago: University of Chicago Press, 1943); Damisch, *The Origin of Perspective,* pp. 169–375; R. Krautheimer, "The Panels in Urbino, Baltimore, and Berlin Reconsidered," in *The Renaissance from Brunelleschi to Michelangelo: The Representation of Architecture,* ed. H. A. Millon and V. M. Lampugnani (London: Thames & Hudson, 1994), pp. 233–259.

173. The idealized iconography of all the three "Urbinate" panels points toward a notion of a universal city, situated in all locations and, in a sense, also in all times. This universality belongs to the urban tradition dominated by the paradigm of the celestial city, which in medieval thought was associated with the vision of Jerusalem located in the center of the earth, while the earth itself was in the middle of the cosmos.

There is a close affinity between the medieval cosmic meaning of the city, its reenactment in the medieval theater, and the pictorial representation of the city at the end of the fifteenth century. The ideal city of the Renaissance is in a sense a new Jerusalem of the Renaissance humanists. This may explain some of the more unusual elements of the Urbinate panels—particularly the Baltimore panel, whose central space is occupied by a paved square with a fountain in the middle and four columns at the corners. The four columns designate an area with the centrally placed source of water and mark the four corners of the imaginary world. This ideal setting—a plausible allegory of paradise—is separated from the real city in the background by a triumphal arch, which is also a gate to the ideal world, situated now on the same level as the rest of the city. The notion of the ideal city is closely linked with the popular Renaissance topos of the "earthly paradise."

See Konigson, *L'espace théâtral médiéval,* pp. 72–110; A. B. Giamatti, *The Earthly Paradise and the Renaissance Epic* (Princeton: Princeton University Press, 1966); H. Levin, *The Myth of the Golden Age in the Renaissance* (1969; reprint, New York: Oxford University Press, 1972).

174. The roles of formal logic in the verbal and in the visual domains are closely related. The formalization of the visual experience leads eventually to the formation of modern aesthetics (M. Dufrenne, "Formalisme logique et formalisme esthétique," in *Esthétique et philosophie* [Paris: Klincksieck, 1967], pp. 113–129).

175. A. Bruschi, *Bramante architetto* (Bari: Laterza, 1969), pp. 865–883; J. Ackerman, *The Cortile del Belvedere* (Vatican City: Biblioteca Apostolico Vaticana, 1954).

176. Julius II's association with Caesar as Pontifex Maximus is discussed in Flavio Biondo's *Roma Instaurata* (1444–1446): see J. Klaczko, *Jules II* (Paris: E. Plon, Nourrit, 1898); J. W. O'Malley, "Fulfilment of the Christian Golden Age under Pope Julius II," *Traditio: Studies in Ancient and Medieval History, Thought and Religion* 25 (1969): 265–338.

177. The most important representations are Perin del Vaga's fresco in Castel S. Angelo (1537–1541) and the drawings by Etienne Duperac (1557) and Giovanni Antonio Dosio (1558–1561). See Bruschi, *Bramante architetto,* p. 373; A. Chastel, "Cortile et theatre," in *Le lieu théâtral à la Renaissance,* 2nd ed. (Paris: Éditions du CNRS, 1968), pp. 41–49.

178. See J. Ackerman, "The Belvedere as a Classical Villa," in *Distance Points: Essays in Theory and Renaissance Art and Architecture* (Cambridge, Mass.: MIT Press, 1991), pp. 325–361; H. Brummer, *The Statue Court in the Vatican Belvedere* (Stockholm: Almquist & Wiksell, 1970).

179. This association became well established following the 1954 publication of Ackerman's influential monograph, *The Cortile del Belvedere.* For a more recent interpretation, see U. Geese, "Antike als Program—Der Statuenhof des Belvedere im Vatikan," in *Natur und Antike in der Renaissance,* [ed. H. Beck and P. C. Bol] (Frankfurt am Main: Liebieghaus, 1985), pp. 24–50.

180. M. Tafuri, "Roma Instaurata: Strategie urbane e politiche pontificie nella Roma del primo '500," in *Raffaelo architetto,* ed. C. L. Frommel, S. Ray, and Tafuri, exhib. cat. (Milan: Electa, 1984), p. 63.

181. "Rome became the centre of Christianity and the successor to Jerusalem," writes Egidio da Viterbo in Aug. Lat. 502, fol. 5v; quoted in J. W. O'Malley, *Giles of Viterbo on Church and Reform* (Leiden: Brill, 1968), p. 124.

182. This argument was anticipated in my earlier discussion of the Baltimore panel; there, as we have seen, the idealized classical forum can be read as a paradisal garden in juxtaposition and contrast with the real city behind the triumphal arch. See note 173.

183. See H. Pfeiffer, *Zur Ikonographie von Raffaels Disputa: Egidio da Viterbo und die christlich-platonische Konzeption der Stanza della Segnatura* (Rome: Università Gregoriana, 1975); J. Shearman, "The Vatican Stanze: Functions and Decoration," *Proceedings of the British Academy* 57 (1971): 369–424.

184. "Truly it was the poets who first proclaimed of themselves that a God existed and who affirmed that God saw everything and ruled over everything. . . . Why otherwise does Father Ennius call the poets sacred but because they are touched by a divine spirit and aflatus?" (E. H. Gombrich, *Symbolic Images* [London: Phaidon Press, 1972], pp. 89–90). See E. Grassi, *Renaissance Humanism: Studies in Philosophy and Poetics* (Binghamton, N.Y.: Medieval and Renaissance Texts and Studies, 1988).

185. Tafuri, "Roma Instaurata," p. 63.

186. A. Bruschi, *Bramante* (London: Thames & Hudson, 1977), p. 104.

187. G. Debord, *Society of the Spectacle* (Detroit: Black & Red, 1983), p. 219.

CHAPTER 4 **THE AGE OF DIVIDED REPRESENTATION**

1. I have chosen the term "transitional" to describe this period of radical mathematization and secularization of knowledge. The transition was a slow process, motivated originally by theological concerns and only later by secular anthropocentric and utilitarian interests. It has been most recently discussed in D. C. Lindberg and R. L. Numbers, eds., *God and Nature: Historical Essays on the Encounter between Christianity and Science* (Berkeley: University of California Press, 1986); A. Funkenstein, *Theology and the Scientific Imagination from the Middle Ages to the Seventeenth Century* (Princeton: Princeton University Press, 1986); S. Toulmin, *Cosmopolis: The Hidden Agenda of Modernity* (Chicago: University of Chicago Press, 1990).

2. In the correspondence, Newton was represented by his disciple Samuel Clarke. See *The Leibniz-Clarke Correspondence,* ed. H. G. Alexander (Manchester: Manchester University Press, 1956); Hans Barth, "Das Zeitalter des Barocks und die Philosophie von Leibniz," in *Die Kunstformen des Barockzeitalters* (Bern: Francke 1956), pp. 413–435.

3. See A. Koyré, *From the Closed World to the Infinite Universe* (Baltimore: Johns Hopkins University Press, 1957); W. Pauli, "The Influence of Archetypal Ideas on the Scientific Theories of Kepler," in *The Interpretation of Nature and the Psyche,* by Pauli and C. Jung (London: Routledge & Kegan Paul, 1955), p. 166.

4. See Funkenstein, *Theology and the Scientific Imagination;* Lindberg and Numbers, eds., *God and Nature.*

5. Claude Perrault, *Ordonnance for the Five Kinds of Columns after the Method of the Ancients,* trans. I. K. McEwen (Santa Monica, Calif.: Getty Center for the History of Art

and the Humanities, 1993); W. Herrmann, *The Theory of Claude Perrault* (London: A. Zwemmer, 1973), pp. 31–70.

6. In this context, Alberti's comments on the principles of comparison in his treatise on painting are of great relevance: "Comparison is made with things most immediately known. . . . Man is the scale and measure of all things" (L. B. Alberti, *On Painting*, trans. C. Grayson [London: Penguin, 1991], p. 53. See also A. C. Crombie, "Science and the Arts in the Renaissance: The Search for Truth and Certainty, Old and New," in *Science and Arts in the Renaissance*, ed. J. W. Shirley and F. W. Hoeniger [Washington, D.C.: Folger Shakespeare Library; London: Associated University Presses, 1985], pp. 15–27); E. Panofsky, "Artist, Scientist, Genius," in *The Renaissance; Six Essays*, by W. K. Ferguson et al. (1953; reprint, New York: Harper & Row, 1962), pp. 121–182.

7. J. L. Vives, *De disciplinis libri XX* (Anvers, 1531), 3:193; trans. in F. Hallyn, *The Poetic Structure of the World: Copernicus and Kepler*, trans. D. M. Leslie (New York: Zone Books, 1990), p. 71.

8. Galileo Galilei, "The Assayer" (*Il Saggiatore*), in *Discoveries and Opinions of Galileo*, trans. S. Drake (Garden City, N.Y.: Doubleday, 1957), p. 274.

9. The term "microcosmos" first appears, in contrast to "macrocosmos" (*megalikosmos*), in Aristotle's *Physics* (252b26). For the historical transformation of the term, see G. P. Conger, *Theories of Macrocosms and Microcosms in the History of Philosophy* (New York: Columbia University Press, 1922); R. Allers, "Microcosmus from Anaximander to Paracelsus," *Traditio: Studies in Medieval and Ancient History, Thought and Religion* 2 (1944): 319–407.

10. S. Ibn Gabirol, *Fons vitae*, trans. [from Arabic] J. Hispanus and D. Gundissalinus, ed. C. Baeumker, Beiträge zur Geschichte der Philosophie des Mittelalters, vol. 3, pt. 2 (Münster: Aschendorff'sche Buchhandlung, 1892), p. 77.

11. St. Ambrose, *Hexaemeron*, in *Patrologiae cursus completus: Series Latina (PL)*, ed. J.-P. Migne (Paris: DeVrayet de Surey, 1845), 14.265.

12. Calcidius, in *Fragmenta Philosophorum Graecorum*, ed. F. Mullach (Paris: Didot, 1881), 2:230.

13. M. Doctor, *Die Philosophie des Josef (ibn) Zaddik: Nach ihren quellen, insbesondere nach ihren beziehungen zu den lauteren Brüdern und zu Gabirol*, Beiträge zur Geschichte der Philosophie des Mittelalters, vol. 2, part 2 (Münster: Aschendorff, 1895), p. 20.

14. H. Crooke, *Mikrocosmographia: A Description of the Body of Man* (London, 1615), pp. 2–3.

15. The breakdown of the ontological nature of analogy and the replacement of the original continuity of reference by a dogmatic equivalent can be seen in the treatises of F. Blondel, *Cours d'architecture enseigné dans l'Académie Royale d'Architecture,* 5 pts. (Paris, 1675–1683); R. Ouvrard, *Architecture harmonique* (Paris, 1679); and C. E. Briseux, *Traité du beau essentiel* (Paris, 1752). The introverted representation of reality is manifested most clearly in the growing interest in collections, botanic gardens, and cabinets of curiosities; see J. von Schlosser, *Die Kunst- und Wunderkammer des Spätrenaissance* (Leipzig: Klinkhardt & Biermann, 1908; G. Olmi, "Dal teatro del mondo ai mondi invetariati, aspetti e forme del collezionismo nell'età moderna," in *Gli Uffizi, quattro secoli di una galleria,* ed. P. Barocchi and G. Ragionieri (Florence: L. S. Olschki, 1983), pp. 5–17; O. Impey and A. MacGregor, eds., *The Origins of Museums: The Cabinet of Curiosities in Sixteenth- and Seventeenth-Century Europe* (Oxford: Clarendon Press, 1985).

16. See G. Boehm, *Studien zur Perspektivität: Philosophie und Kunst in der frühen Neuzeit* (Heidelberg: C. Winter, 1969); J. Pahl, *Die Stadt im Aufbruch der perspectivischen Welt: Versuch über einen neuen Gestaltbegriff der Stadt* (Berlin: Ullstein, 1963).

17. See Panofsky, "Artist, Scientist, Genius"; E. L. Eisenstein, *The Printing Revolution in Early Modern Europe* (Cambridge: Cambridge University Press, 1983); W. J. Ong, *Orality and Literacy: The Technologizing of the Word* (London: Methuen, 1982).

18. E. R. Curtius, *European Literature and the Latin Middle Ages,* trans. W. R. Trask (1953; reprint, New York: Harper & Row, 1963), p. 322.

19. Ibid., pp. 138–144; see also R. Bernheimer, "Theatrum Mundi," *Art Bulletin* 38, no. 4 (December 1956): 225–247; G. Camillo, *L'idea del teatro* (Florence, 1555).

20. See Schlosser, *Die Kunst- und Wunderkammer der Spätrenaissance;* E. Verheyen, *The Paintings in the Studiolo of Isabella d'Este at Mantua* (New York: New York University Press for the College Art Association of America, 1971); L. Cheles, *The Studiolo of Urbino: An Iconographic Investigation* (University Park: Pennsylvania State University Press, 1986).

21. For example, the Teatro Olimpico in Vicenza (1582), Teatro Olimpico in Sabbioneta (1590), and Teatro Farnese in Parma (1618); see R. Klein and H. Zerner, "Vitruve et le théâtre de la Renaissance italienne," in *Le lieu théâtral à la Renaissance,* ed. J. Jacquot (Paris: Éditions du CNRS, 1968), pp. 49–61.

22. The characterization is quoted in J. Prest, *The Garden of Eden: The Botanic Garden and the Re-creation of Paradise* (New Haven: Yale University Press, 1981), p. 44.

23. Camillo, *L'idea del teatro;* F. Yates, *Theatre of the World* (London: Routledge & Kegan Paul, 1969); see also notes 19 and 20.

24. A. Bruschi, *Bramante architetto* (Bari: Laterza, 1969), pp. 122–143; L. Beltrani, "Bramante a Milano," *Rassegna d'Arte* 1 (1901): 33–37.

25. R. G. Hocke, *Die Welt als Labyrinth: Manier und Manie in der europäischen Kunst*, Rowohlts deutsche Enzyklopädie (Hamburg: Rowohlt, 1957). A different, rather unorthodox, interpretation of this transitional period can be found in H. M. Haydn, *The Counter-Renaissance* (New York: Scribner, 1950); M. Tafuri, *L'architettura dell'umanesimo* (Bari: Laterza, 1976), pp. 125–307; E. Battisti, *L'antirinascimento* (Milan: Feltrinelli, 1962); E. Forssman, *Säule und Ornament* (Stockholm: Almquist & Wiksell, 1956).

26. J. Ackerman, "The Ancient Roman Villa," in *The Villa* (London: Thames & Hudson, 1990), pp. 35–63. J. M. André, *L'otium dans la vie morale et intellectuelle romaine, des origines à l'époque augustéene* (Paris: Presses Universitaires de France, 1966).

27. G. Falcone, *La nuova vaga et dilettevole villa* (Brescia, 1564), preface, fol. i; trans. in Ackerman, *The Villa*, p. 113.

28. R. Bentmann and M. Müller, *The Villa as Hegemonic Architecture*, trans. T. Spence and D. Cranem (London: Humanities Press, 1992), p. 113 n. 168.

29. B. Rupprecht, "Villa, zur Geschichte eines Ideals," in *Wandlungen des Paradiesischen und Utopischen: Studien zum Bild eines Ideals*, ed. H. Bauer, Probleme der Kunstwissenschaft, 2 (Berlin: W. de Gruyter, 1966), p. 244.

30. A. Lollio, *La villa: Dialogo di M. Bartolomeo Paegio* (Milan, 1559), folio BIXv; trans. in Ackerman, *The Villa*, p. 117.

31. Bentmann and Müller, *The Villa as Hegemonic Architecture*, p. 55.

32. Quoted in Ackerman, *The Villa*, p. 117.

33. See M. Heidegger, "Letter on Humanism," in *Basic Writings*, ed. D. F. Krell (London: Routledge & Kegan Paul, 1978), pp. 189–243, and the polemical response in E. Grassi, *Heidegger and the Question of Renaissance Humanism* (Binghamton, N.Y.: Center for Medieval and Early Renaissance Studies, 1983).

34. R. Descartes, "Discourse on the Method," in *The Philosophical Works of Descartes*, trans. E. S. Haldane and G. R. T. Ross (1911; reprint, Cambridge: Cambridge University Press, 1982), 1:87, 101.

35. J. Baltrusaitis, *Anamorphic Art*, trans. W. J. Strachan (New York: Abrams, 1977).

36. J. Kepler, *Gesammelte Werke*, ed. W. von Dyck and M. Caspar, 20 vols. (Munich: C. H. Beck, 1937–1997), 6:309.

37. G. B. Riccioli, *Almagestum novum* (Bologna, 1661), 2:469.

38. "In the sphere there are three elements: the center, the surface, and the intervening space. It is the same in the stationary universe: the fixed stars, the sun, and the earth or intervening ether. And it is the same with the Trinity: the Son, the Father, and the Holy Spirit" (Kepler, *Gesammelte Werke,* 13:35).

39. "It is my intention, reader, to demonstrate in this little work that with the creation of this mobile universe and the arrangement of the heavens, God the great creator had in mind these five regular bodies that have been so famous from Pythagoras and Plato to our days and that he caused the number of the heavens, their proportions, and the system of their motions to conform to the motions of the bodies" (ibid., 1:9).

40. Kepler refers to Dürer and Pacioli as direct sources of inspiration, but also to the Platonic tradition transmitted by Euclid and Proclus. For the original role and meaning of the regular solids, see Plato, *Timaeus* 53b, and E. Sachs, *Die fünf platonischen Körper: Zur Geschichte der Mathematik und der Elementenlehre Platons und Pythagoreen* (Berlin: Weidmann, 1917). The best recent interpretation can be found in H. G. Gadamer, *Dialogue and Dialectic: Eight Hermeneutical Studies on Plato,* trans. P. C. Smith (New Haven: Yale University Press, 1980), p. 178.

41. Kepler's interpretation of primary solids is discussed in his *Mysterium cosmographicum* (in *Gesammelte Werke,* 6:117).

42. See Luca Pacioli's *De divina proportione,* discussed in chapter 3.

43. Koyré, *From the Closed World to the Infinite Universe,* chaps. 6–8.

44. See Funkenstein, *Theology and the Scientific Imagination.*

45. F. Manuel, *The Religion of Isaac Newton* (Oxford: Clarendon Press, 1974), p. 37.

46. J. G. Herder, *Älteste Urkunde des menschen Geschlechts,* in *Sämtliche Werke,* ed. B. Suphan, 33 vols. (Berlin: Weidnische Buchhandlung, 1877–1913), 6:202.

47. Pauli, "The Influence of Archetypal Ideas on the Scientific Theories of Kepler," p. 166; Descartes, "Meditations on First Philosophy," in *Philosophical Works,* 1:167.

48. Descartes, "Discourse on the Method," p. 107.

49. Toulmin, *Cosmopolis,* p. 116; he continues, "The scaffolding of modernity was thus a set of provisional and speculative half-truths."

50. The scholastic background of Cartesianism and French classicism is discussed in É. Gilson, *Études sur le rôle de la pensée médiévale dans la formation du système cartésien,* 3rd ed. (Paris: J. Vrin, 1967; see also J. L. Marion, *Sur la théologie blanche de Descartes: Analogie, création des vérités éternelles et fondement* (Paris: Presses Universitaires de France, 1981).

51. B. de Fontenelle, *Histoire de l'Académie Royale de Science depuis le reglement fait en 1699* (Paris, 1702) preface.

52. M. Kline, *Mathematics: The Loss of Certainty* (Oxford: Oxford University Press, 1980), p. 125.

53. Leibniz, quoted in ibid.

54. The process of abstraction appears plainly in the thoughts of a contemporary mathematician, William Oughtred (1574–1660): "The numbers with which we worke, are so, as it were, swallowed up into that new [algebra] which is brought forth, that they quite vanish, not leaving any print or footstep of themselves behind them" (Oughtred, *Clavis mathematicae*, in *The History of Mathematics: A Reader*, ed. J. Fauvel and J. Gray [Basingstoke: Macmillan Education, 1987], p. 302).

55. J. Klein, *Greek Mathematical Thought and the Origin of Algebra,* trans. E. Brann (Cambridge, Mass.: MIT Press, 1968), pp. 184, 185.

56. F. Fichet, *La théorie architecturale à l'âge classique* (Brussels: P. Mardaga, 1978).

57. J. Rykwert, *The First Moderns: The Architects of the Eighteenth Century* (Cambridge, Mass.: MIT Press, 1980); A. Pérez-Gómez, *Architecture and the Crisis of Modern Science* (Cambridge, Mass.: MIT Press, 1983).

58. See *Guarino Guarini e l'internazionalità del Barocco,* 2 vols. (Turin: Accademia della Scienza, 1970), hereafter abbreviated as *GGIB;* N. Carboneri, "Vicende delle Capelle per la Santa Sindone," *Bollettino della Società Piemontese di Archeologia e Belle Arti* [*BSPABA*] 32 (1964): 95–109. For more recent interpretations, see G. A. Ramirez, "Guarino Guarini, Fray Juan Ricci, and the Complete Salomonic Order," *Art History* 4, no. 2 (1981): 175–185; H. A. Meek, *Guarino Guarini and His Architecture* (New Haven: Yale University Press, 1988); J. Gargus, "Guarino Guarini: Geometrical Transformations and the Invention of New Architectural Meanings," *Harvard Architectural Review* 7 (1989): 123–128; E. Robinson, "Optics and Mathematics in the Domed Churches of Guarino Guarini," *Journal of the Society of Architectural Historians* 50, no. 1 (1991): 384–401.

59. G. Claretta, "Inclinazioni artistiche di Carlo Emanuele I di Savoia e dei suoi figli," *Atti della BSPABA* 5, no. 6 (1894): 351.

60. See A. Grabar, *Martyrium: Recherches sur la culte des reliques et l'art chrétien antique,* 2 vols. ([Paris]: Collège de France, 1943–1946); R. Krautheimer, "Introduction to an Iconography of Medieval Architecture," *Journal of the Warburg and Courtauld Institutes* 5 (1942): 1–34.

61. J. B. Scott, "Guarino Guarini: Invention of the Passion Capitals in the Chapel of the Holy Shroud in Turin," *Journal of the Society of Architectural Historians* 54, no. 4 (1995): 418–445.

62. See M. Fagiolo, "La Sindone e l'enigma dell'eclipse," in *GGIB*, 2:209–10. The manuscript of Carlo Emanuele I is in the Archivio di Stato in Turin; quoted in G. Pugno, *La Santa Sindone che si venera a Torino* (Turin: Società Editrice Internazionale, 1961), p. 245, and also in Fagiolo, p. 214.

63. "Eclipsim solis in plano rapresentare data latitudine Lunae ad finum, medium et initium Eclipsis" (G. Guarini, *Placita philosophica* [Paris, 1665], pp. 300–301; hereafter abbreviated *P.Ph.*).

64. C. Balliani, *Regionamenti di Santa Sindone* (Turin, 1610), p. 16.

65. H. Rahner, S. J., *Greek Myths and Christian Mystery* (1963; reprint, New York: Biblo & Tannen, 1971), pp. 89–129, 99ff.

66. Justin Martyr, *Apologia* I.67, in *S. Justini philosophi et martyris opera,* vol. 1 of Corpus apologetarum Christianorum saeculi secundi, ed. J. C. T. von Otto, 2nd ed. (Jena: Mauke, 1872), p. 18.

67. Already at the beginning of the seventeenth century, attempts were being made to reconcile traditional, geocentrically based symbolism with the heliocentric organization of the cosmos. One example is provided by the work of Cardinal Pierre de Bérulle: "An excellent mind of this century wanted to maintain that the sun is at the center of the world and not the earth; that it is immobile and that the earth in proportion to its circular form moves in the sight of the Sun: by this contrary position satisfying all the appearances that oblige our senses to believe that the Sun is in continual motion around the Earth. This new opinion, little followed in the science of the Stars, is useful, and must be followed in the science of salvation. For Jesus is the immobile Sun in His greatness and the mover of all things. Jesus is like his Father and seated to His right he is immobile like Him, and gives motion to all things. Jesus is the true center of the World and the World must be in continual motion toward Him. Jesus is the Sun of our Souls, which receive all grace, light and influence from him. And the Earth of our Hearts must be in continual motion toward Him, to receive in all its powers and parts the favorable countenance, and the benign influence of this great Star" (Bérulle, "Discours de l'état et des grandeurs de Jesus," in *Œuvres* [Paris, 1665], pp. 115–116; trans. in Hallyn, *The Poetic Structure of the World,* p. 143).

68. See K. O. Johnson, "Solomon, Apocalypse, and the Names of God: The Meaning of the Chapel of the Most Holy Shroud in Turin," *Storia Architettura* 8 (1985): 55–80; R. Wittkower, *Art and Architecture In Italy, 1600 to 1750,* 3rd rev. ed. (Harmondsworth: Penguin, 1973), pp. 403–413; Pérez-Gómez, *Architecture and the Crisis of Modern Science,*

pp. 88–94; C. Müller, *Unendlichkeit und Transzendenz in der Sakralarchitektur Guarini's,* Studien zur Kunstgeschichte, 38 (Hildesheim: G. Olms, 1986).

69. *Placita philosophica* was published in Paris in 1665 during Guarini's sojourn there as professor of sacred theology (1662–1666). The work consisted of eight books, of which the most important from our point of view are book 4 (on light) and 8 (on metaphysics). The structure of the *Placita* is based on the standard *cursus philosophicus* of the seventeenth century, most clearly exemplified in Rodriga de Arriaga's *Cursus philosophicus,* written in Prague and published in Antwerp in 1632. Guarini's second most important text is *Euclides adauctus et methodicus mathematicaq(ue) universalis* (Turin, 1671), hereafter abbreviated *E.A.* The work is divided into thirty-five "Tractati," devoted mostly to the problems of continuous quantity, proportions, conic sections, proportional progressions, and surface and solid geometry.

70. "A spiritual quality is not perceived by sense, neither does it extend in the subject nor does it cause corporeal effects; but light poses the contrary, for it is perceived by the senses, it extends in the senses, it causes corporeal effects, for by the mediation of heat it produces fire destructive of the body, etc. Second proof to the first. A spiritual quality must have a spiritual cause; it must be in the same genus of being. The sun and the rest of the sources of light are bodies. Therefore light cannot be a spiritual body" (Guarini, *P.Ph.,* 400Ea). (Translations from *P.Ph.* and *E.A.* unless stated otherwise are by James McQuillan.)

71. Ibid., p. 448, Disp. VII, "De modificationibus lucis." In this section, Guarini continues the discussion of the ambiguous nature of light and its corporeality.

72. "Every luminous body projects rays outside its total sensible sphere[;] . . . therefore, beyond every sphere nature is sensible to the human eye and *lux* propagates its rays" (ibid., 458Ca). The propagation of light beyond the sphere of sensibility (visibility) points toward the existence of invisible light.

73. "When fire is extinguished, light ceases; therefore it is corruptible" (ibid., 460Eb–461Aa).

74. "Essences shining in created intellect (*Essentiae relucentes in intellectu creato)* are actual beings[;] . . . they are beings because they share in created cognition. . . . [T]hings before they are made are known in God" (ibid., 859Da).

75. "The idea is constituted through the verisimilitude of the thing, because it shines in it[;] . . . and as the divine idea produces essences with omnipotence and gives lustre by actuality, therefore it bestows similitude to it" (ibid., 661Ba–Ca).

76. J. McEvoy, *The Philosophy of Robert Grosseteste* (Oxford: Clarendon Press, 1986), pp. 105–113.

77. There is a close affinity between Guarini's and Malebranche's understandings of the intelligibility of geometry seen as a manifestation of divine ideas; the similarity between their thinking is discussed by B. Tavassi La Greca in the appendix to Guarino Guarini, *Architettura civile* (Milan: Polifilo, 1968), pp. 439–459.

78. The analogical background of projection seen as qualitative is discussed in E. J. M. Spargo, *The Category of the Aesthetic in the Philosophy of Saint Bonaventura* (St. Bonaventure, N.Y.: Franciscan Institute, 1953), p. 145; U. Eco, *The Aesthetics of Thomas Aquinas,* trans. H. Bredin (London: Radius, 1988), pp. 82–98.

79. Kepler, *Gesammelte Werke,* 2:92.

80. The development of modern algebra has its origin in the interpretation of book 5 of Euclid's *Elements,* on proportion. Algebra, in turn, made possible infinitesimal calculus and modern mathematical analysis. See C. B. Boyer, *The Concepts of the Calculus: A Critical and Historical Discussion of the Derivative and the Integral* (New York: Columbia University Press, 1939).

81. Proclus, *A Commentary on the First Book of Euclid's Elements,* trans. G. R. Morrow (1970; reprint, Princeton: Princeton University Press, 1992), p. 19.

82. There are three theoretical disciplines, "mathematics, physics, and theology—since it is obvious that if the divine is present anywhere, it is present in this kind of entity" (Aristotle, *Metaphysics* 1026a20; trans. H. Tredennick, Loeb Classical Library [1933–1934; reprint, Cambridge, Mass.: Harvard University Press; London: Heinemann, 1961], 1:297).

83. The tendency to see continuity between the new mathematical representation of reality and the phenomenal world can be found in the works of Mersenne, Malebranche, Clavius, Blancanus, and many lesser-known thinkers, as well as in the works of Guarini. See R. Lenoble, *Mersenne: ou, La naissance du mécanisme,* 2nd ed. (Paris: Vrin, 1971); P. Dear, *Mersenne and the Learning of the Schools* (Ithaca: Cornell University Press, 1988), pp. 62–79; W. A. Wallace, *Galileo and His Sources: The Heritage of the Collegio Romano in Galileo's Science* (Princeton: Princeton University Press, 1984), pp. 136–148; F. Alquié *Malebranche et le rationalisme chrétien* (Paris: Seghers, 1977).

84. In order to penetrate more deeply into the intricacies of Guarini's thinking, we have to follow at least three different lines of thought in his geometry (particularly the one used in the Sindone chapel). The first begins with the experience of identity and difference (the one and the many) and leads through the calculation of identities to the formation of the essences of things. The second subordinates the existence of things to their essence, on the assumption that what exists is what is known to exist. In the formulation of Francisco Suárez, whom Guarini follows very closely, "essence is not a formal cause strictly and properly said; it nevertheless is an intrinsic and formal constituent of what it constitutes" (Suárez, *Disputationes metaphysicae,* 31.5.1; in *Opera*

Omnia, [ed. C. Berton] [Paris: L. Vivès, 1866], 25:122). The third line of thought develops and explains the possibility of identifying the formal essence of things with magnitudes; it depends on faith in the divine knowledge that "essences are like numbers"; M. Mersenne, *Quaestiones celeberrimae in Genesim* (Paris, 1623), p. 437. The relation between numbers and essences of things is sustained not only by divine ideas but also by God's creative power, which in a form of illumination penetrates human intellect and things—not directly, but as a similitude in a continuous proportion of similitudes. The vehicle that can mediate similitudes in a continuous proportion is geometry.

On continuity in representing indivisible qualities, see Aristotle, *Metaphysics* 999a, 1015b35; trans. Tredennick, pp. 121, 229. For more recent interpretations, see W. Breidert, *Das aristotelische Kontinuum in der Scholastik* (Münster: Aschendorff, 1970); J. E. Murdoch, "Infinity and Continuity," in *The Cambridge History of Later Medieval Philosophy: From the Rediscovery of Aristotle to the Disintegration of Scholasticism, 1100–1600,* ed. N. Kretzmann, A. Kenny, and J. Pinborg (Cambridge: Cambridge University Press, 1982), pp. 564–593.

85. Murdoch, "Infinity and Continuity"; Koyré, *From the Closed World to the Infinite Universe.*

86. J. Kepler, "De stella nova in pede serpentarii," in *Opera Omnia,* ed. C. Frisch, 8 vols. (Frankfurt: Heyder & Zimmer, 1858–1871), vol. 2, chap. 21, p. 688; trans. in Koyré, *From the Closed World to the Infinite Universe,* p. 61.

87. B. Pascal, *Pensée* 202 (517); trans. A. J. Krailsheimer in *Pensées* (Harmondsworth: Penguin, 1966), p. 95.

88. "Finitum nullam rationem cum infinito" (No finite thing is said to have a ratio with infinity; Guarini, *E.A.,* p. 108). However, continuity makes possible the similitude between God and the created world: "Eas in Deo dicit similitudinem cum ente creato; conclusio nempe aliquod genus analogationis, tum attributionis, tum proportionis, posse inter Deum et creaturam reperiri" (Being in God is said to have similitude with created being, which leads on to some genus of analogy, either of attribution or proportion, which can be found between God and creature; Guarini, *P.Ph.,* 843Da).

89. "Datis duabis rectis lineis proportiones earum propagare in infinitum" (The proportion can be propagated according to the increase of the smaller to the greater to infinity; Guarini, *E.A.,* p. 243).

90. "Terminus progressionis est serie finis ad quem nulla progressio pertinget licet in infinitum continetur sed ei perpetuo accedet" (Guarini, *E.A.,* p. 256).

91. Renaissance perspective and Guarini's progression of ratios have a common origin in the theorem of similar triangles in the sixth book of Euclid's *Elements* and in Pappus's theorem of the projective similarity of triangles. These also provided the basis of Gérard

Desargues's projective geometry. But while Desargues's is a pure geometry of position and infinity, Guarini's geometry is situated and ontological.

92. "Duplex est series superficierum, qual continuata in infinitum geometrice extendi potest" (Guarini, *E.A.*, p. 495).

93. The drawing is discussed in J. McQuillan, "Geometry and Light in the Architecture of Guarino Guarini" (Ph.D. diss., University of Cambridge, 1991), part 2, p. 237.

94. Hexagonal geometry played an important role in many other Baroque treatises, particularly in the work of Gregorius a Sancto Vincentio (Gregory Saint Vincent). For his life and work, see *Dictionary of Scientific Biography*, ed. C. C. Gillespie (New York: Scribner, 1975), 12:74–76. In his *Opus geometricum*, Gregory demonstrates the principle of continuous summation (progression) to infinity, using hexagons, among other figures; "Terminus of a progression is the end of the series to which the progression does not attain, even if it continued to infinity, but to which it can approach more closely than by any given interval" (Gregorius, *Opus geometricum quadraturae circuli et sectionum coni* [Antwerp, 1647], p. 134). McQuillan, in "Geometry and Light," convincingly establishes an affinity between Guarini's progression to infinity and Gregory's summation to infinity.

95. *Proportione dialectica* expressed in the language of universal mathematics is the main vehicle of discourse in Guarini's *prima philosophia*. Universal mathematics was described by Francesco Barozzi already in the sixteenth century as "divina scienza sine prima philosophia, quae dialectica Platone vocatur." See G. Crapulli, *Mathesis universalis: Genesi di un' idea nel XVI secolo* (Rome: Edizioni dell' Ateneo, 1969), p. 31.

96. There is a particularly close affinity between Guarini's concept of the multiplication of divine perfection emanating from the point of ultimate unity and Cusanus's concept of illumination and vision (discussed in *De visione Dei*). In both cases, the source of projection (emanation) and vision is not the human eye but the absolute and ineffable eye of God. Guarini's geometrical interpretation of *De visione Dei* represents new conditions of visibility based no longer on sensible matter but on the "intelligible matter" (*materia intelligibile*) perceptible only to the intellect. See G. C. Giacobbe, "Epigone in seicento della Quaestio de certitudine mathematicarum Giuseppe Blancani," *Physis* 18, n. 1 (1976): 5–40; Dear, *Mersenne and the Learning of the Schools*, p. 67.

97. The perfection of the circle and circular movement (representing the immortality of the soul) and its distortion due to the imperfection of material bodies are first mentioned in Plato's *Timaeus* 42e, later in Plotinus's *Ennead* II.2 and Proclus's *Commentary* IX.82, and eventually in Kepler, who writes: "because they attached so much importance to the reciprocal relations of the curve and the straight line, and because they dared to compare the curve to God and the straight line to creatures, for this reason alone I hold Nicholas of Cusa and some others as divine" (Kepler, *Gesammelte Werke*, 1:23).

98. Ibid., 7:330.

99. Ibid., 1:23.

100. Because the literature in this field is enormous and still growing, I restrict my references here to the most important publications: C. Ripa, *Iconologia* (Rome, 1603); A. Fletcher, *Allegory: The Theory of a Symbolic Mode* (Ithaca: Cornell University Press, 1964); M. Praz, *Studies in Seventeenth-Century Imagery*, 2 vols., 2nd ed. (Rome: Edizioni di Storia e letteratura, 1964–1974); E. H. Gombrich, "Icones Symbolicae," in *Symbolic Images* (London: Phaidon Press, 1972), pp. 123–191; W. Hekscher, "Emblem und Emblembuch," in *Reallexikon zur deutschen Kunstgeschichte*, ed. O. Schmitt (Stuttgart: J. B. Metzler, 1959), 5:85–228; A. Henkel, and A. Schöne, eds., *Emblemata: Handbuch zur Sinnbildkunst des 16. und 17. Jahrhunderts*, special ed. (Stuttgart: J. B. Metzler, 1978); R. Klein, "The Theory of Figurative Expression in Italian Treatises on the Impressa," in *Form and Meaning: Essays on the Renaissance and Modern Art*, trans. M. Jay and L. Wieseltier (New York: Viking Press, 1979), pp. 3–25; P. M. Daly, ed., *The European Emblem: Towards an Index Emblematicus* (Waterloo, Canada: Wilfred Laurier University Press, 1980); A. Schöne, *Emblematik und Drama in Zeitalter des Barock*, 3rd ed. (Munich: Beck, 1993).

101. See Klein, "The Theory of Figurative Expression," p. 22; G. Ruscelli, *Le impressi illustri* (Venice, 1566); Praz, *Studies in Seventeenth-Century Imagery*.

102. H. G. Gadamer, "The Principle of Effective History," in *Truth and Method*, [trans. W. Glen-Doepel, trans. ed. G. Barden and J. Cumming], 2nd ed. (London: Sheed & Ward, 1975), pp. 267–274.

103. P. Ricoeur, *Figuring the Sacred: Religion, Narrative, and Imagination*, trans. D. Pellauer, ed. M. I. Wallace (Minneapolis: Fortress Press, 1995), p. 52.

104. Ibid., p. 53.

105. Leibniz, quoted in P. Hazard, *The European Mind, 1680–1715*, trans J. L. May (Harmondsworth: Penguin, 1964), p. 261.

106. See R. Zürcher, *Zwiefalten, die Kirche der ehemaligen Benediktinerabtei: Ein Gesamtkunstwerk des süddeutschen Rokoko* (Konstanz: J. Thorbecke, 1967); K. H. Schönnig, *Münster Zwiefalten: Kirche der ehemaligen Reichsabtei*, 3rd ed. (Munich: Schnell & Steiner, 1988).

107. N. Lieb, *Barockkirchen zwischen Donau und Alpen* (Munich: Hirmer, 1953).

108. The mentioned centers of the Marian cult are Genazzano, Einsiedeln, Altötting, Zwiefalten, Fourvière, and Martinsbeg in Hungary (Schönnig, *Münster Zwiefalten*, p. 23).

109. The fragments of the program are preserved as "programm fragmente folio," in Hauptstaatsarchiv, section B551, folder 26, Stuttgart.

110. See W. Mrazek, *Ikonologie der barocken Deckenmalerei* (Vienna: R. M. Rohrer, 1953); H. Tintelnot, *Die barocke Freskomalerei in Deutschland: Ihre Entwicklung und europäische Wirkung* (Munich: F. Bruckmann, 1951); B. Rupprecht, *Die bayerische Rokoko-Kirche* (Kallmünz: M. Lassleben, 1959); H. Bauer, *Der Himmel im Rokoko: Das Fresko im deutschen Kirchenraum des 18. Jahrhunderts* (Regensburg: Pustet, 1965); P. Hawel, *Der spätbarocke Kirchenbau und seine theologische Bedeutung: Ein Beitrag zur Ikonologie der christlichen Sakralarchitektur* (Würzburg: Echter, 1987).

111. F. Boespflug, *Dieu dans l'art: Sollicitudini nostrae de Benoît XIV (1745) et l'affaire Crescence de Kaufbeuren* (Paris: Editions du Cerf, 1984), pp. 22–59.

112. See E. Panofsky, *Idea: A Concept in Art Theory,* trans. J. J. S. Peake (Columbia: University of South Carolina Press, 1968); Gombrich, "Icones Symbolicae." The nature of idea became a dominant topic in the treatises of the late sixteenth and the seventeenth century, most clearly in the writings of Giovanni Paolo Lomazzo, Tadeo Zuccaro, Vincenzo Scamozzi, and Giovanni Pietro Bellori; see P. Barocchi, ed., *Scritti d'arte del Cinquecento,* 9 vols. (1971; reprint, Turin: G. Einaudi, 1977–1979).

113. Gadamer, *Truth and Method,* pp. 379, 387.

114. Gombrich, "Icones Symbolicae," p. 183; E. Tesauro, *Il cannocchiale aristotelico* (Turin, 1670; facsimile ed., Savigliano [Cuneo]: Artistica Piemontese, 2003).

115. See Tesauro, *Il cannocchiale aristotelico,* p. 695; Hekscher, "Emblem, Emblembuch"; H. Bauer, "Concettismo," in *Barock: Kunst einer Epoche* (Berlin: O. Reimer, 1992), pp. 183–217; K. Mösseneder, "Barocke Bildphilosophie und Emblem," introduction to C. F. Menestrier, *L'art des emblêmes* (Paris, 1684; reprint, Mittenwald: Mäander Kunstverlag, 1981)

116. Tesauro, *Il cannocchiale aristotelico,* p. 695.

117. Francis Quarles, *Emblemes* (London, 1635), quoted in Mösseneder, "Barocke Bildphilosophie und Emblem," p. 22.

118. The cult of Mary represents a radical approach to the problem of incarnation, as she overshadows the incarnational role of Christ. The cult swept Europe during twelfth and thirteenth centuries and again after the Council of Trent; see "Mariology," in *Encyclopedia of Theology: A Concise "Sacramentum mundi,"* ed. K. Rahner (1975; reprint, London: Burns & Oates, 1986), pp. 893–905.

119. Gadamer, *Truth and Method,* pp. 378–387. On the meanings of water, see M. Eliade, "The Waters and Water Symbolism," in *Patterns in Comparative Religion,* trans. R.

Sheed (London: Sheed & Ward, 1958), pp. 188–216; H. Rahner, "The Mystery of Baptism," in *Greek Myths and Christian Mystery,* pp. 69–89; J. Danielou, "The Baptismal Rite," in *The Bible and the Liturgy* (Ann Arbor, Mich.: UMI, 1956), pp. 35–54.

120. Anastasius Sinaita, quoted in Rahner, *Greek Myths and Christian Mystery,* p. 163.

121. Rocaille has its origin in the tradition of the grotesque, in the imaginative interpretation of the primary elements and the creative powers of nature. By the beginning of the eighteenth century, rocaille had developed into an ornamental form with unique possibilities of emblematic representation. For the nature and history of the grotesque and rocaille, see H. Bauer, *Rocaille: Zur Herkunft und zum Wesen eines Ornament-Motivs* (Berlin: W. de Gruyter, 1962); W. Kayser, *Das Grotesk* (Oldenburg: G. Stalling, 1957); A. Chastel, *La grottesque* (Paris: Le Promeneur, 1988).

122. Hawel, *Die spätbarocke Kirchenbau,* pp. 325–331.

CHAPTER 5 **THE FOUNDATIONS OF MODERN ARCHITECTURE**

1. G. Gusdorf, *Les principes de la pensée au siècle des Lumières,* vol. 4 of *Les sciences humaines et la pensée occidentale* (Paris: Payot, 1971); P. Hazard, *The European Mind, 1680–1715,* trans. J. L. May (Harmondsworth: Penguin, 1964).

2. B. de Fontenelle, *Histoire de l'Académie Royale des Sciences depuis le reglement fait en 1699* (Paris, 1702), preface.

3. The influence of the Newtonian paradigm of knowledge is discussed most comprehensively by G. Gusdorf, "Le modèle newtonien" and "La généralisation du paradigme newtonien," in *Les principes,* pp. 151–213.

4. The notion that knowledge is cumulative and associated with progress was introduced into modern thinking by Francis Bacon in his *Novum organum* (1620); see P. Rossi, *Francis Bacon: From Magic to Science,* trans. S. Rabinovitch (London: Routledge & Kegan Paul, 1968).

5. A. Koyré, *Newtonian Studies* (London: Chapman & Hall, 1965), p. 24.

6. M. Heidegger, *The Metaphysical Foundations of Logic,* trans. M. Heim (Bloomington: Indiana University Press, 1984), pp. 52–53.

7. See Charles Perrault, *Parallèle des anciens et des modernes* (Paris, 1688); B. de Fontenelle, *Digression sur les anciens et les modernes* (Paris, 1688); J. B. Bury, *The Idea of Progress: An Inquiry into Origin and Growth* (1920; reprint, New York: Dover, 1955). For the most recent bibliography, see J. DeJean, *Ancients against Moderns: Culture Wars and the Making of a Fin de Siècle* (Chicago: University of Chicago Press, 1997).

8. Charles Perrault, *Le siècle de Louis le Grand* (Paris, 1687).

9. Pascal, quoted in Bury, *The Idea of Progress*, p. 68.

10. Mathematical knowledge—its nature and ontology—is discussed in M. Heidegger, "The Modern Mathematical Science of Nature and the Origin of a Critique of Pure Reason," in *What Is a Thing?* trans. W. B. Barton, Jr., and V. Deutsch (Chicago: H. Regnery, 1967), pp. 65–108.

11. At the close of his *Parallèle*, Charles Perrault writes: "Within the last twenty or thirty years more discoveries have been made in natural science than throughout the period of learned antiquity. I own that I consider myself fortunate to know the happiness we enjoy; it is a great pleasure to survey all the past ages in which I can see the birth and the progress of all things, but nothing which has not received a new increase and lustre in our own times. Our age has, arrived at the summit of perfection" (quoted in Bury, *The Idea of Progress*, p. 87).

12. Charles Perrault, *Parallèle des anciens et des modernes,* p. 97.

13. Claude Perrault, *Les dix livres d'architecture de Vitruve* (Paris, 1673); *Ordonnance des cinq espèces de colonnes selon la méthode des anciens* (Paris, 1683).

14. Claude Perrault, *Ordonnance for the Five Kinds of Columns after the Method of the Ancients,* trans. I. K. McEwen (Santa Monica, Calif.: Center for the History of Art and the Humanities, 1993), pp. 58, 60.

15. Ibid., p. 59. Perrault blames the "defective" nature of the copies not on historical circumstances or the changing nature of representation, but only on individual error: "The carelessness of those who build the ancient buildings we see is the only real reason for the failure of these proportions to follow exactly the true ones, which one may reasonably believe were established by the first originators of architecture."

16. I discuss the changing nature of proportions elsewhere, in "The Architectonics of Embodiment," in *Body and Building: Essays on the Changing Relation of Body and Architecture,* ed. G. Dodds and R. Tavernor (Cambridge, Mass.: MIT Press, 2002), pp. 28–44.

17. Claude Perrault, *Ordonnance,* pp. 51, 50. The modern notion of symmetry, unlike classical symmetry (which Perrault calls "proportion"), is bilateral organization and order of parts. It "consists in the relationship the parts have collectively as a result of the balanced correspondence of their size, number, disposition and order" (p. 50). Though Perrault believes such symmetry to be an intrinsic characteristic of all architecture, it is historically determined and therefore relative. See W. Kambartel, *Symmetrie und Schönheit: Über mögliche Voraussetzungen des neueren Kunstbewusstseins in der Architekturtheorie Claude Perraults* (Munich: W. Fink, 1972).

18. In replacing the historical interpretation of orders with a theoretical alternative that unifies the different ratios as new numerical proportions, Perrault was attempting to transform the interpretive creative process into an abstract normative system (W. Herrmann, *The Theory of Claude Perrault* [London: A. Zwemmer, 1973], pp. 95–130).

19. Claude Perrault, *Ordonnance,* p. 61.

20. See K. Löwith, *Meaning in History* (1949; reprint, Chicago: University of Chicago Press, 1967); A. O. Lovejoy, "The Temporalising of the Chain of Being," in *The Great Chain of Being* (1936; reprint, Cambridge, Mass.: Harvard University Press, 1974), pp. 242–287; E. Voegelin, *From Enlightenment to Revolution,* ed. J. H. Hallowell (Durham, N.C.: Duke University Press, 1975), pp. 83–109; R. Koselleck, *Futures Past: On the Semantics of Historical Time,* trans. K. Tribe (Cambridge, Mass.: MIT Press, 1985).

21. See N. Pevsner, *Academies of Art, Past and Present* (1940; reprint, New York: Da Capo Press, 1973); A. Pérez-Gómez, *Architecture and the Crisis of Modern Science* (Cambridge, Mass.: MIT Press, 1983); A. Picon, *French Architects and Engineers in the Age of Enlightenment,* trans. M. Thom (Cambridge: Cambridge University Press, 1988).

22. R. Descartes, "Discourse on Method," in *The Philosophical Works of Descartes,* trans. E. S. Haldane and G. R. T. Ross (1911; reprint, Cambridge: Cambridge University Press, 1982), 1:106.

23. To experimentally reconcile the mathematically structured project of possible reality and phenomenal reality is a subtle imaginative operation: mathematical representation eliminates the distance between the ideal and the phenomenal levels of reality. The nature of the experimental reality of modern science is discussed in E. Husserl, *The Crisis of European Sciences and Transcendental Phenomenology,* trans. D. Carr (Evanston, Ill.: Northwestern University Press, 1970), pp. 21–60; A. Koyré, *Metaphysics and Measurement: Essays in Scientific Revolution* (London: Chapman & Hall, 1968), pp. 44–89; Heidegger, "The Modern Mathematical Science of Nature," pp. 76–95.

24. Husserl, *The Crisis of European Sciences,* p. 51.

25. M. Planck, in a lecture delivered at Leiden University on 9 December 1908, published as "Die Einheit des physikalischen Weltbildes" in *Physikalisches Zeitschrift* 10 (1909): 62–67; trans. as "The Unity of the Physical World-Picture," in *Physical Reality: Philosophical Essays on Twentieth-Century Physics,* ed. S. Toulmin (New York: Harper & Row, 1970), pp. 1–28; quotation, p. 20.

26. Ibid., p. 22.

27. W. Heisenberg, *The Physicist's Conception of Nature,* trans. A. J. Pomerans (New York: Harcourt, Brace, 1958), p. 53.

28. Architecture and art were originally seen as a product of *technē* and *poiēsis* (*technē poiētikē*), where *technē* was creative knowledge and *poiēsis* creativity and symbolic representation. During the seventeenth century, the original unity was dissolved; *technē* became an independent body of instrumental (productive) knowledge and *poiēsis* (symbolic representation) became a new aesthetic reality. The emancipation of *technē* from *poiēsis* coincides with the origin of modern science (technology) and of modern aesthetics; both have a common ground in art understood as *technē poiētikē*. See E. Grassi, *Kunst und Mythos,* Rowohlts deutsche Enzyklopëdie (Hamburg: Rowohlt, 1957), as well as his *Die Theorie des Schönen in der Antike* (Cologne: DuMont, 1962).

29. The group was formed in Auteuil, on the outskirts of Paris, around the personality of Comte Destutt de Tracy, whose *Élémens d'idéologie* (Paris, 1804–1816) remained the most important publication of the movement. See G. Gusdorf, *La conscience révolutionnaire, les idéologues,* vol. 8 of *Les sciences humaines et la pensée occidentale* (Paris: Payot, 1978).

30. The physicalist interpretation of sensations has its precedent in John Locke's *Essay Concerning Human Understanding* (London, 1690). Apart from Locke's *Essay,* the most influential treatise for the Ideologues was Étienne Bonnot de Condillac's *Traité des sensations* (Paris, 1754).

31. The problematic blend of confidence and naivete is clearly evident in the seminal text of the Ideologues: "Locke is, I believe, the first man who attempted to observe and describe human intelligence as one observes and describes the property of a mineral or plant, or the special circumstances of the life of an animal; this study can be a part of physics" (A. L. C. Destutt de Tracy, *Élémens d'idéologie* [Paris: Mme Vve Courcier, 1817], 1:xv).

32. Marquis de Laplace, *A Philosophical Essay on Probabilities,* trans. F. W. Truscott and F. L. Emory (1902; reprint, New York: Dover, 1951), p. 4.

33. See Laplace, *A Philosophical Essay on Probabilities,* p. 4; S. Villari, *J. N. L. Durand (1760–1834): Art and Science of Architecture* (New York: Rizzoli, 1990), p. 33; J. N. L. Durand, *Recueil et parallèle des édifices de tout genre anciens et modernes, remarquables par leur beauté, par leur grandeur, ou par leur singularité, et dessinés sur une même échelle* (Paris: n.p., 1801).

34. J. N. L. Durand, *Précis des leçons d'architecture données à l'École Royale Polytechnique,* 2 vols. (Paris: chez l'auteur, 1809).

35. Ibid., 1:29.

36. G. Semper, *Kleine Schriften,* ed. H. and M. Semper (Berlin: W. Spemann, 1884), p. 262.

37. Gottfried Semper, in H. Semper, *Gottfried Semper: Ein Bild seines Lebens und Wirkens* (Berlin: S. Calvary, 1880), p. 4.

38. "Die Ubereinstimung einer Kunsterscheinung mit ihrer Entstehungsgeschichte mit allen Vorbedingungen und Ummstanden ihres Werdens" (G. Semper, *Kleine Schriften,* p. 402).

39. The possibility of discussing the nature of the artwork or architecture in terms of functional relationships appeared in Semper's "Entwurf eines Systems der vergleichenden Stillehre" (Project for the System of the Comparative Theory of Style). The problem of style is expressed in the formula $Y = F(x, y, z, \ldots)$, where x, etc. are external variable conditions, F stands for the internal and stable conditions, and Y is the work of art (architecture). The formula is meant to be read analogically and not literally, of course.

40. G. W. Leibniz, *Discourse on Metaphysics,* ed. and trans. R. N. D. Martin and S. Brown (Manchester: Manchester University Press, 1988), p. 79.

41. G. W. Leibniz, "The Principles of Nature and of Grace," in *Philosophical Writings,* ed. G. H. R. Parkinson, trans. M. Morris and G. H. R. Parkinson (London: Dent, 1973), pp. 195–205.

42. D. Bouhours, *Les entretiens d'Ariste et d'Eugène* (1671), ed. R. Radouant (Paris: Éditions Bossard, 1920), p. 202; C. Montesquieu, "Essai sur le Goût," in *Encyclopédie; ou Dictionnaire raisonné des sciences, des arts et des métiers,* 17 vols. (Paris, 1751–1765), vol. 7, col. 765b.

43. W. Leibniz, "Monadology," in *Philosophical Writings,* p. 193, par. 83.

44. J. B. Fischer von Erlach, preface to *Entwurff einer historischen Architectur* [2nd ed.; Leipzig, 1725], published trans. by T. Leliard, *A Plan of Civil and Historical Architecture* [London, 1730] (Ridgewood, N.J.: Gregg Press, 1964), n.p. [preface].

45. On the development of the late Baroque theater, the role of theatricality in Baroque art, and the question of aestheticization, see H. Tintelnot, *Barocktheater und barocke Kunst* (Berlin: Gebr. Mann, 1939); K. Harries, *The Bavarian Rococo Church: Between Faith and Aestheticism* (New Haven: Yale University Press, 1983), pp. 250–259; H. Bauer, "Theater und theatralik," in *Barock: Kunst einer Epoche* (Berlin: D. Reimer, 1992), pp. 217–253.

46. M. Dufrenne, "Formalisme logique et formalisme esthétique," in *Esthétique et Philosophie* (Paris: Klinksieck, 1967), pp. 113–129.

47. "Eine Flucht in die Unwirklichkeitssphäre des als 'nur' Kunst deklarierten Bilde zerstört die Ganzheit der barocken illusion" (H. Bauer, *Rocaille: Zur Herkunft und Wesen eines Ornament-Motivs* [Berlin: W. de Gruyter, 1962], p. 72).

48. The discontinuity of perspective illusion seriously interferes with the logic of the illusionistic world, which lies in the continuity between the world of the spectator and the world of representation. The ontological structure of that continuity necessarily provides the foundation of symbolic meaning. Thus, discontinuity reduces the symbolic to a pictorial and secondary (aesthetic) meaning gleaned from an experientially detached visual scene. For a more detailed interpretation, see E. Stadler, "Raumgestaltung im barocken Theater," in *Die Kunstformen des Barockzeitalters,* by H. Barth et al. (Bern: Francke, 1956), pp. 190–227.

49. The key to this analogy is the free play of imagination that establishes an ideal reality, which is then used as an ordering vision (structure) of empirical phenomena. This act is known in science as an "imaginary thought experiment" and in art as "inner design" (*disegno interno*). It was the nature of the common "imaginative project" that guaranteed the close affinity of eighteenth-century art, architecture, and science. That modern aesthetics could be a science of artistic experience was conceivable only in this imaginative project.

50. The principle of artistic disinterestedness, the essence of aesthetic experience, was first formulated by Immanuel Kant in his *Critique of Judgment* (1790); it became the foundation of the modern understanding of art, mostly owing to the influence of Friedrich Schiller's *Letters on the Aesthetic Education of Man* (Berlin, 1793–1795).

51. H. G. Gadamer, *Truth and Method,* [trans. W. Glen-Doepel, trans. ed. G. Barden and J. Cumming], 2nd ed. (London: Sheed & Ward, 1975), p. 74.

52. Ibid., p. 78.

53. Ibid., p. 75.

54. H. Rosenau, *Boullée and Visionary Architecture* (London: Academy Editions, 1976), pp. 83, 33; this work includes both the French text and translation of Boullée's *Architecture, essai sur l'art.* This edition will hereafter be cited parenthetically in the text.

55. Such errors are often produced by an excessive preoccupation with the method of design, which leads theorists to forget that aesthetic appearance and the reality of art are two different things. Boullée's indebtedness to the classical tradition and the use of Egyptian and Gothic elements in his architecture are too obvious to need any commentary. Here it is appropriate to again quote Husserl: "what in truth is merely a method and the results of that method are now taken for 'real nature.'"

56. A. W. Schlegel, *Kritische Schriften und Briefe,* ed. E. Lohner (Stuttgart: W. Kohlhammer, 1963), 2:140: "Die Architektur definieren wir als die Kunst schöner Formen an Gegenstanden, welche ohne bestimmtes Vorbild in der Natur, frei nach einer eigenen ursprünglichen idee des menschlichen Geistes entworfen und ausgeführt werden. Da ihre Werke demnach keinen von den großen ewigen Gedanken, welche die Natur ihren

Schöpfungen eindruckt sichtbar machen; so muß ein menschlicher Gedanke sie bestimmen, d.h. sie mußen aus einen Zweck gerichtet sein."

57. Peyre: "Nous lisions Vitruve sans le comprendre," and Viel: "Ce livre de Vitruve ne pourrait être utile que dans l'Île de Robinson"; both quoted in J. M. Pérouse de Montclos, *Étienne-Louis Boullée, 1720–1799, de l'architecture classique à l'architecture révolutionnaire* (Paris: Arts et Métiers Graphiques, 1969), p. 187.

58. At the beginning of the nineteenth century, style became a key notion in art and in art history, related as closely to historicism as to the new "aesthetic" understanding of art. As the decisive link between art and history, it is better known under its German name, *Stilgeschichte*. For a more comprehensive discussion (and further bibliography), see F. Piel, "Der historische Stilbegriff und die Geschichtlichkeit der Kunst," in *Kunstgeschichte und Kunsttheorie im 19. Jarhhundert*, ed. H. Bauer (Berlin: de Gruyter, 1963), pp. 18–38.

59. E. Grassi, "Ingenium und Scharfsinn," in *Die Macht der Phantasie: Zur Geschichte abendländischen Denkens* (Frankfurt am Main: Syndikat, 1969), pp. 65–70.

60. See R. G. Saisselin, "Genius," in *The Rule of Reason and the Ruses of the Heart: A Philosophical Dictionary of Classical French Criticism, Critics, and Aesthetic Issues* (Cleveland: Press of Case Western Reserve University, 1970), pp. 89–96; P. E. Knabe, "Genie," in *Schlüsselbegriffe des kunsttheoretischen Denkens in Frankreich von der Spätklassik bis zum Ende der Aufklärung* (Dusseldorf: L. Schwann, 1972), pp. 204–238

61. Schinkel, quoted in H. Sedlmayr, *Art in Crisis: The Lost Center*, [trans. B. Battershaw] (London: Hollis & Carter, 1957), p. 33.

62. "Styl in der Architektur durch Reflexion erzeugen zu können"; "Nicht aus einer früheren, sondern aus der gegenwärtigen Beschaffenheit der natürlichen Bildungselemente hervorgehen" (H. Hübsch, *In welchem Style sollen wir bauen?* [Karlsruhe: Chr. Fr. Müller, 1828], pp. 2, p. 13).

63. "Wir leben nicht mehr in der Zeit des unbewußten, naturnothwendigen Schaffens, durch welches früher die Bauordnungen enstanden, sondern in einer Epoche des Denkens, des Forschens und der selbstbewußten Reflexion. Zur Lösung der besprochenen Aufgabe wird es vielleicht hier am Ort seyn, auf die Momente hinzudeuten. welche aut die Architektur der verschiedenen Länder eingewirkt und noch einwirken" (quoted in E. Drüeke, *"Maximilianstil": Zum Stilbegriff der Architektur im 19. Jahrhundert* [Mittenwald: Mäander, 1981], p. 99).

64. "Wichtig ist mir die möglichste Erkenntis der Zukunft wegen des mir in der Gegenwart Anzustrebenden"; "Wir leben in dem Zeitalter der Erfindungen. Warum sollte sich nun nicht auch ein Architekt hinsetzen und einen neuen Baustil erfinden?" (ibid., pp. 37, 25).

65. K. F. Schinkel, *Aus Schinkels Nachlass* (1862), ed. A. von Wolzogen (Mittenwald: Mäander, 1981), 3:161.

66. Ibid., p. 334.

67. "Ein jeder sollte darin gestimmt werden, sich Bilder der Zukunft zu schaffen, durch welche sein Wesen erhöht, und er zum Streben nach Vollendung genöthigt würde" (ibid., p. 161).

68. "Doch soll das Monument für alle Zeiten sein, deshalb im Reich der schönen Kunst gegründet" (K. F. Schinkel, *Das architektonische Lehrbuch*, ed. G. Peschken, Karl Friedrich Schinkel, Lebenswerk [Munich: Deutscher Kunstverlag, 1979], p. 27).

69. "Kunstwerk daher, wenn es nicht auf irgend eine Weise Monument ist und sein will, ist kein Kunstwerk" (Schinkel, *Aus Schinkels Nachlass*, 3:350).

70. Schinkel, *Das architektonische Lehrbuch*, p. 115.

71. "Die hohe Schönheit erregt nie eine der Menschen-Würde widerstrebende Sinnlichkeit, sondern sie zeigt eine Sinnlichkeit höherer Art vom Geiste durchdrungen, daß das Göttliche der irdischen Form beiwohnen kann und muß" (ibid., p. 35).

72. E. Voegelin, *The New Science of Politics: An Introduction* (Chicago: University of Chicago Press, 1952), p. 171.

73. Ibid., p. 150.

74. G. Semper, "Über architektonische Symbole," in *Kleine Schriften*, pp. 292–304.

75. The debates that took place in the Werkbund movement are a good illustration of the ambiguous nature of architecture and art, reflected in the tension between the fine arts and the applied arts. See F. J. Schwartz, *The Werkbund: Design Theory and Mass Culture before the First World War* (New Haven: Yale University Press, 1996); J. Campbell, *The German Werkbund: The Politics of Reform in the Applied Arts* (Princeton: Princeton University Press, 1992).

76. A. Endell, "The Beauty of Form and Decorative Art" (1897–1898), in *Form and Function: A Source Book for the History of Architecture and Design, 1890–1939* by T. and C. Benton, with D. Sharp (London: Crosby Lockwood Staples, 1975), pp. 20–26; quotation, p. 21.

77. J. J. P. Oud, "Architecture and Standardisation in Mass Construction" (1918), in ibid., p. 117.

78. F. Nietzsche, *The Will to Power,* trans. W. Kaufmann and R. J. Hollingdale, ed. W. Kaufmann (New York: Random House, 1967), sec. 800; this work is hereafter cited parenthetically in the text.

79. Monet, quoted in G. Clemenceau, *Claude Monet: Les nymphéas* (Paris: Plon, 1928), pp. 19–20.

80. The intention to impose truth on reality played an important role in the programs of Constructivism, De Stijl, Surrealism, etc. and in their vision of the world as an apocalyptic transformation, pure plastic reality, the occultation of everyday reality, etc.

81. "Picasso Speaks," interview with Marius de Zayas in *The Art,* May 1923, pp. 315–326; quoted in E. F. Fry, *Cubism* (London: Thames & Hudson, 1966), p. 165.

82. By "truth," I understand the capacity of the work of art or architecture to reveal not just the truth of existing reality—the human situation—but also the capacity to preserve it in the work as symbolic representation. In this sense, the nature of truth is almost identical with the classical understanding of *poiēsis* and with Heidegger's understanding of truth in "Origin of the Work of Art" and "The Question Concerning Technology," in his *Basic Writings,* ed. D. F. Krell (London: Routledge & Kegan Paul, 1978), pp. 143–189, pp. 283–319.

83. The crisis in the late eighteenth century to which I refer has been discussed in detail by G. Gusdorf, in vols. 7 and 8 of *Les sciences humaines et la pensée occidentale, Naissance de la conscience romantique au siècle des lumières* (Paris: Payot, 1976) and *La conscience révolutionnaire, les idéologues;* Voegelin, *From Enlightenment to Revolution;* H. Sedlmayr, *Die Revolution der modernen Kunst,* Rowohlts deutsche Enzyklopädie (Hamburg: Rowohlt, 1955).

84. This tendency privileges values established in the context of scientism, historicism, and aestheticism. See C. H. Taylor, *The Sources of the Self: The Making of the Modern Identity* (Cambridge: Cambridge University Press, 1989); R. Sennett, *The Fall of Public Man* (Cambridge: Cambridge University Press, 1976).

85. "I describe what is coming, what can no longer come differently: *the advent of nihilism.* This history can be related even now; for necessity itself is at work here. This future speaks even now in a hundred signs, this destiny announces itself everywhere; for this music of the future all ears are cocked even now. For some time now, our whole European culture has been moving as toward a catastrophe, with a tortured tension that is growing from decade to decade: restlessly, violently, headlong, like a river that wants to reach the end, that no longer reflects, that is afraid to reflect" (Nietzsche, *The Will to Power,* preface, sec. 2).

1. G. Boehm, *Studien zur Perspektivität: Philosophie und Kunst in der frühen Neuzeit* (Heidelberg: C. Winter, 1969), pp. 41–47, 124–137.

2. See P. O. Kristeller, "The Modern System of Arts," in *Renaissance Thought and the Arts* (Princeton: Princeton University Press, 1980), pp. 163–228; P. Rossi, *Philosophy, Technology and the Arts in the Early Modern Era,* trans. S. Attanasio (New York: Harper & Row, 1970).

3. See P. Frankl, "The Secret of the Medieval Masons," *Art Bulletin* 27 (1954): 46–60; J. Ackerman, "'Ars sine Scientia nihil est': Gothic Theory of Architecture at the Cathedral of Milan," *Art Bulletin* 31 (1949): 84–111; V. Ascani, "Le dessin d'architecture médiéval en italie," in *Les bâtisseurs des cathédrales gothiques,* comp. R. Recht ([Strasbourg]: Editions les Musées de la ville de Strasbourg, 1989), pp. 255–279; W. Müller, *Grundlagen gotischer Bautechnik: Ars sine Scientia nihil est* (Munich: Deutscher Kunstverlag, 1990).

4. L. Marx, "The Changing Character of the 'Mechanic Arts' and the Invention of Technology," in *Does Technology Drive History?* ed. M. R. Smith and L. Marx (Cambridge, Mass.: MIT Press, 1994), pp. 242–249.

5. W. Heisenberg, "Rationality in Science and Society," in *Can We Survive Our Future?* ed. G. R. Urban (London: Bodley Head, 1971), p. 84.

6. "I am laboring to lay the foundation not of any sect or doctrine, but of human utility and power." This programmatic formulation first appeared in a well-known passage of Francis Bacon's *Instauratio magna,* in his *New Atlantis; and, The Great Instauration,* ed. J. Weinberger, rev. ed. (Arlington Heights, Ill.: Harlan Davidson, 1989), p. 16.

7. "The basic form of appearance in which the will to will arranges and calculates itself in the unhistorical element of the world of completed metaphysics can be stringently called technology" (M. Heidegger, "Overcoming Metaphysics," in *End of Philosophy,* trans. J. Stambaugh [London: Souvenir Press, 1975], p. 93).

8. Ibid., p. 101.

9. That the will is not absolute is particularly apparent in its situatedness in time—formulated, for instance, by Nietzsche as the attempt to overcome time through the "eternal return." See P. Klossowski, "Nietzsche's Experience of the Eternal Return," in *The New Nietzsche,* ed. D. B. Allison (Cambridge, Mass.: MIT Press, 1986), pp. 107–121.

10. M. Heidegger, *Vorträge und Aufsätze* (Pfullingen: G. Neske, 1959), p. 43.

11. Aristotle, *Metaphysics* 981b14–18.

12. Aristotle, *Physics* 199a7, 9; trans. P. H. Wicksteed and F. M. Cornford, Loeb Classical Library (1929–1934; reprint, Cambridge, Mass.: Harvard University Press; London: W. Heinemann, 1957–1960), 1:173.

13. Aristotle, *Nicomachean Ethics,* 1140a20; trans. H. Rackham, Loeb Classical Library (1925; reprint, Cambridge, Mass.: Harvard University Press; London: W. Heinemann, 1968), p. 335.

14. Aristotle, *Physics* 196b5; trans. Wicksteed and Cornford, 1:147.

15. H. G. Gadamer, *The Relevance of the Beautiful and Other Essays,* trans. N. Walker, ed. R. Bernasconi (Cambridge: Cambridge University Press, 1986), p. 104.

16. Examples of such reenactment can be found in ancient Near Eastern cosmogonies and in the Greeks' understanding of creation, as well as in their refined cosmologies and in the identification of the craftsman and *demiourgos*. In Heidegger's understanding, one of the main characteristics of European metaphysics is the close link between Greek philosophical thinking and *technē*, the knowledge of the craftsmen. See M. Eliade, "The Sacredness of Nature and Cosmic Religion," in *The Sacred and the Profane: The Nature of Religion*, trans. W. R. Trask (New York: Harcourt, Brace, 1959), pp. 116–162; M. Heidegger, "Sketches for a History of Being as Metaphysics," in *The End of Philosophy*, pp. 55–75.

17. "For a science of religion which regards only instrumental action as meaningful, magic is the essence and origin of religion" (W. Burkert, *Greek Religion,* trans. J. Raffan [Oxford: Blackwell, 1985], p. 55). R. Grainger similarly observes, "Science views religion and its manifestations according to its own image and regards everything which refuses to succumb to its techniques as 'magical' and 'primitive'" (*The Language of the Rite* [London: Darton, Longman & Todd, 1974], p. 90).

18. Grainger, *The Language of the Rite,* p. 78.

19. G. van der Leeuw, *Religion in Essence and Manifestation,* trans. J. E. Turner (Gloucester, Mass.: Peter Smith, 1967), 2:548.

20. E. R. Dodds, *The Greeks and the Irrational* (1951; reprint, Berkeley: University of California Press, 1968), p. 288.

21. Pappus of Alexandria, "Revival of Geometry" (mechanics), in *Selections Illustrating the History of Greek Mathematics,* trans. I. Thomas, Loeb Classical Library (1941; reprint, Cambridge, Mass.: Harvard University Press, 1980), p. 616.

22. J. P. Vernant, *Myth and Thought among the Greeks* (London: Routledge & Kegan Paul, 1983), p. 295.

23. Vitruvius, *De architectura* X.1.1.; trans. F. Granger as *On Architecture,* 2 vols., Loeb Classical Library (Cambridge, Mass.: Harvard University Press; London: W. Heinemann, 1931–1934), 2:275.

24. A. Gehlen, *Die Seele im technischen Zeitalter: Sozialpsychologische Probleme in der industriellen Gesellschaft* (Hamburg: Rowohlt, 1957), p. 14.

25. Vitruvius, *De architectura* X.1.4; trans. Granger, 2:277.

26. See, for example, the discussions that followed Frances Yates's explicit claims for the role of magic in the development of modern science and technology, summarized by B. T. Copenhauer in *Reappraisals of the Scientific Revolution,* ed. D. C. Lindberg and R. S. Westman (Cambridge: Cambridge University Press, 1990), pp. 261–303. Scholars seem to have similar difficulties when examining the relationship of art and technique before the seventeenth century, particularly during the late Renaissance. Most interesting here are the discussions about the contributions of prominent individuals—for example, Leonardo da Vinci and his role as artist, engineer, and scientist.

27. For a more detailed discussion of the nature of the arts and their status in the Middle Ages and in the early modern era, see Kristeller, *Renaissance Thought and the Arts,* pp. 163ff; D. L. Wagner, ed., *The Seven Liberal Arts in the Middle Ages* (Bloomington: Indiana University Press, 1986).

28. Characteristically, the arts have very often been referred to as science (*epistēmē*) not only in classical but also in medieval scholarship—for example, the debate on the completion of Milan's cathedral mentioned at the beginning of this chapter (see note 3).

29. In classical ontology, mathematics (and geometry in particular) is seen as a mediating link between metaphysics (theology) and physics, just as the soul (*psychē*) is a mediating link between the intelligible and the sensible realities (P. Merlan, *From Platonism to Neoplatonism,* 3rd ed., rev. [The Hague: Martinus Nijhoff, 1975], pp. 59–87).

30. B. Lorini, *Delle fortificazioni* (Venice, 1596), book 5, p. 172.

31. Further illustrations of the limits of mathematical mechanization and the discussion of the achievements of Leonardo da Vinci can be found in E. J. Dijksterhuis, *The Mechanization of the World Picture,* trans. C. Dikshoorn (Oxford: Clarendon Press, 1961), pp. 37–50.

32. J. C. Pitt, "Galileo and the Use of Geometry," in *New Perspectives on Galileo,* ed. P. E. Butts and Pitt (Dordrecht: D. Reidel, 1978), p. 187; W. A. Wallace, *Galileo and His Sources: The Heritage of the Collegio Romano in Galileo's Science* (Princeton: Princeton University Press, 1984), pp. 126–149.

33. C. B. Boyer, *The Concepts of the Calculus: A Critical and Historical Discussion of the Derivative and the Integral* (New York: Columbia University Press, 1939); G. Crapulli, *Mathesis universalis: Genesi di un'idea nel XVI secolo* (Rome: Edizioni dell'Ateneo, 1969).

34. F. Vieta, "Introduction to the Analytical Art," trans. J. W. Smith, appendix to J. Klein, *Greek Mathematical Thought and the Origin of Algebra,* trans. E. Brann (Cambridge, Mass.: MIT Press, 1968), pp. 315–354.

35. Klein, *Greek Mathematical Thought,* p. 181.

36. Like universal mathematics, *prima philosophia* refers ultimately to the principle of noncontradiction and sufficient reason. The new algebra of a metamathematical kind and physics of a metaphysical kind have the same characteristics.

37. See É. Gilson, *Études sur le rôle de la pensée médiévale dans la formation du système cartésien,* 3rd ed. (Paris: J. Vrin, 1967); Wallace, *Galileo and His Sources,* pp. 338–351; P. Dear, "Aristotelian Science and the Metephysics," in *Mersenne and the Learning of the Schools* (Ithaca: Cornell University Press, 1988), pp. 48–80.

38. R. Descartes, "Letter to Mersenne, 15 April 1630," in *Philosophical Writings,* ed. and trans. E. Anscombe and P. T. Geach (Edinburgh: Nelson, 1954), p. 259.

39. R. Descartes, "Letter to Mersenne, 27 May 1631," in ibid., p. 261.

40. Galileo Galilei, *Dialogue Concerning the Two Chief World Systems, Ptolemaic and Copernican,* trans. D. Stillman, 2nd ed. (Berkeley: University of California Press, 1967), pp. 14, 37–38.

41. "I argue *ex suppositione* about motion, so even though the consequences should not correspond to the events of naturally falling heavy bodies, it would little matter to me, just as it derogates nothing from the demonstrations of Archimedes that no moveable is found in nature that moves along spiral lines. But in this I have been, as I shall say, lucky: for the motion of heavy bodies and its events correspond punctually to the events demonstrated by me from the motion is defined" (Galileo, quoted in E. McMullin, "The Conception of Science in Galileo's work," in Butts and Pitt, *New Perspectives on Galileo,* p. 234).

42. Ibid., p. 232.

43. R. Descartes, *Oeuvres,* ed. C. Adam and P. Tannery, 11 vols. (Paris: J. Vrin, 1974–1982), 11:31, 3:722.

44. R. Descartes, "Objection V," in *Philosophical Writings,* p. 136.

45. D. R. Lachterman, *The Ethics of Geometry: A Genealogy of Modernity* (New York: Routledge, 1989), p. 140.

46. J. Ladrière, "Technique et eschatologie terrestre," in *Civilisation, technique et humanisme* (Paris: Aubier-Montaigne, 1968), pp. 211–245.

47. A. Funkenstein, *Theology and the Scientific Imagination from the Middle Ages to the Seventeenth Century* (Princeton: Princeton University Press, 1986), p. 327. Among those who had this courage are Malebranche and the Occasionalists (Arnold Geulincx, for example)—and, most explicitly, Leibniz.

48. J. Harriss, *The Tallest Tower: Eiffel and the Belle Epoque* (Boston: Houghton Mifflin, 1975).

49. Blaise Cendrars, quoted in R. Barthes, "The Tour Eiffel," in *Structures Implicit and Explicit,* ed. J. Bryan and R. Sauer (Philadelphia: VIA Publications of the Graduate School of Fine Arts, University of Pennsylvania, 1973), 2:220.

50. Le Corbusier, quoted in ibid., p. 226.

51. See E. Husserl, *The Crisis of European Sciences and Transcendental Phenomenology,* trans. D. Carr (Evanston, Ill.: Northwestern University Press), 1970; J. J. Kockelmans, *Heidegger and Science* (Washington, D.C.: Center for Advanced Research in Phenomenology; University Press of America, 1985); M. Polanyi, *Personal Knowledge: Towards a Post-critical Philosophy* (1958; reprint, London: Routledge & Kegan Paul, 1983).

52. H. Bauer, "Architektur als Kunst," in *Kunstgeschichte und Kunsttheorie in 19. Jahrhundert* (Berlin: W. de Gruyter, 1963), pp. 147ff.

53. M. Heidegger, "The Question Concerning Technology," in *The Question Concerning Technology and Other Essays,* trans. W. Lovitt (New York: Harper & Row, 1977), p. 35.

54. Funkenstein, *Theology and the Scientific Imagination,* pp. 290–346.

55. W. J. Mitchell, *City of Bits: Space, Place, and the Infobahn* (Cambridge., Mass.: MIT Press, 1995), p. 167.

56. Ibid., pp. 171–172.

57. S. Toulmin, *Cosmopolis: The Hidden Agenda of Modernity* (Chicago: University of Chicago Press, 1990); M. Heidegger, "The Age of the World Picture," in *The Question Concerning Technology,* pp. 115–155.

58. H. Dreyfus, *What Computers Still Can't Do: A Critique of Artificial Reason* (Cambridge, Mass.: MIT Press, 1992); S. Papert, "One Artificial Intelligence or Many?" in *The Artificial Intelligence Debate,* ed. S. R. Grambard (Cambridge., Mass.: MIT Press, 1988), pp. 1–15.

59. Dreyfus, *What Computers Still Can't Do,* p. xlvi.

60. Ibid., p. 300.

61. Ibid., p. 227.

62. Ibid., p. 280.

63. J. Ellul, *The Technological System,* trans. J. Neugroschel (New York: Continuum, 1980), p. 45.

CHAPTER 7 **THE REHABILITATION OF FRAGMENT**

1. A. Breton, *Surrealism and Painting,* trans. S. W. Taylor (New York: Harper & Row, 1972), p. 275.

2. Giorgio de Chirico, "On Metaphysical Art," in *Metaphysical Art,* ed. M. Carra, P. Waldberg, and E. Rathke, trans. C. Tisdall (New York: Praeger, 1971), p. 91.

3. Conversation with Daniel Libeskind, April 1975.

4. Breton, *Surrealism and Painting,* p. 277.

5. G. W. Leibniz, "Monadology," in *Philosophical Writings,* ed. G. H. R. Parkinson, trans. M. Morris and G. H. R. Parkinson (London: Dent, 1973), p. 179.

6. Diderot, quoted in P. Junod, "Future in the Past," *Oppositions,* no. 26 (spring 1984): 55.

7. W. Oechslin, "Architektur und Alphabet," in *Architektur und Sprache: Gedenkschrift für Richard Zürcher,* ed. C. Braegger (Munich: Prestel-Verlag, 1982), p. 216. "The elements of order are like an alphabet of architecture; and as it is possible to compose from twenty-four letters an unlimited amount of words and speeches, so one can by various composition of elements, which are like letters, create different ornaments in accordance with the five orders" (N. Goldmann, *Civil Baukunst* [Leipzig, 1708], preface).

8. The relationship between letters, words, and discourse is discussed in great depth by Plato as part of the discursive dialectics, in *Theaetetus* 202e, *Cratylus* 427a, and *Sophist* 253a.

9. Nietzsche refers, for the same reasons, to such an epoch as an epoch of decadence, and asks: "What is the sign of decadence? That life no longer dwells in the whole, . . . The whole no longer lives at all: it is composite, calculated, artificial and artifact" ("The Case of Wagner," in *Basic Writings of Nietzsche,* trans. and ed. W. Kaufmann [New York: Modern Library, 1968], p. 626).

10. "The area of obscurity which aphorisms clarify eventually loses some of its puzzling quality and enters our thinking as a stable and lucid insight. Sometimes it may even become a new topic" (J. P. Stern, *Lichtenberg: A Doctrine of Scattered Occasions* [1959;

reprint, London: Thames & Hudson, 1963], p. 217). In most cases, the illumination issues from a fusion of the imaginative reading with the logical or necessitating structure of the potential whole. Aphorism is the most paradoxical mode of discourse, and, like any paradox, it is a formulation of a partial or ostensible contradiction that originates from a particular experience and elicits an abundant range of further insights. The paradoxical nature of aphorism has its source in life situations, from which it also receives its meaning.

11. Some of the best examples can be found in the writings of Georg Christoph Lichtenberg, the first classical author of aphorisms; for example "Reason now rises above the region of dark but warm feelings as the Alpine peaks rise above the clouds. They see the sun more clearly and distinctly but they are cold and infertile. Reason boasts of its light" (quoted in ibid., p. 311).

12. R. Gasche, "Ideality in Fragmentation," in *Philosophical Fragments,* by F. Schlegel, trans. P. Firchow (Minneapolis: University of Minnesota Press, 1991), pp. vii–xxxii.

13. Schlegel, *Athenaeum,* in *Philosophical Fragments,* fr. 24.

14. Ibid., fr. 206.

15. Schlegel, *Critical Fragments,* in *Philosophical Fragments,* fr. 14. "Romantic poetry is progressive universal poetry. Its aim is not merely to reunite all the separate species of poetry and put poetry in touch with philosophy and rhetoric. It tries to and should mix and fuse poetry and prose, inspiration and criticism, the poetry of art and the poetry of nature, and make poetry lively and sociable, and life and society poetical" (Schlegel, *Athenaeum,* fr. 116).

16. "Every good human being is always progressively becoming God. To become God, to be human, to cultivate oneself are all expressions that mean the same thing" (Schlegel, *Athenaeum,* fr. 262).

17. J. P. Richter, *Horn of Oberon: Jean Paul Richter's "School for Aesthetics,"* trans. M. R. Hale (Detroit: Wayne State University Press, 1973), pp. 15–16.

18. "Certain favorite themes might also explain the intense interest of Romantic writers in the prison image: tragic beauty of solitude, glorification of the individual and concern for the problem of identity" (V. Brombert, *The Romantic Prison: The French Tradition* [Princeton: Princeton University Press, 1978], p. 9).

19. J. J. Rousseau, *Reveries of the Solitary Walker,* trans. P. France (Harmondsworth: Penguin, 1979), pp. 82, 89.

20. "Genius," a term identified with human abilities, has its origin in *ingenium,* seen originally as a power of nature. In the Latin tradition, *ingenium* is a "'primal non-reducible

and dominant power'; as such *ingenium* lifts man above the habitual forms of thinking and feeling. It unites man with the Divine and therefore enables him to recognize the laws of the universe which are an expression of the godhead" (E. Grassi, *Renaissance Humanism: Studies in Philosophy and Poetics* [Binghamton, N.Y.: Medieval and Renaissance Texts and Studies, 1988], p. 68. See also G. Vico, *On the Most Ancient Wisdom of the Italians,* trans. L. M. Palmer (Ithaca: Cornell University Press, 1988), p. 96.

21. Inventive interpretation brought together the metamorphosis of rocaille with the primary elements—earth, water, air, and fire—in a form of a new cosmogony, closely linked with the tradition of *ingenium* and the new notion of creative genius. See H. Bauer, *Rocaille: Zur Herkunft und wesen einen Ornament-Motivs* (Berlin: W. de Gruyter, 1962), pp. 32–40; N. Miller, *Archäologie des Traums: Versuch über Giovanni Battista Piranesi* (Munich: Hanser, 1994), pp. 58–76.

22. G. E. Lessing, *Laocoön: An Essay on the Limits of Painting and Poetry,* trans. E. A. McCormick (1962; reprint, Baltimore: Johns Hopkins University Press, 1984), pp. 78–85.

23. A. K. Wiedmann, *Romantic Roots in Modern Art: Romanticism and Expressionism: A Study in Comparative Aesthetics* (Old Working [Eng.]: Gresham Books, 1979), p. 155.

24. See J. A. Schmoll-Eisenwarth, *Das Unvollendete als künstlerische Form* (Bern: Francke, 1959); T. McFarland, *Romanticism and the Forms of Ruin: Wordsworth, Coleridge, and Modalities of Fragmentation* (Princeton: Princeton University Press, 1981).

25. "Romantic poetry is a progressive, universal poetry. Its aim isn't merely to reunite all the separate species of poetry and put poetry in touch with philosophy and rhetoric. It tries to and should mix and fuse poetry and prose, inspiration and criticism, the poetry of art and the poetry of nature; and make poetry lively and sociable, and life and society poetical" (Schlegel, *Athenaeum,* fr. 116).

26. P. Klee, *The Thinking Eye: The Notebooks of Paul Klee,* ed. J. Spiller, [trans. R. Manheim] (New York: G. Wittenborn, 1961), p. 460.

27. See *Goethe on Art,* ed. and trans. J. Gage (London: Scholar Press, 1980), p. 196; H. Bauer, "Architektur als Kunst," in *Kunstgeschichte und Kunsttheorie im 19 Jahrhundert* (Berlin: W. de Gruyter, 1963), pp. 133–172; F. W. J. Schelling, *The Philosophy of Art,* trans. D. W. Stott (Minneapolis: University of Minnesota Press, 1989), pp. 166–170.

28. *Goethe on Art,* p. 197.

29. F. Schlegel, "Aus den Heften zur Poesie und Literatur," in *Kritische Schriften und Fragmente* (Paderborn: F. Schöningh, 1988), fr. 940.

30. It is interesting that even dialogue was interpreted by the Romantics in the light of fragment and system. In Schlegel's words, "A dialog is a chain or garland of fragments.

An exchange of letters is a dialog on a large scale, and memoirs constitute a system of fragments." The vision of wholeness as system was clearly dominant: "Aren't all systems individuals just as all individuals are systems, at least in embryo and tendency? Isn't every real entity historical? Aren't there individuals who contain within themselves whole systems of individuals?" (Schlegel, *Athenaeum,* frs. 77, 242).

31. Schlegel, "Aus den Heften zur Poesie und Literatur," fr. 930.

32. Gasche, "Ideality in Fragmentation," p. IV.

33. F. Schlegel, "Ideas," in *Philosophical Fragments,* frs. 10, 13.

34. See I. Kant, *Critique of Judgment,* trans. J. H. Bernard (New York: Hafner Press, 1951), pp. 82–102; F. Schiller, *Naive and Sentimental Poetry, and On the Sublime,* trans. J. A. Elias (New York: F. Unger, 1966); Schelling, *The Philosophy of Art,* pp. 85–96; Richter, *Horn of Oberon,* pp. 73–76.

35. For the Romantic generation, chaos became an equivalent of cosmos (Wiedmann, *The Romantic Roots of Modern Art,* pp. 197–240).

36. Schelling, *The Philosophy of Art,* p. 88.

37. Ibid., p. 86.

38. Richter, *Horn of Oberon,* p. 73.

39. G. Scobel, "Chaos, Selbstorganisation und das Erhabene," in *Das Erhabene,* ed. C. Pries (Weinheim: VCH, 1989), pp. 277–295.

40. See F. E. D. Schleiermacher, "General Hermeneutics," in *The Hermeneutics Reader: Texts of the German Tradition from the Enlightenment to the Present,* ed. K. Mueller-Vollmer (Oxford: Basil Blackwell, 1985), pp. 73–86; H. G. Gadamer, *Truth and Method,* [trans. W. Glen-Doepel, trans. ed. G. Barden and J. Cumming], 2nd ed. (London: Sheed & Ward, 1975), pp. 162–173, 325–345.

41. M. Merleau-Ponty, "Cézanne's Doubt," in *Sense and Non-Sense,* trans. H. L. Dreyfus and P. A. Dreyfus (Evanston, Ill.: Northwestern University Press, 1964), p. 15.

42. Cézanne, quoted in E. Bernard, "Souvenirs sur Paul Cézanne et lettres inédites," in *Conversations avec Cézanne,* ed. P. M. Doran (Paris: Collection Macula, 1978), p. 158.

43. Bracque, quoted in B. Zürcher, *Georges Braque, Life and Work,* trans. S. Nye (New York: Rizzoli 1988), p. 154.

44. Ibid., p. 155.

45. The term "latent world" is understood and used here to mean a totality of references in which we are always involved and which are most conspicuously articulated in language. This understanding follows the tradition formed by the work of Husserl and Heidegger, which has been enriched more recently by the notion of "effective history" (*Wirkungsgeschichte*) of modern hermeneutics.

46. Braque, quoted in Zürcher, *Georges Braque,* p. 154.

47. Ibid., p. 155.

48. Stern, *Lichtenberg,* p. 275.

49. The question of the universality of civilization and its relation to the life of particular cultures has been discussed by Paul Ricoeur in "Universal Civilization and National Cultures," in *History and Truth,* trans. C. A. Kelbley (Evanston, Ill.: Northwestern University Press, 1965), pp. 271–287.

50. For a recent discussion of the role of metaphor in modern culture, see J. Weinsheimer, "Gadamer's Metaphorical Hermeneutics," in *Gadamer and Hermeneutics,* ed. H. J. Silverman (London: Routledge, 1991), pp. 181–202. The classical work on metaphor is still P. Ricoeur, *The Rule of Metaphor: Multi-disciplinary Studies of the Creation of Meaning in Language,* trans. R. Czerny, with K. McLaughlin and J. Costello (London: Routledge & Kegan Paul, 1978).

51. A. Breton, *La clé des champs* (1953; reprint, Paris: Pauvert, 1979), p. 137.

52. M. Ernst, *Beyond Painting* (New York: Wittenborn, Schultz, 1948), p. 13.

53. P. Reverdy, "L'image," *Nord-Sud* (13 March, 1918); reprinted in Reverdy, *Oeuvres complètes* (Paris: Flammarion, 1975), p. 73.

54. Breton, quoted in Ernst, *Beyond Painting,* p. 13.

55. Breton, *Surrealism and Painting,* p. 205.

56. A. Breton, *Mad Love,* trans. M. A. Caws (Lincoln: University of Nebraska Press, 1986), p. 11.

57. A. Breton, *The Manifestoes of Surrealism,* trans. R. Seaver and H. R. Lane (Ann Arbor: University of Michigan Press, 1974), p. 303.

58. "All the will of the artist is powerless to reduce the opposition that nature's unknown ends set against his own aims. The feeling of being set in motion, not to say being played with, by forces which exceed ours will not, in poetry and in art, cease to become more acute or overwhelming: 'It is false to say: I think. One ought to say: I am thought.' Since then ample room has been given to the question: 'what can we create—is it ours?'" (A. Breton and G. Legrand, *L'art magique* [Paris: Club Français du Livre, 1957], p. 93).

59. See C. Rowe and R. Slutzky, *Transparenz,* trans. B. Hoesli (Basel: Birkhäuser, 1968).

60. The carpet of grass on the floor of the solarium and the low walls, which are too high to be a parapet but too low to be a proper wall, are metaphors of inside and outside, respectively; the fireplace in its relation to the partly visible Arc de Triomphe is a metaphor of monumentalized domesticity; the relationship of the fireplace to the meaning of the solarium is the metaphor of the sun and light; etc.

61. The area of Spitalfields is now available for development because the vegetable and fruit market originally on the site was transferred to the outskirts of London in 1991. Civic and commercial interests have been battling for decades over the nature of the new development.

The alternative project for the development of the Spitalfields market area is a synthesis of individual contributions made by Daphne Becket-Chary, Dominic Cox, David Dernie, Christian Frost, Clare Gerrard, John Hinton, Elspeth Latimer, Charles McKeith, Alberto Micelli, Richard Partington, Adam Robarts, John Ross, Deane Smith, and Ian Taylor.

62. The role of imagination in this kind of transformation was studied and discussed in great detail by Gaston Bachelard under the heading of "material imagination" in his "L'imagination materielle et l'imagination parlée," in *La terre et les revêries de la volonté* (Paris: J. Corti, 1948), pp. 1–17.

CHAPTER 8 **TOWARD A POETICS OF ARCHITECTURE**

1. See P. Eisenman, "Aspects of Modernism: The Maison Domino and the Self-Referential Sign," *Oppositions,* nos. 15–16 (winter–spring 1979): 118–128; *An Architecture of Absence* (London: Architectural Association, 1986); and "Moving Arrows, Eros, and Other Errors," *Precis* 6 (spring 1987): 138–143.

2. This contradiction is closely related to that between the asceticism of production and the abundance of consumption, as discussed by Werner Sombart, Max Weber, Thorstein Veblen, and, most recently, Jean Baudrillard.

3. H. G. Gadamer, *The Relevance of the Beautiful and Other Essays,* trans. N. Walker, ed. R. Bernasconi (Cambridge: Cambridge University Press, 1986), pp. 38, 34, 35.

4. G. Boffrand, *Livre d'architecture* (Paris, 1745); trans. D. Britt as *Book of Architecture,* ed. C. von Eck (Aldershot: Ashgate, 2002), p. 10.

5. Character was known to the Greeks particularly in its relation to ethos. It played an important role in Aristotle's *Rhetoric* and *Poetics,* was developed more explicitly in Theophrastus's *Characters,* and in that form had a great influence on the development of the rhetorics of Cicero and Quintilian and the poetics of Horace. Character became a very important critical term again at the end of the seventeenth century. In 1688, Jean de La Bruyère published his *Les caractères de Théophraste, traduits du grec, avec Les caractères, ou, Les moeurs de ce siècle,* followed by an important second edition of Charles Le Brun's *Conférence sur l'expression générale et particulière,* published in 1698 (originally a lecture delivered in 1669).

6. Boffrand, *Book of Architecture,* p. 8.

7. J. F. Blondel, *Cours d'architecture,* 6 vols. (Paris, 1771–1777), 1:22.

8. Ibid., pp. 337–338.

9. Ibid., 2:xii.

10. Ibid., 4:liv.

11. See H. Bauer, *Kunsthistorik* (Munich: Beck, 1976); L. Venturi, *History of Art Criticism,* trans. C. Marriott, new rev. ed. (New York: E. P. Dutton, 1964); J. Bialostocki, *Stil und Ikonographie: Studien zur Kunstwissenschaft* (Cologne: DuMont, 1981); G. Germann, *Gothic Revival in Europe and Britain: Sources, Influences, and Ideas,* trans. G. Onn (London: Lund Humphries, 1972); W. Hager and N. Knopp, eds., *Beiträge zum Problem des Stilpluralismus* (Munich: Prestel, 1977); K. Döhmer, *In welchem Style sollen wir bauen? Architekturtheorie zwischen Klassizismus und Jugendstil* (Munich: Prestel, 1976); C. van Eck, J. McAllister, and R. van de Vall, eds., *The Question of Style in Philosophy and the Arts* (Cambridge: Cambridge University Press, 1995).

12. K. Schwitters, *Das literarische Werk,* ed. F. Lach, 5 vols. (Cologne: DuMont, 1973–1981), 5:168.

13. E. Jünger, *Strahlungen* (Tübingen: Heliopolis-Verlag, 1949), p. 16.

14. Schwitters, *Das literarische Werk,* 5:187.

15. H. R. Hitchcock and P. Johnson, *The International Style* (1932; reprint, New York: W. W. Norton, 1966), pp. 19, 251.

16. J. F. Blondel, *L'architecture française,* 4 vols. (Paris, 1752–1756), 1:22.

17. For modern discussions of *convenance* and *bienséance,* see P. E. Knabe, *Schlüsselbegriffe des kunsttheoretischen Denkens in Frankreich von der Spätklassik bis zum Ende der Aufklärung* (Düsseldorf: L. Schwann, 1972); A. Röver, *Bienséance: Zur ästhetische Situation im Ancien Régime, dargestellt an Beispielen der Pariser Privatarchitektur* (Hildesheim: G. Olms, 1977); and W. Szambien, *Symétrie, goût, caractère: Théorie et terminologie de l'architecture à l'âge classique* (Paris: Picard, 1986).

18. The French rendering of Vitruvian *decor* as *bienséance* can already be found in Jean Martin's translation of Vitruvius (1547) and in Claude Perrault's (1674).

19. Of particular importance was the tradition of "ut pictura poesis"; see R. W. Lee, *Ut Pictura Poesis: The Humanistic Theory of Painting* (New York: W. W. Norton, 1967), and Knabe, *Schlüsselbegriffe des kunsttheoretischen Denkens in Frankreich,* pp. 463–471.

20. Vitruvius, *De architectura,* I.2.5; trans. F. Granger as *On Architecture,* 2 vols., Loeb Classical Library (Cambridge, Mass.: Harvard University Press; London: W. Heinemann, 1931–1934), 1:27. For example, decor is based on convention "when open air temples are built to the sky god Jupiter and austere Doric temples are built to martial gods and goddesses, like Mars, Minerva and Hercules"; or is based on custom "when harmonious and elegant vestibules are made to fit magnificent interiors in buildings. For if interiors have elegant appearance, but have approaches which are lowly and ugly, they will not be executed with appropriateness (decor)." And finally, decor is based on natural circumstances "when the most salubrious sites for temples are chosen and there are suitable springs in the places," or when "the light for bedrooms and libraries is derived from the east" (ibid., I.2.5–7; trans. Granger, 1:31).

21. In VI.2.5, Vitruvius speaks about the adjustment of symmetry to the requirements of decor: "When the magnitude of this is once determined, there will follow upon it the adjustment of the proportions to the decor so that the appearance of eurythmy may be convincing to the observer" (trans. Granger, 2:23).

22. Decorum and *decet* are terms used in philosophy and in rhetoric as equivalents of the Vitruvian decor. "Decorum more often implies propriety in an ethical sense, decor in an aesthetic sense" (J. J. Pollitt, *The Ancient View of Greek Art: Criticism, History, and Terminology* [New Haven: Yale University Press, 1974], p. 343).

23. "What in Latin may be called decorum (propriety) in Greek is called 'prepon'" (Cicero, *De officiis,* I.93, trans. W. Miller, Loeb Classical Library (1913; reprint, Cambridge, Mass.: Harvard University Press, 1975), p. 97.

24. Ibid., I.94; trans. Miller, p. 97.

25. M. Pohlenz, "To Prepon: Ein Beitrag zur Geschichte des griechischen Geistes," in *Nachrichten von der Gesellschaft der Wissenschaften zu Göttingen* 1 (1933): 92.

26. Plato, *Greater Hippias* 293e.

27. Plato, *Symposium* 204b–6; trans. M. Joyce, in *The Collected Dialogues of Plato,* ed. E. Hamilton and H. Cairns, Bollingen Series, 71 (Princeton: Princeton University Press, 1978), p. 557.

28. Plato's interest was quite clearly in the sphere of truth rather than in the sphere of art. The partiality of his attitude becomes apparent once we have realized that aside from the polemical and rather dogmatic use of "mimesis" (mimesis of appearances), he uses the concept in a great variety of cases, with the deepest understanding of their peculiarities. Examples illustrating this point can be taken from the domain of silent gestures (*Cratylus* 423a), as well as from the domain of dialectical reasoning (*Republic* 532a).

29. For the discussion of the question of "ut pictura poesis," see note 19.

30. Aristotle, *Poetics* 1447a8; trans. W. H. Fyfe, in *The Poetics; On the Sublime; On Style,* Loeb Classical Library (1927; reprint, Cambridge, Mass.: Harvard University Press; London: W. Heinemann, 1965), p. 5. See also E. Grassi, *Die Theorie des Schönen in der Antike* (Cologne: DuMont, 1962), p. 118.

31. Aristotle, *Poetics* 1450b3–4; trans. Fyfe, p. 27.

32. Praxis includes people "as acting" and all things "as in act." See Grassi, *Die Theorie des Schönen in der Antike,* p. 127; P. Ricoeur, *The Rule of Metaphor: Multi-disciplinary Studies of the Creation of Meaning in Language,* trans. R. Czerny, with K. McLaughlin and J. Costello (London: Routledge & Kegan Paul, 1978), pp. 42–43; Aristotle, *Rhetoric* 1411b24.

33. Aristotle, *Poetics* 1451b10; trans. Fyfe, p. 37.

34. Ibid., 1450b21; trans. Fyfe, p. 27. The subordination of character to a situation structured by poetic mythos is an important contrast with the eighteenth century's dominant position of character.

35. On the relation of the chorus to the celebration of the rebirth of Dionysus (cosmic life), see W. F. Otto, *Dionysus, Myth and Cult,* trans. R. B. Palmer (Bloomington: Indiana University Press, 1965), p. 143. On the relation of *chōra* to its origin in chaos, see Aristotle, *Physics* 208b31; Plato, *Timaeus* 62b. Dionysus is also the god of chaos. The relation between chorus as dance and as a place has been discussed most recently in J. Miller, *Measures of Wisdom: The Cosmic Dance in Classical and Christian Antiquity* (Toronto: University of Toronto Press, 1986), pp. 19–31.

36. Plato, *Republic* 607b; trans. P. Shorey, Loeb Classical Library (1930–1935; reprint, Cambridge, Mass.: Harvard University Press; London: W. Heinemann, 1980), 2:465.

37. Plato, *Laws* 817b; trans. A. E. Taylor, in Hamilton and Cairns, eds., *The Collected Dialogues of Plato,* p. 1387.

38. A. G. Baumgarten, *Meditationes philosophicae de nonnullis ad poema pertinentibus* (Halle, 1735) paras. 9, 114.

39. Gadamer, *The Relevance of the Beautiful,* p. 103.

40. W. Heisenberg, *Across the Frontiers,* trans. P. Heath (New York: Harper & Row, 1974), pp. 120–121.

41. I am referring to the classical understanding of praxis as it was preserved mainly in the Aristotelian tradition and brought to light again in modern hermeneutics. See H. G. Gadamer, "The Hermeneutic Relevance of Aristotle," in *Truth and Method,* [trans. W. Glen-Doepel, trans. ed. G. Barden and J. Cumming], 2nd ed. (London: Ward & Sheed, 1975), pp. 278–289, and "What Is Practice," in *Reason in the Age of Science,* trans. F. G. Lawrence (Cambridge, Mass.: MIT Press, 1981), pp. 69–88.

42. Gadamer, "What Is Practice," p. 82.

43. Ibid., p. 83.

44. See H. Frankfort, "The Archetype in Analytical Psychology and the History of Religion," *Journal of the Warburg and Courtauld Institutes* 21 (1958): 166–178; M. Eliade, *Patterns in Comparative Religion,* trans. R. Sheed (London: Sheed & Ward, 1958); M. Eliade, *The Myth of the Eternal Return,* trans. W. R. Trask (Princeton: Princeton University Press, 1954); G. R. Levy, *The Gate of Horn: A Study of the Religious Conceptions of the Stone Age, and Their Influence upon European Thought* (London: Faber & Faber, 1948); P. Wheatley, *The Pivot of the Four Quarters: A Preliminary Inquiry into the Origins and Character of the Ancient Chinese City* (Edinburgh: Edinburgh University Press, 1971).

45. See R. Wittkower, *Architectural Principles in the Age of Humanism,* [3rd rev. ed.] (London: A. Tiranti, 1962); J. Rykwert, *On Adam's House in Paradise: The Idea of the Primitive Hut in Architectural History* (New York: Museum of Modern Art, 1972); A. Pérez-Gómez, *Architecture and the Crisis of Modern Science* (Cambridge, Mass.: MIT Press, 1983); P. von Naredi-Rainer, *Architektur und Harmonie: Zahl, Mass und Proportion in der abendländischen Baukunst* (Cologne: DuMont, 1982); D. Vesely, "The Architectonics of Embodiment," in *Body and Building: Essays on the Changing Relation of Body and Architecture,* ed. G. Dodds and R. Tavernor (Cambridge, Mass.: MIT Press, 2002), pp. 28–44.

46. Gauss, quoted in Morris Kline, *Mathematics: The Loss of Certainty* (Oxford: Oxford University Press, 1980), p. 87.

47. Gadamer, *Truth and Method,* p. 269.

48. "We experience wholeness as an alertness that pervades and casts an horizon vis-à-vis all present things. . . . It is like light that illumines all lighted things as far as one can see. It is like darkness that cannot be grasped or seen through:dark into dark. It is like a tone reaching the limits of audibility and seeming not even to stop there. It is like a silence that is heard with sounds" (C. E. Scott, "Psychotherapy: Being One and Being

Many," in *Heidegger and Psychology,* ed. K. Hoeller ([Seattle]: Review of Existential Psychology and Psychiatry, 1988), p. 90.

49. Gadamer, *Truth and Method,* p. 269.

50. See chapter 2 for a more detailed discussion of the nature of communicative space.

51. H. G. Gadamer, "The Principle of Effective History," in *Truth and Method,* pp. 267–274.

52. E. Straus, "The Upright Posture," in *Phenomenological Psychology: The Selected Papers of Erwin W. Straus,* trans. E. Eng (London: Tavistock, 1966), pp. 142, 147.

53. The building was designed by Eric Parry Architects. For more detailed documentation and commentary, see W. Wang, *Eric Parry Architects,* pref. D. Vesely (London: Black Dog, 2002).

- WORKS CITED -

Abrams, M. H. *The Mirror and the Lamp: Romantic Theory and the Critical Tradition.* Oxford: Oxford University Press, 1953.

Ackerman, J. "'Ars sine Scientia nihil est': Gothic Theory of Architecture at the Cathedral of Milan." *Art Bulletin* 31 (1949): 84–111.

Ackerman, J. *The Cortile del Belvedere.* Vatican City: Biblioteca Apostolica Vaticana, 1954.

Ackerman, J. *Distance Points: Essays in Theory and Renaissance Art and Architecture.* Cambridge, Mass.: MIT Press, 1991.

Ackerman, J. *The Villa.* London: Thames & Hudson, 1990.

Alberti, L. B. *Ludi mathematici.* Vol. 3 of *Opere volgari.* Edited by C. Grayson. Bari: G. Laterza, 1973.

Alberti, L. B. *On Painting.* Translated by C. Grayson. London: Penguin, 1991.

Alberti, L. B. *On the Art of Building in Ten Books.* Translated by J. Rykwert, N. Leach, and R. Tavernor. Cambridge, Mass.: MIT Press, 1988.

Alberti, L. B. *Vita anonima.* In *Opera Volgari de Leon Battista Alberti,* vol. 1. Edited by A. Bonucci. Florence: Tipografia Galileiana, 1843.

Allers, R. "Microcosmus from Anaximander to Paracelsus." *Traditio: Studies in Medieval and Ancient History, Thought, and Religion* 2 (1944): 319–407.

Alquié, F. *Malebranche et le rationalisme chrétien.* Paris: Seghers Philosophie, 1977.

André, J. M. *L'otium dans la vie morale et intellectuelle romaine, des origines à l'époque augustéene.* Paris: Presses Universitaires de France, 1966.

Aragon, L. *Treatise on Style.* Translated by A. Waters. Lincoln: University of Nebraska Press, 1991.

Aristotle. *Metaphysics.* Translated by H. Tredennick. 2 vols. Loeb Classical Library. 1933–1934. Reprint, Cambridge, Mass.: Harvard University Press; London: W. Heinemann, 1961–1962.

Aristotle. *Nicomachean Ethics.* Translated by H. Rackham. Loeb Classical Library. 1926. Reprint, Cambridge, Mass.: Harvard University Press; London: W. Heinemann, 1968.

Aristotle. *Physics.* Translated by P. H. Wicksteed and F. M. Cornford. 2 vols. Loeb Classical Library. 1929–1934. Reprint, Cambridge, Mass.: Harvard University Press; London: W. Heinemann, 1957–1960.

Aristotle. *Poetics.* Translated by W. H. Fyfe. In *The Poetics; On the Sublime; On Style.* Loeb Classical Library. 1927. Reprint, Cambridge, Mass.: Harvard University Press; London: W. Heinemann, 1965.

Arriaga, R. de. *Cursus philosophicus.* Antwerp, 1632.

Ascani, V. "Le dessin d'architecture médiéval en Italie." In *Les bâtisseurs des cathédrales gothiques,* compiled by R. Recht. [Strasbourg:] Éditions les Musées de la ville de Strasbourg, 1989.

Ashton, M. "Allegory, Fact, and Meaning in Giambattista Tiepolo's Four Continents at Wurzburg." *Art Bulletin,* March 1978, pp. 109–125.

Bachelard, G. *Air et songes.* Paris: Corti, 1962.

Bachelard, G. *On Poetic Imagination and Reverie.* Translated by C. Gaudin. Indianapolis: Bobbs-Merrill, 1971.

Bachelard, G. *La terre et les revêries de la volonté.* Paris: J. Corti, 1948.

Bacon, F. *New Atlantis; and, The Great Instauration.* Edited by J. Weinberger. Rev. ed. Arlington Heights, Ill.: Harlan Davidson, 1989.

Bacon, R. *Opus maius.* Translated by R. G. Burke. Philadelphia: University of Pennsylvania Press, 1928.

Bacon, R. *Roger Bacon's Philosophy of Nature: A Critical Edition.* Edited and translated by D. C. Lindberg. Oxford: Clarendon Press, 1983.

Balliani, C. *Regionamenti di Santa Sindone.* Turin, 1610.

Baltrusaitis, J. *Anamorphic Art.* Translated by W. J. Strachan. New York: Abrams, 1977.

Bandmann, G. "Ikonologie der Architektur." In *Politische Architektur in Europa (vom Mittelalter bis heute),* edited by M. Warnke. Cologne: DuMont, 1984.

Bandmann, G. *Mittelalterliche Architektur als Bedeutungsträger.* 5th ed. Berlin: Mann, 1978.

Bann, S., ed. *The Tradition of Constructivism.* Documents of Twentieth-Century Art. London: Thames & Hudson, 1974.

Barocchi, P. *Scritti d'arte del Cinquecento.* 9 vols. 1971. Reprint, Turin: G. Einaudi, 1977.

Barth, Hans. "Das Zeitalter des Barocks und die Philosophie von Leibniz." In *Die Kunstformen des Barockzeitalters.* Bern: Francke, 1956.

Barthes, R. "The Tour Eiffel." In *Structures Implicit and Explicit,* vol. 2. Edited by J. Bryan and R. Sauer. Philadelphia: VIA Publications of the Graduate School of Fine Arts, University of Pennsylvania, 1973.

Battisti, E. *L'antirinascimento.* Milan: Feltrinelli, 1962.

Bauer, H. *Barock: Kunst einer Epoche.* Berlin: D. Reimer, 1992.

Bauer, H. *Der Himmel im Rokoko: Das Fresko im deutschen Kirchenraum des 18. Jahrhunderts.* Regensburg: Pustet, 1965.

Bauer, H. *Kunstgeschichte und Kunsttheorie im 19. Jahrhundert.* Berlin: W. De Gruyter, 1963.

Bauer, H. *Kunsthistorik.* Munich: Beck, 1976.

Bauer, H. *Kunst und Utopie: Studien über das Kunst- und Staadtsdenken in der Renaissance.* Berlin: de Gruyter, 1965.

Bauer, H. *Rocaille: Zur Herkunft und zum Wesen eines Ornament-Motivs.* Berlin: W. de Gruyter, 1962.

Baumgarten, A. G. *Meditationes philosophicae de nonnullis ad poema pertinentibus.* Halle, 1735.

Baur, L. *Das philosophische Lebenswerk des Robert Grosseteste Bishofs von Lincoln.* Cologne: J. P. Bachem, 1910.

Baur, L. *Die philosophischen Werke des Robert Grosseteste Bishofs von Lincoln.* Beiträge zur Geschichte der Philosophie des Mittelalters, vol. 9. Münster: Aschendorff, 1912.

Baxandall, M. *Painting and Experience in Fifteenth Century Italy: A Primer in the Social History of Pictorial Style.* 2nd ed. Oxford: Oxford University Press, 1988.

Behler, E., and J. Hörisch, eds. *Die Aktualität der Frühromantik.* Paderborn: Schöningh, 1987.

Bellandi, S. *Luigi Marsili, degli Agostiniani: Apostolo ed anima del rinascimento letterario in Firenze, An. 1342–1394.* Florence: Tip Arcivescovile, 1911.

Belting, H. *Die Oberkirche von San Francesco in Assisi.* Berlin: Mann, 1977.

Beltrani, L. "Bramante a Milano." *Rasegna d'Arte* 1 (1901): 33–37.

Beltrani, R. "Gli esperimenti prospettichi del Brunelleschi." In *Rendiconti delle Sedute dell'Accademia Nazionale dei Lincei, classe di Scienze morali, storiche e filologiche.* Ser. 28. Rome: Accademia Nazionale dei Lincei, 1974.

Bentmann, R., and M. Müller. *The Villa as Hegemonic Architecture.* Translated by T. Spence and D. Cranem. London: Humanities Press, 1992.

Benton, T., and C. Benton, with D. Sharp, eds. *Form and Function: A Source Book for the History of Architecture and Design, 1890–1939.* London: Crosby Lockwood Staples, 1975.

Bernard, E. "Souvenirs sur Paul Cézanne et lettres inédites." In *Conversations avec Cézanne,* ed. P. M. Doran. Paris: Collection Macula, 1978.

Bernheimer, R. "Theatrum Mundi." *Art Bulletin* 38, no. 4 (December 1956): 225–247.

Bérulle, P. de. *Oeuvres.* Paris, 1665.

Bialostocki, J. *Stil und Ikonographie.* Cologne: DuMont, 1981.

Biemel, W. *Le concept de monde chez Heidegger.* Paris: J. Vrin, 1950.

Boffrand, G. *Book of Architecture.* Edited by C. von Eck. Translated by D. Britt. Aldershot: Ashgate, 2002.

Boyer, M. F. *The French Café.* London: Thames & Hudson, 1994.

Braegger, C., ed. *Architektur und Sprache: Gedenkenschrift für Richard Zürcher.* Munich: Prestel, 1982.

Breidert, W. *Das aristotelische Kontinuum in der Scholastik.* Münster: Aschendorff, 1970.

Breton, A. *La clé des champs.* 1953. Reprint, Paris: Pauvert, 1979.

Breton, A. *The Manifestoes of Surrealism.* Translated by R. Seaver and H. R. Lane. Ann Arbor: University of Michigan Press, 1974.

Breton, A. *Surrealism and Painting.* Translated by S. W. Taylor. New York: Harper & Row, 1972.

Breton, A., and G. Legrand. *L'art magique.* Paris: Club Français du Livre, 1957.

Briseux, C. E. *Traité du beau essentiel.* Paris, 1752.

Brombert, V. *The Romantic Prison: The French Tradition.* Princeton: Princeton University Press, 1978.

Brummer, H. *The Statue Court in the Vatican Belvedere.* Stockholm: Almquist & Wiksell, 1970.

Bruschi, A. *Bramante.* London: Thames & Hudson, 1977.

Bruschi, A. *Bramante architetto.* Bari: Laterza, 1969.

Burkert, W. *Greek Religion.* Translated by J. Raffan. Oxford: Blackwell, 1985.

Burton, H. E., trans. "The Optics of Euclid." *Journal of the Optical Society of America* 35 (1945): 357–372.

Bury, J. B. *The Idea of Progress: An Inquiry into Its Origin and Growth.* 1930. Reprint, New York: Dover, 1955.

Butts, R. E., and J. C. Pitt, eds. *New Perspectives on Galileo.* Dordrecht: D. Reidel, 1978.

Camillo, Giulio. *L'idea del teatro.* Florence, 1555.

Campbell, J. *The German Werkbund: The Politics of Reform in the Applied Arts.* Princeton: Princeton University Press, 1992.

Carboneri, N. "Vicende delle capelle per la Santa Sindone." *Bollettino della Società Piemontese di Archeologia e Belle Arti* 32 (1964): 95–109.

Carrouges, M. *André Breton and the Concepts of Surrealism.* Translated by M. Prendergast. Tuscaloosa: University of Alabama Press, 1974.

Carruthers, M. J. *The Book of Memory: A Study of Memory in Medieval Culture.* Cambridge: Cambridge University Press, 1990.

Cassirer, E. *The Individual and the Cosmos in Renaissance Philosophy.* Translated by M. Dolmandi. 1963. Reprint, Philadelphia: University of Pennsylvania Press, 1972.

Cassirer, E. *Philosophie der symbolischen Formen.* 3 vols. 2nd ed. Darmstadt: Wissenschaftliche Buchgesellschaft, 1953.

Castelli, P. "Ghiberti e gli umanisti." In *Lorenzo Ghiberti, materia e ragionamenti.* Exhib. cat. Florence: Centro Di, 1978.

Charbonnier, G. *Le monologue du peintre, entretiens avec Braque* [etc.]. Paris: R. Julliard, 1959.

Chastel, A. "Cortile et théâtre." In *Le lieu théâtral à la renaissance.* 2nd ed. Paris: Éditions du CNRS, 1968.

Chastel, A. *La grottesque.* Paris: Le Promeneur, 1988.

Cheles, L. *The Studiolo of Urbino: An Iconographic Investigation.* University Park: Pennsylvania State University Press, 1986.

Cicero. *De officiis.* Translated by W. Miller. Loeb Classical Library. 1913. Reprint, Cambridge, Mass.: Harvard University Press, 1975.

Claretta, G. "Inclinazioni artistiche di Carlo Emanuele I di Savoia e dei suoi figli." *Atti della Società Piemontese di Archeologia e Belle Arti* 5, no. 6 (1894): 351–358.

Clark, K. "Leon Battista Alberti." *Proceedings of the British Academy* 30 (1944): 283–303.

Clarke, S. *The Leibniz-Clarke Correspondence.* Edited by H. G. Alexander. Manchester: Manchester University Press, 1956.

Clemenceau, G. *Claude Monet: Les nymphéas.* Paris: Plon, 1928.

Colomina, B. "Mies Not." In *The Presence of Mies,* edited by D. Mertins. New York: Princeton Architectural Press, 1994.

Condillac, E. B. de. *Traité des sensations.* Paris, 1754.

Conger, G. P. *Theories of Macrocosms and Microcosms in the History of Philosophy.* New York: Columbia University Press, 1922.

"Congress of International Progressive Artists." in *The Tradition of Constructivism,* edited by S. Bann. Documents of Twentieth-Century Art. London: Thames & Hudson, 1974.

Coop Himmelblau. *Blaubox.* London: Architectural Association, 1988.

Cooper, H. S. F., Jr. *A House in Space.* New York: Holt, Rinehart, & Winston, 1977.

Copenhauer, B. T. *Reappraisals of the Scientific Revolution.* Edited by D. C. Lindberg and R. S. Westman. Cambridge: Cambridge University Press, 1990.

Cornford, F. M., trans. *Plato and Parmenides.* 1939. Reprint, London: Routledge & Kegan Paul, 1980.

Crapulli, G. *Mathesis universalis: Genesi di un' idea nel XVI secolo.* Rome: Edizioni dell'Ateneo, 1969.

Crombie, A. C. "Science and the Arts in the Renaissance: The Search for Truth and Certainty, Old and New." In *Science and Arts in the Renaissance,* edited by J. W. Shirley and F. W. Hoeniger. London: Associated University Presses; Washington, D.C.: Folger Shakespeare Library, 1985.

Crooke, H. *Microkosmographia: A Description of the Body of Man.* London, 1615.

Curtius, E. R. *European Literature and the Latin Middle Ages.* New York: Harper & Row, 1953.

Dales, R. C. "Robert Grosseteste's Views on Astrology." *Medieval Studies* 29 (1967): 357–363.

d'Alverny, M. T. "Le cosmos symbolique du XIIème siècle." In *AHDLMA [Archives d'histoire doctrinale et littéraire du Moyen Age]* 20 (1953): 31–81.

Daly, P. M., ed. *The European Emblem: Towards an Index Emblematicus.* Waterloo, Canada: Wilfred Laurier University Press, 1980.

Daly-Davis, M. *Piero della Francesca's Mathematical Treatises.* Ravenna: Longo, 1977.

Damish, H. *The Origin of Perspective.* Cambridge, Mass.: MIT Press, 1994.

Danielou, J., S.J. *The Bible and the Liturgy.* Ann Arbor, Mich.: UMI, 1956.

David, C. "The Science of Optics." In *Science in the Middle Ages,* edited by D. C. Lindberg. Chicago: University of Chicago Press, 1978.

Davy, M. M. *Initiation à la symbolique romane, XIIe siècle.* Paris: Flammarion, 1964.

Dear, P. *Mersenne and the Learning of the Schools.* Ithaca: Cornell University Press, 1988.

Debord, G. *Society of the Spectacle.* Detroit: Black & Red, 1983.

DeJean, J. *Ancients against Moderns: Culture Wars and the Making of a Fin de Siècle.* Chicago: University of Chicago Press, 1997.

Delaporte, M. Y. *Les vitraux de la cathédrale de Chartres.* Chartres: E. Houvet, 1926.

Dempsey, C. "Masaccio's Trinity: Altarpiece or Tomb?" *Art Bulletin* 54 (1972): 279–281.

Descartes, R. *Oeuvres.* 11 vols. Edited by C. Adam and P. Tannery. New ed. Paris: J. Vrin, 1974–1982.

Descartes, R. *The Philosophical Works of Descartes*. Translated by E. S. Haldane and G. R. T. Ross. 2 vols. 1911. Reprint, Cambridge: Cambridge University Press, 1982.

Descartes, R. *Philosophical Writings*. Edited and translated by E. Anscombe and P. T. Geach. Edinburgh: Nelson, 1954.

Destutt de Tracy, A. L. C., comte. *Élémens d'idéologie*. 4 vols. 2nd ed. Paris: Courcier, 1804–1818.

Devotio Moderna: Basic Writings. Translated by J. Van Engen. New York: Paulist Press, 1988.

Dijksterhuis, E. J. *The Mechanization of the World Picture*. Translated by C. Dikshoorn. Oxford: Clarendon Press, 1961.

Dillon, J. *The Middle Platonists*. London: Duckworth, 1977.

Doctor, M. *Die Philosophie des Josef (ibn) Zaddik: Nach ihren Quellen, insbesondere nach ihren Beziehungen zu den lauteren Brüdern und zu Gabirol*. Beiträge zur Geschichte der Philosophie des Mittelalters, vol. 2, part 2. Münster: Aschendorff, 1895.

Dodd, B. G. "Aristoteles Latinus." In *The Cambridge History of Later Medieval Philosophy: From the Rediscovery of Aristotle to the Disintegration of Scholasticism, 1100–1600*, edited by N. Kretzmann, A. Kenny, and J. Pilburg. Cambridge: Cambridge University Press, 1982.

Dodds, E. R. *The Greeks and the Irrational*. 1951. Reprint, Berkeley: University of California Press, 1968.

Doesburg, Theo van. *Art Concret, no.* 1 (April 1931): 1–2.

Döhmer, K. *In welchem Style sollen wir bauen? Architekturtheorie zwischen Klassizismus und Jugendstil*. Munich: Prestel, 1976.

Dreyfus, H. L. "Misrepresenting Human Intelligence." In *Artificial Intelligence*. London: Croom Helm, 1987.

Dreyfus, H. L. *What Computers Still Can't Do: A Critique of Artificial Reason*. Cambridge, Mass.: MIT Press, 1992.

Drüeke, E. *"Maximilianstil": Zum Stilbegriff der Architektur im 19. Jahrhundert*. Mittenwald: Mäander, 1981.

Dubos, R. *Man Adapting*. New Haven: Yale University Press, 1965.

Duby, G. *The Age of the Cathedrals: Art and Society, 980–1420*. Translated by E. Levieux and B. Thompson. Chicago: University of Chicago Press, 1981.

Dufrenne, M. "Formalisme logique et formalisme esthétique." In *Esthétique et philosophie*. Paris: Klincksieck, 1967.

Durand, J. N. L. *Précis des leçons d'architecture données à l'École Royale Polytechnique*. 2 vols. Paris: chez l'auteur, 1809.

Durand, J. N. L. *Recueil et parallèle des édifices de tout genre anciens et modernes, remarquables par leur beauté, par leur grandeur, ou par leur singularité, et dessinés sur une même échelle*. Paris: n.p., 1801.

Eck, C. van, J. McAllister, and R. van de Vall, eds. *The Philosophy of Style in Philosophy and the Arts*. Cambridge: Cambridge University Press, 1983.

Eco, U. *The Aesthetics of Thomas Aquinas.* Translated by H. Bredin. London: Radius, 1988.

Edgerton, S. Y. *The Renaissance Rediscovery of Linear Perspective.* New York: Harper & Row, 1975.

Eisenman, P. *An Architecture of Absence.* London: Architectural Association, 1986.

Eisenman, P. "Aspects of Modernism: The Maison Domino and the Self-Referential Sign." *Oppositions,* nos. 15–16 (winter-spring 1979): 118–128.

Eisenman, P. "Moving Arrows, Eros, and Other Errors." *Precis* 6 (spring 1987): 138–143.

Eisenstein, Elizabeth L. *The Printing Revolution in Early Modern Europe.* Cambridge: Cambridge University Press, 1983.

Eliade, M. *The Myth of the Eternal Return.* Translated by W. R. Trask. Princeton: Princeton University Press, 1954.

Eliade, M. *Patterns in Comparative Religion.* Translated by R. Sheed. London: Sheed & Ward, 1958.

Eliade, M. *The Sacred and the Profane.* New York, 1959.

Ellul, J. *The Technological System.* New York: Continuum, 1980.

Endell, A. "The Beauty of Form and Decorative Art" (1897–1898). In *Form and Function,* edited by T. and C. Benton, with D. S. Sharp. London: Crosby Lockwood Staples, 1975.

Ernst, M. *Beyond Painting.* New York: Wittenborn, Schultz, 1948.

Euclid. *L'optique et la catoptrique.* Translated by P. Ver Eecke. New ed. Paris: A. Blanchard, 1959.

Fagiolo, M. "La Sindone e l'enigma dell'eclipse." In *Guarino Guarini e l'internazionalità del Barocco,* vol. 2. Turin: Accademia della Scienza, 1970.

Falcone, G. *La nuova vaga et dilettevole villa.* Brescia, 1564.

Fauvel, J., and J. Gray, eds. *The History of Mathematics: A Reader.* Basingstoke: Macmillan Education in association with the Open University, 1987.

Fichet, F. *La théorie architecturale à l'âge classique.* Brussels: P. Mardaga, 1978.

Filarete. *Treatise on Architecture.* Translated by J. R. Spencer. New Haven: Yale University Press, 1965.

Fischer von Erlach, J. B. *Entwurff einer historischen Architectur* [2nd ed.; Leipzig, 1725]. German text reprinted, with translation by T. Lediard, *A Plan of Civil and Historical Architecture* [London, 1730], Ridgewood, N.J.: Gregg Press, 1964.

Fletcher, A. *Allegory: The Theory of a Symbolic Mode.* Ithaca: Cornell University Press, 1964.

Fontenelle, B. de. *Digression sur les anciens et les modernes.* Paris, 1688.

Fontenelle, B. de. *Histoire de l'Académie Royale de Science depuis le reglement fait en 1699.* Paris, 1702.

Forssman, E. "Ikonologie und allgemeine Kunstgeschichte." In *Ikonographie und Ikonologie,* edited by E. Kaemmerling. Cologne: DuMont, 1979.

Forssman, E. *Säule und Ornament.* Stockholm, 1956.

Frank, E. E. *Literary Architecture: Essays toward a Tradition*. 1979. Reprint, Berkeley: University of California Press, 1983.

Frankfort, H. "The Archetype in Analytical Psychology and the History of Religion." *Journal of the Warburg and Courtauld Institutes* 21 (1951): 166–178.

Frankl, P. "The Secret of the Medieval Masons." *Art Bulletin* 27 (1954): 46–60.

Freeden, M. H. von, and C. Lamb. *Das Meisterwerk des Giovanni Battista Tiepolo: Die Fresken der Würzburger Residenz*. Munich: Hirmer, 1956.

Fry, E. F. *Cubism*. London: Thames & Hudson, 1966.

Funkenstein, A. *Theology and the Scientific Imagination from the Middle Ages to the Seventeenth Century*. Princeton: Princeton University Press, 1986.

Gadamer, H. G. *Dialogue and Dialectic: Eight Hermeneutical Studies on Plato*. Translated by P. C. Smith. New Haven: Yale University Press, 1980.

Gadamer, H. G. *Reason in the Age of Science*. Translated by F. G. Lawrence. Cambridge, Mass.: MIT Press, 1981.

Gadamer, H. G. *The Relevance of the Beautiful and Other Essays*. Translated by N. Walker. Edited by R. Bernasconi. Cambridge: Cambridge University Press, 1986.

Gadamer, H. G. "The Science of the Life World." In *Philosophical Hermeneutics*. Edited and translated by D. E. Linge. Berkeley: University of California Press, 1976.

Gadamer, H. G. *Truth and Method*. [Translation by W. Glen-Doepel. Translation edited by G. Barden and J. Cumming.] 2nd ed. London: Sheed & Ward, 1975.

Galileo Galilei. "The Assayer" (*Il Saggiatore*). In *Discoveries and Opinions of Galileo*. Translated by D. Stillman. Garden City, N.Y.: Doubleday, 1957.

Galileo Galilei. *Dialogue Concerning the Two Chief World Systems, Ptolemaic and Copernican*. Translated by D. Stillman. 2nd ed. Berkeley: University of California Press, 1967.

Gargus, J. "Geometrical Transformations and the Invention of New Architectural Meanings." *Harvard Architectural Review* 7 (1989): 117–131.

Garin, E. *Italian Humanism: Philosophy and Civic Life in the Renaissance*. Translated by P. Munz. Westport, Conn.: Greenwood Press, 1965.

Garin, E. "Ritratto di Paolo del Pozzo Toscanelli." In *Ritratti di umanisti*. Florence: Sansoni, 1967.

Gasche, R. "Ideality in Fragmentation." In *Philosophical Fragments,* by F. Schlegel. Translated by P. Firchow. Minneapolis: University of Minnesota Press, 1971.

Geese, U. "Antike als Program—Der Statuenhof des Belvedere im Vatikan." In *Natur und Antike in der Renaissance*. Frankfurt am Main: Liebieghaus, 1985.

Gehlen, A. *Man, His Nature and Place in the World*. Translated by C. Macmillan and K. Pilliner. New York: Columbia University Press, 1988.

Gehlen, A. *Die Seele im technischen Zeitalter*. Hamburg: Reinbeg, 1957.

Germann, G. *Gothic Revival in Europe and Britain: Sources, Influences, and Ideas*. Translated by G. Onn. London: Lund Humphries, 1972.

Ghiberti, L. *Der dritte Kommentar Lorenzo Ghibertis: Naturwissenschaften und Medizin in der Kunsttheorie der Frührenaissance.* Edited and translated by K. K. Bergdolt. Weinheim: VCH, 1988.

Giacobbe, G. C. "Epigone in seicento della Quaestio de certitudine mathematicarum Giuseppe Blancani." *Physis* 18, no. 1 (1976): 5–40.

Giamatti, A. B. *The Earthly Paradise and the Renaissance Epic.* Princeton: Princeton University Press, 1966.

Gilson, É. *Études sur le rôle de la pensée médiévale dans la formation du système cartésien.* 3rd ed. Paris: J. Vrin, 1967.

Gilson, É. *The Philosophy of St. Bonaventura.* Translated by I. Trethowan and F. J. Sheed. Paterson, N.J.: St. Anthony's Guild Press, 1965.

Gioseffi, D. *Perspectiva artificialis per la storia della prospettiva spigolature e appunti.* Trieste: Facoltà di Lettere e Filosofia, 1957.

Goethe, J. W. von. *Goethe on Art.* Translated by J. Gage. London: Scholar Press, 1980.

Goffen, R., ed. *Masaccio's Trinity.* Cambridge: Cambridge University Press, 1998.

Goldmann, N. *Civil Baukunst,* Leipzig, 1708.

Goldstein, K. "L'analyse de l'aphasie et l'essence du langage." *Journal de Psychologie* 28 (1933): 430–496.

Goldstein, K. "Autobiography." In *A History of Psychology in Autobiography,* vol 5. Edited by E. G. Boring and G. Lindzey. New York: Russell & Russell, 1967.

Goldstein, K. *Language and Language Disturbances.* New York: Grune & Stratton, 1948.

Goldstein, K. *Selected Papers—Ausgewählte Schriften.* Edited by A. Gurwitsch, E. Haudek, and W. E. Haudek. The Hague: Nijhoff, 1971.

Gombrich, E. *Art and Illusion.* Bollingen Series, 35. A. W. Mellon Lectures in the Fine Arts, no. 5. New York: Pantheon, 1960.

Gombrich, E. *Symbolic Images.* Phaidon Press, London, 1972.

Goodman, N. *Languages of Art.* 2nd ed. Indianapolis: Hackett Publishing, 1976.

Grabar, A. *Martyrium: Recherches sur la culte des reliques et l'art chrétien antique.* 2 vols. [Paris]: Collège de France, 1943–1946.

Grainger, R. *The Language of the Rite.* London: Darton Longman & Todd, 1974.

Grant, E., ed. *A Source Book in Medieval Science.* Cambridge, Mass.: Harvard University Press, 1974.

Grassi, E. *Heidegger and the Question of Renaissance Humanism.* Binghamton, N.Y.: Center for Medieval and Early Renaissance Studies, 1983.

Grassi, E. *Kunst und Mythos.* Rowohlts deutsche Enzyklopädie. Hamburg: Rowohlt, 1957.

Grassi, E. *Die Macht der Phantasie: Zur Geschichte abendländischen Denkens.* Frankfurt am Main: Hain, 1984.

Grassi, E. *Renaissance Humanism: Studies in Philosophy and Poetics.* Binghamton, N.Y.: Medieval and Renaissance Texts and Studies, 1988.

Grassi, E. *Die Theorie des Schönen in der Antike.* Cologne: Du Mont, 1962.

Gregorius a Sancto Vincentio. *Opus geometricum quadraturae circuli et sectionum coni.* Antwerp, 1647.

Groethuysen, B. *Anthropologie philosophique.* Gallimard, Paris, 1953.

Gross, W. *Die abendländische Architektur um 1300.* Stuttgart: W. Kohlhammer, 1948.

Grosseteste, R. *De lineis, angulis et figuris seu de fractionibus et reflexionibus radiorum.* In *Die philosophischen Werke,* edited by L. Baur. Beiträge zur Geschichte der Philosophie des Mittelalters, vol. 9. Münster: Aschendorff, 1912.

Grosseteste, R. *On Light (De Luce).* Translated by C. C. Riedl. Milwaukee: Marquette University Press, 1978.

Guarini, G. *Euclides adauctus et methodicus mathematicaq(ue) universalis.* Turin, 1671.

Guarini, G. *Placita philosophica.* Paris, 1665.

Guarino Guarini e l'internazionalità del Barocco. 2 vols. Turin: Accademia della Scienza, 1970.

Gusdorf, G. *La conscience révolutionnaire, les idéologues.* Vol. 8 of *Les sciences humaines et la pensée occidentale.* Paris: Payot, 1978.

Gusdorf, G. *Naissance de la conscience romantique au siècle des lumières.* Vol. 7 of *Les sciences humaines et la pensée occidentale.* Paris: Payot, 1976.

Gusdorf, G. *Les principes de la pensée au siècle des lumières.* Vol. 4 of *Les sciences humaines et la pensée occidentale.* Paris: Payot, 1971.

Habermas, J., ed. *Observations on "the Spiritual Situation of the Age": Contemporary German Perspectives.* Translated by A. Buchwalter. Cambridge, Mass.: MIT Press, 1985.

Hadamard, J. *The Psychology of Invention in the Mathematical Field.* 1945. Reprint, New York: Dover, 1954.

Hager, W., and N. Knopp, eds. *Beiträge zum Problem des Stilpluralismus.* Munich: Prestel, 1977.

Hallyn, F. *The Poetic Structure of the World: Copernicus and Kepler.* Translated by D. M. Leslie. New York: Zone Books, 1990.

Harries, K. *The Bavarian Rococo Church: Between Faith and Aestheticism.* New Haven: Yale University Press, 1983.

Harriss, J. *The Tallest Tower: Eiffel and the Belle Epoque.* Boston: Houghton Mifflin, 1975.

Havelock, E. A. *The Muse Learns to Write: Reflections on Orality and Literacy from Antiquity to the Present.* New Haven: Yale University Press, 1986.

Hawel, P. *Der spätbarocke Kirchenbau und seine theologische Bedeutung: Ein Beitrag zur Ikonologie der christlichen Sakralarchitektur.* Würzburg: Echter, 1987.

Haydn, H. M. *The Counter-Renaissance.* New York: Scribners, 1950.

Hazard, P. *The European Mind, 1680–1715.* Translated by J. L. May. Harmondsworth: Penguin, 1964.

Hedwig, K. *Sphaera Lucis: Studien zur Intelligibilität des Seienden in Kontext der mittelalterlichen Lichtspekulation.* Münster: Aschendorff, 1980.

Heer, F. *The Intellectual History of Europe.* Translated by J. Steinberg. London: Weidenfeld & Nicolson, 1966.

Heidegger, M. *Basic Writings.* Edited by D. F. Krell. London: Routledge & Kegan Paul, 1978.

Heidegger, M. *Being and Time.* Translated by J. Macquarrie and E. Robinson. Oxford: Basil Blackwell, 1967.

Heidegger, M. *End of Philosophy.* Translated by J. Stambaugh. London: Souvenir Press, 1975.

Heidegger, M. *History of the Concept of Time: Prolegomena.* Translated by T. Kisiel. Bloomington: Indiana University Press, 1985.

Heidegger, M. *Kant and the Problem of Metaphysics.* Translated by R. Taft. 4th ed. Bloomington: Bloomington University Press, 1989.

Heidegger, M. *The Metaphysical Foundations of Logic.* Translated by M. Heim. Bloomington: Indiana University Press, 1978.

Heidegger, M. "The Origin of the Work of Art." In *Poetry, Language, Thought.* Translated by A. Hofstadter. New York: Harper & Row, 1971.

Heidegger, M. *The Question Concerning Technology and Other Essays.* Translated by W. Lovitt. New York: Harper & Row, 1977.

Heidegger, M. *Vorträge und Aufsätze.* Pfullingen: G. Neske, 1959.

Heidegger, M. *What Is a Thing?* Translated by W. B. Barton, Jr., and V. Deutsch. Chicago: H. Regnery, 1967.

Heideloff, C. *Die Bauhütte des Mittelalters in Deutschland.* Nuremberg: Johann Adam Stein, 1844.

Heisenberg, W. *Across the Frontiers.* Translated by P. Heath. New York: Harper & Row, 1974.

Heisenberg, W. *The Physicist's Conception of Nature.* Translated by A. J. Pomerans. New York: Harcourt, Brace, 1958.

Heisenberg, W. "Rationality in Science and Society." In *Can We Survive Our Future?* edited by G. R. Urban. London: Bodley Head, 1971.

Hekscher, W. "Emblem und Emblembuch." In *Reallexikon zur deutschen Kunstgeschichte,* edited by O. Schmitt. Vol. 5. Stuttgart: J. B. Metzler, 1959.

Hempel, E. "Nikolaus von Cues in seinen Beziehungen zur Bildenden Kunst." *Berichte über die Verhandlungen der Sächsischen Akademie der Wissenschaften zu Leipzig* 100, no. 3 (1953): 3–42.

Heninger, S. K., Jr. *The Cosmographical Glass: Renaissance Diagrams of the Universe.* San Marino, Calif.: Huntington Library, 1977.

Henkel, A., and A. Schöne, eds. *Emblemata: Handbuch zur Sinnbildkunst des 16. und 17. Jahrhunderts.* Special ed. Stuttgart: J. B. Metzler, 1978.

Herder, J. G. *Sämmtliche Werke.* Edited by B. Suphan. 33 vols. Berlin: Weidmannsche Buchhandlung, 1877–1913.

Herrmann, W. *The Theory of Claude Perrault.* London: A. Zwemmer, 1973.

Hersey, G. *The Lost Meaning of Classical Architecture.* Cambridge, Mass.: MIT Press, 1988.

Hills, P. *The Light of Early Italian Painting.* New Haven: Yale University Press, 1987.

Hine, R. V. *Second Sight.* Berkeley: University of California Press, 1993.

Hitchcock, H. R., and P. Johnson. *The International Style.* 1932. Reprint, New York: W. W. Norton, 1966.

Hocke, R. G. *Die Welt als Labyrinth.* Rowohlts deutsche Enzyklopädie. Hamburg: Rowohlt, 1957.

Hohl, H. *Lebenwelt und Geschichte.* Freiberg: Karl Alher, 1962.

Holly, M. A. *Panofsky and the Foundations of Art History.* Ithaca: Cornell University Press, 1984.

Holt, E. G., ed. *Documentary History of Art.* Vol. 1. 2nd ed. Garden City, N.Y.: Doubleday, 1957.

Honey, S. *Mies van der Rohe. European Works.* London: Academy Editions, 1986.

Horn-Oncken, A. *Über das Schickliche: Studien zur Geschichte der Architekturtheorie.* Göttingen: Vandenhoeck & Ruprecht, 1967.

Hübsch, H. *In welchem Style sollen wir bauen?* Karlsruhe: Chr. Fr. Müller, 1828.

Husserl, E. *The Crisis of European Sciences and Transcendental Phenomenology.* Translated by D. Carr. Evanston, Ill.: Northwestern University Press, 1970.

Hvattum, M. "Poetics and Practical Aesthetics in the Writing of Gottfried Semper." Ph. D. diss., University of Cambridge, 1999.

Ibn Gabirol, S. *Fons vitae.* Translated [from Arabic] by J. Hispanus and D. Gundissalinus. Edited by C. Baeumker. Beiträge zur Geschichte der Philosophie des Mittelalters. Vol. 1, pt. 2. Münster: Aschendorff'sche Buchhandlung, 1892.

Impey, O., and A. McGregor, eds. *The Origins of Museums: The Cabinet of Curiosities in Seventeenth- and Eighteenth-Century Europe.* Oxford: Clarendon Press, 1985.

Iversen, E. *The Myth of Egypt and Its Hieroglyphs in European Tradition.* 1961. Reprint, Princeton: Princeton University Press, 1993.

Jamnitzer, W. *Perspectiva corporum regularium.* Nuremberg, 1548.

Janofske, E. *Architektur-Räume: Idee und Gestalt bei Hans Scharoun.* Braunschweig: F. Vieweg & Sohn, 1984.

Johnson, K. O. "Solomon, Apocalypse, and the Names of God: The Meaning of the Chapel of the Most Holy Shroud in Turin." *Storia Architettura* 8 (1985): 55–80.

Johnson, P. *Mies van der Rohe.* New York: Museum of Modern Art, 1947.

Jonas, H. *The Phenomenon of Life: Toward a Philosophical Biology.* New York: Harper & Row, 1966.

Jünger, E. *Strahlungen.* Tübingen: Heliopolis-Verlag, 1949.

Junod, P. "Future in the Past." *Oppositions,* no. 26 (1984): 43–63.

Justin Martyr. *S. Justini philosophi et martyris opera.* Vol. 1 of Corpus apologetarum Christianorum saeculi secundi. Edited by J. C. T. von Otto. 2nd ed. Jena: Mauke, 1872.

Kambartel, W. *Symmetrie und Schönheit: Über mögliche Voraussetzungen des neueren Kunstbewusstseins in der Architekturtheorie Claude Perraults.* Munich: W. Fink, 1972.

Kant, I. *Critique of Judgment.* Translated by J. H. Bernard. New York: Hafner Press, 1951.

Katz, David. "Der Aufbau der Tastwelt." *Zeitschrift für Pyschologie* 2 (1925): 104–145.

Kayser, W. *Das Grotesk*. Oldenburg: G. Stalling, 1957.

Keller, H. *The Story of My Life*. 1903. Reprint, New York: Bantam, 1980.

Kemp, M. "Science, Non-Science, and Nonsense: Brunelleschi's Perspective." *Art History* 1, no. 2 (1978): 134–161.

Kepler, J. "De stella nova in pede serpentarii." In *Opera Omnia*. Vol. 2. Edited by C. Frisch. Frankfurt: Heyder & Zimmer, 1859.

Kepler, J. *Gesammelte Werke*. Edited by W. von Dyck and M. Caspar. 20 vols. Munich: C. H. Beck, 1937–1997.

Kernodle, G. R. *From Art to Theatre: Form and Convention in the Renaissance*. Chicago: University of Chicago Press, 1943.

Kimball, F. "Luciano Laurana and the High Renaissance." *Art Bulletin* 10 (1927): 124–151.

Kisiel, T. "Aphasiology, Phenomenology, Structuralism." In *Language and Language Disturbances*, edited by E. W. Straus. *Fifth Lexington Conference on Pure and Applied Phenomenology*. Pittsburgh: Duquesne University Press, 1974.

Klaczko, J. *Jules II*. Paris: E. Plon, Nourrit, 1898.

Klee, P. *The Thinking Eye: The Notebooks of Paul Klee*. Edited by J. Spiller. [Translated by R. Manheim.] New York: G. Wittenborn, 1961.

Klein, J. *Greek Mathematical Thought and the Origin of Algebra*. Translated by E. Brann. Cambridge, Mass.: MIT Press, 1968.

Klein, R. *Form and Meaning: Essays on the Renaissance and Modern Art*. Translated by M. Jay and L. Wieseltier. New York: Viking Press, 1979.

Klein, R., and H. Zerner. "Vitruve et le théâtre de la Renaissance italienne." In *Le lieu théâtral à la Renaissance*, edited by J. Jacquot. Paris: Éditions du CNRS, 1968.

Kline, M. *Mathematics: The Loss of Certainty*. Oxford: Oxford University Press, 1980.

Klossowski, P. "Nietzsche's Experience of the Eternal Return." In *The New Nietzsche*, edited by D. B. Allison. Cambridge, Mass.: MIT Press, 1986.

Knabe, P. E. *Schlüsselbegriffe des kunsttheoretischen Denkens in Frankreich von der Spätklassik bis zum Ende der Aufklärung*. Düsseldorf: L. Schwann, 1972.

Kockelmans, J. J. *Heidegger and Science*. Washington, D.C.: Center for Advanced Research in Phenomenology; University Press of America, 1985.

Köhler, W. *The Gestalt Psychology*. London: G. Bell, 1930.

Konigson, E. *L'espace théâtral médiéval*. Paris: Éditions du CNRS, 1975.

Koselleck, R. *Futures Past: On the Semantics of Historical Time*. Translated by K. Tribe. Cambridge, Mass.: MIT Press, 1985.

Koyré, A. *Études d'histoire de la pensée philosophique*. Paris: Gallimard, 1971.

Koyré, A. *From the Closed World to the Infinite Universe*. Baltimore: Johns Hopkins University Press, 1957.

Koyré, A. *Metaphysics and Measurement: Essays in Scientific Revolution*. London: Chapman & Hall, 1968.

Koyré, A *Newtonian Studies*. London: Chapman & Hall, 1965.

Marion, J-L. *Sur la théologie blanche de Descartes: Analogie, création des vérités éter-nelles et fondement.* Paris: Presses Universitaires de France, 1981.

Marx, L. "The Changing Character of the 'Mechanic Arts' and the Invention of Tech-nology." In *Does Technology Drive History?*, edited by M. R. Smith and L. Marx. Cambridge, Mass.: MIT Press, 1994.

Maurois, A. *The Quest for Proust.* Translated by G. Hopkins. London: Cape, 1968.

McEvoy, J., ed. "Grosseteste R. Com. in Hier. Cael." M. A. thesis. Queen's University, Belfast, 1967.

McEvoy, J. *The Philosophy of Robert Grosseteste.* Oxford: Clarendon Press, 1986.

McEvoy, J. "The Sun as Res and Signum: Grosseteste's Commentary on Ecclesiasticus, chap. 43, vv. 1–5." *Recherches de Théologie Ancienne et Médiévale* 41 (1974): 38–91.

McFarland, T. *Romanticism and the Forms of Ruin: Romanticism, Coleridge, and the Modalities of Fragmentation.* Princeton: Princeton University Press, 1981.

McMullin, E. "The Conception of Science in Galileo." In *New Perspectives on Galileo,* edited by R. E. Butts and J. C. Pitt. Boston: D. Reidel, 1978.

McQuillan, J. "Geometry and Light in the Architecture of Guarino Guarini." Ph.D. diss., University of Cambridge, 1991.

Meek, H. A. *Guarino Guarini and His Architecture.* New Haven: Yale University Press, 1988.

Merlan, P. *From Platonism to Neoplatonism.* 3rd ed., rev. The Hague: Martinus Nijhoff, 1975.

Merleau-Ponty, M. *Consciousness and the Acquisition of Language.* Translated by H. J. Silverman. Evanston, Ill.: Northwestern University Press, 1973.

Merleau-Ponty, M. *Phenomenology of Perception.* Translated by C. Smith. London: Routledge & Kegan Paul, 1962.

Merleau-Ponty, M. "The Primacy of Perception and Its Philosophical Consequences." Translated by J. M. Edie. In *Primacy of Perception and Other Essays.* Edited by Edie. 1964. Reprint, Evanston, Ill.: Northwestern University Press, 1971.

Merleau-Ponty, M. *Sense and Non-Sense.* Translated by H. L. Dreyfus and P. A. Dreyfus. Evanston, Ill.: Northwestern University Press, 1964.

Mersenne, M. *Quaestiones celeberrimae in Genesim.* Paris, 1623.

Miller, N. *Archäologie des Traums: Versuch über Giovanni Battista Piranesi.* Munich: C. Hanser, 1994.

Minkowski, E. "Imagination." In *Readings in Existential Phenomenology.* Edited by N. Lawrence and D. O'Connor. Englewood Cliffs, N.J.: Prentice-Hall, 1967.

Minkowski, E. *Vers une cosmologie.* Paris: Aubier-Montaigne, 1936.

Mitchell, W. J. *City of Bits: Space, Place, and the Infobahn.* Cambridge, Mass.: MIT Press, 1995.

Montesquieu, C. "Essai sur le goût." In vol. 7 of *Encyclopédie; ou Dictionnaire rais-sonné des sciences, des arts et des métiers.* 17 vols. Paris, 1751–1760.

Mösseneder, K. "Barocke Bildphilosophie und Emblem." Introduction to *L'art des emblêmes,* by C. F. Menestrier. 1684. Reprint, Mittenwald: Mäander Kunstverlag, 1981.

Mrazek, W. *Ikonologie der barocken Deckenmalerei.* Vienna: R. M. Rohrer, 1953.

Muckle, J. T. "The *Hexaemeron* of Robert Grosseteste." *Medieval Studies,* no. 6 (1944): 151–174.

Mullach, F., ed. *Fragmenta Philosophorum Graecorum.* 3 vols. Paris: Didot, 1875–1881.

Müller, Claudia. *Unendlichkeit und Transzendenz in der Sakralarchitektur Guarini's.* Studiem zur Kunstgeschichte, 38. Hildesheim: G. Olms, 1986.

Müller, W. *Grundlagen gotischer Bautechnik: Ars sine Scientia nihil est.* Munich: Deutscher Kunstverlag, 1990.

Murdoch, J. E. "Infinity and Continuity." In *The Cambridge History of Later Medieval Philosophy: From the Rediscovery of Aristotle to the Disintegration of Scholasticism, 1100–1600,* edited by N. Kretzmann, A. Kenny, and J. Pilborg. Cambridge: Cambridge University Press, 1982.

Naredi-Rainer, P. von. *Architektur und Harmonie: Zahl, Mass und Proportion in der abendländischen Baukunst.* Cologne: DuMont, 1982.

Nascimento, Carlos A. R. do. "Une théorie des opérations naturelles fondée sur l'optique: Le *De multiplicatione specierum* de Roger Bacon." Ph.D. diss. Université de Montreal, 1975.

Neumeyer, F. *The Artless World: Mies van der Rohe on the Building Art.* Translated by M. Jarzombek. Cambridge, Mass.: MIT Press, 1991.

Nicholas of Cusa. *De coniecturis.* Ed. J. Koch, C. Bormann, and I. G. Senger. Vol. 3 of *Nicolai de Cusa Opera Omnia.* Hamburg: Felix Meiner, 1972.

Nicholas of Cusa. *Opera Omnia.* 3 vols. Paris, 1514.

Nicholas of Cusa. *Opera Omnia.* Vol. 11. Edited by L. Baur. Hamburg: F. Meiner, 1940.

Nicholas of Cusa. *Selected Spiritual Writings.* Translated by H. L. Bond. New York: Paulist Press, 1997.

Nicholls, S. G., Jr. *Romanesque Signs. Early Medieval Narrative and Iconography.* New Haven: Yale University Press, 1983.

Nietzsche, F. *Basic Writings.* Translated and edited by W. Kaufmann. New York: Modern Library, 1968.

Nietzsche, F. *The Will to Power.* Translated by W. Kaufmann and R. J. Hollingdale. Edited by W. Kaufmann. New York: Random House, 1967.

Nisbet, H. B. *Goethe and the Scientific Tradition.* London: Institute of Germanic Studies, University of London, 1972.

Oechslin, W. "Architektur und Alphabet." In *Architektur und Sprache: Gedenkenschrift für Richard Zürcher,* edited by C. Braegger. Munich: Prestel, 1982.

Ohly, F. "Deus Geometra." In *Interdisziplinäre Forschungen zur Geschichte des frühen Mittelalters,* edited by N. Kemp. Berlin: de Gruyter, 1982.

Olmi, G. "Dal teatro del mondo ai mondi inventariati, aspetti e forme del collezionismo nell'età moderna." In *Gli Uffizi, quattro secoli di una galleria,* edited by P. Barocchi and G. Ragionieri. Florence: L. S. Olschki, 1983.

O'Malley, J. W. "Fulfilment of the Christian Golden Age under Pope Julius II." *Traditio: Studies in Ancient and Medieval History, Thought and Religion* 25 (1969): 265–338.

O'Malley, J. W. *Giles of Viterbo on Church and Reform.* Leiden: Brill, 1968.

Ong, W. J. *Orality and Literacy: The Technologizing of the Word.* London: Methuen, 1982.

Osborne, H. *Abstraction and Artifice in Twentieth-Century Art.* Oxford: Clarendon Press, 1979.

Otto, W. F. *Dionysus, Myth and Cult.* Translated by R. B. Palmer. Bloomington: Indiana University Press, 1965.

Oud, J. J. P. "Architecture and Standardisation in Mass Construction" (1918). In *Form and Function: A Source Book for the History of Architecture and Design, 1890–1939,* edited by T. and C. Benton, with D. Sharp. London: Crosby Lockwood Staples, 1975.

Oughtred, W. *Clavis mathematicae.* In *The History of Mathematics: A Reader,* edited by J. Fauvel and J. Gray. Basingstoke: Macmillan Education, 1987.

Ouvrard, R. *Architecture harmonique.* Paris, 1679.

Pacioli, L. *Divine proportion.* Translated by G. Duchesne and M. Giraud. Paris: Compagnonnage, 1980.

Pahl, J. *Die Stadt im Aufbruch der perspektivischen Welt: Versuch über einen neuen Gestaltbegriff der Stadt.* Berlin: Ullstein, 1963.

Panofsky, E. "Artist, Scientist, Genius." In *The Renaissance: Six Essays,* by W. K. Ferguson et al. 1953. Reprint, New York: Harper & Row, 1962.

Panofsky, E. "Facies illa Rogeri Maximi Pictoris." In *Late Classical and Medieval Studies in Honor of Albert Mathias Friend Jr.,* edited by K. Weitzmann. Princeton: Princeton University Press, 1955.

Panofsky, E. *Idea: A Concept in Art Theory.* Translated by J. J. S. Peake. Columbia: University of South Carolina Press, 1968.

Panofsky, E. "Die Perspektive als symbolische Form." *Vorträge der Bibliothek Warburg* 4 (1924–1925): 258–330.

Papert, S. "One Artificial Intelligence or Many?" In *The Artificial Intelligence Debate,* edited by S. R. Grambard. Cambridge, Mass.: MIT Press, 1988.

Pappus of Alexandria. "Revival of Geometry." In *Selections Illustrating the History of Greek Mathematics,* vol. 1. Translated by I. Thomas. Loeb Classical Library. 1941. Reprint, Cambridge, Mass.: Harvard University Press, 1980.

Parronchi, A. "Le due tavole prospettiche del Brunelleschi." *Paragone,* no. 107 (1958): 3–32; no. 109 (1959): 3–31.

Parronchi, A. *Studi su la dolce prospettiva.* Milan: A. Martello, 1964.

Pascal, B. *Pensées.* Translated by A. J. Krailsheimer. Harmondsworth: Penguin, 1966.

Patocka, J. *Le monde naturel comme problème philosophique.* Translated by J. Danek and H. Declève. The Hague: Martin Nijhoff, 1976.

Patocka, J. "The Natural World and Phenomenology." In *Jan Patocka: Philosophy and Selected Writings,* by E. Kohak. Chicago: University of Chicago Press, 1989.

Pauli, W. "The Influence of Archetypal Ideas on the Scientific Theories of Kepler." In *The Interpretation of Nature and the Psyche,* by Pauli and C. Jung. London: Routledge & Kegan Paul, 1955.

Payot, D. *Le philosophe et l'architecte.* Paris: Aubier-Montaigne, 1982.

Peckham, J. *John Pecham and the Science of Optics: Perspectiva communis.* Edited with an introduction, translation, and critical notes by D. C. Lindberg. Madison: University of Wisconsin Press, 1970.

Pérez-Gómez, A. *Architecture and the Crisis of Modern Science.* Cambridge, Mass.: MIT Press, 1983.

Pérouse de Montclose, J. M. *Étienne-Louis Boullée, 1728–1799, de l'architecture classique à l'architecture révolutionnaire.* Paris: Arts et Métiers Graphiques, 1969.

Perrault, Charles. *Parallèle des Anciens et des Modernes.* Paris, 1688.

Perrault, Charles. *Le siècle de Louis le Grand.* Paris, 1687.

Perrault, Claude. *Les dix livres d'architecture de Vitruve.* Paris, 1673.

Perrault, Claude. *Ordonnance de cinq espèces de colonnes selon la méthode des anciens.* Paris, 1683.

Perrault, Claude. *Ordonnance for the Five Kinds of Columns after the Method of the Ancients.* Translated by I. K. McEwen. Santa Monica, Calif.: Getty Center for the History of Art and the Humanities, 1993.

Pevsner, N. *Academies of Art Past and Present.* 1840. Reprint, New York: Da Capo Press, 1973.

Pfeiffer, H. *Zur Ikonographie von Raffaels Disputa: Egidio da Viterbo und die christlich-platonische Konzeption der Stanza della Segnatura.* Rome: Università Gregoriana, 1975.

Pico della Mirandola, G. *"De hominis dignitate," "Heptaplus," "De ente et uno," e scritti vari.* Edited by E. Garin. Florence: Vallechi, 1942.

Picon, A. *French Architects and Engineers in the Age of Enlightenment.* Translated by M. Thom. Cambridge: Cambridge University Press, 1988.

Piel, F. "Der historische Stilbegriff und die Geschichtlichkeit der Kunst." In *Kunstgeschichte und Kunsttheorie im 19. Jarhhundert,* edited by H. Bauer. Berlin: de Gruyter, 1963.

Piero della Francesca. *De prospectiva pingendi.* Edited by G. Nicco-Fasola. 1942. Reprint, Florence: Casa Editrice Lettera, 1989.

Piero della Francesca. *L'opera "De corporibus regularibus" di Pietro Franceschi detto Della Francesca usurpata da fra Luca Pacioli.* Edited by G. Mancini. Rome: [n.p.], 1916.

Pitt, J. C. "Galileo and the Use of Geometry." In *New Perspectives on Galileo,* edited by R. E. Butts and Pitt. Boston: D. Reidel, 1978.

Planck, M. "Die Einheit des physikalischen Weltbildes." *Physikalisches Zeitschrift* 10 (1909): 62–67. Translated as "The Unity of the Physical World-Picture" in *Physical Reality: Philosophical Essays on Twentieth-Century Physics,* edited by S. Toulmin (New York: Harper & Row, 1970), pp. 1–28.

Plato. *Laws*. Translated by A. E. Taylor. In *The Collected Dialogues of Plato*. Edited by
E. Hamilton and H. Cairns. Bollingen Series, 71. Princeton: Princeton University Press, 1978.

Plato. *Plato's Cosmology: The Timaeus of Plato*. Translated by F. M. Cornford. London:
Routledge & Kegan Paul, 1937.

Plato. *Republic*. Translated by P. Shorey. 2 vols. Loeb Classical Library. 1930–1935.
Reprint, Cambridge, Mass.: Harvard University Press; London: W. Heinemann, 1980.

Plato. *Symposium*. Translated by M. Joyce. In *The Collected Dialogues of Plato*. Edited
by E. Hamilton and H. Cairns. Bollingen Series, 71. Princeton: Princeton University Press, 1978.

Platz, G. "Elements in the Creation of a New Style." In *Form and Function: A Source
Book for the History of Architecture and Design, 1890–1939*, edited by T. and C. Benton, with D. Sharp. London: Crosby Lockwood Staples, 1975.

Plotinus. *Enneads*. Translated by A. H. Armstrong. 7 vols. Loeb Classical Library. Cambridge, Mass.: Harvard University Press; London: Heinemann, 1966–1988.

Pöggeler, O. "Topology of Being." In *Martin Heidegger's Path of Thinking*. Translated
by D. Magurshak and S. Barber. Atlantic Highlands, N.J.: Humanities Press International, 1989.

Poggioli, R. *The Theory of the Avant-Garde*. Translated by G. Fitzgerald. Mass.: Harvard University Press, 1968.

Pohlenz, M. "To Prepon: Ein Beitrag zur Geschichte des griechischen Geistes." *Nachrichten von der Gesellschaft der Wissenschaften zu Göttingen* (1933): 53–93.

Polanyi, M. *Personal Knowledge: Towards a Post-critical Philosophy*. 1958. Reprint,
London: Routledge & Kegan Paul, 1983.

Polanyi, M. *The Tacit Dimension*. New York: Doubleday, 1967.

Pollitt, J. J. *The Ancient View of Greek Art: Criticism, History, and Terminology*. New
Haven: Yale University Press, 1974.

Polzer, J. "The Anatomy of Masaccio's Holy Trinity." *Jahrbuch der Berliner Museen* 93
(1971): 18–59.

Post, R. R. *The Modern Devotion: Confrontation with Reformation and Humanism*.
Leiden: E. J. Brill, 1968.

Praz, M. *Studies in Seventeenth-Century Imagery*. 2 vols. 2nd ed. Rome: Edizioni di
Storia e Letteratura, 1964–1974.

Prest, J. *The Garden of Eden: The Botanic Garden and the Re-creation of Paradise*.
New Haven: Yale University Press, 1981.

Proclus. *A Commentary on the First Book of Euclid's Elements*. Translated by G. R.
Morrow. 1970. Reprint, Princeton: Princeton University Press, 1992.

Proust, M. *À la recherche du temps perdu*. 1914–1927. Reprint, 3 vols. Paris: Gallimard, 1964.

Pugno, G. *La Santa Sindone che si venera a Torino*. Turin: Società Editrice Internazionale, 1961.

Rahner, H., S.J. *Greek Myths and Christian Mystery*. 1963. Reprint, New York: Biblo & Tannen, 1971.

Rahner, K., ed. *Encyclopedia of Theology: The Concise "Sacramentum Mundi."* 1975. Reprint, Tunbridge Wells: Burns & Oates, 1986.

Ramirez, G. A. "Guarino Guarini, Fray Juan Ricci, and the Complete Salomonic Order." *Art History* 4, no. 2 (1981): 175–185.

Reverdy, P. "L'image" (1918). In *Oeuvres complètes*. Paris: Flammarion, 1975.

Révész, G. *Psychology and Art of the Blind*. Translated by H. A. Wolff. London: Longmans, Green, 1950.

Riccioli, G. B. *Almagestum novum*. Bologna, 1661.

Richter, J. P. *Horn of Oberon: Jean Paul Richter's "School for Aesthetics."* Translated by M. R. Hale. Detroit: Wayne State University Press, 1973.

Ricoeur, P. *Figuring the Sacred: Religion, Narrative, and Imagination*. Translated by D. Pellauer and M. I. Wallace. Minneapolis: Fortress Press, 1995.

Ricoeur, P. *The Rule of Metaphor: Multi-disciplinary Studies of the Creation of Meaning in Language*. Translated by R. Czerny, with K. McLaughlin and J. Costello. London: Routledge & Kegan Paul, 1978.

Ricoeur, P. "Universal Civilization and National Cultures." In *History and Truth*, translated by C. A. Kelbley. Evanston. Ill.: Northwestern University Press, 1965.

Ripa, C. *Iconologia*. Rome, 1603.

Robison, E. "Optics and Mathematics in the Domed Churches of Guarino Guarini." *Journal of the Society of Architectural Historians* 50, no. 1 (1991): 384–401.

Roland, W. P. *Being Blind in-the-World: A Phenomenological Analysis of Blindness*. Pretoria, South Africa: National Council for the Blind, 1985.

Rose, P. L. *The Italian Renaissance and Mathematics: Studies on Humanists and Mathematicians from Petrarch to Galileo*. Geneva: Droz, 1975.

Rosenau, H. *Boullée and Visionary Architecture*. London: Academy Editions, 1976.

Rossi, P. *Francis Bacon: From Magic to Science*. Translated by S. Rabinovitch. London: Routledge & Kegan Paul, 1968.

Rossi, P. *Philosophy, Technology, and the Arts in the Early Modern Era*. Translated by S. Attanasio. New York: Harper & Row, 1970.

Rousseau, J. J. *Reveries of the Solitary Walker*. Translated by P. France. Harmondsworth: Penguin, 1979.

Röver, A. *Bienséance: Zur ästhetische Situation im Ancien Régime, dargestellt an Beispielen der Pariser Privatarchitektur*. Hildesheim: G. Olms, 1977.

Rowe, C., and R. Slutzky. *Transparenz*. Translated by B. Hoesli. Basel: Birkhäuser, 1968.

Rupprecht, B. *Die bayerische Rokoko-Kirche*. Kallmünz: M. Lassleben, 1959.

Rupprecht, B. "Villa, zur Geschichte eines Ideals." In *Wandlungen des Paradiesischen und Utopischen: Studien zum Bild eines Ideals*, edited by H. Bauer. Probleme der Kunstwissenschaft, 2. Berlin: W. de Gruyter, 1966.

Ruscelli, G. *Le impressi illustri*. Venice, 1566.

Rykwert, J. *The First Moderns: The Architects of the Eighteenth Century*. Cambridge, Mass.: MIT Press, 1980.

Rykwert, J. *On Adam's House in Paradise: The Idea of the Primitive Hut in Architectural History*. New York: Museum of Modern Art, 1972.

Sachs, E. *Die fünf platonischen Körper: Zur Geschichte der Mathematik und der Elementenlehre Platons und Pythagoreen.* Berlin: Weidmann, 1917.

Sacks, O. *A Leg to Stand On.* New York: Summit Books, 1984.

Sacks, O. *Seing Voices.* London: Picador, 1991.

Saisselin, R. G. *The Rule of Reason and the Ruses of the Heart: A Philosophical Dictionary of Classical French Criticism, Critics, and Aesthetic Issues.* Cleveland: Press of Case Western Reserve University, 1970.

Sanpaolesi, P. *Brunelleschi.* [Florence]: G. Barbèra, 1962.

Santinello, C. N. "Cusano e L. B. Alberti: Pensieri sul bello e sull'arte." In *Nicolò da Cusa, Relazioni tenute al convegno interuniversitario di Bressanone nel 1960.* Florence: G. C. Sansoni, 1962.

Sartre, J-P. *Imagination.* Translated by F. Williams. Ann Arbor: University of Michigan Press, 1962.

Scharoun, H. "Bauen und Leben." *Bauwelt* 58 (1967): 154–157.

Schelling, F. W. J. *The Philosophy of Art.* Translated by D. W. Stott. Minneapolis: University of Minnesota Press, 1989.

Schilder, P. *The Image and Appearance of the Human Body: Studies in the Constructive Energies of the Psyche.* 1935. Reprint, New York: Science Editions, J. Wiley & Sons, 1950.

Schiller, F. *Letters on the Aesthetic Education of Man.* Berlin, 1793–1795.

Schiller, F. *Naive and Sentimental Poetry, and On the Sublime.* Translated by J. A. Elias. New York: F. Unger, 1966.

Schinkel, K. F. *Das architektonische Lehrbuch.* Edited by G. Peschken. Munich: Deutscher Kunstverlag, 1979.

Schinkel, K. F. *Aus Schinkels Nachlass* (1862). Edited by A. von Wolzogen. 4 vols. in 2. Mittenwald: Mäander, 1981.

Schlegel, A. W. *Kritische Schriften und Briefe.* Edited by E. Lohner. 7 vols. Stuttgart: W. Kohlhammer, 1962–1974.

Schlegel, F. *Kritische Schriften und Fragmente.* Paderborn: F. Schöningh, 1988.

Schlegel, F. *Philosophical Fragments.* Translated by P. Firchow. Minneapolis: University of Minnesota Press, 1991.

Schleiermacher, F. E. D. "General Hermeneutics." In *The Hermeneutics Reader: Texts of the German Tradition from the Enlightenment to the Present,* edited by K. Mueller-Vollmer. Oxford: Basil Blackwell, 1985.

Schlosser, J. von. *Die Kunst- und Wunderkammer des Spätrenaissance.* Leipzig: Klinkhardt & Biermann, 1908.

Schmoll-Eisenwarth, J. A. *Das Unvollendete als künstlerische Form.* Bern: Francke, 1959.

Schöne, A. *Emblematik und Drama in Zeitalter des Barock.* 3rd ed. Munich: Beck, 1993.

Schönnig, K. H. *Münster Zwiefalten: Kirche der ehemaligen Reichsabtei.* 3rd ed. Munich: Schnell & Steiner, 1988.

Schwartz, F. J. *The Werkbund: Design Theory and Mass Culture before the First World War.* New Haven: Yale University Press, 1996.

Schwitters, K. *Das literarische Werk.* Edited by F. Lach. 5 vols. Cologne: DuMont, 1973–1981.

Scobel, G. "Chaos, Selbstorganisation und das Erhabene." In *Das Erhabene.* Edited by C. Pries. Weinheim: VCH, 1989.

Scott, C. E. "Psychotherapy: Being One and Being Many." In *Heidegger and Psychology,* edited by K. Hoeller. [Seattle]: Review of Existential Psychology and Psychiatry, 1988. Originally published as a special issue of the *Review of Existential Psychology and Psychiatry* (16, nos. 1–3 [1978–1979]).

Scott, J. B. "Guarino Guarini: Invention of the Passion Capitals in the Chapel of the Holy Shroud in Turin." *Journal of the Society of Architectural Historians* 54 no. 4 (1995): 418–445.

Sedlmaier, R., and R. Pfister. *Die fürstbischöfliche Residenz zu Würzburg.* 2 vols. in 1. Munich: G. Müller, 1923.

Sedlmayr, H. *Art in Crisis: The Lost Center.* [Translated by B. Battershaw.] London: Hollis & Carter, 1957.

Sedlmayr, H. *Epochen und Werke: Gesammelte Schriften zur Kunstgeschichte.* Vienna: Herold, 1959.

Sedlmayr, H. *Kunst und Wahrheit: Zur Theorie und Methode der Kunstgeschichte.* Rowohlts, deutsche Enzyklopädie. Hamburg: Rowohlt, [1958].

Sedlmayr, H. *Die Revolution der modernen Kunst.* Rowohlts deutsche Enzyklopädie. Hamburg: Rowohlt, 1958.

Semper, G. *Kleine Schriften.* Edited by H. and M. Semper. Berlin: W. Spemann, 1884.

Semper, H. *Gottfried Semper: Ein Bild seines Lebens und Wirkens mit Benutzung der Familienpapier.* Berlin: S. Calvary, 1880.

Senden, M. von. *Space and Sight: The Perception of Space and Shape in the Congenitally Blind Before and After Operation.* Translated by P. Heath. London: Methuen, 1960.

Sennett, R. *The Fall of Public Man.* Cambridge: Cambridge University Press, 1976.

Seuphor, M. *Cercle et carré.* Collections Art—Action—Architecture. Paris: P. Belfond, 1971.

Seymour, P. "One Artificial Intelligence or Many?" In *The Artificial Intelligence Debate,* edited by S. R. Graubard. Cambridge, Mass.: MIT Press, 1988.

Shearman, J. "The Vatican Stanze: Functions and Decoration." *Proceedings of the British Academy* 57 (1971): 369–424.

Shelby, L. R., ed. and trans. *Gothic Design Techniques: The Fifteenth-Century Design Booklets of Mathes Roriczer and Hanns Schmuttermayer.* Carbondale: Southern Illinois University Press, 1977.

Simson, O. G. von. *The Gothic Cathedral: Origins of Gothic Architecture and the Medieval Concept of Order.* Bollingen Series, 48. 1956. Reprint, New York: Pantheon, 1965.

Smith, C. *Architecture in the Culture of Early Humanism: Ethics, Aesthetics, and Eloquence, 1400–1470.* New York: Oxford University Press, 1992.

Spargo, E. J. M. *The Category of the Aesthetic in the Philosophy of Saint Bonaventura.* St. Bonaventure, N.Y.: Franciscan Institute, 1953.

Stackhouse, M. L. *Ethics and the Urban Ethos: An Essay in Social Theory and Theological Reconstruction.* Boston: Beacon Press, 1972.

Stadler, E. "Raumgestaltung im barocken Theater." In *Die Kunstformen des Barockzeitalters,* by H. Barth et al. Bern: Francke, 1956.

Stern, J. P. *Lichtenberg: A Doctrine of Scattered Occasions.* 1959. Reprint, London: Thames & Hudson, 1963.

Stock, B. *Myth and Science in the Twelfth Century.* Princeton: Princeton University Press, 1972.

Straus, E. "Aesthesiology and Hallucinations." In *Existence: A New Dimension in Psychiatry and Psychology.* Edited by R. May, E. Angel, and H. F. Hellenberger. New York: Simon and Schuster, 1958.

Straus, E. "Born to See, Bound to Behold: Reflections on the Function of Upright Posture in the Aesthetic Attitude." In *The Philosophy of the Body: Rejections of Cartesian Dualism,* edited by S. F. Spicker. Chicago: Quadrangle Books, 1970.

Straus, E. *Phenomenological Psychology: The Selected Papers of Erwin W. Straus.* Translated by E. Eng. London: Tavistock, 1966.

Suárez, F. *Disputationes metaphysicae.* [Edited by C. Berton.] Vols. 25–26 of *Opera Omnia.* Paris: L. Vivès, 1866.

Summers, D. *The Judgment of Sense: Renaissance Naturalism and the Rise of Aesthetics.* Cambridge: Cambridge University Press, 1987.

Szambien, W. *Symétrie, goût, caractère: Théorie et terminologie de l'architecture à l'âge classique.* Paris: Picard, 1986.

Tafuri, M. *L'architettura dell'Umanesimo.* Bari: Laterza, 1976.

Tafuri, M. "Roma Instaurata: Strategie urbane e politiche pontificie nella Roma del primo '500." In *Raffaelo architetto,* edited by C. L. Frommel, S. Ray, and Tafuri. Exhib. cat. Milan: Electa, 1984.

Tavassi La Greca, B. Appendix to Guarino Guarini, *Architettura civile.* Milan: Polifilo, 1968.

Taylor, C. H. *The Sources of the Self: The Making of the Modern Identity.* Cambridge: Cambridge University Press, 1989.

Tegethoff, W. "From Obscurity to Maturity." In *Mies van der Rohe: Critical Essays,* edited by F. Schulze. New York: Museum of Modern Art, 1989.

Teige, K. "Konstruktivismus a likvidace 'umění'" (Constructivism and the liquidation of art, 1925). In *Svět stavby a básně* (The world of building and poetry). Prague: Československý Spisovatel, 1966.

Tesauro, E. *Il cannocchiale aristotelico.* Turin, 1670. Facsimile ed. Savigliano (Cuneo): Artistica Piemontese, 2003.

Theisen, W. R., ed. and trans. "The Mediaeval Tradition of Euclid's Optics." Ph.D. diss., University of Wisconsin, 1972.

Theophrastus. *The Characters of Theophrastus.* Edited and translated by J. M. Edmonds. Loeb Classical Library. 1929. Reprint, Cambridge, Mass.: Harvard University Press, 1967.

Thomson, M. "Architecture and the Depth of Visibility." Dipl. diss., University of Cambridge, 1999.

Thomson, M. "The Nature of Space and the Blind." Third-year diss., University of Cambridge, 1996.

Tintelnot, H. *Die barocke Freskomalerei in Deutschland: Ihre Entwicklung und europäische Wirkung.* Munich: F. Bruckmann, 1951.

Tintelnot, H. *Barocktheater und barocke Kunst.* Berlin: Gebr. Mann, 1939.

Toulmin, S. *Cosmopolis: The Hidden Agenda of Modernity.* Chicago: University of Chicago Press, 1990.

Toulmin, S., ed. *Physical Reality: Philosophical Essays on Twentieth-Century Physics.* New York: Harper & Row, 1970.

van der Leeuw, G. *Religion in Essence and Manifestation.* Translated by J. E. Turner. Gloucester, Mass.: P. Smith, 1967.

Vasari, G. "Brunelleschi." In *The Lives of the Artists: A Selection.* Translated by G. Bull. Harmondsworth: Penguin, 1965.

Vattimo, G. *The End of Modernity.* Translated by J. Snyder. Cambridge: Polity Press, 1988.

Veltman, K. H. *Linear Perspective and the Visual Dimensions of Science and Art.* Munich: Deutscher Kunstverlag, 1986.

Venturi, L. *History of Art Criticism.* Translated by C. Marriott. New rev. ed. New York: E. P. Dutton, 1964.

Verheyen, E. *The Paintings in the Studiolo of Isabella d'Este at Mantua.* New York: New York University Press for the College Art Association of America, 1971.

Vernant, J. P. *Myth and Thought among the Greeks.* London: Routledge & Kegan Paul, 1983.

Vernon, Jack A. *Inside the Black Room.* 1963. Reprint, Harmondsworth: Penguin, 1966.

Vescovini, G. F. "Biaggio Pelacani da Parma." *Rivista di Filosofia* 51 (1960): 179–185.

Vescovini, G. F. "La prospettiva del Brunelleschi, Alhazen e Biaggio Pelacani a Firenze." In *Filippo Brunelleschi: La sua opera e il suo tempo.* [Edited by P. Ragionieri.] Florence: Centro Di, 1980.

Vescovini, G. F. *Studi sulla prospettiva medievale.* Turin: G. Giappichelli, 1965.

Vesely, D. "The Architectonics of Embodiment." In *Body and Building: Essays on the Changing Relation of Body and Architecture,* edited by G. Dodds and R. Tavernor. Cambridge, Mass.: MIT Press, 2002.

Vesely, D. "Surrealism, Myth, and Modernity." *Architectural Design,* nos. 2/3 (1978): 87–95.

Vespasiano da Bisticci. *The Vespasiano Memoirs: Lives of Illustrious Men from the Fifteenth Century.* Translated by W. George and E. Waters. London: Routledge & Sons, 1926.

Vico, G. *On the Most Ancient Wisdom of the Italians*. Ithaca: Cornell University Press, 1988.

Vietta, F. "Introduction to the Analytical Art." Translated by J. W. Smith. Appendix to *Greek Mathematical Thought and the Origin of Algebra,* by J. Klein. Cambridge, Mass.: MIT Press, 1968.

Villari, S. *J. N. L. Durand. (1760–1834): Art and Science of Architecture*. New York: Rizzoli, 1990.

Vitruvius. *On Architecture*. Translated by F. Granger. 2 vols. Loeb Classical Library. Cambridge, Mass.: Harvard University Press: London; W. Heinemann, 1931–1934.

Vives, J. L. *De disciplinis libri XX*. Anvers, 1531.

Voegelin, E. *From Enlightenment to Revolution*. Edited by J. H. Hallowell. Durham, N.C.: Duke University Press, 1975.

Voegelin, E. *The New Science of Politics: An Introduction*. Chicago: University of Chicago Press, 1952.

Vygotsky, L. S. *Thought and Language*. Edited and translated by E. Hanfmann and G. Vakar. 1962. Reprint, Cambridge, Mass.: MIT Press, 1981.

Wackernagel, M. *The World of the Florentine Renaissance Artist*. Translated by A. Luchs. Princeton: Princeton University Press, 1981.

Wagner, D. L. ed., *The Seven Liberal Arts in the Middle Ages*. Bloomington: Indiana University Press, 1986.

Wallace, W. A. *Galileo and His Sources: The Heritage of the Collegio Romano in Galileo's Science*. Princeton: Princeton University Press, 1984.

Wang, W. *Eric Parry Architects*. Preface by D. Vesely. London: Black Dog, 2002.

Waszink, J. H. *Timaeus a Calcidio translatus*. London: Warburg Institute; Leiden: E. J. Brill, 1962.

Watts, P. M. *Nicolaus Cusanus, a Fifteenth-Century Vision of Man*. Leiden: Brill, 1982.

Weelden, J. V. *On Being Blind: An Ontological Approach to the Problem of Blindness*. Amsterdam: Netherlands Society for the Blind, 1967.

Weidle, W. *Gestalt und Sprache des Kunstwerkes*. Mittenwald: Mäander, 1981.

Weizsäcker, V. von. *Der Gestaltkreis: Theorie der Einheit von Wahrnehmen und Bewegen*. Frankfurt am Main: Suhrkamp, 1973.

Wheatley, P. *The Pivot of the Four Quarters: A Preliminary Inquiry into the Origins and Character of the Ancient Chinese City*. Edinburgh: Edinburgh University Press, 1971.

White, J. *The Birth and Rebirth of Pictorial Space*. 3rd ed. London: Faber & Faber, 1987.

White, J. "Cavallini and the Last Frescoes in San Paolo." *Journal of the Warburg and Courtauld Institutes* 19 (1956): 84–95.

Wiedmann, A. K. *Romantic Roots in Modern Art: Romanticism and Expressionism: A Study in Comparative Aesthetics*. Old Woking [Eng.]: Gresham Books, 1979.

Wittkower, R. *Architectural Principles in the Age of Humanism*. London: A. Tiranti, 1962.

Wittkower, R. *Art and Architecture in Italy, 1600 to 1750.* 3rd rev. ed. Harmondsworth: Penguin, 1973.

Wittkower, R. "Brunelleschi and 'Proportion in Perspective.'" *Journal of the Warburg and Courtauld Institutes* 16 (1953): 275–291.

Wittkower, R., and M. Wittkower. *Born under Saturn: The Character and Conduct of Artists: A Documented History from Antiquity to the French Revolution.* New York: Random House, 1963.

Yates, F. *The Art of Memory.* 1966. Reprint, Harmondsworth: Penguin, 1969.

Yates, F. *Theatre of the World.* London: Routledge & Kegan Paul, 1969.

Zimler, J., and J. M. Keenan. "Imagery in the Congenitally Blind: How Visual Are Visual Images?" *Journal of Experimental Psychology: Learning, Memory and Cognition* 9, pt. 1 (1983): 269–282.

Zuccaro, F. *L'idea de' pittori, scultori e architetti.* Turin, 1607.

Zurcher, B. *Georges Braque, Life and Work.* Translated by S. Nye. New York: Rizzoli 1988.

Zürcher, R. *Zwiefalten, die Kirche der ehemaligen Benediktinerabtei: Ein Gesamtkunstwerk des süddeutschen Rokoko.* Konstanz: J. Thorbecke, 1967.

Soprintendenza Speciale per il Polo Museale Napoletano, 3.20

The Walters Art Museum, Baltimore, 3.24

By courtesy of the Trustees of Sir John Soane's Museum, 3.26

Bibliothèque Nationale de France, 4.1, 6.1

Archivio di Stato, Torino, 4.16

By courtesy of the Board of Trustees of the Alfred Beit Foundation, 5.1

Institut Géographique National, 5.4

Faculty of Architecture and History of Art Library, University of Cambridge, 5.5, 5.6, 5.7, 5.12, 7.6, 8.2

Musée National de Versailles, 5.8

Galleria degli Uffizi, Florence, 5.13

Staatliche Museen zu Berlin Kunstbibliothek, 5.14

The Royal Collection, © 2002 Her Majesty Queen Elizabeth II, 6.2

Bibliothèque Royale de Belgique, Brussels, 6.7

Graduate School of Fine Arts, University of Pennsylvania (photo Rolf Sauer), 6.11

By courtesy of Bryan Avery, 6.13

Musée Carnavalet, Paris, 7.4

Staatliche Museen zu Berlin-Preussischer Kulturbesitz, Nationalgalerie, 7.7

National Gallery, Prague, 7.9

Fondation Le Corbusier, 7.11

By courtesy of Chris Wong, 7.12

Museum of Modern Art, New York, 8.3

Technical Museum Prague, 8.7

By courtesy of Ernst Scheidegger, 8.10

Eric Parry Architects (photo David Grandorge), 8.11

Eric Parry Architects, 8.12, 8.13

Eric Parry Architects (photo Martin Charles), 8.14

- INDEX -

abstraction, 24–25

aesthetic, 255, 269, 273

    aesthetization, 251, 360

aesthetics, 249, 372

Alberti, Leon Battista, 6, 134–137, 147–
    150, 156, 159, 163, 165

Alexander, Friedrich Carl Christian, 93

algebra, 195, 294

Alhazen, 160

allegory, 221–222

Altichiero da Zevio, 141–143

Ambrose, Saint, 180

amnesia, 75

analogy, 135, 181, 341, 342

anthropology, 123

Aphaia, temple of, 365

aphorism, 325–326, 340

Apollo, 88, 172

Aragon, Louis, 37

archē, 52

architectonics, 92

Architectonisches Alphabeth, 93

architecture, 5, 371

    artistic element of, 268

    autonomy of, 244

    as communicative power, 68

    as construction, 266

    and cosmology, 236

    order of, 384

    poetics, 258–259, 330, 386–387

    self-referential, 356

    and technology, 16, 282

Aristotelianism, 121, 202, 206, 207

Aristotle, 118, 181, 204, 287, 367, 368

ars fabricandi, 282

Art Deco, 306

articulation. *See* embodiment

artificial intelligence, 310

artistic truth, 274

Art Nouveau, 14, 270, 334

Askandar, Adela, 374, 389

Auteuil, group of, 242

automatism, 37, 290

avant-garde, 30, 33, 37

Averroes, 160

Avery, Bryan, 314

Avicenna, 160

Bachelard, Gaston, 88

Bacon, Roger, 117, 120, 121–131, 160

    optical works, 410 n.61

Badrashi, Jemal, 379

Balliani, Camillo, 199

Baltimore panel, 168, 423 n.173

Baroque, 210–218

    dynamism, 212

    Gesamtkunstwerk, 218

    representation, 214, 216

    rocaille, 328

    space, 212

Bauhaus, 18, 248

Baumgarten, Alexander Gottlieb, 372

Baumgartner, Johann Wolfgang, 329

beauty, 249–251, 267

    arbitrary and positive, 235

    of the machine, 36

    and style, 271

Beistegui, Charles de, apartment, 344,
    345

Benedict, Saint, 218

Benedict XIV (pope), 220

Berlage, H. P., 248

Berlin

    Kulturforum, 35

    National Gallery, 33, 34

    Philharmonie, 30, 31, 34

    Schloss Charlottenhof (Potsdam),
        264, 265, 267

Bernini, Gian Lorenzo, 107

beryl, 161

Biagio da Parma (Pelacani), 138

Bibiena, Fernandino Galli da, 254, 255

bienséance, 363

Bingen, Hildegard von, 179

Bleu (Bles), Hendrik, 295

blindness, and space, 48–49

Blondel, François, 196

Blondel, Jacques-François, 360, 361, 363

Boffrand, Germain, 358, 360

Bolles + Wilson, 61, 62

Bosse, Abraham, 321

Bouhours, Dominique, 251

Boullée, Étienne-Louis, 257–260

Bramante, Donato, 168–172, 184–186

Braque, Georges, 337–339

Breton, André, 318–320, 340, 342, 343

Briseux, Charles-Étienne, 196

Bruegel, Pieter, the Elder, 299

Brunelleschi, Filippo, 131, 137, 138, 139,
     142–145, 159
     experiments, 143

Cambridge Botanical Gardens, 47

Carlo di Castelmonte, 197

Carlo Emanuele (duke of Savoy), 198

Carrogis, Louis (Carmontelle), 324

Cartesianism, 57, 178, 190, 193, 195,
     299. *See also* Descartes, René
     and space, 113

categorical intuition, 69

Cato, Marcus Porcius, the Elder, 186

Cavallini, Pietro, 140

Cendrars, Blaise, 305

Cesariano, Cesare, 115, 133

Cézanne, Paul, 335, 336

character, 259–260, 358
     emancipation of, 360
     and style, 261, 358–363

Charlemagne, 124, 125

Chartres, cathedral, 64–67, 86, 96–98,
     124, 125
     last judgment, 64–66
     west façade, 64

chōra, 370

chōrion, to, 113

Christ, 64, 172, 198–200, 221–223

Christianity, 172, 199, 220, 376

Cicero, Marcus Tullius, 186, 364

Cimabue, Giovanni, 140

classicism, 32, 178

cogito, 190

collage, 341

Columella, Lucius Junius Moderatus, 186

commercial and civic interests, 346

common sense, unifying faculty of
     senses, 138

common world, disintegration of, 231

communication, 44
     in the articulated world, 215

communicative movement, 70, 90–91,
     345

communicative space, 100, 196, 216, 363
     rules of, 349
     structure of, 377

computer programs, 311

Concorsi Clementini, 256

Condillac, Étienne Bonnot de, 258

conic sections, 212–213

Constructivism, 14, 18, 28, 340

content, 32

continuity, 48, 206, 207

convenance, 363

Coop Himmelblau, 37, 38, 39, 357

Cordemoy, Jean-Louis de, 196

corporeality, 46, 80, 140

correctness of sight, 132

cosmology, 94, 118, 216, 236, 288
     classical, 104, 378
     geometrical structure, 200
     heliocentric, 192
     new, 431 n.67
     Platonic, 153, 155, 156

costruzione legittima, 130, 137, 139, 148,
     165
     experimental demonstration, 147

Cousin, Jean, 152

creativity, 3, 7, 30, 327, 374, 387. *See also*
     invention
     and production, 19, 329

crisis of the object, 318

Crooke, Helkiah, 180

Crusoe, Robinson, 261

crystal, 343
Cubism
    Analytic, 336–338
    new structure of space, 337–338, 339, 342
    Synthetic, 318, 334–341
Cuningham, William, 291
Cusanus, Nicolaus (Nicholas of Cusa), 6, 156–158, 161–163, 166, 210
Cuvier, Georges, 247

Dadaism, 341
De Chirico, Giorgio, 318, 319
deconstruction, 361
deconstructive constructions, 21, 319–320
decor, 93–94, 328, 363–364
decorum, 363–364
deep spatial structures, 52
deep structures of reality, 379
Delafosse, Jean-Charles, 359
Delage automobile, 268, 269
Delaunay, Robert, 305
Desargues, Girard, 321
Descartes, René, 190, 193–194, 203–204, 240, 296–299. *See also* Cartesianism
design process, 8, 37
De Stijl, 18
diaphanous bodies, 160
Dientzenhofer, Christoph, 105, 212
Dientzenhofer, Kilian Ignaz, 196, 212
Dies Solis, 200
discontinuity, cultural, 34, 195
disegno interno, 134
Disneyland, 322
displacement of meaning, 356
divided representation, 6, 177–178, 179
divine illumination, 205
divine intellect, 162
Dodds, E. R., 289
Doesburg, Theo van, 20
Donatello, 137

Dubos, René, 26
Duccio di Buoninsegna, 140
Durand, Jean-Nicolas-Louis, 244–247, 265
Dürer, Albrecht, 156
dwelling, 26, 376
Dymaxion House, 376

earth
    as embodiment of world, 106
    as primary reference, 49
Eck, Johan, 181
École Polytechnique, 242
Einstein, Albert, 70
electronic revolution, 308
Ellul, Jacques, 315
emblem, 215, 221–222
embodiment, 29, 60, 76–77, 86, 91–106, 314
    architectural, 62–66, 96, 103–105, 183–184
    articulation and, 62–66, 73–74, 91, 96, 99, 184, 191
Empedocles, 180
Endell, August, 270
Endless House, 376
engineering structures, 306
Enlightenment, 27, 71
environment, 39, 55, 58
ergon, 71
Ernst, Max, 341, 342
essential form, 29
ethos, 363–364, 367, 370
Euclid, 73, 113, 122, 318
    elements, 118, 119, 206, 209
    optics, 118
Europe, 93
    architecture, 14
    culture, 104, 110, 137, 195
experimental method, 240, 297
Expressionism, 28, 29, 329, 334, 360

Falcone, Giuseppe, 186
Farell, Terry, 278

fine arts and practical arts, 257
Fischer, Johann Michael, 217
Fischer von Erlach, Johann Bernhard, 252, 253
Florence, 110, 159
    baptistery, 131, 145, 164, 165
    Palazzo della Signoria, 131
    Santa Croce, 140, 141
    Santa Maria Novella, 147
    Santo Spirito, 159
    Scuola del Abaco, 159
Fontenelle, Bernard de, 195, 230
formal content, 273
fragment, 318, 322, 340
    as element, 323
    modern, 324
    role of, 325–326, 335
    as self-sufficient, 320
    unfinished character, 330
Francesco di Giorgio Martini, 137
Frémin, Michel de, 196
French café, as typical situation, 77, 78, 382
French Revolution, 243
Frost, Christian, 351
Fuller, R. Buckminster, 376
Funder, factory (St. Veit/Glan), 357

Gadamer, Hans-Georg, 13, 94, 221, 257, 358, 372–374, 380, 382
Gaddi, Taddeo, 140, 141
Galileo Galilei, 156, 178, 203, 296, 297
Gauss, Karl Friedrich, 113, 380
Gehlen, Arnold, 63, 78, 82
Genesis, 122, 194
genius, 29, 251, 262, 328
geometry, 23, 71–74, 92, 204
    and cosmos, 200
    Euclidean, 113, 118
    and language, 156
    medieval, 118
    and optics, 116–118, 127
    of primary solids, 154

reasoning, 194
    and space, 192, 212
German culture, 28, 264
German Werkbund, 248
Gesamtkunstwerk, 86, 94, 218, 330, 334
Gestalt, 29, 84
gesture, 71
Ghiberti, Lorenzo, 121, 150
    and contemporary humanism, 159
    judgment of sense, 160, 161–166
Giacometti, Alberto, 383
Gilly, Friedrich, 260, 261
Giotto di Bondone, 140
Glass Chain, 30
Goethe, Johann Wolfgang von, 16, 248, 330
Goldstein, Kurt, 57, 69
gray zone of modernity, 34
Gregory of St. Vincent, 210, 211
Grosseteste, Robert, 113, 121–129, 132, 136
Guarini, Guarino, 176, 196–197, 198, 200–212, 221, 232
    Euclides adauctus, 202, 204–210
    Placita philosophica, 202–204, 211
    reasoning, outline, 433 n.84

Habermas, Jürgen, 37
hallucinations, 39–40
Häring, Hugo, 29
Heidegger, Martin, 106, 189, 307
Heidelberg, 83
Heisenberg, Werner, 241, 284, 372
heliocentric system, 192
Helios, 199–200
Hellenism, 371
Herder, Johann Gottfried von, 194
hermeneutics, 6, 215, 220, 339
Hildebrandt, Johann Lucas von, 102, 212
historia, 150, 151
historicism, 187, 261

history, 19, 215
   relativity of, 273–274
   transformation into theory, 245
Hitchcock, Henry-Russell, 362
Holy Ghost, 223
Holy Sepulchre, 197
Horace (Horatius Quintus Flaccus), 360
horizon of visibility, 85
Hortus Palatinus, 83
Houston, 323
Hübsch, Heinrich, 262
human emancipation, 25
Husserl, Edmund, 240
Huygens, Christiaan, 176, 203

iconology, 68
idealization and disembodiment, 314
idéologie, 242
illusion, 21, 172, 173, 184
imagination, 38, 60–61, 84–85, 88, 119,
   333, 338, 343
   representative power, 21
impoverishment of culture, 312
impresa, 214
Impressionism, 334
individual expression, 358
infinity, 157, 203, 206, 207–208, 210,
   221, 230, 332–333
Innocent VIII, villa of, 169
instrumental thinking, 282
intelligibility, 114, 230
invention, 21, 253, 263, 328
   dialectics of, 264
inverted vision, 46
Isidore of Seville, 199
Isocrates, 188
isolated elements, 324

Jacopo de' Barbari, 154
Jamnitzer, Wenzel, 156
je ne sais quoi, 251
Jerusalem, 111, 170
Johnson, Philip, 362

Jonas, Hans, 82
judgment of sense (*iudicium sensus*), 144
Julius II (pope), 169, 172
Justin Martyr, Saint, 199

Kandinsky, Wassily, 270
Keller, Helen, 74
Kepler, Johannes, 156, 182, 191–193,
   207, 212, 238
Kiesler, Frederick, 376
Klee, Paul, 330
Klenze, Leo von, 261, 263
kosmopoiēsis, 94
kosmos, 94
Koyré, Alexandre, 231

laboratory, as a paradigm, 298
Ladrière, Jean, 24
Lajoue, Jacques de, 233
language
   and geometry, 156
   and light, 115
   nonverbal, 399 n.56
   visual, 149
Laplace, Pierre-Simon, marquis de, 243
Latimer, Elspeth, 352
Lautréamont, comte de, 318
Lebenswelt, 76
Le Clerc, Sebastien, 177, 283
Le Corbusier, 268, 269, 305, 344, 345
Ledoux, Claude-Nicolas, 243
Legrand, Jacques-Guillaume, 265
Leibniz, Wilhelm, 176, 195, 216, 249–
   251, 321, 372
Lencker, Hans, 156
Leonardo da Vinci, 146, 150, 153, 155,
   286
liberal arts, 292
Libeskind, Daniel, 21–23, 341
light
   action, 125
   corporeality of, 112
   cosmogonic role, 122, 154

light (continued)
geometrical representation of, 116
independent reality of, 203
and language, 115
and natural philosophy, 126
paradigm of intelligibility, 114
pyramidal propagation, 129
as universal medium, 202
lineamenti, 134–135, 139
Lodoli, Carlo, 196
Lollio, Alberto, 188
London
Camden Town, 278, 303
Spitalfields Market, 346–348, 350, 351
Loos, Adolf, 248
Louvain, 45
Luise (queen of Prussia), 265, 267
Luria, Aleksandr Romanovich, 75

magic, 288
and technique, 291
Malevich, Kazimir, 270
Mannerism, 134, 371
and space, 368
Marsigli, Luigi, 159
Mary, 217–223
cult of, 218
as *fons et origo,* 222
as mediatrix, 218, 222–223
Masaccio (Tommaso di Giovanni Guidi),
137, 147
material transformation, 16
mathēma, 286
mathematics, 23, 238, 293, 297–298
universal, 206, 295
Maximilian II (king of Bavaria), 263
mécanisme de la composition, 244
mechanical arts, 292
mechanics, 293
and magic, 290
modern, 296
memory
art of, 98, 402 n.86

engram theory, 99
room, 102
Merleau-Ponty, Maurice, 38, 40, 48, 57,
72, 100, 144, 335
Mersenne, Marin, 203
metaphor, 214, 338
microcosmos, 179
human body as, 180
Middle Ages, 110, 122, 180, 207, 263,
322, 376, 409 n.57
optics, 120–131, 408 n.46
middle sciences, 292
Mies van der Rohe, Ludwig, 16, 18, 24,
32–34, 36, 268
Milan
cathedral, 282
S. Maria presso S. Satiro, 184–186
mimesis, 13, 287, 366–367
and nonmimetic arts, 367
of praxis, 367
mind, as a measure of things, 178
Minkowski, Eugène, 91
mirror, 144, 145
and perspective, 416 n.103
Mondrian, Piet, 270
Monet, Claude, 273
Montefeltro, Federigo da, 152
Montefeltro, Guidobaldo da, 152
Montesquieu, Charles de Secondat, baron
de, 251
monument, 266
Moscow, 25
movement
animating power of, 82
circular, 435 n.97
communicative, 70, 90–91, 345
divine origin of, 296
experience and, 79
participation in, 88
Munich
House of German Art, 272
Münster, library, 61, 62
museum, 94, 349

National Aeronautics and Space Administration (NASA), 53, 309, 376
  sky laboratory, 376
Neoplasticism, 340
Neoplatonism, 114, 121, 126, 202, 212
Neumann, Balthasar, 86, 196, 212
Newton, Sir Isaac, 176, 194, 213, 230
Nicéron, Jean-François, 191
Nietzsche, Friedrich, 270–274
nihilism, 277–278
number symbolism, 372

occasionalism, 300
ontological disorientation, 240
optics
  Euclidean, 118
  and geometry, 116–118, 127
  medieval, 120–131, 408 n.46
order
  architectural, 384
  prereflective, 82–83
  search for, 185
organic, 331
orientation, 48
  in zero gravity, 52
originality, 37, 312
Oud, J. J. P., 270
Ouvrard, René, 196

Pacioli, Luca, 153–156
  De divina proportione, 155
Padua
  Basilica del Santo, 142
  Capella Arena, 112
  Oratorio di San Giorgio, 142
Palladio, Andrea, 187
Panofsky, Erwin, 162
Pappus of Alexandria, 290
Paris
  Boulevard Saint-Germain, 78
  Eiffel Tower, 268, 304, 305, 306
  Parc Monceau, 324, 326
Parnassus, 170–172

Parousia, 64
Parry, Eric, 385–388
Parthenon, 268, 269
Pascal, Blaise, 207, 232, 233
Patel, Pierre, 250
Peckham, John, 121, 160
perception, 49, 60–61, 84, 123–124
Perin del Vaga, 169
Perrault, Charles, 176–177, 196, 232–236
Perrault, Claude, 202, 234, 236–237, 242, 251
perspective, 139–149
  perspectiva artificialis, 130
  perspectiva naturalis, 112, 132, 405 n.19
  as phenomenal experience, 144
  and proportion, 136
  as relationship of human bodies, 163
  sectional projection, 148
  as symbolic form, 162
  as visual knowledge, 166
Peyre, Marie-Joseph, 261
physica sacra, 194
physiognomy of structures, 356
Picasso, Pablo, 275
Piero della Francesca, 150–154, 162, 163
Piranesi, Giovanni Battista, 213, 256–257
Pittone, Giovanni Battista, 213
Planck, Max, 241
Plato, 113, 119, 180, 366–367, 370–371
  Timaeus, 180
Platonic solids, 151, 153, 156, 192
Platonism, 118, 151, 192, 378
  academy, 118
  cosmology, 153, 155, 156
Pliny the Younger (Gaius Plinius Caecilius Secundus), 186
Plotinus, 113
poetics, 6, 389. See also architecture: poetics
poetry, 16, 170–171, 266, 327, 341–343, 368, 371
poiēsis, 13, 287, 366

Pointillism, 334

postmodernism, 272

practical world, 12

Prague

    project for, 379

    St. Nicholas Church, 105

praxis, 82–83, 367, 368, 372–373

prepon, 365

prison, as cultural paradigm, 328

Proclus, 73, 119, 206, 210

productive knowledge, 30, 241

proportion, 135, 136

    continuous, 206

    direct visibility, 165

    Divine, 153

    projective, 210

    universal, 207

proportione dialectica, 210

Proust, Marcel, 103

Purism, 18

Quadri, Bernardino, 197

querelle of ancients and moderns, 232,
    234

railways, as engineering systems, 300–
    303

Ramelli, Agostino, 294

Ranke, Leopold von, 263

Raphael (Raffaello Sanzio), 170, 171

recognition, 100

reconciliation of interests, 348

Reformation, 187

regular and irregular bodies, 152

    transformation, 156

relief (*Entlastung*) law, 63

religious drama, 111

Renaissance, 110–112, 116, 124, 133–
    134, 151, 156, 327

    art, 160, 162

    culture, 162, 170

    individualism, 158

    new sense of space, 403 n.3

perspective, 6, 113, 127, 128, 132, 136

    representation, 140

    treatises, 144

renovatio Romae, 170

representation

    anthropocentric mode, 326–327

    appropriative, 184

    Baroque, 214, 216

    of the context, 311

    divided, 6, 177–178, 179

    electronic, 310

    emancipated, 5, 168, 326

    empirically based, 132

    idealized, 238

    illusionistic, 173

    introverted, 182, 189

    mathematical, 238

    mediating role of, 19, 92

    participatory function of, 4

    perspectival, 139–149

    Renaissance, 140

    and revelation, 124

res cogitans, 57, 178

resistance, 104

resonance, 91

reverberation, 91

Reverdy, Pierre, 342

rhetoric, 94, 130, 214, 218, 220

    rhetorical space, 226

Richter, Jean Paul, 327, 333

Ricoeur, Paul, 215

Riemann, Bernhard, 113

Rimbaud, Arthur, 318

Robarts, Adam, 350

rocaille, 224–225, 328

Rogier van der Weyden, 157

Roman architecture, 263

Roman Empire, 172

Romanticism, 28, 178, 264, 320, 332, 372

Rome. *See also* Vatican

    Fontana dei Fiumi, Piazza Navona, 107

    Palazzo dei Tribunali, 172

    St. Peter's, 172

rooms
    concept and paradigm, 140
    as embodiment of culture, 183–184
Rousseau, Jean-Jacques, 328
Ruysdael, Jacob van, 381

Sacks, Oliver, 57
Saint-Denis
    cathedral, 111
Santini, Giovanni, 196
Saturn, 200
scenography, 254
    science as, 176
    and space, 212, 217, 328, 368, 370
    vision of the world, 215–216
Scharoun, Hans, 29–34
Schelling, Friedrich Wilhelm Joseph von, 263, 333
Schinkel, Karl Friedrich, 16, 261–268, 332
Schlegel, August Wilhelm von, 261
Schlegel, Friedrich von, 326, 331
Schwitters, Kurt, 361, 362
science, 176, 240, 241
Scripture, 66. *See also* Genesis
Semper, Gottfried, 16, 247–248, 268
sensory deprivation, 75
Seuphor, Michel, 24
shadow theater, 349, 350
Sindone. *See* Turin: SS. Sindone
situatedness, 88, 387
situations
    artificial, 54
    constancy of, 79
    hidden conditions, 46
    identity of, 382
    as language and metaphor, 370
    and otherness, 82
    paradigmatic, 368
    pattern, 45
    practical nature of, 373, 377
    as primary paradigm, 377
    as receptacle of experience, 369
    spatiality and temporality, 75, 380

    structure, 58, 345
    typical, 72, 77, 78, 104, 376, 382
sky, figure of, 215
Sol Invictus, 200
Sophists, 367
space, 21, 30, 54, 85, 110, 142
    abstract organization of, 375
    and body, 140, 141
    Cartesian, 113
    configuration of, 45, 164
    Cubist, 337–338, 339, 342
    Euclidean, 113, 122
    Mannerist, 368
    Renaissance, 403 n.3
    and scenography, 212, 217, 328, 368, 370
    and situations, 380
    structure, 40, 47
    topography of, 49
species (in optics), 125, 128–130
spectacle, 173
spontaneity, 37
Stackhouse, Max, 12
Steinhuber, Johann David, 93
Stirling, James, 276, 277
Stockley Park, 384–388
Straus, Erwin, 82, 99, 384
studiolo, 183
Stuttgart
    Staatsgalerie, 276, 277
style, 261, 262, 271, 361
    and character, 261, 358–363
sublime, 258, 333
Summers, David, 138
Surrealism, 28, 318, 329, 340–346, 349, 372, 375
symbolic representation, 17, 74, 85, 216

technē and instrumentality, 242
technē poiētikē, 285
technology, 15
    adaptation, 27, 194, 252, 261
    and architecture, 16, 282

technology (continued)
    and art, 307
    and culture, 306
    essence of, 285
    rationality, 27, 276, 284
    technological systems, 302, 303
    and tectonics, 401 n.81
Teige, Karel, 36
telepresence, 309
Tesauro, Emanuele, 222, 224, 225–226
Tiepolo, Giovanni Battista, 86
topology, 52
Toscanelli, Paolo, 156, 159
transparency, phenomenal, 313–314, 344
Traversari, Ambrosio, 159
Trinity, 192, 198, 220, 221. *See also* Holy
    Ghost
trompe l'oeil, 337
Troost, Paul Ludwig, 272
Turin
    Palazzo Reale, 198
    SS. Sindone, 196–205, 208–210

Uccello, Paolo, 137
Ulm, cathedral, 135
universal intelligence, 243
universality, 33
    of technical thinking, 283
Urbinate panels, 167–168
Urbino, ducal library, 152

Vatican
    Cortile del Belvedere, 168, 169–172
    Stanza della Segnatura, 170, 171
    Vatican Palace, 172
veduta per angolo, 254
Vernant, Jean-Pierre, 290
Veronese, Paolo, 189
Versailles, 239, 250
verticality, 384–385
Viel de Saint Maux, Charles-François,
    261

Vienna
    Piaristenkirche Maria Treu, 102
    project for, 389
villa, as way of life, 186–188
Villa Barbaro (Maser), 188, 189
Villard de Honnecourt, 119
virtuality, 4, 48, 310
visibility of reality, 400 n.71
visual language, 149
Vitruvius Pollio, Marcus, 115, 133, 160,
    290, 363–364, 366
Vittone, Bernardo, 196
Vives, Juan, 178
Voegelin, Eric, 268

Wagner, Otto, 248
Weinbrenner, Friedrich, 262
Weston-Thomas, David, 289, 369
Wirkungsgeschichte, 215
Witelo, 121, 160
Wood, Robert, 319
world, 12, 49, 60, 215, 301
    beauty of, 251
    in Heidegger, 106
    latent, 83, 338, 343, 378
    natural, 76–77, 94, 126, 398 n.54
    perspectival, 149
    of reference, 51
    structures of, 58, 133, 338
    as theater, 183
    virtual, 309
    visible, 132, 139
Wren, Christopher, 176, 202
Würzburg, residence, 86, 87, 88, 89–93

Yates, Frances, 98, 103
Young, Melanie, 27, 59

Žák, Ladislav, 377
zero gravity, 52, 395 n.14
Zuccaro, Federigo, 134
Zwiefalten, church, 95, 217–225, 232, 254